SOFT LAW AND PUBLIC AUTHORITIES

This book considers the phenomenon of soft law employed by domestic public authorities. Lawyers have long understood that public authorities are able to issue certain communications in a way that causes them to be *treated* like law, even though these are neither legislation nor subordinate legislation. Importantly for soft law as a regulatory tool, people tend to treat soft law as binding even though public authorities know that it is not. It follows that soft law's 'binding' effects do not apply equally between the public authority and those to whom it is directed. Consequently, soft law is both highly effective as a means of regulation, and inherently risky for those who are regulated by it. Rather than considering soft law as a form of regulation, this book examines the possible remedies when a public authority breaches its own soft law upon which people have relied, thereby suffering loss. It considers judicial review remedies, modes of compensation which are not based upon a finding of invalidity, namely tort and equity, and 'soft' challenges outside the scope of the courts, such as through the Ombudsman or by seeking an ex gratia payment.

Volume 11 in the series Hart Studies in Comparative Public Law

Hart Studies in Comparative Public Law

Recent titles in this series:

The Use of Foreign Precedents by Constitutional Judges
Edited by Tania Groppi and Marie-Claire Ponthoreau

Israeli Constitutional Law in the Making
Edited by Gideon Sapir, Daphne Barak-Erez and Aharon Barak

Judicial Decision-Making in a Globalised World
A Comparative Analysis of the Changing Practices of Western Highest Courts
Elaine Mak

Constitutionalising Secession
David Haljan

Parliaments and Human Rights
Redressing the Democratic Deficit
Edited by Murray Hunt, Hayley Hooper and Paul Yowell

The Right to Freedom of Assembly
A Comparative Study
Orsolya Salát

An Inquiry into the Existence of Global Values
Through the Lens of Comparative Constitutional Law
Edited by Dennis Davis, Alan Richter and Cheryl Saunders

The Scope and Intensity of Substantive Review
Traversing Taggart's Rainbow
Edited by Hanna Wilberg and Mark Elliott

Entick v Carrington
250 Years of the Rule of Law
Edited by Adam Tomkins and Paul Scott

Administrative Law and Judicial Deference
Matthew Lewans

Soft Law and Public Authorities

Remedies and Reform

Greg Weeks

•HART•

OXFORD • LONDON • NEW YORK • NEW DELHI • SYDNEY

HART PUBLISHING
Bloomsbury Publishing Plc
Kemp House, Chawley Park, Cumnor Hill, Oxford, OX2 9PH, UK

HART PUBLISHING, the Hart/Stag logo, BLOOMSBURY and the Diana logo are trademarks of Bloomsbury Publishing Plc
First published in Great Britain 2016

First published in hardback, 2016
Paperback edition, 2018

A catalogue record for this book is available from the British Library.

Library of Congress Cataloging-in-Publication Data

Names: Weeks, Greg (Law teacher), author.

Title: Soft law and public authorities : remedies and reform / Greg Weeks.

Description: Oxford ; Portland, Or. : Hart Pubishing Ltd, 2015. | Series: Hart studies in comparative public law | Based on author's thesis (doctoral—University of New South Wales, 2013), issued under title: Australian public authorities which breach their soft law : remedies and suggested reforms. | Includes bibliographical references and index.

Identifiers: LCCN 2015041540 | ISBN 9781782256885 (hardback : alk. paper)

Subjects: LCSH: Administrative law—Australia. | Administrative responsibility—Australia. | Soft law—Australia.

Classification: LCC KU2450.W44 2015 | DDC 342.94/06—dc23 LC record available at http://lccn.loc.gov/2015041540

ISBN: PB: 978-1-50992-206-2
HB: 978-1-78225-688-5

Typeset by Compuscript Ltd, Shannon

Foreword

A lay person may think that LAW is all about commands backed up with civil or criminal sanctions. But there has always been a lot more, if only because law does not exist in a vacuum. It is a tool of government that operates in a social context. (Laws can of course be good or bad; effective or ineffective; honoured in spirit, or letter, or in the breach.) The 'command theory' of law is also deficient because law also facilitates and educates.

Much of constitutional law, contract law and succession law will guide participants to achieve desired outcomes with the minimum of fuss, while leaving it up to them to choose. This is the facilitative function. Thus, if an Australian government wanted to raise an excise tax it must get it enacted by the federal parliament. If a citizen wants an effective sale of land (without risky litigation) he or she should use a written, signed contract. To maximise the prospects of an effective passing of property on death, a testator should comply with the formalities of a valid will and (in the hope of staving off a family provision claim) leave a statement explaining why his or her nearest and dearest will be getting less than they might desire.

This excellent monograph by Dr Greg Weeks explores the role of soft law in the domain of public authorities. It is a comparative law study with an Australian focus. Much of soft law facilitates and educates, but occasionally it shows its teeth.

Soft law (in the public law realm) appears in codes of practice, guides, circulars, management manuals, policy notes and practice directions. These are all tools capable of guiding and educating both those (including judges) who administer hard (usually statute) law and those for whom hard law is primarily enacted. Only a handful of these instruments will have express statutory authorisation. Most will have been promulgated to educate 'the governed' and 'the governors' how best to work with a complex pattern of hard laws. This education frequently goes beyond the facile guidance of an explanatory memorandum or ministerial speech. For one thing it will present its message in plain English, using headings and concepts that a lay person will comprehend.

It has taken hundreds of years, and is still a work in progress, but public law now recognises that discretion is not the same as arbitrariness and it is not necessarily inimical to the rule of law. Practitioners of Equity have understood this for a long time. Discretionary decision-making by administrators and judges may occur because it is beyond the wit of man to formulate rules for every conceivable situation; and because sharp-edged rules may encourage evasion and hair-splitting. But consistency remains a hallmark of justice and good administration, so long as it is not offered in a Procrustean form.

Soft law in the form of guidelines issued by and for administrators can explain how discretions are likely to be exercised and the factors intended to be taken into account. Of course, statutes can do this as well, but modern statutes tend to offer an open-ended check list of mutually inconsistent goals designed to help legislators claim to have satisfied the discrepant demands of vocal interest groups. A guideline can actually telegraph the likely outcome of a discretion, while leaving the administrator free of the charge of fettering discretion. Such information may properly be designed to discourage persons likely to fall outside the ambit of a favourable exercise of the discretion. At least it may focus their attention and that of their advisers so as not to waste the time of administrators.

As Dr Weeks demonstrates, soft law has advantages, at least for administrators. Its promulgation, review and withdrawal occur without the formality, delay and direct scrutiny of the parliamentary process. Courts will seldom be able to review soft law instruments, because by their very nature they do not directly create rights and because a well-drawn guideline will have left ample wriggle room for administrators to demonstrate that discretions have not been unlawfully fettered (at least not by the text of the guideline). Failure to pay regard to soft law instruments is unlikely to attract judicial review for the very reason that there is no statutory or common law *obligation* to give them any attention. Some governmental policies can thus be experimented with, modified or withdrawn. In this sense their expression in soft law instruments can be exceedingly 'soft'. Procedural fairness may require notice to be given before policies are withdrawn, but this does not mean that they are fixed like the laws of the Medes and Persians or even like legislation itself.

Under Australian law, this is entirely consistent with the High Court's rejection of substantive due process and its unwillingness to allow notions of estoppel to fetter administrative decision-making. This retired solicitor-general and counsel for the Attorney-General in *Quin's Case* happens to see much good in this state of affairs. It keeps judges away from governmental policy areas where they are unlikely to understand the range of issues at stake or to have the experience to weigh them within the confines of adversary litigation.

It would be fallacious to argue from the proposition that 'soft law' must contain elements of 'law' in order to justify its examination. But, as Dr Weeks demonstrates, instruments of soft law are relied upon, like signs erected on a highway, and they may form factual elements going to make up causes of action in tort or proprietary estoppel or even (in extreme cases) contractual rights—so long as the general principles of tort, proprietary estoppel, misleading conduct, contract, are themselves satisfied. Given that there is nothing unlawful in promulgating soft law instruments, governmental liability to compensate for loss may ensue in this modern era that is hostile to immunities. Since, however, soft law operates in contexts where it is generally known that governments change their minds and use experience in administration to modify policies (unless constrained by legislation from doing so), it will always be difficult to erect legal claims directly on the back of soft law instruments.

Soft law may therefore be a relatively one-sided phenomenon. But whether, as Dr Weeks suggests (p 112) it is dangerously so may lie in the eye of the beholder. Information on the internet can also be dangerous, and it can be vexing for medical practitioners to be confronted by patients citing 'Dr Google'. But in this modern era, arguments against *excessive* information are difficult to muster. Those who attempt to sue others simply for what they have said or written face many hurdles.

This work operates at several levels. It introduces the reader to the idea of soft law. It tests its theses against a thorough review of modern administrative law across several jurisdictions. And it presents powerfully the case for detecting hard rights in the interstices of soft law.

The Hon Keith Mason AC QC

Acknowledgements

This book could not have been written without the help and support of a large number of people. I owe a debt of gratitude to my current and former colleagues at the University of New South Wales Faculty of Law, in particular Lyria Bennett-Moses, Phil Burgess, Shipra Chordia, Denis Harley, Cameron Holley, Andrew Lynch, Keith Mason, Linda Pearson, Prue Vines and George Williams, who all advised me in their areas of expertise. I learned much from the experience of teaching with Joanna Davidson, Sarah-jane Morris and Richard Travers. Stephen Argument, John Basten, Cora Hoexter, Alistair McKeough, John McMillan, Anita Stuhmcke and Gareth Tilley were immensely generous with their time, encouragement and advice, as were Jill Hunter and Jill McKeough, whose encouragement and support was manifested at least in part by never allowing me to pay for coffee. I should make particular mention of Simone Degeling, Matthew Groves, Carol Harlow, Jessica Hudson and Christopher Rossiter, each of whom spent considerable time and effort making and discussing with me their notes on particular chapters. I am grateful to Keith Mason for kindly supplying a Foreword to this book. Finally, my great thanks are owed to Robin Creyke and Christopher Forsyth, who examined the thesis on which this book is based and whose thoughtful comments have allowed me to build on the foundations I laid in that thesis. The usual caveat applies with respect to each of those who generously gave their advice.

The greatest assistance that anybody who writes a thesis can receive comes from his or her supervisors. I was fortunate to have two supervisors, Mark Aronson and Theunis Roux, whose styles of research supervision were almost perfectly complementary. Theunis' immense knowledge of legal theory and instinctive understanding of the 'broad sweep' of the narrative arc required by a lengthy piece of writing were invaluable to me. Additionally, he has a wonderful talent for identifying flaws in an argument and has never spared me the benefit of it. I am very grateful to Theunis for all his help and support.

Mark Aronson has been a mentor to me since he taught me administrative law as an undergraduate in 2004. I was immediately captivated because Mark is, like most great thinkers, a great teacher. Since that first course and an elective course, through an undergraduate thesis and several articles on which Mark offered me the benefit of his guidance, our relationship has evolved, but Mark still teaches me, and I still learn from him, almost constantly. Mark's advice on this book is in many ways nothing more than an extension of the interest he has always taken in my academic pursuits. There is little I can say about Mark Aronson that has not been said before. He is a demanding taskmaster but an incredibly generous one. His intellect is staggering but he is patient with those, like me, who cannot quite move at his blinding conceptual pace. Sometimes, it has taken me months to figure out the meaning of a comment that Mark has made but he never betrays impatience at my intellectual tardiness.

Mark's involvement with me has been a constant source of pleasure to me over many years and it is no exaggeration to say that I would not have achieved a fraction of what I have without his help.

Finally, and most importantly, I wish to thank my family. My parents, Lyn and Brian, have always supported me and I owe them immense thanks. My father-in-law, Stephen Smith, has valiantly faked an interest in areas of law far beyond his expertise in the Western Australian Criminal Code for my benefit (and, more importantly, has demanded no reciprocity on my part) and I appreciate his consistent efforts in this regard. My greatest debt of gratitude is owed to my beloved wife, Rachael, and my children, Emily and James. They have been patient with me as I wrote this book, and many other things which have kept me from them, and have shown me unstinting love and support. I dedicate this book to them as a very small gesture towards part-payment.

The law in this book is accurate to 18 August 2015.

Greg Weeks
Senior Lecturer, Faculty of Law,
University of New South Wales

Contents

Table of Cases

Australia

Canada

South Africa

United Kingdom

United States

Other

Table of Legislation

Australia

Commonwealth

Australian Capital Territory

New South Wales

Northern Territory

Queensland

South Australia

Tasmania

Victoria

Western Australia

EU

South Africa

New Zealand

United Kingdom

United States of America

1

Introduction

> The expression 'soft law' is, at first sight, a *non sequitur*. Law is either 'hard'—that is, enforceable, ultimately by the state—or it is not law. A norm that lacks formal consequences is foreign to the lexicon applied to describe a domestic legal system. Nonetheless ... it may be the paucity of our legal lexicon, rather than the expression itself, which is deficient.[1]

> Catch-22 did not exist, he was positive of that, but it made no difference. What did matter was that everyone thought it existed, and that was much worse, for there was no object or text to ridicule or refute, to accuse, criticize, attack, amend, hate, revile, spit at, rip to shreds, trample upon or burn up.[2]

SOME NORMS HAVE consequences which are not formal but nonetheless remain powerful. Consider an agency's formal statement of how it will interpret certain legislation, such as precedential views provided by the Australian Taxation Office (ATO) which represent the ATO's interpretation of any laws administered by the Commissioner of Taxation.[3] Alternatively, consider a Department's guidelines as to how it will interpret certain ordinary English words, such as those which appear in legislative instruments in relation to a reference to the annual 'turnover' of a business, which are not defined in legislation.[4] Consider further a revenue authority, which implemented guidelines contrary to legislation setting limits to the authority's powers designed to collect tax in excess of that presently owed, in order to prevent the taxpayer (a building society) from receiving a windfall.[5] For a variety of reasons, instruments like those described above effectively compel compliance, not only from the legally naïve or unwary, but also from relatively sophisticated parties.[6] There can be little doubt that soft law has consequences and that they are significant.

Are these consequences formal? In one sense, they are not: soft law is not directly enforceable in court proceedings. This is the orthodox understanding of the effect of soft law. However, there are two ways in which soft law has effects which cannot

[1] R Creyke and J McMillan, 'Soft Law versus Hard Law' in L Pearson, C Harlow and M Taggart (eds), *Administrative Law in a Changing State: Essays in Honour of Mark Aronson* (Oxford, Hart Publishing, 2008) 377, 378.

[2] J Heller, *Catch-22* (50th Anniversary edition, Vintage, 2011) 494.

[3] Australian Taxation Office, *ATO Practice Statement Law Administration PS LA 2003/3* (2003), [1].

[4] *Cheng v Minister for Immigration and Citizenship* (2013) 213 FCR 362.

[5] See eg *Woolwich Equitable Building Society v Inland Revenue Commissioners* [1993] AC 70. *Woolwich* was not itself a soft law case, since Woolwich Equitable Building Society made the relevant tax payments in response to a statutory instrument: see G Weeks, 'The Public Law of Restitution' (2014) 38 *Melbourne University Law Review* 198, 202.

[6] See eg *Woolwich* [1993] AC 70; *R (on the application of Davies) v Commissioners for Her Majesty's Revenue and Customs* [2011] 1 WLR 2625.

be dismissed as merely informal. The first is that courts take notice of soft law. It is over 20 years since the Full Federal Court noted that 'the proposition that government policy cannot bind [a public authority] does not imply that the policy can be ignored'.[7] Soft law, particularly in the form of policy, can be effective in delivering the connected benefits of predictability and consistency. These are issues closely connected to the operation of the rule of law. The operation of the law should be understood prior to decisions, either administrative or judicial, being made. Likewise, arbitrary decision-making is opposed to the rule of law. Soft law is a recognised way of ensuring consistency between decisions on like sets of facts.[8] Australian courts do not defer to administrative decision-makers on any legal issue, and specifically rejected the US Supreme Court's *Chevron* doctrine.[9] However, the Administrative Appeals Tribunal (AAT) has recognised since the earliest days of its existence that, in the exercise of its *de novo* merits review jurisdiction, it is generally better to apply a lawful administrative policy in reaching a decision on review than to risk the 'inelegance' of inconsistency.[10]

The second 'formal' effect of soft law is connected to the first: people will be subjected to real and legally effective consequences as a result of the operation of soft law. This may be, as discussed above, because soft law is given something close to normative operation by tribunals and courts. It may also be because people structure their dealings in reliance upon soft law which either undergoes a change or is subsequently interpreted in an unexpected way.[11] Consequences which materially affect individuals are in no way reduced or removed because they are not characterised as legally 'formal'.

Soft law can also have effects which are harder to trace to precise outcomes but which are nevertheless significant. For example, soft law is frequently used as a method of confining the discretion of administrative decision-makers. In part, this is designed to bring consistency to those decisions, but soft law is also used as a method of ensuring that discretionary power is exercised accountably. Part I of this volume attempts to deal with these issues by looking at what soft law is and how it is used within domestic legal settings. It is already well understood in international legal scholarship, at least in part because the comparatively limited scope of primary legislation in international law has caused soft law to be an important and effective method of regulation.[12]

[7] *Minister for Immigration, Local Government and Ethnic Affairs v Gray* (1994) 50 FCR 189, 206 (French and Drummond JJ).

[8] See E Johnson, 'Should "Inconsistency" of Administrative Decisions Give Rise to Judicial Review?' (2013) 72 *AIAL Forum* 50.

[9] *Corporation of the City of Enfield v Development Assessment Commission* (2000) 199 CLR 135, 151–54 (Gleeson CJ, Gummow, Kirby & Hayne JJ); cf *Chevron USA Inc v Natural Resources Defense Council, Inc* 467 US 837 (1984).

[10] *Re Drake and Minister for Immigration and Ethnic Affairs (No 2)* (1979) 2 ALD 634, 639 (Brennan J). See eg *Segal v Waverley Council* (2005) 64 NSWLR 177.

[11] See eg *Macquarie Bank Limited v Commissioner of Taxation* (2013) 89 ATR 262; *HTV Ltd v Price Commission* [1976] ICR 170; *Davies v HM Revenue & Customs* [2011] 1 WLR 2625.

[12] See eg O Dilling, M Herberg and G Winter (eds), *Transnational Administrative Rule-Making: Performance, Legal Effects and Legitimacy* (Oxford, Hart Publishing, 2011); D Shelton (ed), *Commitment and Compliance: The Role of Non-Binding Norms in the International Legal System* (Oxford, Oxford University Press, 2000).

This book does not, however, have the definition and categorisation of soft law as its only—or even its main—concern. Rather, it seeks to explore the possibility that people who have been exposed to soft law regulation, and particularly those who have relied on soft law only to suffer detriment when it is breached, altered or removed, might be able to obtain legal redress for their losses. This possibility is dealt with in Parts II and III.

Judicial review is considered in Chapters five, six and seven as a potential source of remedies for people adversely affected by relying on soft law. In the Australian context, it is an ill fit for two main reasons. The first is that judicial review's remedies attach to invalidity and soft law does not give them any purchase because it operates outside the valid/invalid dichotomy. The second is that judicial review's remedies, as they apply in Australia, are procedural in nature and tend to provide no greater benefit to an applicant than the opportunity to have the decision-maker remake the decision according to law.

One of the key battlegrounds in common law judicial review over the last two decades—whether or not courts can or should give substantive remedies to otherwise successful claimants in judicial review matters—can be located within the broader debate as to whether every problem must have a court-centred solution. The affirmative response to this proposition is typified by Lord Bingham's *dictum* that 'the rule of public policy which has first claim on the loyalty of the law [is] that wrongs should be remedied'.[13] Lord Bingham's approach has not been followed uncritically.[14] However, it is undoubtedly the case that England has embraced a broad judicial capacity to grant remedies for conspicuous unfairness amounting to an abuse of power.[15] This is a path down which England has been followed by various common law countries, with the notable exception of Australia.[16]

The Australian reluctance to accept the proposition that every wrong must have a (legal) remedy can, as usual, be traced to the Constitution, but to a certain extent this feels like more than just a formalist excuse to stop an unwelcome debate before it starts.[17] It is disingenuous to contend that the Australian judiciary as a whole (or at least a majority of the High Court) does not have a genuine concern about courts being invited to remedy unfairness which is 'conspicuous' (to whom?); or to intervene in matters featuring a 'potentially unjust decision' (by what standard?).[18] The orthodox judicial view in Australia is that such broad judicial discretion is apt to be misused, taking individual judges genuinely motivated to prevent injustice outside the limits of the acceptable judicial role. There is no compelling evidence that this

[13] *X and others (minors) v Bedfordshire County Council* [1995] 2 AC 633, 663.

[14] See eg Lord Hoffmann, 'Reforming the Law of Public Authority Negligence' (Speech delivered at the Bar Council Law Reform Lecture, London, UK, 17 November 2009) [20].

[15] *R v Inland Revenue Commissioners; ex parte Unilever plc* [1996] STC 681, 695 (Simon Brown LJ); *Secretary of State for the Home Department; ex parte Zeqiri* [2002] Imm AR 296, [44] (Lord Hoffmann).

[16] K Stern, 'Substantive Fairness in UK and Australian Law' (2007) 29 *Australian Bar Review* 266, 266.

[17] cf M Taggart, '"Australian Exceptionalism" in Judicial Review' (2008) 36 *Federal Law Review* 1, 27.

[18] ibid, 20; referring to *Griffith University v Tang* (2005) 221 CLR 99; cf Chapter 5.B.(i) below.

is part of a political agenda.[19] But does it amount to sacrificing justice on the altar of consistency? Not at all, once we are prepared to accept that sometimes serious issues will be exposed in legal proceedings which are then remedied outside those proceedings.

Compensation generally has nothing to do with proving invalidity in either tort or equity, and Chapters eight, nine and ten examine whether remedies in these disciplines have the capacity to assist people who have suffered loss as a result of having relied on soft law. Chapter eight deals with important threshold questions regarding whether public authorities can ever be liable in tort; whether they can be liable where private individuals would not be liable; the particular difficulties in proposing public authority liability for pure omissions; and whether public authorities can be liable in equity where an estoppel is raised.

Chapters nine and ten use hypothetical scenarios to cover two main issues. The first of these is whether and how soft law might create a common law duty of care, how it would be used to do so, and how knowledge of the terms of the soft law might affect the previous answers. The second examines the importance of a plaintiff's subjective reliance on a soft law instrument, both as a matter of tort and of equity. A public authority will be held liable in negligence for loss caused by the failure to apply a soft law instrument if the soft law in question includes a misrepresentation that the authority will act in accordance with it and an individual has relied reasonably on that representation to his or her detriment. However, this ground of claim is difficult to make out, reflecting the traditional reluctance of the common law to attach a duty of care to words rather than acts. At first blush, equity is even less promising, since the usual remedy where a person has relied to his or her detriment on a non-contractual statement or instrument is promissory estoppel. England allowed the creation of a doctrine of public law estoppel, later absorbed into the public law doctrine of substantive enforcement of legitimate expectations.[20] By contrast, Australia has been at best lukewarm on the issue and there has been no judicial consideration of the subject since 1990.[21] It is generally held that an estoppel will not be enforced where it would cause a public authority either to act ultra vires or to fetter its statutory discretion.[22] However, I suggest in Chapter ten that it is possible to harness the 'remedial flexibility [which] is a characteristic of equity jurisprudence' to fashion another response.[23] This is possible in as much as an estoppel is not a remedy but a circumstance which allows equity to be granted, usually in the form

[19] cf T Poole, 'Between the Devil and the Deep Blue Sea: Administrative Law in an Age of Rights' in L Pearson et al (eds), *Administrative Law in a Changing State* (Oxford, Hart Publishing, 2008) 15, 33.

[20] *R v East Sussex County Council; ex parte Reprotech (Pebsham) Ltd* [2003] 1 WLR 348. See G Weeks, 'Holding Government to its Word: Legitimate Expectations and Estoppels in Administrative Law' in M Groves (ed), *Modern Administrative Law in Australia: Concepts and Context* (Melbourne, Cambridge University Press, 2014) 224.

[21] *Attorney-General (NSW) v Quin* (1990) 170 CLR 1; *Minister for Immigration and Ethnic Affairs v Kurtovic* (1990) 21 FCR 193.

[22] *Maritime Electric Co Ltd v General Dairies Ltd* [1937] AC 610; *Southend-on-Sea Corporation v Hodgson (Wickford) Ltd* [1962] 1 QB 416.

[23] *Harris v Digital Pulse Pty Ltd* (2003) 56 NSWLR 298, 304 (Spigelman CJ). See also G Weeks, 'Estoppel and Public Authorities: Examining the Case for an Equitable Remedy' (2010) 4 *Journal of Equity* 247.

of an order to hold the representor to the substance of his or her representation.[24] It could also be an order for equitable compensation, which is a remedy that has fallen into disuse, but need not have done. Nonetheless, these chapters' conclusion, which is inescapable, is that, although private law remedies are in some circumstances available for the failure of public authorities to adhere to their own soft law, they are severely limited, both in scope and regularity of occurrence. These remedies provide inadequate protection for individuals who have acted on the strength of soft law.

In many ways, Part III is an appropriate note on which to end this book, because it concludes that the most effective remedies to soft law issues are, themselves, 'soft'. The non-judicial remedies considered are: intervention by the Ombudsman in Chapter eleven; and payments under one of the various discretionary compensation schemes provided for by government in Chapter twelve. The Ombudsman is a consistently underestimated institution, often on the basis that it lacks the capacity to make binding declarations of right and is therefore a 'toothless tiger'.[25] However, the Ombudsman has 'a potential for *systemic* impact beyond any court's capacity' (emphasis added) and is able to use it to effect change where soft law is being misused by public authorities.[26] Ombudsmen are flexible and can recommend a wide variety of remedial action, including things that are beyond the capacity of the courts. Furthermore, ombudsmen's recommendations are usually followed by government and are most unlikely to be the subject of judicial review proceedings in Australia.[27] Either by examining the use of soft law at a systemic level or by investigating an individual complaint, ombudsmen are more likely than courts to obtain a satisfactory result.

Chapter twelve examines one remedy which the Ombudsman might well recommend where a person has relied on soft law to his or her detriment, namely a payment under a discretionary scheme. These schemes are designed to allow government to make payments to deserving parties without running afoul of the legal limitations on the capacity of government to remedy injustice by spending from consolidated revenue.[28] At Commonwealth level, there are discretionary statutory mechanisms under which the Finance Minister may authorise compensatory 'act of grace' payments or waive or set off debts.[29] Another non-legislative remedial scheme, which relies on the Commonwealth's executive powers under section 61 of the Constitution and is exercised by individual portfolio Ministers or their delegates,

[24] *Commonwealth v Verwayen* (1990) 170 CLR 394, 443 (Deane J); *Giumelli v Giumelli* (1999) 196 CLR 101, 123–24; cf *Waltons Stores (Interstate) Ltd v Maher* (1988) 164 CLR 387, 416 (Brennan J); A Robertson, 'Satisfying the Minimum Equity: Equitable Estoppel Remedies after *Verwayen*' (1996) 20 *Melbourne University Law Review* 805, 821.

[25] R Creyke and J McMillan, *Control of Government Action: Text, Cases and Commentary*, 3rd edn (New South Wales, LexisNexis, 2012) 217.

[26] M Aronson and M Groves, *Judicial Review of Administrative Action*, 5th edn (Sydney, Thompson Reuters, 2013) [1.90].

[27] J McMillan, 'Re-thinking the Separation of Powers' (2010) 38 *Federal Law Review* 423, 427.

[28] *Auckland Harbour Board v R* [1924] AC 318. See also *Brown v West* (1990) 169 CLR 195; *British American Tobacco Australia Ltd v Western Australia* (2003) 217 CLR 30; *Combet v Commonwealth of Australia* (2005) 224 CLR 494; *The State of Victoria v The Commonwealth of Australia and Hayden* (1975) 134 CLR 338, ('*The AAP Case*').

[29] Respectively: Public Governance, Performance and Accountability Act 2013 (Cth) ss 65, 63 and 64.

is the Scheme for Compensation for Detriment caused by Defective Administration (the CDDA Scheme), under which a government agency may make a payment to an applicant which it has 'directly caused to experience detriment as a result of defective administration' in circumstances where the agency bears no legal liability and 'there is no other viable avenue to provide redress'.[30] These schemes are all intended to be used to remedy *exceptional* losses, rather than merely as a method of expenditure for providing compensation which has not been envisaged by the relevant statute. Given that payments under these discretionary schemes generally require that an applicant have no other legal rights which s/he could exercise in order to obtain redress, they are in many ways the ideal response to the issues thrown up by the use of soft law. The ambiguous nature of soft law as law/non-law is precisely what makes it attractive as a regulatory instrument. But should Australian public authorities be able to rely on such a convenient regulatory device without accepting some responsibility for adverse impact suffered by those who have been influenced to their detriment by soft law? This issue, and in particular what remedies might be available for breach of soft law, are considered throughout this book.

[30] Commonwealth Department of Finance and Deregulation, '*The Scheme for Compensation for Detriment caused by Defective Administration*', available at www.finance.gov.au/resource-management/discretionary-financial-assistance/cdda-scheme/information-for-applicants-cdda.html, ('*CDDA Fact Sheet*').

Part I

The Rise of Soft Law: Definitions and Issues

INTRODUCTION

Part I introduces the concept of soft law and considers both previous analyses of it as a phenomenon in domestic law and some of the doctrinal issues which it raises. It looks at what soft law is, what it is intended to do, and what happens when it is used. The final section of Chapter four considers two particular examples of soft law in regulatory regimes.

This book looks at soft law only as it applies within domestic legal systems. Although it is true that there are many different approaches to considering soft law, most of the academic writing is confined to its roles in international law, often looking at soft law's success in attracting political consensus in international relations where harder forms of regulation would likely have been resisted.[1] However, the role, meaning and very existence of international soft law are all still contested. Blutman describes soft law, in its international senses, as a 'a vague, redundant and unfounded notion, [whose] use may not be justified and can hardly withstand Ockham's razor'.[2] His view, essentially, is that soft law is a mere 'label', which must be looked behind in order to yield meaning, but which constitutes a 'trap' for the unwary. On the other hand, soft law and other 'informal standards' have an undeniable effect in transnational dealings, sometimes obtaining a 'quasi-binding status'.[3] All of these observations are worth heeding, and indeed Chapter two looks behind the 'labels' to examine the issue of what soft law is. However, I leave to others an examination of soft law in the context of international law.

Another burgeoning academic field is the study of regulation. For reasons that will be considered below, soft law can be a highly effective form of regulation and much has been written about using soft law as a means of regulating conduct. In a little over a decade, there were two prominent Australian considerations of soft law, between which the concept of domestic soft law seemed to 'sleep'.[4] The first of these was the Report of the Commonwealth Interdepartmental Committee on Quasi-regulation (IDC), which reported in December 1997.[5] The second was the report by the Administrative Review Council (ARC) in November 2008 on *Administrative Accountability in Business Areas Subject to Complex and Specific Regulation*.[6] These reports bookended the time in office of the government led by then-Prime Minister John Howard; the Grey-Letter Law Report was commissioned in the government's first

[1] M Cini, 'From Soft Law to Hard Law? Discretion and Rules-making in the Commission's State Aid Regime' (2000) *Working Paper 35*, European University Institute, p 4.

[2] L Blutman, 'In the Trap of a Legal Metaphor: International Soft Law' (2010) 59 *ICLQ* 605, 606–7.

[3] O Dilling, M Herberg and G Winter, 'Exploring Transnational Administrative Rule-Making' in O Dilling et al (eds), *Transnational Administrative Rule-Making* (Oxford, Hart Publishing, 2011) 1, 5.

[4] For the purpose of awaking soft law from its slumber, Creyke and McMillan cast Mark Aronson in the role of Prince Charming: R Creyke and J McMillan, 'Soft Law versus Hard Law' in L Pearson et al (eds), *Administrative Law in a Changing State* (Oxford, Hart Publishing, 2008) 377, 377. This analogy is not wholly novel; see M Kirby, 'Professor Mark Aronson: Doyen of Australian Administrative Law' (2006) 50 *AIAL Forum* 4, 6.

[5] Commonwealth Interdepartmental Committee on Quasi-regulation, *Grey-Letter law: Report of the Commonwealth Interdepartmental Committee on Quasi-regulation* (1997) ('*Grey-Letter Law Report*').

[6] Administrative Review Council, *Administrative Accountability in Business Areas Subject to Complex and Specific Regulation*, Report No 49, (2008), ('*Complex Regulation Report*').

year in power and the reference to the ARC from Commonwealth Attorney-General Phillip Ruddock which led to the Complex Regulation Report came just before the start of the government's final year in office.

Both reports focused predominantly on soft law as a regulatory instrument. The reference to the IDC was the result of concerns raised in the report of the Small Business Deregulation Task Force in November 1996.[7] The ARC's reference followed up on the report of the Taskforce on Reducing Regulatory Burdens on Business.[8] It was not intended to result in a report which would cover the same ground as the Grey-Letter Law Report, but picked up from the point at which that report ended, placing a greater focus on review than on processes for developing regulations. Both reports defined soft law by reference to a specific focus on the regulatory effects and compliance burdens associated with its use.[9]

The Grey-Letter Law Report concluded that there is a place for soft law (which it described as 'quasi-regulation') in the spectrum of available regulatory forms and discussed in detail strategies for developing effective and successful 'quasi-regulatory arrangements'. Its concern was the situation in which it is appropriate to use of soft law, and provided a checklist of the factors it perceived as relevant to whether and when the use of soft law is appropriate.[10] The Grey-Letter Law Report's approach to the use of soft law is concerning in so far as its authors seemed to view regulation as akin to a formal garden, in which everything grows in its appointed place. Soft law does not really fit this model; it is more akin to a weed—or, more generously, a wild-flower—which crops up opportunistically rather than always in the place it is expected. It thrives despite the disapprobation which may be directed to it because it is so effective *without* requiring either sanction or structure. While the Grey-Letter Law Report devoted much space to ensuring that soft law is applied in an orderly fashion, remarking that government may need 'to insist on, assist with, or put into place, appropriate arrangements for monitoring and review' of soft law schemes, the passage of time has shown that dealing with the effects of soft law remains a point of concern for the business community.[11]

The central recommendation made in the Complex Regulation Report was that administrative law values should apply 'to business rules at the development, application, monitoring and review stages, regardless of whether the rules have been developed and applied by government agencies, industry bodies or other non-government entities'.[12] In one sense, this recommendation broke no new ground. After all, judicial review's principles—although not its remedies—have long been available in circumstances completely unrelated to administrative decision-making

[7] Recommendation 57 of the Small Business Deregulation Task Force, *Time for Business: Report of the Small Business Deregulation Task Force* (1996).

[8] Taskforce on Reducing Regulatory Burdens on Business, *Rethinking Regulation: Report of the Taskforce on Reducing Regulatory Burdens on Business*, (2006). See *Complex Regulation Report* (2008), 1.

[9] See *Grey-Letter Law Report* (1997), xi–xii and Table 1; *Complex Regulation Report* (2008), 5–8.

[10] *Grey-Letter Law Report* (1997), 55–56; cf Keyes' argument that soft law is only appropriate 'in two types of situations': JM Keyes, *Executive Legislation*, 2nd edn (New South Wales, Butterworths, 2010) 77.

[11] *Grey-Letter Law Report* (1997), 82.

[12] *Complex Regulation Report* (2008), 40.

governed by statute, typically to provide procedural fairness to members of private sector associations.[13] Nonetheless, it is notable that the ARC's recommendations, taken broadly, are swimming against the tide of recent High Court jurisprudence.[14]

The application of administrative law values was the first of three support structures which, together, the ARC considered capable of providing regulatory accountability where judicial review's procedures and remedies are unavailable.[15] The second was that 'redress mechanisms available in business areas should be responsive to changes in regulatory needs as business areas evolve', which could allow soft law instruments to be reviewable without removing their great advantage of regulatory flexibility and speed.[16] The third support structure for accountability proposed by the ARC was that there should be improved consultation and drafting practices and regular internal and external review of rules once they are in effect.[17] These structures repeated the concerns stated in the Grey-Letter Law Report.

The ARC conceded that (apart from limited exceptions under privacy and human rights legislation) 'soft law administered by industry bodies and other non-government entities falls completely outside the scope of administrative law'.[18] Accountability and review measures in self-regulatory systems are therefore also 'soft'. Another example of the point that the most effective controls on soft law seem, themselves, to be 'soft' arose in regard to whether and when decisions made by public decision-makers in relation to soft law regulation should be subject to merits review. The ARC affirmed the recommendation from its earlier report that, with the exception of a small category of decisions which are unsuitable for merits review, 'a decision that will or is likely to affect the interests of a person should be subject to merits review'.[19] However, it added some further comments with respect to review of regulation in particular, in order to avoid 'the imposition of unnecessary red tape or additional burdens on business'.[20] Specifically, it recommended that tribunals invested with merits review functions be given the capacity to respond to the issues thrown up by review of decisions relating to soft law instruments with efficiency, flexibility and responsiveness. This could be achieved, for example, by ensuring that tribunal members are selected based on having a level of expertise in the matters before the tribunal. The ARC noted the Administrative Appeals Tribunal (AAT) as an exemplar of flexibility and said that this approach is to be preferred to the relatively inflexible approach of adapting merits review procedures with legislation.[21]

[13] M Aronson and M Groves, *Judicial Review of Administrative Action*, 5th edn (Sydney, Thompson Reuters, 2013) [3.210]–[3.230].

[14] *Griffith University v Tang* (2005) 221 CLR 99. See M Aronson, 'Soft Law in the High Court' (2007) 35 *Federal Law Review* 1; M Aronson and M Groves, *Judicial Review of Administrative Action*, 5th edn (Sydney, Thompson Reuters, 2013) [3.290].

[15] Guideline principle 3: *Complex Regulation Report* (2008), xiii.

[16] ibid, xi; Guideline principle 4: ibid, xiii.

[17] Guideline principles 1, 2 and 5: ibid, xii–xiii.

[18] ibid, 14.

[19] ibid, 35. See Administrative Review Council, *What Decisions Should be Subject to Merit Review?*, Booklet (1999).

[20] *Complex Regulation Report* (2008), 36.

[21] ibid, 39.

The ARC took a pragmatic approach to the complicated problem of how to impose accountability upon soft law regulation in calling for the application of administrative law values to the development, monitoring and review of soft law and decisions thereunder, regardless of whether it originates from within government or an external industry or body. Not for nothing was the report entitled 'Administrative Accountability in Business Areas subject to Complex and Specific Regulation'. However, as the ARC well understood, this approach is fraught with limitations where soft law instruments neither originate from within government nor are susceptible to control by government, such as by a regulator imposing certain standards in order to register an instrument. This book does not delve into the question of whether regulation is necessary where there is effective competition. While the ARC found that most self-regulatory schemes are run in a way that applies administrative law's values, it is difficult to know whether this remains the case for soft law regimes which have not attracted government attention or are otherwise under minimal threat of being replaced with legislation.

The reports by the IDC and ARC are not central to this book, which does not analyse how and why soft law is so effective as a regulatory tool. As is the case in regard to international law, others are better equipped for that job and there is already a burgeoning literature on the subject. Rather, this book is written from the point of view of those who are subject to government's soft law regulation and, more specifically, those who feel as though they have suffered as a result of their reliance on it. I take it as read that there are limits to what can be done with legislation and that soft law responds directly to some of those limitations. The limits of legislative responses are particularly evident in fast-moving areas of technological change.[22] Similarly, while soft law creates some interesting and peculiar interpretive challenges, we need to engage with the issues it creates on the understanding that soft law is unlikely to disappear from the regulatory landscape.[23]

[22] L Bennett Moses, 'Understanding Legal Responses to Technological Change: The Example of *In Vitro* Fertilization' (2005) 6 *Minnesota Journal of Law, Science & Technology* 505, 607.

[23] See eg C Harlow and R Rawlings, *Law and Administration*, 3rd edn (Cambridge, Cambridge University Press, 2009) 203–22.

2

Defining Soft Law

SOFT LAW MEANS different things to different people. Indeed, 'one of the most difficult issues in dealing with quasi-legislation is to work out exactly what sort of creature quasi-legislation *is*'.[1] As a generic term, there is an argument that soft law conceals as much as it reveals, making it at best unhelpful and at worst a 'misleading simplification'.[2] It is convenient to begin this chapter's analysis of what is included under the heading of soft law by first excluding that which is not.

First, soft law is not conclusively determinative of legal outcomes. What it affects, it affects by influence. The success of the concept of soft law in international law is probably directly attributable to this fact.[3] Assuming that the public can know whether guidance is prescriptive at all, soft law is less likely to provoke the development of a culture of resistance than prescriptive and overtly coercive forms of regulation.[4] On the contrary, Rupp and Williams claimed that many regulated parties will in fact internalise the values that are inherent in or otherwise promoted by soft law and thereby move 'beyond compliance' to the extent that justice becomes a 'social contagion' within an organisation.[5] As an effective means of regulation, soft law might be considered to speak for itself in this regard. However, the feeling of security in complying as readily—or more so—with soft law as with hard law in the positivist sense also presents significant risks to the regulated party.

Secondly, soft law as it is defined in this book is fundamentally not delegated legislation. In their authoritative work on the subject in Australia, Pearce and Argument defined 'delegated legislation' as comprising instruments of legislative effect made pursuant to the authority of Parliament.[6] Baldwin described this as 'secondary legislation', which he distinguished from 'primary' legislation (passed by Parliament) and 'tertiary' legislation.[7] The last of these he defined as 'usually' being made without

[1] S Argument, 'Quasi-legislation: Greasy Pig, Trojan Horse or Unruly Child?' (1994) 1 *Australian Journal of Administrative Law* 144, 144.

[2] CM Chinkin, 'Challenge of Soft Law' (1989) 38 *ICLQ* 850, 850. See also L Blutman, 'In the Trap of a Legal Metaphor' (2010) 59 *ICLQ* 605.

[3] See text accompanying fn 1 to the Introduction to Part I of this volume above.

[4] DE Rupp and CA Williams, 'The Efficacy of Regulation as a Function of Psychological Fit: Reexamining the Hard Law/Soft Law Continuum' (2011) 12 *Theoretical Inquiries in Law* 581, 586; cf C Harlow and R Rawlings, *Law and Administration*, 3rd edn (Cambridge, Cambridge University Press, 2009) 194.

[5] DE Rupp and CA Williams, 'The Efficacy of Regulation as a Function of Psychological Fit' (2011) 12 *Theoretical Inquiries in Law* 581, 595–96.

[6] D Pearce and S Argument, *Delegated Legislation in Australia*, 4th edn (Sydney, LexisNexis, 2012) 1; approved in *Latitude Fisheries Pty Ltd v Minister for Primary Industries and Energy* (1992) 110 ALR 209, 228–29 (French J).

[7] R Baldwin, *Rules and Government* (Oxford, Clarendon Press, 1995) 60–80.

an express power to legislate conferred by an Act of Parliament, without which there is no, or at least unclear, statutory authorisation 'to make directly enforceable rules'.[8] This rather begs the question of when legislation will fail to amount to secondary legislation as 'usual'. There are nonetheless demonstrable differences between codes of practice issued and published subject to statutory authority on the one hand and mere 'guidance' on the other.[9] These are not only differences which go to legal enforceability. Greenberg has characterised soft law as 'the third bite of the cherry', through which the executive attempts continuously to control the interpretation of primary and secondary legislation by means of guidance that can be revised or replaced at will.[10] On this interpretation, soft law actively constrains the judiciary but is subject to none of the requirements of clear drafting or accessibility which are imposed on primary and secondary legislation.

Thirdly, treaties are not soft law. This point is more contentious than those preceding it because treaties sometimes look as though they share some of the characteristics of soft law and analogies can be drawn between them as a result. Like soft law, treaties mean *something*, even if they have not been adopted into domestic legislation.[11] However, the important difference between the two types of instrument is that treaties are regulatory instruments as between states. The government does not intend that they should have the effect of regulating the behaviour of individuals. If it did, it would be more likely to take steps to give treaties explicit status in domestic law, as is the case with the Refugee Convention.[12] Treaties are not intended to regulate behaviour *within* a country in the same way that soft law is and, for that reason, do not fall within the definition of soft law employed in this book.

One potentially difficult issue is whether soft law and policy are the same and, if not, how they differ.[13] Certainly, policies are widely seen as being a form of soft law.[14] Without seeking to reach a definitive position, the approach taken in this book is to regard policies which seek to affect behaviour as manifestations of soft law. To the extent that a policy is not motivated by the intention to modify or affect conduct, it might not be considered to be soft law. This definitional point might not matter very much if people are not apt to *follow* such an instrument in any event, whatever it is called.

Soft law has been a topic of mainstream academic consideration for at least 70 years.[15] Indeed, Craig traced the use of the term 'quasi-legislation' back to the nineteenth century.[16] However, soft law is not a term whose content is agreed beyond

[8] ibid, 80.

[9] See C Harlow and R Rawlings, *Law and Administration*, 3rd edn (Cambridge, Cambridge University Press, 2009) 193–94.

[10] D Greenberg, 'Dangerous Trends in Modern Legislation' [2015] *PL* 96, 99–100.

[11] eg *Minister for Immigration and Ethnic Affairs v Teoh* (1995) 183 CLR 273; *Re Tracey* (2011) 80 NSWLR 261. See Chapter 6.A.(iii) of this volume.

[12] See J Vrachnas, M Bagaric, P Dimopoulos and A Pathinayake, *Migration and Refugee Law: Principles and Practice in Australia*, 3rd edn (Melbourne, Cambridge University Press, 2012) 182.

[13] I am indebted to Robin Creyke for raising this issue with me.

[14] See eg D Greenberg, 'Dangerous Trends in Modern Legislation' [2015] *PL* 96, 99.

[15] See RE Megarry, 'Administrative Quasi-Legislation' (1944) 60 *LQR* 125.

[16] PP Craig, *Administrative Law*, 7th edn (London, Sweet and Maxwell, 2012) 472 (fn 219).

argument: unlike 'delegated legislation', it is not 'a term of art'.[17] This is particularly the case in regard to whether it includes delegated legislation or is restricted to 'tertiary rules'.[18] In the Complex Regulation Report, the ARC expressly defined soft law to be limited to 'non-legislative' materials.[19] It nonetheless included a diagram which suggested that subordinate legislation might be included within the definitions of both soft law and 'black letter' law. The reasoning behind this conclusion is readily understandable: soft law has long been acknowledged to have the capacity to operate in the manner of legislation, even though it lacks legal force.[20] Indeed, the ARC reported that a number of participants in its research had 'agreed that in practice soft law can be as influential in modifying behaviour as black letter law'.[21] To the extent that the Complex Regulation Report might be understood as including delegated legislation within the definition of soft law, this book will respectfully depart from its reasoning, regardless of whether such instruments are registered under the Legislation Act 2003.[22]

One reason for which soft law stands apart from secondary rules is that it is not reliant on power delegated by the legislature and, hence, is not directly enforceable.[23] It is practically more difficult to assess the legal force of soft law.[24] However, as noted above, a feature of soft law is that it takes effect through influence rather than as an expression of positive law.[25] The difficulties raised thereby are the main focus of this book.

As long ago as the nineteenth century, issues of political responsibility 'reduced the ability of administrators to act autonomously' in formulating rules and regulations, and this responsibility was increasingly reserved to those who were politically accountable.[26] This phenomenon would now be described as delegated legislation. Even on a formalist approach, delegated legislation has always been 'law', since it is made subject to the express authority of Parliament. Of course, at Commonwealth level in Australia, its legitimacy is bolstered by the effect of the Legislation Act, which has been described as the 'single most important development in delegated legislation for at least half a century'.[27] That Act has its own definition of a 'legislative instrument', determined on the basis of an instrument's function.[28] Delegated legislation includes any instrument 'of a legislative character' which 'was made in

[17] G Ganz, *Quasi-legislation: Recent Developments in Secondary Legislation* (London, Sweet and Maxwell, 1987) 1.

[18] R Baldwin, *Rules and Government* (Oxford, Clarendon Press, 1995) 4.

[19] *Complex Regulation Report* (2008) xi, 5.

[20] See eg RE Megarry, 'Administrative Quasi-Legislation' (1944) 60 *LQR* 125, 126.

[21] *Complex Regulation Report* (2008), 5.

[22] Legislation Act 2003 (Cth) s 31(1). Amendments to the Legislative Instruments Act 2003 (Cth), along with a change of title, come into effect no later than 12 months after Royal Assent (which was 5 March 2015).

[23] R Baldwin, *Rules and Government* (Oxford, Clarendon Press, 1995), 60.

[24] ibid, 80.

[25] R Creyke and J McMillan, 'Soft Law versus Hard Law' in L Pearson et al (eds), *Administrative Law in a Changing State* (Oxford, Hart Publishing, 2008) 377, 379.

[26] HW Arthurs, '*Without the Law*'*: Administrative Justice and Legal Pluralism in Nineteenth-Century England* (Toronto, University of Toronto Press, 1985) 136.

[27] S Argument, 'Delegated Legislation' in M Groves and HP Lee (eds), *Australian Administrative Law: Fundamentals, Principles and Doctrines* (Melbourne, Cambridge University Press, 2007) 134, 135.

[28] Legislation Act 2003 s 5.

the exercise of a power delegated by the Parliament' or is within a list of nominated instruments.[29] In practice, most statutes now specify whether the Act is to apply, causing much of the debate that previously surrounded the difference between secondary and tertiary legislation at Commonwealth level in Australia to be moot.[30]

Are instruments which are not legislative instruments for the purposes of the Legislation Act thereby precluded from being 'law'? Creyke and McMillan concluded that law in the positivist sense is both designed to control and to be enforceable and 'from that one can draw a proposition that a soft law instrument, if it is to be so described, must be intended to influence or control behaviour, and that intention is backed up by some form of enforcement'.[31] On this understanding, hard law differs from soft law in form more than substance. Hard law binds and exerts its influence through the threat of a concrete sanction; soft law applies influence in some less tangible form. Heydon J noted the additional phenomenon of 'tough law', as an example of which he gave the 'specific and detailed rules of criminal procedure which exist under the general law' as compared to 'mass of detailed anti-discrimination and other human rights legislation' which has been introduced in recent decades.[32] Harlow and Rawlings displayed greater ambivalence about 'whether or not a lawyer would characterise … informal [guidance] documents as "rules"' but noted that 'they are certainly intended by their authors to have some practical effect'.[33] Regardless of the *legal* status of soft law, there has been a widespread outbreak of furious agreement that it is 'real'.[34] Soft law must mean something.

It is often possible to impute to agencies which use soft law the intention for it to influence or control behaviour. In reasoning which departed from the rest of the Appellate Committee of the House of Lords in *McFarland*, Lord Steyn stated that:[35]

> in respect of the many kinds of 'soft laws' with which we are now familiar, one must bear in mind that citizens are led to believe that the carefully drafted and considered statements truly represent government policy which will be observed in decision-making unless there is good reason to depart from it. It is an integral part of the working of a mature process of public administration.

It is uncontroversial in England that judicial review might be available for decisions made under soft law.[36] It is similarly accepted that government decision-makers must adhere to policy statements unless there is a 'good reason' for departing from them.[37] Lord Steyn seems to have proposed something greater: that a policy statement issued

[29] Legislation Act 2003 ss 5(1)(b), 5(2), 6. The Act also specifies certain categories of instrument which have been expressly declared not to be legislative instruments under the Act: ibid, s 7.

[30] D Pearce and S Argument, *Delegated Legislation*, 4th edn (Sydney, LexisNexis, 2012) 33.

[31] R Creyke and J McMillan, 'Soft Law versus Hard Law' in L Pearson et al (eds), *Administrative Law in a Changing State* (Oxford, Hart Publishing, 2008) 377, 383.

[32] *Momcilovic v The Queen* (2011) 245 CLR 1, 152.

[33] C Harlow and R Rawlings, *Law and Administration*, 3rd edn (Cambridge, Cambridge University Press, 2009) 194.

[34] D Greenberg, 'Dangerous Trends in Modern Legislation' [2015] *PL* 96, 99.

[35] *In re McFarland* [2004] 1 WLR 1289, 1299.

[36] See eg *Gillick v West Norfolk and Wisbech Area Health Authority* [1986] AC 112, 163 (Lord Fraser); 177–78 (Lord Scarman).

[37] This point was reiterated on several occasions by both Lord Hope and Baroness Hale in *R (Kambadzi) v Secretary of State for the Home Department* [2011] 1 WLR 1299.

for the purpose of giving 'guidance to the public' should entitle a citizen 'to rely on the language of the statement, seen as always in its proper context'. Unless or until the Minister responsible for such a policy retracts it for a 'good reason',[38]

> the citizen is entitled to ask in a court of law whether he fairly comes within the language of the publicly announced policy. *That question, like all questions of interpretation, is one of law.* And on such a question of law it necessarily follows that the court does not defer to the minister: the court is bound to decide such a question for itself, paying, of course, close attention to the reasons advanced for the competing interpretations. This is not to say that policy statements must be construed like primary or subordinate legislation. It seems sensible that a broader and wholly untechnical approach should prevail. But what is involved is still an interpretative process conducted by a court which must necessarily be approached objectively and without speculation about what a particular minister may have had in mind (emphasis added).

Lord Steyn's preference for treating statements of policy as containing issues of law which courts can interpret and determine did not attract majority support in *McFarland*, although more recent judgments do not rule out such a position being adopted. Likewise, regardless of what is intended when agencies use soft law, in Australia, mere 'influence' does not cause soft law to be enforceable in the manner of hard law.[39] Perhaps, in the absence of a genuine claim to be 'law', the presence of practical effect is the explanation behind Pearce and Argument's statement that soft law and rules often 'go by the name "quasi-legislation", on the basis that they are *almost* laws'.[40] Likewise, Keyes stated that courts are now prepared to view soft law as both significant and persuasive to the extent that it 'often has something approaching [binding legal effect]', even though its effect is in fact neither binding nor legal.[41] This approach is consistent with the argument of this book that soft law is best understood as occupying a space between instruments so soft as not to be law on one hand and hard law of the positivist variety on the other. Further, it is consistent with another central theme of this book, namely that the tension within any rule of law system between allowing sufficient discretion to do justice in individual circumstances and requiring sufficient structure that exercises of discretion are broadly predictable is integral. This tension cannot be resolved, nor is it desirable that it should be. However, soft law can be seen as a means of *managing* this tension.

A. TYPES OF SOFT LAW

Soft law instruments occupy a broad section of the spectrum between unstructured discretion and legislation.[42] As time has gone by, the problem has been one

[38] *McFarland* [2004] 1 WLR 1289, 1299.

[39] cf fns 327–328 in Chapter 5.D.(i) of this volume below.

[40] D Pearce and S Argument, *Delegated Legislation*, 4th edn (Sydney, LexisNexis, 2012) 15. See C Harlow and R Rawlings, *Law and Administration*, 3rd edn (Cambridge, Cambridge University Press, 2009) 192; L Sossin and CW Smith, 'Hard Choices and Soft Law: Ethical Codes, Policy Guidelines and the Role of the Courts in Regulating Government' (2003) 40 *Alberta Law Review* 867, 871.

[41] JM Keyes, *Executive Legislation*, 2nd edn (New South Wales, Butterworths, 2010) 51.

[42] G Ganz, *Quasi-legislation* (London, Sweet and Maxwell, 1987) 1; M Cini, 'From Soft Law to Hard Law?' (2000) *Working Paper 35*, European University Institute p 4.

of ascertaining which of this 'wide variety of instruments' are included within quasi-legislation and by what other names it—and its constituent parts—might be called.[43] Indeed, the two matters are related.[44] I have chosen to use the term 'soft law', which is common in the literature (to the extent that it considers the phenomenon of soft law in a domestic setting at all), albeit very rarely in judicial writing.[45]

Many attempts to classify soft law have been compelled simply to list various examples of soft law instruments.[46] This approach, while instructive, does not lead to a definition but usually serves only to nominate instruments which could be either delegated legislation on one hand or soft law on the other, depending on whether their creation has been expressly authorised by Parliament. Codes of practice, guidance, guidance notes, circulars, policy notes, development briefs, practice statements, tax concessions, codes of conduct, codes of ethics and conventions all generally fall into the latter category.[47] Writing from a British perspective, McHarg would also have included constitutional conventions which lack legislative force.[48] Rawlings, by contrast, simply reflected that soft law finds a 'natural habitat' in an uncodified constitution which has a long history of constitutional conventions.[49]

No broader guiding principles can be derived from an approach based on lists of instruments. Lists tend 'to be over-inclusive, while not giving sufficient information to enable a classification to be made'.[50] They are therefore unsatisfactory for defining what soft law *is*, but can provide examples of what soft law *includes*, although 'it is what an instrument does, not what it is called, that is important'.[51] The most productive approach is typified by Sossin and Smith, who listed soft law's forms as including '[r]ules, manuals, directives, codes, guidelines, memoranda, correspondence, circulars, protocols, bulletins, employee handbooks and training materials' *because* each of the those instruments 'may have a substantial influence over decision-making'.[52] Harlow and Rawlings pointed out that defining soft law in terms of 'procedural distinctions', as many commentators have done (and as this book also does), is not the only suitable mode of classification because theorists would distinguish rules from principles.[53] Provided that soft law is considered on the

[43] S Argument, 'Quasi-legislation' (1994) 1 *Australian Journal of Administrative Law* 144, 144.

[44] R Rawlings, 'Soft Law Never Dies' in D Feldman and M Elliott (eds), *The Cambridge Companion to Public Law* (Cambridge, Cambridge University Press, 2015) 215, 218–23.

[45] cf *Thamotharem v Canada (Minister of Citizenship and Immigration)* [2008] 1 FCR 385, [55].

[46] See eg *Complex Regulation Report* (2008), 5; J Houghton and R Baldwin, 'Circular Arguments: the Status and Legitimacy of Administrative Rules' [1986] *PL* 239, 240–45; L Sossin and CW Smith, 'Hard Choices and Soft Law' (2003) 40 *Alberta Law Review* 867, 871; G Ganz, *Quasi-legislation* (London, Sweet and Maxwell, 1987) 1–2.

[47] D Pearce and S Argument, *Delegated Legislation*, 4th edn (Sydney, LexisNexis, 2012) 4–5; G Ganz, *Quasi-legislation* (London, Sweet and Maxwell, 1987).

[48] A McHarg, 'Reforming the United Kingdom Constitution: Law, Convention, Soft Law' (2008) 71 *MLR* 853. See also AV Dicey, *Introduction to the Study of the Law of the Constitution*, 8th edn (1915) 413.

[49] R Rawlings, 'Soft Law Never Dies' in D Feldman and M Elliott (eds), *The Cambridge Companion to Public Law* (Cambridge, Cambridge University Press, 2015) 215, 215.

[50] R Creyke and J McMillan, 'Soft Law versus Hard Law' in L Pearson et al (eds), *Administrative Law in a Changing State* (Oxford, Hart Publishing, 2008) 377, 380.

[51] ibid.

[52] L Sossin and CW Smith, 'Hard Choices and Soft Law' (2003) 40 *Alberta Law Review* 867, 871.

[53] C Harlow and R Rawlings, *Law and Administration*, 3rd edn (Cambridge, Cambridge University Press, 2009) 203–4.

basis of its effect rather than any more superficial consideration, I do not think that this issue is crucial to the argument being put forward here.

Soft law is best understood as including a range of different instruments along a spectrum rather than a collection of like objects.[54] In other words, soft laws have variable degrees of 'softness'. A rigid, taxonomic approach to determining what is included under the canopy of the term soft law would ignore that fact. The softness of law may differ between, for example, mere guidance or statements about an agency's general practices on one hand and, on the other, soft law which is all but compulsory to follow because, for example, it sets out the process to be followed if you wish to obtain a licence. This approach would answer Blutman's query 'Why is it soft, if it is law?'.[55] 'Soft' and 'hard' are meaningless adjectives to the extent that the (international) legal system can be divided into things which are 'law' and those which are not. In fact, between law which is 'hard', in the sense that it is enforceable by and against government, and edicts which are so 'soft' as not to be considered law at all, there is a range of instruments which mix softness with legality in varying concentrations.

Keyes argued that the 'principal distinction between executive legislation and quasi-legislation lies in their legal effect. Quasi-legislation has a hortatory, rather than mandatory, effect' on the decision-making process.[56] As a consequence, 'the persons whom [soft law instruments] address are both freer to ignore them and less able to rely on them as a legal basis for their actions'.[57] This statement is simultaneously true and inaccurate. It is true that people may not be bound by soft law as though it were hard law, although this chapter includes several examples of soft law with hard legal consequences. The flaw in Keyes' claim is more akin to that of Lord Diplock when he stated that people were free simply to ignore invalid decisions.[58] Such statements ignore the very real and persuasive power that instruments have when they bear some kind of official stamp. People tend not to ignore such instruments but *do* tend instead to rely on them as a legal basis for the actions they take. These very tendencies are what make soft law both so effective and so dangerous to people who do not realise the difference, in this context, between hard and soft.[59] Indeed, general compliance with soft law is usually a positive good, reducing disputes and litigation, and enhancing the ability of third parties to order their own affairs.

As long ago as 1944, Megarry noted that a legal world previously 'bounded by Acts of Parliament, Statutory Rules and Orders and judicial decisions' had been invaded by 'administrative quasi-legislation'.[60] He divided this phenomenon into two categories: 'the State-and-subject type, consisting of announcements by

[54] cf ibid, 203.

[55] L Blutman, 'In the Trap of a Legal Metaphor' (2010) 59 *ICLQ* 605, 609.

[56] JM Keyes, *Executive Legislation*, 2nd edn (New South Wales, Butterworths, 2010) 50. See also G Ganz, *Quasi-legislation* (London, Sweet and Maxwell, 1987) 24.

[57] JM Keyes, *Executive Legislation*, 2nd edn (New South Wales, Butterworths, 2010) 51.

[58] *Dunlop v Woollahra Municipal Council* [1982] AC 158, 172.

[59] See text accompanying fn 6 in Chapter 1 above.

[60] RE Megarry, 'Administrative Quasi-Legislation' (1944) 60 *LQR* 125, 125–26. See now D Greenberg, 'Dangerous Trends in Modern Legislation' [2015] *PL* 96.

administrative bodies of the course which it proposed to take in the administration of particular statutes' and 'the subject-and-subject type, consisting of arrangements made by administrative bodies which affect the operation of the law between one subject and another'.[61] Several examples of 'codified discretion' have been observed from even earlier than this.[62]

The proliferation of legislation produced outside of Parliament which concerned Megarry in 1944 has not abated. Pearce and Argument have observed that there are not only problems with the use of delegated legislation but also 'attendant problems of that use':[63]

> Outside of the established categories of delegated legislation ... a great body of instruments developed that apparently fit within the accepted definition of delegated legislation but in relation to which no discernible logic or discipline exists. From the 1980s, Australian parliaments (and particularly the Commonwealth Parliament) have passed into law an enormous number of provisions authorising the making of delegated instruments which were legislative in character but which do not obviously fit within the established categories of delegated legislation.

However, while the volume of delegated legislation has increased, its 'attendant problems' have been extensively reduced in Australia by the enactment of the Legislation Act, at least at the Commonwealth level.[64]

Aronson defined soft law as including rules and other instruments which guide and influence behaviour but have neither statutory nor contractual force.[65] Within this definition, which is the most appropriate in the Australian context, soft law does not denote a cohesive body of legal instruments, but refers to a number of different types of rule, within a broad spectrum.[66] Baldwin listed eight different types of soft law under the heading of tertiary rules classified by function: procedural rules, interpretive guides, instructions to officials, prescriptive rules, evidential rules, commendatory rules, voluntary codes and rules of practice.[67] In an earlier co-written article, Baldwin had also listed eight classifications of rules, but had combined prescriptive and evidential rules under a single heading.[68] The eighth classification

[61] RE Megarry, 'Administrative Quasi-Legislation' (1944) 60 *LQR* 125, 126. See also D Pearce and S Argument, *Delegated Legislation*, 4th edn (Sydney, LexisNexis, 2012) 15–16; C Harlow and R Rawlings, *Law and Administration*, 3rd edn (Cambridge, Cambridge University Press, 2009) 190–91.

[62] HW Arthurs, *Without the Law* (Toronto, Toronto University Press, 1985) 136; E Page, *Governing By Numbers: Delegated Legislation and Everyday Policy-Making* (Oxford, Hart Publishing, 2001) 13. For accounts of the history of rule-making, see CM Kerwin, *Rulemaking: How Government Agencies Write Law and Make Policy*, 2nd edn (Thousand Oaks CA, CQ Press, 1999) 7–22 (the USA) and PP Craig, *Administrative Law*, 7th edn (London, Sweet and Maxwell, 2012) 434–37 (England).

[63] D Pearce and S Argument, *Delegated Legislation*, 4th edn (Sydney, LexisNexis, 2012) 15. See the discussion accompanying n 40 above.

[64] See R Creyke and J McMillan, 'Soft Law versus Hard Law' in L Pearson et al (eds), *Administrative Law in a Changing State* (Oxford, Hart Publishing, 2008) 377.

[65] M Aronson, 'Private Bodies, Public Power and Soft Law in the High Court' (2007) 35 *Federal Law Review* 1, 3.

[66] See the text accompanying n 55 above.

[67] R Baldwin, *Rules and Government* (Oxford, Clarendon Press, 1995) 81–85.

[68] J Houghton and R Baldwin, 'Circular Arguments' [1986] *PL* 239, 240–45.

was 'Consultative Devices and Administrative Pronouncements', about which the authors noted:[69]

> [A] statement may have normative effects in certain circumstances or from some perspectives and it may lack them in a different context. To adhere to rigid definitions or conceptual distinctions is therefore to fall into a trap. Our final group is thus something of a safety-net. It covers those pronouncements which fit into none of the other groups but which have a significance that goes beyond the individual case. Principal amongst these are consultative statements. These often involve draft outlines of agency or departmental policy and invite comments. As such, they form a halfway house in the rule-making or adjudicative processes. They allow an expression of policy views without undertaking a rigid commitment.

Within the sub-categories of rules proposed by Baldwin, soft law may be used for a variety of purposes. Baldwin's classification of tertiary rules was focused on intention rather than effect: by definition, tertiary rules have no direct enforceability but are put in place in order to have some kind of practical effect. Baldwin divided them based upon the effect which rule-makers intend for them to have. By contrast, Greenberg argued that 'neither the Executive nor the Parliament is entitled to gloss the statute or to substitute its motives and intentions for those apparent from the text of the legislation that has been enacted'.[70]

Baldwin's approach contrasts with Megarry's earlier bipartite classification, based on whether regulation affected dealings between an entity of the state and another party or between two (or more) non-state parties. Writing some 50 years before Baldwin, in the infancy of the recognition of soft law, Megarry was understandably more concerned with the effect of soft law than its aims. Consequently, he was able to praise practice notes issued by the War Damage Commission as being 'shining examples of official helpfulness' in so far they 'deal with procedure or state the official view of a doubtful point that will be taken until the Courts rule otherwise'.[71] In this respect, Megarry departed from the traditional post-Diceyan approach to the administrative state, which would not likely have been prepared to concede any positive aspects to guidelines being issued by executive agencies, regardless of their benign intention or positive effect.[72]

In the USA, Anthony and Kerwin have both attempted to categorise rule-making, although Kerwin noted at the outset of his consideration of this topic that to do so is 'very difficult'.[73] To begin with, it is important to note that the Administrative Procedure Act 1946 (APA) specifies that rules are divided by function, although the classification of rules by function in fact predates that legislation by many years.[74] The first of these are 'legislative' or 'substantive' rules, which must be made in accordance with the APA's notice and comment procedures and, once made, 'bind the agency and

[69] ibid, 245.
[70] D Greenberg, 'Dangerous Trends in Modern Legislation' [2015] *PL* 96, 101.
[71] RE Megarry, 'Administrative Quasi-Legislation' (1944) 60 *LQR* 125, 126.
[72] See eg Lord Hewart, *The New Despotism* (Westport CT, Greenwood Press, 1975) 37.
[73] For example, the US *Code of Federal Regulations* organises rules into 50 distinct categories: CM Kerwin, *Rulemaking*, 2nd edn (Thousand Oaks CA, CQ Press, 1999) 22.
[74] ibid, 23–24.

the public'.[75] Due to this mutually binding effect, legislative rule-making of this kind is analogous to delegated legislation in Australia rather than to soft law.[76]

The APA exempts 'interpretative rules, general statements of policy, or rules of agency organisation, procedure, or practice' from its 'notice and comment' requirements.[77] Anthony divided the 'non-legislative' rules which fall within this exemption into two sub-categories: 'interpretive' and 'procedural' rules.[78] 'Interpretive' rules are generally published in the Federal Register of Legislative Instruments.[79] Unlike legislative rules, they need not be.

Furthermore, subject to the US Supreme Court's decision in *Chevron*, which has the effect that some interpretive rules will not be overturned by the courts if they are reasonably open, 'interpretive' rules do not impose new legal obligations on the agency which has issued them.[80] The agency can adopt a different interpretive rule if it is still reasonable. Interpretive rules generally take the form of guidelines, policy statements, technical manuals and the like, which are 'intended to advise the public how the agencies [interpret] their legal obligations' under certain legislation or court cases in which they have been considered.[81] 'Procedural' rules, on the other hand, define and describe the internal operations of administrative agencies. This information remains important to the public, particularly when it describes how members of the public may interact with an agency or participate in rule-making.[82]

Another method of classifying rule-making is not by function but by purpose, asking whom the rules are intended to 'influence and direct'.[83] Predominantly, those affected by rules are businesses and much of the work that has gone into assessing the impact of rule-making has been focused on business regulation.[84] Although government's capacity to involve itself in the way that private businesses are operated is virtually limitless, the methods by which this involvement can manifest itself *are* limited.[85] Most rules either prohibit behaviour or things outright, put limitations on them or set standards. Each of the latter two forms of regulation essentially allows a private actor to do as it pleases, 'within certain boundaries'.[86] Another form of rule which may be used to supplement any of the other types named above

[75] APA 1946 (US) 5 USC § 553. See CM Kerwin, *Rulemaking*, 2nd edn (Thousand Oaks CA, CQ Press, 1999) 23.

[76] RA Anthony, 'Interpretive Rules, Policy Statements, Guidances, Manuals, and the Like: Should Federal Agencies Use Them to Bind the Public?' (1992) 41 *Duke Law Journal* 1311, 1322.

[77] APA 1946 5 US Code § 553(b)(3)(A).

[78] RA Anthony, 'Interpretive Rules, Policy Statements, Guidances, Manuals, and the Like' (1992) 41 *Duke Law Journal* 1311, 1321.

[79] See Office of the Federal Register, *Federal Register*, available at www.archives.gov/federal-register/.

[80] RA Anthony, 'Interpretive Rules, Policy Statements, Guidances, Manuals, and the Like' (1992) 41 *Duke Law Journal* 1311, 1313–14. See *Chevron USA, Inc v Natural Resources Defense, Inc* 467 US 837 (1984); *City of Arlington v Federal Communications Commission* 133 SCt 1863 (2013).

[81] CM Kerwin, *Rulemaking*, 2nd edn (Thousand Oaks CA, CQ Press, 1999), 23.

[82] ibid; cf D Greenberg, 'Dangerous Trends in Modern Legislation' [2015] *PL* 96, 100.

[83] CM Kerwin, *Rulemaking*, 2nd edn (Thousand Oaks CA, CQ Press, 1999), 24.

[84] *Complex Regulation Report* (2008); CM Kerwin, *Rulemaking*, 2nd edn (Thousand Oaks CA, CQ Press, 1999) 24–26; Productivity Commission, *Annual Review of Regulatory Burdens on Business: Social and Economic Infrastructure Services*, Research Report (2009); G Pearson, *Financial Services Law and Compliance in Australia* (New York, Cambridge University Press, 2008).

[85] CM Kerwin, *Rulemaking*, 2nd edn (Thousand Oaks CA, CQ Press, 1999), 26.

[86] ibid, 27.

is one which obliges private actors to submit information about their activities to government, allowing their activities to be monitored.[87] In particular, this might be a pre-condition for parties who wish to enter into contracts with government.[88]

Classification of rules by purpose as opposed to function implies a less benign effect from soft law instruments. The structure imposed under the APA suggests that rules which are not 'legislative' are in place merely to inform the public or as a courtesy. It does not take account of the reality that, even where rules do not have a legally binding effect (as is the case with all soft law as defined by this book), they are nonetheless able to influence outcomes. The wealth of soft law regulation to which businesses are subject stands as a testament to this proposition.

Many soft law instruments which have an effect on businesses, particularly industry codes of conduct, *do* bind organisations, but achieve this end as a matter either of contract or consent rather than due to the binding effect of the soft law instrument per se. In effect, adherence to an industry code of conduct is a condition of membership of the industry body which has issued the code. A particularly demanding example can be observed in relation to providers of *in vitro* fertilisation (IVF) services. Certain activities can only be performed by certified members of the industry body, the Fertility Society of Australia (FSA). Certification is demanding and requires that an accredited Certification Body assess the compliance of a party which wishes to provide IVF services with the standards in the FSA Reproductive Technology Accreditation Committee's Certification Scheme.[89] The FSA additionally publishes its own Code of Practice, which is a hard and 'rule-like' example of soft law.[90] While these instruments fall within the definition of soft law in as much as they are not legislative, there can also be no doubt that they are both mandatory (rather than merely influential) and highly effective.[91] This is more typical of an industry scheme than of schemes which are designed to operate more broadly.

Governments are also able to set standards through the medium of placing certain requirements on the parties with whom they contract.[92] The Complex Regulation Report noted that the effect of these standard-setting instruments is analogous to decisions of the Superannuation Complaints Tribunal (SCT), to whose jurisdiction trustees of superannuation funds bind their trusts by contract in order to allow the

[87] ibid. See the discussion at nn 92–96 below.

[88] C Scott, 'Standard-Setting' in R Baldwin et al (eds), *Oxford Handbook of Regulation* (Oxford, Oxford University Press, 2010) [6.2.1]; cf N Seddon, *Government Contracts: Federal, State and Local*, 5th edn (Sydney, Federation Press, 2013) 45–46.

[89] Joint Accreditation System of Australia and New Zealand, *JAS-ANZ—RTAC Certification Scheme*, available at www.jas-anz.com.au/index.php?option=com_content&task=view&id=108; Fertility Society of Australia, '*Reproductive Technology Accreditation Committee Certification Scheme*' (2010).

[90] Fertility Society of Australia, '*Reproductive Technology Accreditation Committee: Code of Practice for Assisted Reproductive Technology Units*' (2010), available at www.fertilitysociety.com.au/rtac/. See L Bennett Moses, 'Understanding Legal Responses to Technological Change' (2005) 6 *Minnesota Journal of Law, Science & Technology* 505, 597.

[91] Particularly by comparison to the USA; see L Bennett Moses, 'Understanding Legal Responses to Technological Change' (2005) 6 *Minnesota Journal of Law, Science & Technology* 505, 597–99.

[92] CM Kerwin, *Rulemaking*, 2nd edn (Thousand Oaks CA, CQ Press, 1999) 28; C Scott, 'Standard-Setting' in R Baldwin et al (eds), *Oxford Handbook of Regulation* (Oxford, Oxford University Press, 2010) [6.2.1].

trusts to obtain certain tax concessions.[93] The ARC sought to make the point that, to the extent that the operation of these codes is subject to accountability mechanisms, those mechanisms are outside the scope of administrative law. This analogy is imperfect, mainly due to the fact that, although the SCT obtains jurisdiction by consent, this is at the option of the trustee of a superannuation fund rather than the beneficiary who brings a complaint to the SCT.[94] Additionally, a High Court majority recognised that, while the trustee of a fund might elect to submit to the jurisdiction of the SCT, trustees are frequently left with no practical option to do otherwise and 'cases may be readily imagined where it would be a breach of trust not to exercise the election so as to obtain the revenue benefits which follow'.[95] Nonetheless, the substance of the comparison between the SCT and many nominally voluntary industry codes of conduct is instructive.

Notwithstanding the various beneficial aspects of soft law which he was prepared to concede, Megarry considered the phenomenon to be a 'curate's egg', which is to say that the negative aspects of soft law nullified any benefits which its positive aspects might otherwise have provided.[96] He described as 'regrettable' 'quasi-legislative' official announcements which contradicted or were inconsistent with statutory provisions, with the effect that 'the statute remains unaltered on the statute book but ceases to represent the effective law'. This was because:[97]

> although no Court would enforce [the official announcements], no official body would fail to honour them, and as they are not merely concessions in individual cases but are intended to apply generally to all who fall within their scope, the description of 'quasi-legislation' is perhaps not inept.

Megarry's complaint can therefore be understood to be that state entities were able to issue announcements which had the practical status of legislation, even in the absence of legal status, without legislative scrutiny, and which, while open to challenge in court, were unlikely to be so challenged. The effect of this quasi-legislative influence was considered to be of greater import than the purpose for which it might be employed. In this sense, Megarry expressed a concern with the damage done to legal 'symmetry' that is reminiscent of Dicey's view that judges 'are much more concerned than Parliament to maintain "the logic or the symmetry of the law"', although no less valid for it.[98]

[93] *Complex Regulation Report* (2008), 14.

[94] See G Pearson, *Financial Services Law and Compliance* (New York, Cambridge University Press, 2008) 490; G Weeks, 'Superannuation Complaints Tribunal and the Public / Private Distinction in Australian Administrative Law' (2006) 13 *Australian Journal of Administrative Law* 147.

[95] *Attorney-General (Cth) v Breckler* (1999) 197 CLR 83, 111. See *Complex Regulation Report* (2008) 14.

[96] RE Megarry, 'Administrative Quasi-Legislation' (1944) 60 *LQR* 125, 127.

[97] ibid, 126.

[98] HW Arthurs, 'Rethinking Administrative Law: a Slightly Dicey Business' (1979) 17 *Osgoode Hall Law Journal* 1, 15; quoting AV Dicey, *Lectures on the Relation between Law and Public Opinion in England during the Nineteenth Century*, 2nd edn (London, Macmillan, 1962) 364.

B. DISCRETIONARY POWER

This section examines some of the reasons why soft law regulation has remained (and become increasingly) attractive to administrators as a method of controlling behaviour.

There is a lengthy history of delegating decision-making to those better equipped than the legislative drafters to exercise discretion appropriate to the circumstances.[99] Arthurs used the example of emigration officers who understood maritime engineering being better able than Parliament to decide whether ships were 'seaworthy', a term whose variable legal content has subsequently been noted.[100] Parliament, in turn, recognised the expertise of the officers and transferred its responsibility to them as members of the administration; they in turn formulated technical manuals as a means of structuring their discretion.[101] Where Parliament has decided to delegate its legislative authority in this way, the exercise of that authority must be (and, in recent decades, generally has been) recognised as 'law', in the sense of encapsulating a norm of positive law.[102] There is a strong argument that so too must the policy instruments or guidelines which are developed as a means of exercising, structuring and controlling delegated authority, particularly since (for good or ill) these forms of soft law have an immense capacity both to inform and to induce reliance.[103]

This section considers the issues which are raised when administrative officers are granted discretion to exercise power and how these issues affect (and are affected by) the use of soft law. For example, might a level of residual discretion serve to mitigate the unsympathetic application of soft law in exceptional cases?[104]

(i) The Diceyan View

Dicey was both the author of what remains the most influential work on English constitutional theory and famously opposed to administrative law.[105] Those of Dicey's theoretical cast were marked by their distaste for administrative law on two bases. First, it was a French concept (*droit administratif*) without any English analogue.[106] Secondly, it was fundamentally opposed to the notion that members of the executive should be held accountable under the 'ordinary law of the realm and amenable to the jurisdiction of the ordinary tribunals', rather than in specialised

[99] HW Arthurs, *Without the Law* (Toronto, Toronto University Press, 1985) 137.

[100] *HongKong Fir Shipping Co Ltd v Kawasaki Kisen Kaisha Ltd* [1962] 2 QB 26.

[101] HW Arthurs, *Without the Law* (Toronto, Toronto University Press, 1985) 137.

[102] See C Harlow and R Rawlings, *Law and Administration*, 3rd edn (Cambridge, Camrbidge University Press, 2009) 191.

[103] JM Keyes, *Executive Legislation*, 2nd edn (New South Wales, Butterworths, 2010) 55–56.

[104] See C Harlow and R Rawlings, *Law and Administration*, 3rd edn (Cambridge, Cambridge University Press, 2009) 217.

[105] AV Dicey, *Introduction to the Study of the Law of the Constitution*, 10th edn, ECS Wade (ed) (London, Palgrave, 1959). See generally C Harlow and R Rawlings, *Law and Administration*, 3rd edn (Cambridge, Cambridge University Press, 2009) 4–25.

[106] AV Dicey, *Introduction to the Law of the Constitution*, 10th edn, ECS Wade (ed) (London, Palgrave, 1959) 336–38.

administrative tribunals.[107] This vein of criticism is said to have resulted in 'generations of lawyers … being brought up to believe … that administrative law was repugnant to the British constitution'.[108]

Much has been made of the almost nationalistic tone of Dicey's stated opposition to the French *droit administratif*, which his numerous critics have often put down to a fundamental misunderstanding on his part of the tenets of that system.[109] This does Dicey a disservice: he was clearly very familiar with the *droit administratif*.[110] He was, however, philosophically opposed to specialist administrative courts, which were a feature of the French system, and it was in preference to these separate courts that Dicey advocated the role of 'ordinary courts' applying the 'ordinary law'. This analysis came against a background of 'notably formalist' English case law at the start of the twentieth century.[111]

Another reason for Dicey's antipathy towards administrative law was the breadth of the discretionary powers given to the administrative state, which he saw as a threat to the rule of law. He took the view that discretion was the antithesis of law, although this proposition has been described even by those generally sympathetic to Dicey's views as 'difficult to accept'; more so with the passage of time since Dicey first expressed it.[112] In his introduction to the 10th edition of Dicey's *Introduction to the Study of the Law of the Constitution*, Wade noted that:[113]

> Dicey's interest in discretions is not in their control by the courts, whether they could be challenged, in particular by certiorari, but in denying their existence. *Yet discretions are the most important of all topics for the modern constitutional lawyer* (emphasis added).

Harlow and Rawlings contended that Dicey's concern with discretionary powers was based on his elision of 'discretionary' with 'arbitrary' powers.[114] Nonetheless, Dicey's view that discretionary power is arbitrary per se had the effect of making suspicion of discretionary power a cornerstone principle of administrative law, in both England and America.[115] Certainly, the dichotomy between discretion and the

[107] ibid, 187–96.
[108] HWR Wade and C Forsyth, *Administrative Law*, 11th edn (Oxford, Oxford University Press, 2014) 14.
[109] See eg HW Arthurs, 'Rethinking Administrative Law: a Slightly Dicey Business' (1979) 17 *Osgoode Hall Law Journal* 1, 6–7.
[110] AV Dicey, '*Droit Administratif* in Modern French Law' (1901) 17 *LQR* 302; C Harlow, 'The Influence of Léon Duguit on Anglo-American Legal Thought' in F Melleray (ed), *Autour de Léon Duguit: Colloque commémoratif du 150e anniversaire de la naissance du doyen Léon Duguit tenu à Bordeaux les 29-30 Mai 2009* (Brussels, Bruylant, 2011) 227, 231–32.
[111] C Harlow, 'Duguit and Anglo-American Legal Thought' in F Melleray (ed), *Autour de Léon Duguit* (Brussels, Bruylant, 2011) 227, 232.
[112] ECS Wade, 'Introduction' to AV Dicey, *Introduction to the Law of the Constitution*, 10th edn (London, Palgrave, 1959) cxxv. See also HW Arthurs, 'Rethinking Administrative Law: a Slightly Dicey Business' (1979) 17 *Osgoode Hall Law Journal* 1, 23.
[113] ECS Wade, 'Introduction' to AV Dicey, *Introduction to the Law of the Constitution*, 10th edn (London, Palgrave, 1959) cxvii.
[114] C Harlow and R Rawlings, *Law and Administration*, 3rd edn (Cambridge, Cambridge University Press, 2009) 17. See also HW Arthurs, 'Rethinking Administrative Law: a Slightly Dicey Business' (1979) 17 *Osgoode Hall Law Journal* 1, 23–25; ibid.
[115] See J Dickinson, *Administrative Justice and the Supremacy of Law* (Cambridge MA, Harvard University Press, 1927) 35.

rule of law was reinforced in England by the Franks Committee.[116] Davis described this as 'the extravagant version of the rule of law'.[117] The contention that an exercise of discretion would only be arbitrary if the decision-maker lacked good faith is relatively modern.[118]

The difference between discretionary powers and arbitrariness is clearly articulated by Wade and Forsyth, who contended that the former are compatible with the principle of legality and the rule of law when 'conducted within a framework of recognised rules and principles which restrict discretionary power'.[119] The structural tension within the rule of law—between the value of predictability through adherence to law on the one hand, and flexibility and the capacity to do justice in individual cases on the other—is inescapable. It is, however, manageable once one concedes that discretionary power is now always subject to limits. Hence, while essential to the function of modern government, broadly expressed legislative powers must be controlled by common law principles of administrative law in order to be acceptable to the rule of law, rather than being left to mere political control.[120]

(ii) The Perils of Skeletal Legislation

Most modern legislation includes a capacity to make delegated legislation, usually, in Australia, through the agency of the relevant vice-regal officer. The reasoning behind creating this capacity is that legislation is slow to make, due to the high level of oversight and debate to which it is subjected, and that Parliamentary time is limited. Primary legislation, while being held to a high standard of accountability, is therefore not very responsive or flexible. Delegated legislation is able to be made more easily, with more limited parliamentary oversight, although the efficacy of this oversight has been queried.[121] There is a tendency to draft legislation in minimalist or 'skeletal' form and to leave issues of detail or uncertainty 'to the Regs'.[122] Detailed guidance about material which is more appropriate for consideration by Parliament is provided by a Handbook issued by the Department of Prime Minister and Cabinet.[123] To the extent that such material is nonetheless left to be the subject

[116] Franks Committee, (Committee on Administrative Tribunals and Enquiries), *Report of the Committee on Administrative Tribunals and Enquiries*, Command Paper No 218, (1957) 6.

[117] KC Davis, *Discretionary Justice* (Baton Rouge, Louisiana State University Press, 1969) 28–29.

[118] See eg *Buck v Bavone* (1976) 135 CLR 110, 118 (Gibbs J).

[119] HWR Wade and C Forsyth, *Administrative Law*, 11th edn (Oxford, Oxford University Press, 2014) 15.

[120] ibid, 16.

[121] PL Strauss, 'Legislation that Isn't—Attending to Rulemaking's "Democracy Deficit"' (2010) 98 *California Law Review* 1351, 1353.

[122] See S Argument, '"Leaving it to the Regs"—The Pros and Cons of Dealing with Issues in Subordinate Legislation' (Paper presented at the Australia-New Zealand Scrutiny of Legislation Conference, Brisbane, 26–28 July 2011), available at: www.parliament.qld.gov.au/documents/committees/SLC/2011/SLC_Conference/SLCConf-Sess11-Argument.pdf; D Pearce and S Argument, *Delegated Legislation*, 4th edn (Sydney, LexisNexis, 2012) 12–15; M Aronson, 'The Great Depression. This Depression and Administrative Law' (2009) 37 *Federal Law Review* 165, 166.

[123] See D Pearce and S Argument, *Delegated Legislation*, 4th edn (Sydney, LexisNexis, 2012) 119–20.

of delegated legislation in Australia, the operation of Parliamentary scrutiny committees mitigates that choice (although they could do more).[124]

The question of whether skeletal legislation is constitutionally valid in Australia was decided more than 80 years ago, when the High Court held in *Dignan* that the Commonwealth Parliament was competent to delegate legislatively the entirety of the law-making function under an enactment to the executive.[125] By contrast, in other countries, such as South Africa, there are constitutional principles which prevent excessively broad delegation of powers. In *Dawood*, the Constitutional Court held that if an overbroad grant of legislative discretion (without legislative criteria to guide its exercise) threatens to violate constitutional rights, the ambit of the discretion needs to be accompanied by more detailed criteria than where constitutional rights are not so threatened. A failure to provide such criteria may offend constitutionally entrenched rights.[126] If the capacity to delegate law-making power to the executive were the only relevance of *Dignan*, it would hardly rate a mention here. However, it is also notable—and arguably more important—for reminding us that skeletal legislation is not new and that modern legislatures and governments are not the first to employ it from questionable, openly political, or even positively malign, motives.[127]

Having said that, the problem of skeletal legislation appears to be more widespread than was formerly the case. Strauss made this point in relation to comparable legislation in the USA by comparing the Railway Safety Appliances Act 1893 (US) to the National Traffic and Motor Vehicle Safety Act 1966 (US).[128] He determined that at the time of the earlier Act, Congress saw it as its business to maintain a 'sharp focus on precise definition of the appropriate legal response to the problem at hand' but that this focus had been lost by the time of the later Act.[129] Aronson concluded that 'members of Congress used to be directly involved in formulating an Act's content, which they debated amongst themselves. That sort of work these days is left to huge congressional bureaucracies supervised by staffers'.[130] The devolution of political authority from elected representatives to agencies and administrators has been blamed on 'the complexities of contemporary society, and our understanding of the resulting needs for social order', with the result that 'placing the power to create law in other hands [is] inevitable'.[131] The world is simply more complicated than it used to be and, if we want government to regulate it in considerable detail, we face the problem that Parliament lacks the expertise to deal with matters of detail which

[124] ibid, 121–23; 144.

[125] *Victorian Stevedoring and General Contracting Co Pty Ltd v Dignan* (1931) 46 CLR 73.

[126] *Dawood v Minister of Home Affairs* 2000 (3) SA 936 (CC), [46]–[56] (O'Regan J). See C Hoexter, *Administrative Law in South Africa*, 2nd edn (Claremont, Juta & Co, 2012) 264–65.

[127] See R Creyke and J McMillan, *Control of Government Action*, 3rd edn (Sydney, LexisNexis, 2012) 316–17; EL Rubin, 'The Myth of Accountability and the Anti-Administrative Impulse' (2005) 103 *Michigan Law Review* 2073, 2074.

[128] PL Strauss, 'Legislative Theory and the Rule of Law: Some Comments on Rubin' (1989) 89 *Columbia Law Review* 427, 428–30.

[129] ibid, 429.

[130] M Aronson, 'The Great Depression' (2009) 37 *Federal Law Review* 165, 178 (fn 83).

[131] PL Strauss, 'Legislation that Isn't' (2010) 98 *California Law Review* 1351, 1353. See also EL Rubin, 'Law and Legislation in the Administrative State' (1989) 89 *Columbia Law Review* 369.

may arise under legislation.[132] There is also some suggestion that Parliament simply lacks the time to do more than set out principles in many cases, and leaves scrutiny of the operational law which is ultimately created to other oversight mechanisms, such as parliamentary committees.[133]

American concerns about increased devolution of law-making power to the executive creating a 'democracy deficit' have never exercised the same hold on Australian or English administrative lawyers. Indeed, they do not even cause a universal degree of concern amongst American administrative lawyers: 'American legislation these days typically leaves *everything* (even policy at the broadest level) to the executive branch and its agencies' (emphasis added).[134] Rubin was prepared to see 'rule-making' by agencies as an intrinsic sign of how the administrative state had developed:[135]

> The power to make rules is the power of the legislature itself, and a grant of this power represents at least a partial surrender of the legislature's own prerogatives. But rule-making power cannot be equated with legislation in a modern administrative state.

Nonetheless, there are some issues with which administrative lawyers generally might legitimately concern themselves. One is that, the Constitutional determination in *Dignan* notwithstanding, there is some legislation that is so skeletal that, whether or not it is 'an Act of Parliament', it no longer sits comfortably with any accepted normative definition of 'law'.[136] Another is that, increasingly, it is not mechanical provisions but also issues of policy which are left to delegated legislation or, indeed, soft law.[137]

Neither of these points directly concerns this book, although both are important. What is of concern is the likelihood that not all of the vast amount of law-making power which is 'left to the Regs' in fact results in a legislative instrument. Some of what Parliament leaves for administrators and agencies to do is better done through the mechanism of soft law rather than subordinate legislation; the sheer proliferation of soft law instruments leads inevitably to this conclusion.[138] Soft law *is* used. What is more, soft law instruments may possess 'a generality of application such that if they were juxtaposed to real statutory instruments they would be indistinguishable in terms of their nature or content'.[139]

As a practical matter, there is no prospect of this changing, and there are good practical reasons why it ought not. As I have discussed above, the use of soft law is not likely to carry a cost in terms of *effectiveness*, since many people comply with

[132] D Pearce and S Argument, *Delegated Legislation*, 4th edn (Sydney, LexisNexis, 2012) 18.
[133] See D Pearce, 'Legislative Scrutiny: Are the ANZACs Still the Leaders?' (Paper presented at the Australia-New Zealand Scrutiny of Legislation Conference: Scrutiny and Accountability in the 21st Century, Parliament House, Canberra, Australia, 6–8 July 2009), available at: www.aph.gov.au/~/media/Committees/Senate/sl_conference/papers/pearce.pdf.
[134] M Aronson, 'Great Depression' (2009) 37 *Federal Law Review* 165, 178.
[135] EL Rubin, 'Law and Legislation' (1989) 89 *Columbia Law Review* 369, 391.
[136] ibid, 380–85; M Aronson, 'Great Depression' (2009) 37 *Federal Law Review* 165, 178.
[137] S Argument, '"Leaving it to the Regs"' (Paper presented at the Australia-New Zealand Scrutiny of Legislation Conference, 26–28 July 2011); C Harlow and R Rawlings, *Law and Administration*, 3rd edn (Cambridge, Cambridge University Press, 2009) 196.
[138] D Pearce and S Argument, *Delegated Legislation*, 4th edn (Sydney, LexisNexis, 2012) 16–18.
[139] PP Craig, *Administrative Law*, 7th edn (London, Sweet and Maxwell, 2012) 467.

soft law as though it were legislative in any case. It does however have a cost in terms of *accountability*, since soft law is not even subject to the minimal scrutiny of being tabled in Parliament, or the exposure of being placed on the Federal Register of Legislative Instruments.[140] It further carries a higher level of risk simply because the drafting standards of soft law instruments are inconsistent and inferior to those used by legislative drafters.[141]

(iii) Confining and Structuring Discretion

That discretion can be exercised other than arbitrarily is now well understood. Davis observed to this end that rules and discretion occupy a spectrum, rather than being two mutually exclusive options (although he was still prepared to describe a broad discretion as 'arbitrary' when it had no more than the *potential* for misuse).[142] Within this spectrum:[143]

> a standard, principle or rule can be so vague as to be meaningless, it can have a slight meaning or a considerable meaning, it can have some degree of controlling effect, or it can be so clear and compelling as to leave little or no room for discretion.

It was Davis' thesis that the confinement and structuring of discretion are as relevant as how it was granted to administrators in the first place, and that discretion could be confined through the structure provided by rules as effectively as by restricting grants of discretion from the legislature.[144] Furthermore, Davis argued that, while administrative rule-making has a legislative aspect, it '*need not contain any generalisation*', should not shy away from being very specific and should build a body of rules case by case if necessary.[145] In this regard, he can be seen as favouring (at least in some circumstances) an incrementalist, 'judicial' approach to rule-making, rather than an exclusively 'legislative' approach which sees administrators frame rules only at a high level of abstraction.[146]

Davis' highly influential central thesis in *Discretionary Justice* should not be understood in strictly Diceyan terms.[147] Davis favoured discretion over rules in circumstances where it is important to counter legal rigidity, and stated that 'law' and 'discretion' do not form a dichotomy but that there is a 'zone' between them,

[140] Legislation Act 2003 s 20. See www.licencerecognition.gov.au/Mutual%20recognition/Pages/Federal-Register-of-Legislative-Instruments.aspx and www.comlaw.gov.au/Browse/ByTitle/LegislativeInstruments/; C Harlow and R Rawlings, *Law and Administration*, 3rd edn (Cambridge, Cambridge University Press, 2009) 192.

[141] D Pearce and S Argument, *Delegated Legislation*, 4th edn (Sydney, LexisNexis, 2012) 19; D Greenberg, 'Dangerous Trends in Modern Legislation' [2015] *PL* 96, 99–100.

[142] KC Davis, *Discretionary Justice* (Baton Rouge, Louisiana State University Press, 1969) 78.

[143] ibid, 15. See text accompanying fns 54–55 in Chapter 2.A of this volume above.

[144] ibid, 55–57.

[145] KC Davis, *Discretionary Justice* (Baton Rouge, Louisiana State University Press, 1969) 60, cf text accompanying fns 144–147 in Chapter 2.B.(ii) of this volume above. See C Harlow and R Rawlings, *Law and Administration*, 3rd edn (Cambridge, Cambridge University Press, 2009) 201.

[146] KC Davis, *Discretionary Justice* (Baton Rouge, Louisiana State University Press, 1969) 57–60.

[147] C Harlow and R Rawlings, *Law and Administration*, 3rd edn (Cambridge, Cambridge University Press, 2009) 201–2.

much as the dawn separates night and day.[148] Nonetheless, the bulk of the book is concerned with applying limits to administrative discretion. There is a long tradition of suspicion towards discretion, in which Davis was a central (but by no means the only) figure, and which has developed in the USA independently of Diceyan influence.[149] Davis strongly advocated executive rule-making as a response to grants of discretionary power in the United States. His influence in this regard was immense.[150] However, his approach was more 'pluralist' than most in at least one aspect: he argued that rules and guidelines about the enforcement of legislation which amount to the 'substantial reformulation of enacted law' can have the practical effect of changing the law.[151] Davis justified this position, specifically in regard to police enforcement of criminal legislation (which, it is conceded, carries its own specific issues) on the basis that it is preferable to a situation where the enacted law is not enforced in practice but the discretion not to enforce the law is exercised on an ad hoc basis rather than in accordance with a stated policy.[152]

Dicey would have abhorred the use of soft law as an exercise of discretion. He objected, after all, to 'official law', the term by which he described law administered by official bodies.[153] However, this was generally imposed by legislation and was saved, in Dicey's view, from violating the rule of rule of law only because the decisions of any such official body were reviewable by the 'ordinary courts' applying 'ordinary law'.[154] Soft law, by comparison, amounts to the voluntary adoption by state administrative agencies of informal rules and processes which may be applied in some circumstances as though they were law, but generally without recourse to a court to review their application, absent jurisdictional error by the administrative body in question.

In an oft-cited appraisal of Dicey's theoretical approach to administrative law, Arthurs was extremely critical of the approach taken by Dicey and his followers (most notably, Lord Hewart) to the legitimacy of administrative law.[155] While Arthurs' criticisms of Dicey's exposition of the theoretical underpinnings of the rule of law are well reasoned and in the main difficult to dispute, there is a sense in which such attacks amounted to taking aim at a target which has long since ceased to move. Indeed, Arthurs conceded that focusing his article on Dicey's work might be seen 'to belabour a horse which is thought to have died so long ago, after assaults so numerous and savage, that humane considerations might dictate another line of investigation'.[156] Furthermore, while Arthurs' deconstruction of the Diceyan concept

[148] KC Davis, *Discretionary Justice* (Baton Rouge, Louisiana State University Press, 1969) 19, 106–7; cf AM Gleeson, 'Judicial Legitimacy' (2000) 20 *Australian Bar Review* 1, 8.

[149] See PL Strauss, 'Legislation that Isn't' (2010) 98 *California Law Review* 1351, 1355 (fn 17).

[150] See RM Levin, 'The Administrative Law Legacy of Kenneth Culp Davis' (2005) 42 *San Diego Law Review* 315, 324–25.

[151] KC Davis, *Discretionary Justice* (Baton Rouge, Louisiana State University Press, 1969) 93–94.

[152] ibid, 94.

[153] AV Dicey, *Introduction to the Study of the Law of the Constitution*, 8th edn (London, Macmillan, 1902) 190–91.

[154] HW Arthurs, 'Rethinking Administrative Law: a Slightly Dicey Business' (1979) 17 *Osgoode Hall Law Journal* 1, 26–27.

[155] ibid.

[156] ibid, 4 (citation omitted).

of the rule of law is essentially sound, this need not justify a wholesale repudiation of Dicey's work, which still retains much that is attractive, particularly when understood as a set of aspirations for equality of justice between government and citizens.

The reason that Dicey's approach to discretion must be discarded is that the functions of government have long since moved beyond what the legislature has the capacity to handle alone. Representative democracy is limited in this regard, which only causes a problem to those who equate the *direct* responsibility of the legislature for all non-judicial law-making functions as a pre-requisite of the rule of law.[157] In this regard, Davis submitted that, apart from the fact that legislatures are limited in their capacity to govern every aspect of modern life directly, they had also recognised that to do so was undesirable in many circumstances.[158] Where Parliament is unable to anticipate the detailed requirements of law, Davis argued that it is better to legislate at a higher level of generality and have administrative agencies, with the expertise garnered from applying legislation in a certain field, add the necessary level of detail. This was to be done in the form of 'rules', a word whose imprecision he found 'unsatisfactory' but which limitations of the language compelled him to use.[159]

Davis' proposal was for the courts to declare the appropriate extent to which administrative discretion should be structured by rules in order to satisfy the rule of law, and even to compel administrators to formulate rules which supply 'the desired standards' if they fail to do so as a matter of their own initiative.[160] These thoughts subsequently obtained fresh relevance, some 40 years after they were first published by Davis, when the Appellate Committee of the House of Lords (in its final judicial decision prior to the establishment of the Supreme Court of the United Kingdom) considered the criminal offence of 'aid[ing], abet[ting], counsel[ling] or procur[ing] the suicide of another' by arranging for a terminally ill person to travel to a clinic in Switzerland.[161] The interesting (although deeply unfortunate) consequence of such legislation is that, although suicide and attempted suicide have long ceased to attract criminal sanctions in England, *assisting* someone to commit suicide remains a criminal act in its own right, not merely ancillary to the offence of the person who commits suicide.[162] Their Lordships ordered the Director of Public Prosecutions to 'promulgate an offence-specific policy identifying the facts and circumstances which he will take into account in deciding … whether or not to consent to a prosecution' for breach of the legislative provision above.[163]

This approach leaves some open questions, such as the level of specificity which will suffice to satisfy a court order to formulate soft law and the amount of discretion that the DPP might justifiably leave to himself. The prospect also looms that the inevitably difficult and frequently heart-rending cases that will be covered by the proposed soft law will be dealt with through 'selective enforcement' of not only the Suicide Act 1961 but also of the DPP's guidelines, which cannot, after

157 See eg KC Davis, *Discretionary Justice* (Baton Rouge, Louisiana State University Press, 1969) 48.
158 ibid, 45–51.
159 ibid, 56 (fn 4).
160 ibid, 50–51; 58.
161 Suicide Act 1961 (UK) s 2(1).
162 See Chapter 5.A.(i) of this volume below.
163 *R (Purdy) v Director of Public Prosecutions* [2009] 1 AC 345, 396.

all, bind the DPP to commence a prosecution. There is often a danger of selective [non]-enforcement of the law, especially against sympathetic subjects in 'hard cases'.[164] Most significantly, it raises the question of what remedies are available in the event that an administrative body formulates soft law from which it later seeks to depart. The potential answers to these questions are the focus of the subsequent chapters of this book.

Davis did not see discretion as an absolute evil but argued that, to be useful, it needed to be curtailed in three ways: by confining it, structuring it and checking it.[165] Over 40 years after its initial publication, much of what Davis had to say about checking discretion is moot in the Australian federal context as a result of the 'new administrative law' reforms of the 1970s. Specifically, the wide jurisdiction of the Administrative Appeals Tribunal, in addition to 'super' tribunals in most States, means that there are institutionalised checking measures over executive discretionary decisions in addition to whatever internal review processes an administrative agency may have. However, not every need to structure discretion is solved by the availability of a checking mechanism in the form of merits review. Davis' view was that the acts of confining and structuring discretion 'may overlap' but are purposively different because the 'purpose of confining is to keep discretionary power within designated boundaries' and the 'purpose of structuring is to control the manner of the exercise of discretionary power within the boundaries'.[166]

Baldwin strongly criticised the paradigm embodied in Davis' belief that previously announced rules are the most appropriate means of regulating discretion, on the basis that:[167] 'to structure or confine discretion at one point without attention to the shaping of that discretion often leads to the phenomenon of displacement. Squeeze in one place and, like a tube of toothpaste, discretion will bulge at another'. As with the outlook espoused by Dicey, Davis was focused strongly on justice in individual cases (without favouring broad discretion, which is usually seen as the best means of providing individual justice) but did not consider the issues of 'collective consumption', beyond an assessment that procedural limits on discretion would be of general benefit.[168] Davis took pains to differentiate his views from the 'extravagant version of the rule of law' espoused by Dicey and Hayek.[169]

Baldwin made his critique of Davis on the basis that a legalist/formalist view of the world, which interprets the rule of law such that every flaw in administration can be remedied with more rules, fails to take account of the possibility that the 'failings of a particular governmental process may be fundamental and may require substantial rethinking of such matters as broad government strategy, schemes of accountability, scrutiny procedures, organisational frameworks and goals'.[170] In other words,

164 See C Harlow and R Rawlings, *Law and Administration*, 3rd edn (Cambridge, Cambridge University Press, 2009) 208.

165 KC Davis, *Discretionary Justice* (Baton Rouge, Louisiana State University Press, 1969) chs III, IV and V respectively.

166 ibid, 97.

167 R Baldwin, *Rules and Government* (Oxford, Clarendon Press, 1995) 26.

168 KC Davis, *Discretionary Justice* (Baton Rouge, Louisiana State University Press, 1969) 31–33; P McAuslan, 'Administrative Law, Collective Consumption and Judicial Policy' (1983) 46 *MLR* 1, 7.

169 KC Davis, *Discretionary Justice* (Baton Rouge, Louisiana State University Press, 1969) 32.

170 R Baldwin, *Rules and Government* (Oxford, Clarendon Press, 1995) 19.

where Davis was content to limit discretion and rules to either end of a spectrum, Baldwin was prepared to see them as a legal issue forming only one part of a broader set of political and organisational queries. This difference in approach is exemplified by Baldwin's point that, so far from being an 'apolitical benchmark' as Davis had seen it, the very concept of justice is essentially subjective.[171]

Baldwin made a further potent criticism of the model suggested by Davis by querying whether the increased amount of structure provided by rules has any effect in reducing the practical exercise of administrative discretion.[172] He argued that it may not, because a highly detailed regulatory regime (such as the US taxation laws, which were cited by both Davis and Baldwin) can often allow administrators to choose *between* competing tenable decisions. If this analysis is correct, a highly detailed, fact-specific body of rules in a particular area will in fact *increase* the discretion of administrators to choose between applicable rules. There is much to support this view, including empirical evidence cited by Baldwin.[173] Every lawyer knows that, of the many thousands of cases which are decided every year, added to an already massive body of case law, it frequently occurs that there is no case on all fours with the factual scenario being considered. In such cases, lawyers will argue that a court should apply certain authorities and distinguish others, meaning that there is a discretionary choice as to what case to apply. Baldwin's argument regarding very rule-heavy administration is analogous to this situation.

It follows from this that Davis' proposal that a body of rules should be built up in the smallest increments necessary is flawed to the extent that it relies on the same factual scenarios recurring.[174] Unless there is a high degree of factual recurrence in a particular area, the capacity to develop rules and also the value of those rules will be impaired by this method.[175] If that statement is accurate, it significantly undermines one of Davis' central findings: that rules are generally, even if not universally, preferable to unstructured discretions. Davis, of course, readily conceded that it is undesirable to be so completely rule-bound that judicious use of discretion is unable to impose a just decision in circumstances unanticipated by existing rules.[176] While Baldwin recognised this concession, he pressed further, arguing that the somewhat Diceyan tendency to characterise discretionary decision-making as 'arbitrary' and 'capricious' is inaccurate in so far as it is based on a narrow conception of a 'decision'.[177] The thrust of Baldwin's argument was that, even if discretion in the absence of rules is less structured, it has the concomitant advantage of greater flexibility which allows administrators to be more responsive in times of rapid or unanticipated change.[178] The issue returns again to the tension between the rule of law principles of flexibility and predictability.

[171] ibid, 22.
[172] ibid, 23.
[173] ibid.
[174] KC Davis, *Discretionary Justice* (Baton Rouge, Louisiana State University Press, 1969) 60.
[175] DJ Gifford, 'Decisions, Decisional Referents and Administrative Justice' (1972) 37 *Law and Contemporary Problems 3*; cited in R Baldwin, *Rules and Government* (Oxford, Clarendon Press, 1995) 24.
[176] KC Davis, *Discretionary Justice* (Baton Rouge, Louisiana State University Press, 1969) 106–7.
[177] R Baldwin, *Rules and Government* (Oxford, Clarendon Press, 1995) 25–26.
[178] ibid, 28.

Further to this, there are practical limitations on the capacity of agencies to issue prospectively binding rules. Mantel noted that:[179]

> because agencies operate in a world of imperfect information where they cannot anticipate all scenarios that may arise in the course of implementing a statutory and regulatory scheme, an agency cannot define and set forth in its legislative rules every nuance of its policies.

Rules of this sort are effectively no better than legislation set out in general terms. Leaving some breadth of discretion also allows for creative responses to the problems which regulation seeks to address, rather than encouraging those subject to rules simply to 'tick the appropriate boxes'.[180] Flexibility, therefore, can be seen not only as a benefit allowing for a higher quality of regulation but a practical necessity, since both administrative and legislative foresight are limited.

Having said that, flexibility carries with it a greater level of risk than mandatory procedures. Stewart asked that proponents of flexibility remember that:[181]

> there may be a trial and error process in [an administrative agency] finding the best means of achieving the posited goal, but persons subject to the administrator's control are no more liable to his arbitrary will than are patients remitted to the care of a skilled doctor.

The capacity to experiment with administrative approaches should be understood as carrying with it a heavy responsibility.

In relation to judicial, rather than administrative decision-making, Haack noted that there is frequently a range within which different decisions are able to be logically and morally supported. Judicially, this is illustrated by the fact that dissenting judgments need not necessarily betray a want of logic, although they are not binding as precedent.[182] This extends by analogy to administrative exercises of discretion. Haack's point goes to the fact that there is moral legitimacy to structuring democratic power through indeterminate rules, if there is something *other than* those rules which also structures discretion, such as legal and cultural values.

The requirement that rules be made (as opposed to the effectiveness of those rules) changes with the administrative body to which they would be applied. Greater levels of administrative expertise, externality from government and other means of control (usually under contract and including audits, inspections and targets) will influence whether rules are in fact appropriate means by which to regulate administrative discretions.[183]

[179] J Mantel, 'Procedural Safeguards for Agency Guidance: a Source of Legitimacy for the Administrative State' (2009) 61 *Administrative Law Review* 343, 351; see also NA Mendelson, 'Regulatory Beneficiaries and Informal Agency Policymaking' (2007) 92 *Cornell Law Review* 397, 410.

[180] C Scott, 'Standard-Setting' in R Baldwin et al (eds), *Oxford Handbook of Regulation* (Oxford, Oxford University Press, 2010) [6.2.2].

[181] RB Stewart, 'The Reformation of American Administrative Law' (1975) 88 *Harvard Law Review* 1667, 1678.

[182] S Haack, 'Pluralistic Universe of Law' (2008) 21 *Ratio Juris* 453, 470–71; OW Holmes, 'The Path of the Law' (1896) 10 *Harvard Law Review* 457, 465. See S Gageler and B Lim, 'Collective Irrationality and the Doctrine of Precedent' (2015) 38 *Melbourne University Law Review* 525, 548.

[183] See eg *Australian Retailers' Association v Reserve Bank of Australia* (2005) 148 FCR 446; G Weeks, 'Litigating Questions of Quality' (2007) 14 *Australian Journal of Administrative Law* 76, 83; I Harden, *The Contracting State* (Milton Keynes, Open University Press, 1992) ch 5.

(iv) Alternative Approaches

Davis wanted a body of precedent which both confines and adds structure to administrative discretion. Baldwin opposed this vision on the basis that it would serve to increase the amount of discretion available to administrators in practice. However, others have taken an alternative approach. Arthurs noted that research had shown that administrative decision-makers 'may tend to allow discretion to crystallise so completely into rules that they sometimes cease to function effectively, or at least as originally mandated'.[184] Both Farmer and Nonet wrote to this effect within five years of the initial publication of Davis' *Discretionary Justice*.[185]

Nonet described the welfare state as having been designed to avoid the 'rigid constraints that paralysed initiative and prevented effective action to solve the problems of society', constraints that were born of the 'burdensome formalism of legal procedure'.[186] By contrast, he portrayed its critics as employing Diceyan 'rule of law' reasoning to argue for a restrictive approach to administrative power, which was to be subject to 'public authority'.[187] Nonet argued that the imposition of external restraints on administrative action, in the form of judicial review, both obscured 'opportunities for securing *internal* restraints in government, by building legal control within the administrative process' and 'ruled out the possibility that, through the courts from without or through built-in legal processes, law might *positively* contribute to the capacities of government and further the realisation of public purposes'.[188] This in turn was seen as diminishing the scope and import of legal criticism because, by separating substantive issues of policy from procedural issues of legality, the legal limitations placed upon the exercise of discretion serve only to place checks on decision-makers who exceed their authority and not on those who stray from the policy basis for which their discretionary powers were granted.

Nonet saw dual consequences of this approach. First, challenges to existing policies at an administrative level would have a reduced scope, thus binding decision-makers to execute policies docilely without exercising any discretion of their own. Secondly, legal criticism would be focused on the process rather than the substance of administrative decision-making.[189] Nonet proposed that 'legal criticism' be extended to administrative decision-making to ensure, not simply that discretion be constrained, but that it is exercised 'consistent with the aims of public welfare' following legal argument.[190]

Nonet asserted that, by making exercises of discretion follow legal argument, people can ensure that they obtain 'rights' to benefits provided by government through

[184] HW Arthurs, 'Rethinking Administrative Law: a Slightly Dicey Business' (1979) 17 *Osgoode Hall Law Journal* 1, 24.

[185] JA Farmer, *Tribunals and Government* (London, Weidenfeld and Nicolson, 1974); P Nonet, *Administrative Justice: Advocacy and Change in a Government Agency* (New York, Russell Sage, 1969).

[186] P Nonet, *Administrative Justice* (New York, Russell Sage, 1969) 3.

[187] ibid, 4. See AV Dicey, *Introduction to the Law of the Constitution*, 10th edn, ECS Wade (ed) (London, Palgrave, 1959) 328–405.

[188] P Nonet, *Administrative Justice* (New York, Russell Sage, 1969) 4.

[189] ibid, 5.

[190] ibid, 6.

administrative discretion.[191] However, one of the reasons for the increasing use of soft law is precisely to bypass onerous procedures of this type. Exercising discretion subsequent to legal argument would be unlikely to contribute to the goal of making administrative decision-making swift, efficient, effective, economical and responsive to change. It would carry with it *additional* procedural burdens and, inevitably, expose administrative decisions to a greater likelihood of challenge by way of judicial review. This may be seen as an effect of the APA's informal 'notice and comment' procedures, since Davis' influential approach required courts to distinguish between adjudicative and legislative facts, providing a focus for potential disputes even as the formal rule-making 'trial' procedure fell into disuse.[192] In Australia, additional procedural burdens might follow the Legislation Act's requirement that legislative instruments be tabled in Parliament, although in reality the Act has a negligible impact on validity.[193]

Farmer's work specifically considered the degree to which judicial and tribunal decision-making each apply precedent. He noted that, during the 1960s, the House of Lords and English Court of Appeal became less inclined to apply the doctrine of precedent as stringently as they had previously done, with the effect that new common law doctrines developed.[194] However, this did not alter the sovereignty of the English Parliament and Farmer argued that courts became even less willing to make new law as an exercise of policy: the increased inclination of Parliament to find legislative solutions to questions of policy was in general treated with appropriate deference by the judicial branch.[195] Farmer linked this trend to the expansion of tribunal decision-making, particularly where pressure on parliamentary time meant that not every important issue could be legislated for in full.[196]

However, Farmer further argued that tribunal justice tends *in practice* to 'bind' itself to precedent.[197] It is true that tribunals generally are not bound to apply previous tribunal findings as precedents, since every matter is decided on its own merits and not by the application of precedent. Nonetheless, Farmer noted that, while 'flexibility is the ideal', demands for consistent and predictable decision-making lead to 'an informal *de facto* system of precedent'.[198] Adopting Dworkin's terminology, Farmer distinguished between 'rules' which require decision-makers to conform to them and 'principles' which indicate issues of importance without compelling a particular decision.[199] His purpose was to distinguish between informal 'precedent', of

[191] ibid. See also CA Reich, 'The New Property' (1964) 73 *Yale Law Journal* 733, 786; cf R Stevens, *Torts and Rights* (Oxford, Oxford University Press, 2007) Ch 10.

[192] RM Levin, 'Legacy of K.C. Davis' (2005) 42 *San Diego Law Review* 315, 325–26. See Administrative Procedure Act 1946 (US) 5 USC § 553.

[193] D Pearce and S Argument, *Delegated Legislation*, 4th edn (Sydney, LexisNexis, 2012) 34–35.

[194] eg *Hedley Byrne & Co Ltd v Heller & Partners Ltd* [1964] AC 465. See JA Farmer, *Tribunals and Government* (London, Weidenfeld and Nicolson, 1974) 172.

[195] cf *Dutton v Bognor Regis Urban District Council* [1972] 1 QB 373, 397 (Lord Denning MR).

[196] JA Farmer, *Tribunals and Government* (London, Weidenfeld and Nicolson, 1974) 173.

[197] See fn 40 in Chapter 4.A of this volume below.

[198] JA Farmer, *Tribunals and Government* (London, Weidenfeld and Nicolson, 1974) 174.

[199] RM Dworkin, 'The Model of Rules' (1967) 35 *University of Chicago Law Review* 14, 22–29. One may query to what extent this adoption was apposite, since tribunal rules may be very 'rule-like' in the sense employed by Dworkin, in which rules have an 'all or nothing' application.

the kind found in tribunals, and precedents which bind, or must be distinguished by, judges in court proceedings. On this view, tribunal members are guided, judges are bound.

The notion that tribunal decisions made on the facts have precedential value abuts the question of what constitutes law. This is a significant issue, about which it currently suffices simply to compare the traditional view with the realities of tribunal justice.[200] The Diceyan approach that only Parliament and (preferably) the 'ordinary law courts' have the power to make law has been questioned. By any practical definition, tribunals also set precedents which might well be included in a functionalist definition of 'law':[201]

> Tribunals are under the same pressures as the courts to decide like cases alike, to explain their understanding of the law, and to confine themselves to the case at hand. Their decisions are widely published, and read not just by anyone who is to appear before them, but also by anyone wanting to discover and study the substantive law with which they deal … In any practical sense, their decisions are surely authoritative.

Likewise, the APA:[202]

> seems to imagine that the impact of a publication rule will be rather like that of an agency adjudicatory precedent—not itself 'law', yet establishing a principle to which the public may be held unless the agency is persuaded not to apply it, and constraining the judgment of the agency itself in the absence of some demonstrated reason for departing from it.

It is instructive that Strauss describes both the agency *and* the public as being bound by such a precedent. His broader point was later approved by a majority of the Supreme Court in *US v Mead Corp*.[203]

The practical reality identified in the excerpts above serves to emphasise the concern raised by Farmer that the balance between consistency and flexibility is tipped too far in favour of the former if tribunals bind themselves to 'informal precedents'. In Australia, Deane J commented to similar effect that, 'while consistency may properly be seen as an ingredient of justice, it does not constitute a hallmark of it'.[204] However, the role of informal precedents in tribunals has been settled for many years, since the highly influential decision of Brennan J, sitting as President of the AAT, in *Drake (No 2)*.[205] In *Babaniaris*, the High Court was called upon to consider whether a decision of the Chairman of the Workers' Compensation Board, a judicial officer, was binding as precedent on later decisions of the Board.

200 See Chapter 3 of this volume below.

201 M Aronson et al, *Judicial Review of Administrative Action*, 4th edn (Sydney, Thompson Reuters, 2009) 189. See now M Aronson and M Groves, *Judicial Review of Administrative Action*, 5th edn (Sydney, Thompson Reuters, 2013) [4.70].

202 PL Strauss, 'The Rulemaking Continuum' (1992) 41 *Duke Law Journal* 1463, 1472–73. More precisely, Strauss should have referred to a 'norm' rather than a principle.

203 *United States v Mead Corporation* 533 US 218 (2001), 232.

204 *Nevistic v Minister for Immigration and Ethnic Affairs* (1981) 51 FLR 325, 334. See also C Harlow and R Rawlings, *Law and Administration*, 3rd edn (Cambridge, Cambridge University Press, 2009) 207–8.

205 *Drake (No 2)* (1979) 2 ALD 634.

Brennan and Deane JJ held that the issue turned on whether the Chairman's decision was 'an administrative opinion' about the intention of Parliament or a judicial determination which declared the same, concluding that:[206]

> When a tribunal which has exclusive jurisdiction to determine claims between parties for the enforcement of a statutory right construes the statute in order to determine a claim, the construction placed on the statute is not a mere administrative opinion; it is a judicial determination.

This approach further reinforced the distinction between informal (tribunal) and formal (judicial) precedents.

Both Farmer and Nonet reached the conclusion that executive decision-makers tend to allow discretion which is confined or structured by rules to be 'crystallised' by those rules (to use Arthurs' term), with the effect that discretionary decision-making is not markedly different from non-discretionary decision-making. As such, it may have none of the risks that Davis noted as being inherent in discretion, but perhaps also none of its advantages, such as responsiveness, flexibility, the 'potential for interpretation' and 'the development of innovative ways of addressing' the problem with which the soft law in question purports to deal.[207] Furthermore, to the extent that previous decisions have not been made in light of new information which will inevitably become known and which may demand a more 'nuanced' policy, this method of restricting administrative discretion will result in decision-making with additional deficiencies, such as not only being unresponsive but also essentially backward-looking.[208] Finally, it is inevitable that soft law, whose métier is influence, will continue to thrive and that the public will continue to be exposed to it, albeit below the level of the formerly-soft law which has been 'hardened' or 'crystallised' into law of a more formal, positivist kind.

The post-Dicey common ground on the issue of discretion is that the administrative state cannot be run from the floor of Parliament (or indeed from Ministerial offices) alone. Indeed, Sunstein cited 'the shift from regulation through common law courts to regulation through administrative agencies' in support of the *Chevron* doctrine of judicial deference to administrative statutory interpretation, a doctrine which Dicey would have placed wholly outside the rule of law.[209] A majority of the Australian High Court firmly rejected *Chevron* in *Enfield Corporation*, although it was not strictly necessary to do so on the facts of the case. It also endorsed criticism of the doctrine on the basis that it is 'indicative of a "delegalisation" of the

[206] *Babaniaris v Lutony Fashions Proprietary Limited* (1987) 163 CLR 1, 31–32.

[207] C Scott, 'Standard-Setting' in R Baldwin et al (eds), *Oxford Handbook of Regulation* (Oxford, Oxford University Press, 2010) [6.2.1].

[208] J Mantel, 'Procedural Safeguards for Agency Guidance' (2009) 61 *Administrative Law Review* 343, 351.

[209] CR Sunstein, 'Beyond *Marbury*: the Executive's Power to Say What the Law Is' (2006) 115 *Yale Law Journal* 2580, 2583; see *Chevron* 467 US 837 (1984).

administrative process'.[210] This fact will be considered significant by critics of the Court's supposedly 'formalist' and 'legalist' tendencies.[211]

The undeniable development of the administrative state means that some degree of discretionary decision-making is inevitable and this is not wholly undesirable. Discretion allows flexibility in decision-making and this is necessary to allow for greater speed in responding to changing circumstances than is possible through the more rigorous process of legislation, and also to ensure that justice is able to be done in unusual cases which have not been considered in formulating rules. While most agree that some level of structure is desirable in the exercise of discretion, particularly in circumstances where substantially similar factual situations recur frequently, the imposition of regulations under a statutory scheme by government is beyond the scope of this book.

The tension between consistency and flexibility is also inevitable and not undesirable. Soft law emerges in the context of that inevitable tension as a device that tries to have it both ways: to be both hard, consistent, inflexible law and soft, adaptable, flexible non-law. The questions which remain are therefore to what extent soft law can succeed in this aim and what specific problems may be present in using soft law thus understood. For example, should public authorities structure their own discretions by making them subject to rules and, having done so, when and how are they able to reach a decision which is contrary to a self-imposed rule?

[210] *Enfield Corporation* (2000) 199 CLR 135, 152 (Gleeson CJ, Gummow, Kirby & Hayne JJ); citing K Werhan, 'Delegalizing Administrative Law' [1996] *University of Illinois Law Review* 423, 457. See M Aronson and M Groves, *Judicial Review of Administrative Action*, 5th edn (Sydney, Thompson Reuters, 2013) [4.60].

[211] See eg T Poole, 'Between the Devil and the Deep Blue Sea' in L Pearson et al (eds), *Administrative Law in a Changing State* (Oxford, Hart Publishing, 2008) 15; M Taggart, 'Australian Exceptionalism' (2008) 36 *Federal Law Review* 1; cf J Boughey and G Weeks, '"Officers of the Commonwealth" in the Private Sector: Can the High Court Review Outsourced Exercises of Power?' (2013) 36 *University of NSW Law Journal* 316, 329.

3

The Regulatory Purpose of Soft Law

THE ARGUMENTS RAISED in Chapter two about the nature of law lead to further questions. What part of administrative rule-making leads to law or legal rules (as opposed to 'secondary rules', delegated legislation or (in England) Statutory Instruments)?[1] What part merely results in soft law?[2] A further question, the answer to which will clarify the role and status of soft law, is to what extent can soft law simply be described as 'rules'? If we accept as a starting point that the category of 'rules' is broader than that of 'law', what part of 'rules' is outside the definition of 'law'? Soft law differs from law in that it does not have legally *binding* consequences. Likewise, rules are 'law' to the extent that they are legally enforceable. Rules can therefore be divided into categories of those which are binding and those which are not; the latter of these can just as accurately be described as soft law. However, soft law cannot be adequately defined in a purely negative way. The above reasoning explains why soft law is 'soft', but not why, without binding force, it is able to be described as 'law' despite being an essentially 'bureaucratic phenomenon'.[3] The answer is that, even without the capacity to bind, soft law is created with the capacity to have some kind of practical, normative effect. Soft law is *in fact* a regulatory tool.

Much has been written about rule-making in the course of the last 50 years, particularly by American authors, starting with the work of Davis and including, for example, the work of Kerwin.[4] Black and Baldwin have each also written about rule-making from the British perspective.[5] Braithwaite has done so from the Australian perspective.[6] At least one major British administrative law text dedicates a chapter to rule-making.[7] An increasing amount of space was dedicated to the subject in each successive edition of Davis' *Administrative Law Treatise*.[8] Finally, rule-making has

[1] See R Baldwin, *Rules and Government* (Oxford, Clarendon Press, 1995).

[2] Regarding the distinction between rules and law, see C Harlow and R Rawlings, *Law and Administration*, 3rd edn (Cambridge, Cambridge University Press, 2009) 192.

[3] R Baldwin, *Rules and Government* (Oxford, Clarendon Press, 1995) 196.

[4] KC Davis, *Discretionary Justice* (Baton Rouge, Louisiana State University Press, 1969); CM Kerwin, *Rulemaking*, 2nd edn (Thousand Oaks CA, CQ Press, 1999).

[5] J Black, 'Constitutionalising Self-Regulation' (1996) 59 *MLR* 24; J Black, *Rules and Regulators* (Oxford, Clarendon Press, 1997); J Houghton and R Baldwin, 'Circular Arguments' [1986] *PL* 239; R Baldwin and D Horne, 'Expectations in a Joyless Landscape' (1986) 49 *MLR* 685; R Baldwin, *Rules and Government* (Oxford, Clarendon Press, 1995).

[6] J Braithwaite, 'Rules and Principles: a Theory of Legal Certainty' (2002) 27 *Australian Journal of Legal Philosophy* 47.

[7] PP Craig, *Administrative Law*, 7th edn (London, Sweet and Maxwell, 2012) ch 15.

[8] KC Davis, *Administrative Law Treatise*, 1st edn (St Paul MN, West Publishing, 1958); KC Davis and JP Wilson, *Administrative Law Treatise*, 2nd edn (1979); KC Davis and RJ Pierce, *Administrative Law Treatise*, 3rd edn (San Diego CA, KC Davis Publishing Co, 1994).

been the subject of a report by the Administrative Review Council in Australia.[9] These works have focused mainly on rule-making as a *method* of imposing regulation. This book instead explores the *consequences* of the use of rules to regulate behaviour.

An argument against the legal status of soft law rules may be derived by extension from the fact that delegated legislation obtains legitimacy, at least in part, from Parliament (although query whether and to what extent political legitimacy attaches itself to delegated legislation formulated generally in seclusion from public scrutiny).[10] Soft law rules which are developed without express parliamentary delegation beforehand or approval afterwards might be seen as illegitimate because they have not been exposed to political accountability processes. Indeed, this is often the very point: soft law can be implemented and have effect without the difficulty of the legislative process, something which has been true since the nineteenth century:[11]

> Administrators became increasingly reluctant to embark upon legislative campaigns, and their political masters increasingly restrained such activity. Where they could enact regulations or improvise using their own quasi-legislation by the imaginative use of existing statutes, they did so. Where new or amending legislation was clearly needed, it was often limited to the specific situation at hand: 'we provided a plaster for the wound, but we do not make it any larger than the wound.' This attitude represented a retreat from the early Benthamite legislative ideal of comprehensive and formal specification. But it was a tactical retreat only. Comprehensiveness and specificity flourished in the regulations, rules, and practices developed under the protective umbrella of the general enabling legislation. What parliament could not or would not enact, what judges could not or would not read into legislation, might be provided by commissioners and inspectors themselves, through subordinate law-making and the daily routine of administration.

While such practices may have been intended as no more than a 'tactical retreat' from the ideal of comprehensive, specific legislation, they amounted to a more fundamental departure from positivist notions about the source of law. Administrative rule-making in lieu of legislation is *effective* only if those rules will have consequences comparable to the legislation in whose place they stand. In this practical sense, soft law rules are 'law', although whether or not they have the legitimacy that attaches to that term is a separate question.

Craig, who is this respect generally representative of the other commentators on this topic, nominated four main reasons why soft law might be used in preference to delegated legislation:[12]

> First, even where no explicit power to make regulations is granted to an agency, it will often make rules to indicate how it will exercise its discretion. This is a natural tendency for bureaucracies when faced with a recurring problem ... Second, non-legal rules facilitate the use of non-technical language, exemplified by the Highway Code, and the Health

[9] Administrative Review Council, *Rule Making* (1992).

[10] E Page, *Governing By Numbers* (Oxford, Hart Publishing, 2001) 7. See also M Aronson, 'Great Depression' (2009) 37 *Federal Law Review* 165, 175.

[11] HW Arthurs, *Without the Law* (Toronto, Toronto University Press, 1985) 160 (footnotes omitted). See also E Page, *Governing By Numbers* (Oxford, Hart Publishing, 2001) 13; C Stebbings, *Legal Foundations of Tribunals in Nineteenth-Century England* (Cambridge, Cambridge University Press, 2006).

[12] PP Craig, *Administrative Law*, 7th edn (London, Sweet and Maxwell, 2012) 467–68.

> and Safety Codes. Third, such rules may be preferred because they are more flexible than statutory instruments, and hence can be changed more easily. Finally, these rules may be preferred to delegated legislation precisely because they are not legally binding. They enable policies to be developed voluntarily in the sense that 'persuasion may be preferable to compulsion'.

It is in the nature of rules that they tend either to be over-inclusive or under-inclusive, even though it is clearly preferable that a 'rule should apply to all the circumstances within the intent of a policy maker and to none that fall outside that intent'.[13] This ideal is not realised because the purpose of rules has been to confine discretionary decision-making (the first of the considerations listed by Craig).[14] One of the reasons that discretions are granted in the first place is that the relevant issues cannot be determined far enough in advance to make their regulation the subject of sufficiently detailed legislation; hence Brennan J's comment in *Drake (No 2)* that some discretions, such as the discretion reposed in the Minister for Immigration by the Migration Act to deport certain individuals held not to be of good character, 'cannot be exercised according to broad and binding rules'.[15] There are circumstances which are beyond the capacity of rule-makers to predict and attempts to do so may result in the relevant discretion being unsatisfactorily exercised.

Generally, however, rule-making has come to be seen as an appropriate method by which discretionary powers are able to be guided.[16] The push towards rule-making as a means of controlling administrative discretion is several decades old in America. Literature which focuses on English rule-making, by contrast, talks more about the greater facility of governing without legislation as the genesis of the increase in rule-making.[17] There is a fundamental difference between rule-making which is motivated by a desire to control undemocratic power and rule-making which is designed to circumvent the inconvenience of dealing with the central organ of democracy. A third motivation, much considered in Australia, is that soft law is an effective means of controlling discretion in a manner that allows it to retain its flexibility but reduces inconsistency, which carries with it the suspicion of arbitrariness.[18]

Anthony contended that agencies tend to use rules to 'avoid the procedural rigours of legislative rule-making', although he is by no means the only one to make this point.[19] Craig argued that soft law may be chosen as the method by which a

[13] C Scott, 'Standard-Setting' in R Baldwin et al (eds), *Oxford Handbook of Regulation* (Oxford, Oxford University Press, 2010) [6.2.2]. See J Black, *Rules and Regulators* (Oxford, Clarendon Press, 1997) 6.

[14] See Chapter 2.B.(iii) of this volume above.

[15] *Drake v Minister for Immigration and Ethnic Affairs (No 2)* (1979) 2 ALD 634, 640 (Brennan J). See also *Re Pochi and Minister for Immigration and Ethnic Affairs* (1979) 2 ALD 33; cf Migration Act 1958 (Cth) ss 501, 501A.

[16] KC Davis, *Discretionary Justice* (Baton Rouge, Louisiana State University Press, 1969).

[17] See eg E Page, *Governing By Numbers* (2001) ch 1.

[18] See *Drake (No 2)* (1979) 2 ALD 634, 639 (Brennan J).

[19] RA Anthony, 'Interpretive Rules, Policy Statements, Guidances, Manuals, and the Like' (1992) 41 *Duke Law Journal* 1311, 1327. See also *Grey-Letter Law Report* (1997), xii; CM Kerwin, *Rulemaking*, 2nd edn (Thousand Oaks CA, CQ Press, 1999) 24; L Sossin, 'The Politics of Soft Law: How Judicial Decisions Influence Bureaucratic Discretion in Canada' in M Hertogh and S Halliday (eds), *Judicial Review and Bureaucratic Impact: International and Interdisciplinary Perspectives* (Cambridge, Cambridge University Press, 2004) 129, 138; Stenning and Associates Pty Ltd (Department of Industry, Science and Tourism), *Codes of Practice Project Stage 1: Scoping Study*, Scoping Study (1997) 5.

policy is implemented, either because it is more efficacious or because it exemplifies the outcome of direct negotiation between the executive and a major stakeholder with which a majority of the legislature may not agree. It may equally be used by:[20]

> a powerful executive [to implement] a code or rule which the relevant interest groups oppose, but which they are powerless to fight. Legislative scrutiny can be avoided, and the minimum of legal formalism troubles the executive in pursuit of its aim. Not all informal rules are therefore necessarily more truly consensual in nature than those norms which emerge as legislation.

In stark contrast to this comment, Cini regarded one of the strengths of soft law in the international context as being that it is more likely to be supported by political consensus than harder forms of regulation.[21]

It is not unduly cynical to make the point that one of the major attractions of soft law in a domestic setting is that, unlike legislation, it requires *no* political consensus in order to be implemented. Indeed, there is nothing more natural for the executive arm of government, increasingly used to power for over a century, than to seek to avoid dealing with an obstructive Parliament. The ship of state turns very slowly and members of the executive may believe, with entirely clear consciences, that to avoid the scrutiny of the legislature is a more effective means of responding to rapidly changing circumstances. They may in this way justify using soft law as a less democratic but more efficacious method of regulating public behaviour. Of course, they may ask themselves none of these questions of political morality at all and simply see soft law as an easier way to govern. The question which is inevitably left to be answered following any discussion of formulating rules in such a way as to avoid democratic scrutiny is whether a rule made with the latter purpose is lawful at all. Determining the true purpose behind an exercise of executive power, particularly where it may differ from the avowed purpose, is very difficult.[22] This difficulty is increased where there are numerous people responsible for exercising the power, not all of whom may share the same purpose or purposes.[23]

The short answer is that it is very difficult to establish whether an administrator has made soft law in order to avoid legislative scrutiny, although establishing the intention to bind creates specific problems in the USA because it brings the Administrative Procedure Act (APA)'s notice and comment procedures into force.[24] In Australia and England at least, provided that the capacity to make rules is within that administrator's powers and the rules do not disclose an improper purpose which takes them beyond the extent of those powers, the soft law will not be 'illegal'. After all, since soft law does not have a *legally* binding effect, 'to quash it seems to mean

[20] PP Craig, *Administrative Law*, 7th edn (London, Sweet and Maxwell, 2012) 468.

[21] M Cini, 'From Soft Law to Hard Law?' (2000) *Working Paper 35*, European University Institute, p 4; cf L Blutman, 'In the Trap of a Legal Metaphor' (2010) 59 *ICLQ* 605.

[22] See eg *Minister for Immigration and Citizenship v Haneef* (2007) 163 FCR 414, 450 (Black CJ, French & Weinberg JJ); cf *Padfield v Minister of Agriculture, Fisheries and Food* [1968] AC 997.

[23] See R Creyke and J McMillan, *Control of Government Action*, 3rd edn (Sydney, LexisNexis, 2012) 502; M Aronson and M Groves, *Judicial Review of Administrative Action*, 5th edn (Sydney, Thompson Reuters, 2013) [5.510]–[5.580].

[24] RA Anthony, 'Interpretive Rules, Policy Statements, Guidances, Manuals, and the Like' (1992) 41 *Duke Law Journal* 1311, 1331–32; 1355ff.

nothing. How can it be *ultra vires* if it has no *vires* to be *ultra*'?[25] The legal status of a soft law instrument depends on issues apart from it being ultra vires.[26]

Any treatment of a soft law instrument by an agency as though it *were* legally binding and therefore 'as dispositive of the issues that it addresses' means that the instrument has binding effect in practice, although arguably not for reasons of 'law'.[27] Soft law policies which purport to determine the exercise of legislative powers must be consistent with the governing legislation or will otherwise result in an invalid exercise of power.[28] Any challenge to soft law which is binding as a matter of practice rather than of law would be on the basis that the administrator in question had unlawfully fettered his or her discretion.[29]

However, having a judicial review remedy is not satisfactory per se if agencies choose to misuse soft law to control most people's behaviour but come to an alternative arrangement with the few who have the knowledge, the resources or the pugnacity to pose a challenge. The situation is of course worse where there is no immediate right to seek judicial review because, for example, an applicant is required to exhaust certain internal review processes first.[30] The alternatives to this limitation on judicial review's utility in Australia and England are few once it is understood that what would be called 'legislative' rules (under the APA) are already subject to parliamentary supervision. Craig proposed possible solutions, but all depend on either legislative or judicial scrutiny.[31] It is the very nature of soft law that it operates outside the scope of what is 'legislative' and is therefore not legally binding unless it amounts to an exercise of prerogative power or executive power (including, in Australia, under section 61 of the Constitution).

While much has been written on the benefits of rule-making, the relative strengths and limitations involved in using soft law can, in light of the discussion above, be seen as a matter of perspective.[32] For example, to the extent that a soft law instrument lacks binding force, this represents a limitation from the perspective of entities who seek to rely on that instrument but a strength from the perspective of the body which has issued the instrument but may later wish to resile from its effect, a fortiori if it is accepted that 'in practice soft law can be as influential in modifying behaviour as black letter law'.[33] Indeed, it was suggested in argument before the High Court on behalf of the Commonwealth in *Plaintiff S157*:[34]

> that the Parliament might validly delegate to the Minister 'the power to exercise a totally open-ended discretion as to what aliens can and what aliens cannot come to and stay in

[25] HWR Wade, 'Beyond the Law: A British Innovation in Judicial Review' (1991) 43 *Administrative Law Review* 559, 561.

[26] PP Craig, *Administrative Law*, 7th edn (London, Sweet and Maxwell, 2012) 468–69.

[27] RA Anthony, 'Interpretive Rules, Policy Statements, Guidances, Manuals, and the Like' (1992) 41 *Duke Law Journal* 1311, 1328.

[28] See eg *Green v Daniels* (1977) 13 ALR 1.

[29] See eg JM Keyes, *Executive Legislation*, 2nd edn (New South Wales, Butterworths, 2010) 56–58; Chapter 6.A.(i) of this volume below.

[30] RA Anthony, 'Interpretive Rules, Policy Statements, Guidances, Manuals, and the Like' (1992) 41 *Duke Law Journal* 1311, 1330.

[31] PP Craig, *Administrative Law*, 7th edn (London, Sweet and Maxwell, 2012) 469–72.

[32] See eg CM Kerwin, *Rulemaking*, 2nd edn (Thousand Oaks CA, CQ Press, 1999) 29–36.

[33] *Complex Regulation Report* (2008), 5.

[34] *Plaintiff S157/2002 v Commonwealth* (2003) 211 CLR 476, 512. See also *Plaintiff M79/2012 v Minister for Immigration and Citizenship* (2013) 252 CLR 336, 367 (Hayne J).

> Australia', subject only to this Court deciding any dispute as to the 'constitutional fact' of alien status. Alternatively, it was put that the Act might validly be redrawn to say, in effect, '[h]ere are some non-binding guidelines which should be applied', with the 'guidelines' being the balance of the statute.

Without deciding the issue, the Court doubted that the Parliament could so delegate. The purpose behind such a legislative approach would be to remove even the application of the constitutional writs under section 75(v) of the Constitution to decisions made under the relevant statute by, effectively, placing every decision so made within the discretion of the decision-maker.[35]

The largely self-imposed restraint of the AAT in reviewing policy decisions since *Drake (No 2)* explains much about the appeal of soft law as a method of regulation in Australia. It has been the established orthodoxy over a great many years that courts exercising a judicial review jurisdiction will rarely, if ever, inquire into the merits of a decision.[36] However, the reluctance of administrative tribunals to oppose a proper exercise of policy by an administrative decision-maker, notwithstanding that they are empowered to do so, has served to make soft law instruments 'harder' in practice than is the case in theory (as I have discussed above).

There is a beneficial role for soft law in causing executive discretion to be subject to judicial precedent.[37] Sossin has argued that it is one of the functions of soft law to ensure that executive decision-makers have taken account of the latest judicial findings and dicta on any given issue. In support of this, he pointed out the difference between hard and soft law:[38]

> whereas statutes and regulations are meant to define the boundaries and mandates of public authority, soft law is intended to ensure coherence and consistency in the implementation of those mandates.

The APA characterises soft law so described as 'non-legislative'. The least that can be said of soft law of this character is that it is benign. At best, it is an important aid to guiding administrative decision-making. However, as I have noted above, soft law is neither benign nor malign per se. Its benefits and dangers are almost entirely due to the purpose for which it is made and used. Just as soft law has numerous incarnations, ranging from aspirational statements of policy to highly prescriptive instruments, so too are there different reasons why and how soft law is used.[39]

[35] L McDonald, 'The Entrenched Minimum Provision of Judicial Review and the Rule of Law' (2010) 21 *Public Law Review* 14.

[36] See G Weeks, 'The Expanding Role of Process in Judicial Review' (2008) 15 *Australian Journal of Administrative Law* 100.

[37] L Sossin, 'The Politics of Soft Law' in M Hertogh and S Halliday (eds), *Judicial Review and Bureaucratic Impact* (Cambridge, Cambridge University Press, 2004) 129, 134.

[38] ibid, 139.

[39] Interestingly, a diagram in the *Complex Regulation Report* excludes 'aspirational edicts' from soft law, placing them below soft law: *Complex Regulation Report* (2008), x. This classification is open to debate.

4

The Regulatory Effect of Soft Law

THE PREVIOUS CHAPTER looked at the *purposes* which might lie behind using soft law as a regulatory mechanism and what they might reveal. This chapter is concerned with the *effects* of using soft law as a regulatory mechanism. It picks up from my earlier consideration of the possibility that soft law might crystallise discretion into law of a more positivist kind.[1] I will consider the operation of soft law in the context of tribunal justice and will conclude by examining two detailed examples of the application of soft law with a regulatory effect.

A. THE 'HARDENING' OF SOFT LAW

Can soft law assume a 'hardened' status as a result of its application, whether or not it applies to both parties? In addressing this question, this section looks at the effects of Brennan J's iconic judgment in *Drake (No 2)* and considers whether tribunal decisions made since that judgment have the effect of hardening the soft law which they consider, due to the informal—but undeniable—precedential value of tribunal decisions.

I have referred above to the work of Farmer regarding the extent to which judicial and tribunal decision-making applies precedent.[2] The theory behind this question is simple enough. Judicial decision-making is based on deciding questions of fact and of legality in relation to particular sets of facts. The doctrine of stare decisis states that similar fact situations will be decided in substantially the same way—that is, by applying the precedent of previous cases—unless a higher court distinguishes or overturns the approach of the prevailing relevant cases. There is nonetheless much acrimony about the proper judicial approach to precedent.[3] What is 'proper' is also subject to change, as when English superior courts started to apply the doctrine of stare decisis less stringently by the second half of the twentieth century, leading to greater development in the common law.[4]

[1] See Chapter 2.B.(iv) of this volume above.

[2] JA Farmer, *Tribunals and Government* (London, Weidenfeld and Nicolson, 1974).

[3] See M Aronson, 'Process, Quality, and Variable Standards: Responding to an *Agent Provocateur*' in D Dyzenhaus, M Hunt and G Huscroft (eds), *A Simple Common Lawyer: Essays in Honour of Michael Taggart* (Oxford, Hart Publishing, 2009) 5, 25–28.

[4] See fns 194–196 in Chapter 2.B.(iv) of this volume above; JA Farmer, *Tribunals and Government* (London, Weidenfeld and Nicolson, 1974) 172.

Farmer argued that English courts had largely ceased to make new law as an exercise of policy by the 1960s, deferring instead to legislative solutions to questions of policy, due in part to the greater availability of tribunal decision-making.[5] This is now seen as no more than the judicial branch restricting itself to its proper constitutional role and has nothing to do with deferring to administrative interpretations of law.[6] Tribunal decision-making, on the other hand, is typically not restricted to questions of law but enables the tribunal to exercise the jurisdiction of the original administrative decision-maker and to reach the correct or preferable decision on the merits of the case.[7] Such predominantly fact-based decisions have generally been assumed to contain little precedential value. However, unlike courts which—in Australia and England, at least—owe no duty of deference to executive interpretations of law, it was decided very early in the history of the Administrative Appeals Tribunal (AAT) that Tribunal members should generally apply any lawful Ministerial policy in reaching a decision on review.[8]

Regardless of these general principles, Farmer's concern was that tribunals do in practice follow earlier decisions of the same tribunal as precedents, with the result that they are unable to exercise discretion in a flexible manner.[9] Such flexibility is inherent in the design of a tribunal authorised to come to the 'correct or preferable' decision on the facts, which is one of the hallmarks of merits review.[10] The Diceyan concern, by contrast, would have been somewhat less functionalist and focused on Dicey's view that only 'ordinary law courts' had the power to make law by binding subsequent or subordinate courts with decisions accorded the status of precedent. This concern is outdated, since it is now generally accepted that the definition of 'law' extends beyond legislation and the binding decisions of superior courts. A functionalist definition of law might well extend to tribunal decisions which are accorded the status of binding precedent on the basis that they are authoritative.[11]

There are, of course, some differences between precedent as it applies in court hearings and the species of 'precedent' which applies to tribunal proceedings. Tribunals are obliged to decide each matter which comes before them on the merits and must therefore not fetter themselves to a reduced 'range of discretion' by following a precedent or policy which results in anything other than the correct or preferable decision being reached.[12] However, there are also strong expectations that tribunal decisions will be largely consistent, since 'inconsistency is not merely inelegant: it brings the process of deciding into disrepute, suggesting an arbitrariness which

[5] JA Farmer, *Tribunals and Government* (London, Weidenfeld and Nicolson, 1974) 173.

[6] See AM Gleeson, 'Judicial Legitimacy' (2000) 20 *Australian Bar Review* 1.

[7] See *Administrative Appeals Tribunal Act 1975* (Cth) s 43; *Shi v Migration Agents' Registration Authority* (2008) 235 CLR 286, 327 (Kiefel J).

[8] *Drake v Minister for Immigration and Ethnic Affairs* ('*Drake (No 2)*') (1979) 2 ALD 634.

[9] JA Farmer, *Tribunals and Government* (London, Weidenfeld and Nicolson, 1974) 174.

[10] *Drake v Minister for Immigration and Ethnic Affairs* (1979) 46 FLR 409, 589 (Bowen CJ & Deane J). See P Cane, 'Merits Review and Judicial Review: the AAT as Trojan Horse' (2000) 28 *Federal Law Review* 213; MD Kirby, 'Administrative Review on the Merits: The Right or Preferable Decision' (1980) 6 *Monash University Law Review* 171.

[11] M Aronson and M Groves, *Judicial Review of Administrative Action*, 5th edn (Sydney, Thompson Reuters, 2013) [4.70].

[12] *Drake (No 2)* (1979) 2 ALD 634, 641.

is incompatible with commonly accepted notions of justice'.[13] Those expectations come with a set of complex and contradictory pressures.[14]

Individual decision-makers within the executive, such as Ministers, do not of course need to strive towards consistency in the same way that tribunals with numerous members must. To the extent that Ministers delegate their decision-making functions, consistency is achieved by the formulation of policy. This result has been described as 'inevitable and desirable'.[15] In *Drake (No 2)*, Brennan J stated that, in order to bring consistency to decision-making standards and values, the AAT ought also to make its decisions in such a way that it is 'guided' but not fettered by any relevant Ministerial policy.[16] On this view, the AAT is in fact 'at liberty to adopt whatever policy it chooses, or no policy at all, in fulfilling its statutory function', although Brennan J regarded doing so as unwise.[17] Soft law is able to promote consistent decision-making without being binding, an aspiration which is often stated expressly.[18]

It should therefore be understood that tribunals which follow 'precedent' *strive* towards consistency without being bound to it as courts subject to the doctrine of stare decisis are. This is a position strengthened by decisions of single judges of the Federal Court to the effect that tribunal members cannot be *bound* to follow earlier decisions in like cases.[19] Despite the constitutional requirement that the AAT be a Chapter II body (rather than a Chapter III court), it has to some extent always followed a 'judicial' model since the time that Brennan J was its first President, although this was probably not the intention of the Kerr Committee, which had recommended its creation.[20] In England, which imposes no constitutionally mandated separation of tribunals from courts, a preference for a judicial model of tribunal justice has consistently been shown. The word 'tribunal' traditionally carried 'judicial connotations' and first commonly replaced terms like 'commission' and 'board' at a time when those bodies began to follow a more 'judicial' model of operation.[21] From the eport of the Franks Committee to the Leggatt Review of Tribunals, a preference

[13] ibid, 639 (Brennan J). See Chapter 7.A.(iii) of this volume below.

[14] See E Johnson, '"Inconsistency" of Administrative Decisions' (2013) 72 *Australian Institute of Administrative Law Forum* 50.

[15] P Bayne, 'Policy Guidelines and Law—Some Intersections' (1991) 65 *Australian Law Journal* 607, 607.

[16] *Drake (No 2)* (1979) 2 ALD 634, 642. See JM Keyes, *Executive Legislation*, 2nd edn (New South Wales, Butterworths, 2010) 58–59.

[17] *Drake (No 2)* (1979) 2 ALD 634, 642. See n 33 below.

[18] See eg Australian Taxation Office, *ATO Practice Statement Law Administration PS LA 2003/11* (2003), [21].

[19] *NARY v Minister for Immigration and Multicultural and Indigenous Affairs* [2003] FCA 1255 [10] (Moore J); *SGBB v Minister for Immigration and Multicultural and Indigenous Affairs* (2003) 199 ALR 364, 372 (Selway J). The NSW Court of Appeal reached a similar conclusion in *Segal v Waverley Council* (2005) 64 NSWLR 177. See M Aronson and M Groves, *Judicial Review of Administrative Action*, 5th edn (Sydney, Thompson Reuters, 2013) [6.610].

[20] Commonwealth Administrative Review Committee, *Commonwealth Administrative Review Committee Report*, Parliamentary Paper No 144 (1971), ('*Kerr Report*').

[21] C Stebbings, *Legal Foundations of Tribunals in Nineteenth-Century England* (Cambridge, Cambridge University Press, 2006), 329.

for a judicial model of tribunal justice has long been evident, as it is now in the operation of the First Tier and Upper Tribunals.[22]

The raison d'être of tribunals is to do 'justice in the individual case'.[23] By comparison, justice on the facts is irrelevant to the function of courts exercising judicial review.[24] Regardless of this broad distinction, the 'realities of tribunal justice' demand recognition of the fact that tribunals strive for consistency and are therefore under the same pressures as the courts to decide similar cases consistently with each other, to provide reasons which reveal the tribunal's understanding of the law and to decide only the case before the tribunal.[25] Tribunal decisions have at the very least the de facto status of precedent as a result of the expectation that like cases will be decided alike and that any variation from a previous like case will need to be explained by the tribunal (although, at a practical level, even factual scenarios which are to all intents and purposes identical might be decided differently).[26] These realities point persuasively to the fact that tribunals are now a source of 'hard law' and do nothing to assuage the fears expressed by Farmer over 30 years ago that some of the benefits of flexibility are being lost from tribunal decision-making. It cannot be argued, however, that *all* benefits of tribunal decision-making are being lost.

It is strongly arguable that the AAT in Australia has been a source of law for the three decades since the decision in *Drake (No 2)*.[27] In that case, Brennan J was called upon to review the decision of the Minister to deport Mr Drake, who had been incarcerated for drug trafficking offences.[28] The case was heard during the infancy of the AAT and Brennan J accordingly took the opportunity to make a statement of general principle about the role of precedent in deciding cases before the Tribunal. His Honour's position was that tribunals should strive for consistency without unduly fettering their discretion, although he realised that in practice consistency demands some fettering of discretion.[29] *Drake (No 2)* is taken to express the conclusion that consistency is in insoluble tension with the flexibility of discretion.[30] Brennan J sought to promote a balance between them. Consistency is a function of policy where numerous individuals are collectively responsible for decision-making. Brennan J's view was that, since policy-making is inconsistent with the other functions of adjudicative tribunals, they would be well-advised to follow any policy on

[22] *R (Cart) v Upper Tribunal* [2012] 1 AC 663; *R (Jones) v First Tier Tribunal (Social Entitlement Chamber)* [2013] 2 WLR 1012. See Committee on Administrative Tribunals and Enquiries, *Report of the Committee on Administrative Tribunals and Enquiries*, Command Paper No 218 (1957); A Leggatt, *Tribunals for Users: One System, One Service*, Report of the Review of Tribunals (2001); P Cane, *Administrative Tribunals and Adjudication* (Oxford, Hart Publishing, 2009), 108–10.

[23] *Drake* (1979) 46 FLR 409, 590 (Bowen CJ & Deane J).

[24] *Attorney General (NSW) v Quin* (1990) 170 CLR 1, 35–36 (Brennan J).

[25] M Aronson and M Groves, *Judicial Review of Administrative Action*, 5th edn (Sydney, Thompson Reuters, 2013) [4.70]. See also PL Strauss, 'The Rulemaking Continuum' (1992) 41 *Duke Law Journal* 1463, 1472–73; *US v Mead Corp* 533 US 218 (2001), 232.

[26] E Johnson, '"Inconsistency" of Administrative Decisions' (2013) 72 *Australian Institute of Administrative Law Forum* 50, 53–54.

[27] *Drake (No 2)* (1979) 2 ALD 634.

[28] cf *Re Pochi and Minister for Immigration and Ethnic Affairs* (1979) 2 ALD 33.

[29] cf M Aronson and M Groves, *Judicial Review of Administrative Action*, 5th edn (Sydney, Thompson Reuters, 2013) [5.270].

[30] See fns 119–120 in Chapter 2.B.(i) of this volume above.

a matter within a department's responsibilities where to do so does not preclude the tribunal from reaching the correct or preferable decision.[31]

It is important to note that Brennan J's comments about the general desirability of tribunals applying policy formulated by the executive were preceded by an affirmation that a Minister should not adopt—and the AAT would not apply—a policy which would lead the tribunal to commit a jurisdictional error. This includes a policy which would truncate the tribunal member's discretion to reach the proper decision on the merits of each matter, or would take into account irrelevant considerations, or would preclude consideration of relevant arguments or is inconsistent with the statute which provides jurisdiction.[32] His Honour declared that the AAT was free to come to the correct or preferable decision regardless of a Minister's statement of policy but advised that tribunals would be 'manifestly imprudent' to adopt their own policies where there already existed a Ministerial policy, which had been subject to the scrutiny and sanction of the political process in a way that a tribunal-generated policy could not be.[33] His Honour justified this position by arguing that, for the sake of consistency, some kind of policy is generally desirable, particularly where there is a high volume of decision-making, in order to structure executive discretions.[34] Many years after *Drake (No 2)*, the AAT remains deeply reluctant to exercise its freedom to come to the correct or preferable decision without applying ministerial policy, where such exists. It adheres instead to Brennan J's recommendation that such a policy, scrutinised and approved by parliament, be departed from only cautiously and sparingly.

Drake (No 2) must be understood in the context of the early days of the AAT and the debate which surrounded its role and function.[35] It was presided over by a President who was a judge of the Federal Court but 'stood in the shoes' of the original decision-maker and was able to exercise all the powers and discretions conferred on that person.[36] *Drake (No 2)* settled whatever ambiguity was raised by these provisions by giving firm encouragement to the AAT to behave more like a court than an administrator, although Cane noted that 'the assimilationist logic implicit in this situation cannot be carried through to a conclusion because of the constitutionally mandated distinction between judicial and non-judicial functions'.[37]

Cane noted that one of the benefits of Australia's system of merits review tribunals being located within the executive branch of government was supposed to be that, unlike the courts, they are not compelled to refrain from overturning a decision if that would not 'be the best of the available options'.[38] Rather, they are able to

[31] *Drake (No 2)* (1979) 2 ALD 634, 643–44; cf *Hneidi v Minister for Immigration and Citizenship* (2010) 182 FCR 115, 121.

[32] *Drake (No 2)* (1979) 2 ALD 634, 640–41.

[33] *Drake (No 2)* (1979) 2 ALD 634, 642–44.

[34] See W Gummow, 'Rationality and Reasonableness as Grounds for Review' in D Mortimer (ed), *Administrative Justice and its Availability* (Sydney, Federation Press, 2015) 13, 18.

[35] See P Cane, 'Understanding Administrative Adjudication' in L Pearson et al (eds), *Administrative Law in a Changing State* (Oxford, Hart Publishing, 2008) 273, 293 (fn 73).

[36] *AAT Act 1975* (Cth) ss 7(1), 43(1).

[37] P Cane, 'Administrative Adjudication' in L Pearson et al (eds), *Administrative Law in a Changing State* (Oxford, Hart Publishing, 2008) 273, 293.

[38] P Cane, 'Judicial Review in the Age of Tribunals' [2009] *PL* 479, 490. See also P Cane, *Administrative Tribunals and Adjudication* (Oxford, Hart Publishing, 2009) 57–67.

take advantage of greater resources and investigative capacity to balance the various issues in question and thereby come to the correct or preferable decision. In so doing, they need not defer to the opinion reached on that subject by the original decision-maker. However, in practice, merits review since *Drake (No 2)* has generally been applied with a reluctance to exercise the theoretical power to disagree with government policy: 'Brennan J's caution has been more influential than his strong statement of the law'.[39]

One of the problems with courts (as opposed to tribunals) being guided by soft law is that it is difficult to assess the weight that is assigned to individual instruments in individual cases. Much soft law in England arises from that country's membership in the European Union.[40] It has been noted that courts merely declaring that they are 'assisted' by any such soft law instrument which has no explicit treaty basis effectively treat it as having no greater worth than, for example, academic books or articles. On the other hand, the solution to that problem has generally been for the soft law in question to be 'hardened', not by the manner of its application in court proceedings but by adoption into domestic legislation.

Similarly, guidelines made pursuant to statutory authorisation have previously been seen as something less than 'hard law' in both England and Australia. Australian guidelines have previously been held not to be of a 'legislative character'.[41] However, the power of Parliament to give a word like 'guidelines' 'any meaning it wishes', notwithstanding the inconvenience that might cause, has been judicially noted.[42] The problems encountered in such cases would now be addressed in practice by the Legislation Act if the instrument were also 'made in the exercise of a power delegated by the Parliament'.[43]

In England, however, courts still assess whether codes of practice have binding effect on the basis of whether they purport to offer guidance or instruction.[44] It should follow that any guideline which is not specifically anticipated in legislation cannot be given any greater weight than one which is. However, even though soft law is made without statutory authority, this does not mean that it lacks legal effect. Some soft law can be useful to courts in determining 'the standard that can reasonably be expected having regard to the norms within an industry' in order to establish negligence.[45] Where soft law has the function of informing the public about the law in a manner which is more accessible than the operative legislation, breach of the soft law may in practice amount to a criminal offence.[46] Conversely, reliance

[39] P Cane, 'Judicial Review in the Age of Tribunals' [2009] *PL* 479, 489.

[40] See C Harlow and R Rawlings, *Law and Administration*, 3rd edn (Cambridge, Cambridge University Press, 2009) 199–200.

[41] See P Bayne, 'Policy Guidelines and Law' (1991) 65 *Australian Law Journal* 607, 608.

[42] *Smoker v Pharmacy Restructuring Authority* (1994) 53 FCR 287, 289 (Wilcox J).

[43] Legislation Act 2003 s 5(1)(b).

[44] See eg *R (Munjaz) v Mersey Care NHS Trust* [2006] 2 AC 148, 189 (Lord Bingham). See also D Greenberg, *Craies on Legislation: A Practitioner's Guide to the Nature, Process, Effect and Interpretation of Legislation*, 9th edn (London, Sweet and Maxwell, 2008) 146.

[45] D Greenberg, *Craies on Legislation*, 9th edn (London, Sweet and Maxwell, 2008) 147. See *Benton v Tea Tree Plaza* (1995) 64 SASR 494.

[46] The Highway Code (UK) is a good example; see C Harlow and R Rawlings, *Law and Administration*, 3rd edn (Cambridge, Cambridge University Press, 2009) 195.

on legally flawed soft law by a decision-maker causes decisions based on it also to be unlawful.[47] Applying legally flawed soft law may itself result in a subsequent negligence claim.[48]

However, it need not necessarily follow that soft law will fall within the parameters set out in *Drake (No 2)*, which has the practical effect of 'hardening' soft law guidelines for the purpose of merits review proceedings before the AAT due to Brennan J's dicta regarding the wisdom of generally following executive policies.

B. TWO EXAMPLES OF THE REGULATORY EFFECTS OF SOFT LAW

This chapter concludes by considering two examples of soft law with regulatory effects.

The first example arose in *Hua-Aus*, in which Edmonds J heard an application for the Federal Court to use its discretion to extend the time for appeal against a decision in a taxation matter heard in the AAT.[49] The proposed appeal was from the decision of a Senior Member of the AAT to affirm (with some variation) a decision of the Australian Taxation Office (ATO) in relation to payments of Goods and Services Tax (GST) by the applicant company, which provided escort services.[50] The applicant had objected to a Notice of Assessment of GST which it had received from the ATO. It had further objected to a Notice of Penalty 'for failure to withhold related amounts from payments made to his suppliers'.[51] The obligation to withhold GST from payments made by the applicant to its escorts was imposed by legislation.[52] Failure to comply enlivened a discretion in the Commissioner to impose a penalty in the amount equal to that which the applicant had failed to withhold.[53] The ATO issued a soft law practice statement which explained the criteria for reducing the presumptive penalty, which included a guide to when penalties would be remitted by the ATO for the express purpose of maintaining 'consistency with other tax penalties'.[54] A Deputy Commissioner reduced the amount of GST payable and reduced the penalty payable to 50 per cent but upheld the decision to impose a penalty on the applicant.[55]

The Deputy Commissioner's decision was reviewable in the AAT.[56] The applicant there argued for a further reduction of the penalty on the basis that the calculations of taxable supplies for both the GST assessment and the penalty were excessive.

[47] See eg *Plaintiff M61/2010E v Commonwealth of Australia* (2010) 243 CLR 319 ('*Offshore Processing Case*'); *Newbury District Council v Secretary of State for the Environment* [1981] AC 578.
[48] *Sami v Roads Corporation (Vic)* (2008) 51 MVR 118, 146.
[49] *Hua-Aus Pty Ltd v Federal Commissioner of Taxation* (2009) 75 ATR 886.
[50] *Re Hua-Aus Pty Ltd and Federal Commissioner of Taxation* [2008] AATA 1033.
[51] ibid, [1].
[52] Division 12 of Schedule 1 to the Taxation Administration Act 1953 (Cth).
[53] Under s 16–30 of Schedule 1 to the Taxation Administration Act 1953 (Cth): *Re Hua-Aus* [2008] AATA 1033, [46].
[54] Australian Taxation Office, *PS LA 2003/11* (2003), [21].
[55] *Re Hua-Aus* [2008] AATA 1033, [48].
[56] Taxation Administration Act 1953 (Cth) s 14ZZA.

To this end, he relied on the ATO's practice statement.[57] The Deputy Commissioner had held that the applicant's conduct was 'reckless', as that term had previously been defined by the ATO.[58] Specifically, the applicant had demonstrated 'gross carelessness showing a disregard or indifference to [his] obligations'.[59] The merits of the Deputy Commissioner's finding are hard to dispute when it is understood that the ATO website provides specific advice on the subject.[60]

The AAT had complete discretion over the penalty that would be imposed following its hearing but the Senior Member simply applied the ATO's soft law, for the same reasons as the Deputy Commissioner had done.[61] The applicant then sought judicial review of the AAT's decision in the Federal Court, including on the ground that the AAT had affirmed the decision under review 'without undertaking its own independent assessment or making its own findings in order to re-exercise the discretion to further remit the penalty for failure to withhold afresh'.[62] The issue before the Federal Court in *Hua-Aus* was dealt with in short order. Edmonds J held that, because the AAT had made findings which were open to it, the pleading extracted above did not raise a question of law.[63] This decision was both obvious and certainly correct.

The point of interest for this book is the extent to which a soft law instrument may have 'hardened' in the course of its consideration by the AAT as a result of *Drake (No 2)*. Given the conclusions reached above regarding both the precedential value of AAT case law and the application of Brennan J's dictum in *Drake (No 2)* to soft law (particularly when it has been developed by a very large and independent administrative agency such as the ATO, for which no single Minister is responsible), soft law must harden, at least in regard to subsequent treatments of the same soft law instrument in the AAT.

Of course, it remains open for a court to overturn the soft law instrument that the AAT has effectively 'hardened'; in that sense, it is no harder than any other policy considered by the AAT.[64] Indeed, the Commissioner has been chastised by the Full Federal Court for failing to give effect to a court's understanding of a statute in preference to the understanding reached by the ATO.[65] Regardless of this obvious and natural limitation, what is clear from the analysis above is that soft law applied by

[57] Australian Taxation Office, *PS LA 2003/11* (2003).

[58] See Australian Taxation Office, *ATO Taxation Ruling TR 94/4: Income tax: tax shortfall penalties: reasonable care, recklessness and intentional disregard* (1994). TR 94/4 has since been withdrawn and has been replaced by Australian Taxation Office, *ATO Miscellaneous Taxation Ruling MT 2008/1: Penalty relating to statements: meaning of reasonable care, recklessness and intentional disregard* (2008), [99]–[116].

[59] Australian Taxation Office, *PS LA 2003/11* (2003), [21], [23].

[60] *GST and the sex industry—questions and answers* (2008), available at: www.ato.gov.au/Business/GST/In-detail/Your-industry/Other-industries/GST-and-the-sex-industry/.

[61] *Re Hua-Aus* [2008] AATA 1033, [45].

[62] *Hua-Aus v FCT* (2009) 75 ATR 886, [22].

[63] AAT Act 1975 (Cth) s 44. See *Hua-Aus v FCT* (2009) 75 ATR 886, [24].

[64] M Aronson and M Groves, *Judicial Review of Administrative Action*, 5th edn (Sydney, Thompson Reuters, 2013) [4.80].

[65] *Federal Commissioner of Taxation v Indooroopilly Children Services (Qld) Pty Ltd* (2007) 158 FCR 325, 326–27.

the AAT cannot be denied the status of authoritative legal precedent until such time as it is overruled in court proceedings. Cane has commented in this regard that[66]

> although the AAT can set decisions aside for error of law—in other words, it can decide questions of law—it cannot do so 'conclusively' because conclusive resolution of issues of law is (according to the High Court) a judicial function that only courts can perform. In other words, the AAT cannot make law—or, perhaps more precisely, it cannot make hard law, although it can (and does) make soft law; and in practice, soft law made by the AAT is generally treated as if it were hard law.

Cane identified a further point of difference between the application of law and policy by administrators and review tribunals respectively which derives from the inexact nature of the metaphor that a tribunal empowered to review the merits of an administrative decision 'stands in the shoes' of the original decision-maker.[67] He pointed out that these decision-makers have essentially different functions:[68]

> The basic responsibility of the bureaucrat is to promote the social purposes of general rules—hard and soft law—by deciding individual cases, whereas the basic responsibility of the merits reviewer is to afford to the interests of the individual applicant for review maximum protection compatible with fidelity to relevant hard and soft law. Although only a matter of priority or emphasis, this difference between implementation and adjudication is fundamental and significantly reduces the value of the shoe metaphor as a description of the [juridical basis] of merits review.

Of course, the issues raised by the application of policy in the course of merits review differ in various jurisdictions. English administrative tribunals are considered part of the 'machinery of justice' alongside the courts.[69] By contrast, in America, Administrative Law Judges are embedded within the administrative departments whose decisions they review.[70] Cane contended that, notwithstanding these differences, merits review in each of the three jurisdictions is exercised in practice by attaching significant weight to soft law.

Australian tribunals are 'technically' part of the executive as a result of the High Court's interpretation of the constitutional separation of judicial power.[71] Indeed, there is significant support for the approach of treating tribunals as executive bodies with regard to the performance of 'integrity' functions.[72] Cane once argued that the

[66] P Cane, 'Judicial Review in the Age of Tribunals' [2009] *PL* 479, 496.

[67] ibid, 485–87. See *Shi v Migrant Agents Registration Authority* (2008) 235 CLR 286, 296–99 (Kirby J), 326–27 (Kiefel J); P Cane, *Administrative Tribunals and Adjudication* (Oxford, Hart Publishing, 2009) 144–76.

[68] P Cane, 'Judicial Review in the Age of Tribunals' [2009] *PL* 479, 487; cf *Drake (No 2)* (1979) 2 ALD 634, 639.

[69] P Cane, 'Judicial Review in the Age of Tribunals' [2009] *PL* 479, 484; *Franks Committee Report* (1957), [40]; *Cart v Upper Tribunal* [2012] 1 AC 663.

[70] P Cane, 'Judicial Review in the Age of Tribunals' [2009] *PL* 479, 483.

[71] ibid, 484. See *R v Kirby; ex parte Boilermakers' Society of Australia* (1956) 94 CLR 254, ('*Boilermakers' Case*'); P Cane, 'Administrative Adjudication' in L Pearson et al (eds), *Administrative Law in a Changing State* (Oxford, Hart Publishing, 2008) 273, 289–93.

[72] See eg M Aronson and M Groves, *Judicial Review of Administrative Action*, 5th edn (Sydney, Thompson Reuters, 2013) [1.90]; J McMillan, 'Re-thinking the Separation of Powers' (2010) 38 *Federal Law Review* 423.

AAT and the courts could be seen as more similar in practice than has traditionally been believed and that 'merits review can plausibly be described as judicial review in disguise'.[73] He pointed out the ironic fact that 'despite the bright-line constitutional distinction between courts and tribunals ... in reality the AAT inhabits an uncomfortable limbo somewhere between the judicial and executive branches'.[74] The constitutional basis for tribunals being located within the executive, rather than designated as Chapter III courts, goes back so far that it has taken on a level of permanence.[75] This is the only ground on which one might query regarding tribunals' status as part of the executive as merely 'technical'. In the AAT, soft law is approached much as it would be in a court and those who would challenge a policy's application face strong practical limitations. Cane noted that a 'decision may not be the preferable one if it is based on a policy that is *Wednesbury* unreasonable; but the AAT appears even less willing than the courts to set aside a decision on this ground'.[76]

Likewise, Cane stated that in England a tribunal had no jurisdiction to review the 'discretionary application, non-application or misapplication' of soft law by a decision-maker and, where the application of a soft law instrument was 'not in accordance with the law', the applicant had nothing more than a procedural right to have the decision made again according to law.[77] The law with regard to the English tribunal system was in a state of flux at least until the Tribunal Procedure Committee made rules for the First Tier and Upper Tribunals, which replaced a range of separate tribunals.[78] Additionally, new hard law has been handed down with regard to those tribunals.[79] To compare English tribunals to the AAT is nonetheless at best an uncertain business, since their model seems to be judicial in both style and substance.

In the USA, the 'prime function' of an Administrative Law Judge 'is to apply and give effect to soft law developed by the agency' in which s/he is embedded, although Cane remarked in passing that 'the limited freedom of agencies to disagree with the ALJ about the proper inferences to be drawn from agreed facts may confer on the

[73] P Cane, 'The AAT as Trojan Horse' (2000) 28 *Federal Law Review* 213.

[74] P Cane, 'Administrative Adjudication' in L Pearson et al (eds), *Administrative Law in a Changing State* (Oxford, Hart Publishing, 2008) 273, 291.

[75] *British Imperial Oil Co Ltd v Federal Commissioner of Taxation* (1925) 35 CLR 422. See P Cane, 'Administrative Adjudication' in L Pearson et al (eds), *Administrative Law in a Changing State* (Oxford, Hart Publishing, 2008) 273, 291.

[76] P Cane, 'Judicial Review in the Age of Tribunals' [2009] *PL* 479, 489; cf *Minister for Immigration and Citizenship v Li* (2013) 249 CLR 332.

[77] P Cane, 'Judicial Review in the Age of Tribunals' [2009] *PL* 479, 491. See *Attorney General and Others (Policies; Executive Discretions; Tribunal's Powers) Kosovo v Secretary of State for the Home Department* [2007] UKAIT 00082, [44].

[78] HWR Wade and CF Forsyth, *Administrative Law*, 11th edn (Oxford, Oxford University Press, 2014) 775; cf HWR Wade and C Forsyth, *Administrative Law*, 10th edn (Oxford, Oxford University Press, 2009) 783.

[79] See eg *Cart v Upper Tribunal* [2012] 1 AC 663; *Jones v First Tier Tribunal* [2013] 2 WLR 1012. See also R Carnwath, 'Tribunal Justice: A New Start' [2009] *PL* 48; R Carnwath, 'Tribunal Justice: Judicial Review by Another Route' in C Forsyth, M Elliott, S Jhaveri, M Ramsden and A Scully-Hill (eds), *Effective Judicial Review: a Cornerstone of Good Governance* (Oxford, Oxford University Press, 2010) 143; M Aronson and M Groves, *Judicial Review of Administrative Action*, 5th edn (Sydney, Thompson Reuters, 2013) [10.260].

ALJ a degree of *de facto* power to develop policy without interference from their agencies'.[80] In general, then, it is accurate to say that soft law is treated by tribunals in each of these jurisdictions as though it were hard.

A second example of how soft law is able to be 'hardened' in Australia can be observed in the operation of Part II of the Commonwealth Freedom of Information Act.[81] Part II of the FOI Act creates an impetus for agencies to be active in publishing government information.[82] This is consistent with the objects of the FOI Act which state that 'information held by the Government is to be managed for public purposes, and is a national resource'.[83] For many years, open government had been something of a punchline, on the basis that 'you can either be open, or have government' or that government should be open 'but not gaping'.[84] The changes to Part II introduced by the Freedom of Information Amendment (Reform) Act 2010 (Cth) were intended to secure political and Public Service support for open government in an unprecedented fashion, but have largely been nullified by the decision in 2014 first to defund and subsequently to abolish the Office of the Australian Information Commissioner.[85]

The FOI Act requires agencies to publish 'operational information', which is

> information held by the agency to assist the agency to perform or exercise the agency's functions or powers in making decisions or recommendations affecting members of the public (or any particular person or entity, or class of persons or entities),

provided that such information is not already publicly available.[86] Where an agency fails to publish operational information 'in relation to a function or power of the agency', and 'a person engages in conduct relevant to the performance of the function or the exercise of the power' without being 'aware of the unpublished information', the FOI Act provides that:[87]

> [t]he person must not be subjected to any prejudice only because of the application to that conduct of any rule, guideline or practice in the unpublished information, if the person could lawfully have avoided that prejudice had he or she been aware of the unpublished information.

[80] P Cane, 'Judicial Review in the Age of Tribunals' [2009] *PL* 479, 493–94.

[81] Freedom of Information Act 1982 (Cth) ('FOI Act'). See M Aronson and M Groves, *Judicial Review of Administrative Action*, 5th edn (Sydney, Thompson Reuters, 2013) [5.250]; JM Keyes, *Executive Legislation*, 2nd edn (New South Wales, Butterworths, 2010) 55.

[82] See R Creyke and J McMillan, *Control of Government Action*, 3rd edn (Sydney, LexisNexis, 2012) 1018–19.

[83] FOI Act s 3(3). See Office of the Australian Information Commissioner, *Guide to the Freedom of Information Act 1982* (2011) 64–67: www.oaic.gov.au/publications/agency_resources/guide_freedom_of_information_act_1982.html; J McMillan, 'Freedom of Information Reform—The Australian Government' (2011) 65 *Australian Institute of Administrative Law Forum* 31, 33–34.

[84] A Jay and J Lynn, *The Complete 'Yes, Minister': The Diaries of a Cabinet Minister* (London, BBC, 1984) 27.

[85] See G Weeks, 'Comment on Australia: A Disappointing Backward Step in Information Policy', (6 September 2014) *UK Constitutional Law Association Blog*: ukconstitutionallaw.org/2014/09/06/greg-weeks-comment-on-australia-a-disappointing-backward-step-in-information-policy/.

[86] FOI Act s 8A(1).

[87] FOI Act s 10. The relevant legislation in Queensland, NSW and Victoria features an equivalent provision; see R Creyke and J McMillan, *Control of Government Action*, 3rd edn (Sydney, LexisNexis, 2012) 672–73.

This provision acknowledges the fact that some administrative decision-makers use soft law guidelines, in practice impossible for the public to get but with the de facto status of 'law', to fetter their exercise of statutory discretions.[88] It does not, however, 'harden' soft law in the sense that it becomes binding. In this regard, it cannot be said to have the same effect as *Drake (No 2)* has on decisions in the AAT. Rather, the FOI Act requires that soft law instruments which have a practical effect on the way public bodies make administrative decisions are known to those who may be affected by their content.

As the decision of the High Court majority in *Tang* demonstrates, this does not mean that such persons are able to bind that public body to act consistently with their published guidelines, nor are those guidelines elevated 'to the status of law' such that they are enforceable under section 5(1)(b) of the Administrative Decisions (Judicial Review) Act 1977 (ADJR).[89] However, a person may not suffer prejudice by an agency's failure to publish operational information under Part II of the FOI Act, depending, of course, on such a person being able to establish that they had standing to challenge in court proceedings the failure of the agency to produce its soft law instruments.[90] Furthermore, the failure to publish information as required under Part II is a 'decision' for ADJR purposes, in respect of which a 'person aggrieved' could seek to obtain redress, subject to the relief sought providing 'real practical consequences'.[91]

More generally, the requirement that law must be promulgated before it can be applied adversely to an individual is nothing less than a rule of law principle, which has been recognised for 120 years in England in legislation which requires the publication of every statutory instrument. From 1946, the legislation was expanded to cover the 'flood tide of rules and regulations which arrived with the welfare state'.[92] Fuller took the view, writing over 50 years ago, that this principle should apply to both hard and soft law:[93]

> Deciding agencies, especially administrative tribunals, often take the view that, though the rules they apply to controversies ought to be published, a like requirement does not attach to the rules and practices governing their internal procedures. Yet every experienced attorney knows that to predict the outcome of cases it is often essential to know, not only the formal rules governing them, but the internal procedures of deliberation and consultation by which these rules are in fact applied.

The UK Supreme Court has applied this reasoning in holding that, by adopting and acting upon a secret policy, the Home Office acted ultra vires.[94] The policy at issue in

[88] M Aronson and M Groves, *Judicial Review of Administrative Action*, 5th edn (Sydney, Thompson Reuters, 2013) [5.250], [5.290]. See Chapter 6.A.(i) of this volume below.

[89] *Griffith University v Tang* (2005) 221 CLR 99; *Bryant v Deputy Commissioner of Taxation* (1993) 25 ATR 419, [8]. See G Weeks, 'Expanding Role of Process' (2008) 15 *Australian Journal of Administrative Law* 100, 102–3.

[90] *Duncan v Chief Executive Officer, Centrelink* (2008) 244 ALR 129, 135.

[91] ibid, 137–38.

[92] HWR Wade and C Forsyth, *Administrative Law*, 11th edn (Oxford, Oxford University Press, 2014) 752.

[93] LL Fuller, *The Morality of Law* (New Haven, Yale University Press, 1964) 50. See RE Megarry, 'Administrative Quasi-Legislation'(1944) 60 *LQR* 125, 125–26.

[94] *R (Lumba) v Secretary of State for the Home Department* [2012] 1 AC 245.

Lumba v Home Secretary was not one with which the claimants were able to comply actively, but was merely one whose application affected them. This distinction was not considered to be of any consequence by the Supreme Court. To the extent that the rule of law demands that we be informed in advance of any law which might be applied adversely to us, the FOI Act upholds that principle by severely constraining the administrative benefits of leaving information unpublished.

C. CONCLUSION

It should not come as a surprise that soft law is hard to define. It can be—and frequently has been—characterised by listing examples of how soft law has manifested in the past but, although helpful to a certain extent, this method of definition is imprecise. Soft law is not best considered alone, since it takes so much of its character from what is left after primary and secondary legislative instruments have been applied. Law-makers are welcome to create as much hard law as they choose. However, what is important is that once that choice has been made, only a trained and experienced eye will notice that some law remains which is not hard. Most people will only see law, and this is the cause of soft law's great influence. The following chapters look at what remedies are available to those who have been influenced by soft law to act to their detriment.

Part II

Court-based Remedies

INTRODUCTION

The aims and content of judicial review are hard to define. Even a base-level desire for 'a legal system which addresses the ideals of good government according to law' leaves open the question of what is covered by the concept of 'law'.[1] As I have demonstrated in Part I above, soft law operates like law even though it cannot be enforced like law. It is lawful in the jurisprudential sense (because it is governed by a rule of recognition).[2] However, it is only 'law' (as opposed to hard law) because it is not derived from any of the three sources of law accepted by our rule of recognition: the Constitution, the legislatures or the courts. Soft law is not judicially reviewable on this definition, since judicial review currently operates as a check on exercises of power by public authorities only if they are both legally supported and legally enforceable. In order for soft law to fall within the scope of judicial review, its conception would need to be reassessed.

Chapter five considers whether judicial review's purpose is to civilise law, or power. In other words, it asks whether judicial review is merely about enforcing government adherence to law, or whether it also extends to enforcing symmetrical adherence to all the means by which government asserts power over us? It also considers remedial processes where breach of soft law is held to be relevant to judicial review proceedings having first examined the relevance of soft law to judicial review proceedings, the role of the Australian *Constitution* and the 'province of judicial review'.[3] Chapter six looks at the orthodox, procedural judicial review remedies and Chapter seven analyses the developing role of substantive remedies in judicial review and their relevance to soft law.

Part II then examines the possibility of obtaining a remedy in respect of applications of soft law which are probably irremediable by judicial review, but which nonetheless cause loss. Judicial review remedies are not universally appropriate: as Keane J noted extra-judicially, while 'one may accept that "public power begets public accountability" ... [it] does not follow ... that judicial review is the only mechanism for ensuring public accountability, much less that it is the best available mechanism'.[4]

Chapter eight examines the possibility of obtaining monetary remedies in tort or equity for the application of, or failure to apply, soft law. It addresses some threshold issues to obtaining private law remedies from public authorities, setting out the legal principles of tort and equitable liability which are applicable to Chapters nine and ten. These chapters consider two hypothetical case scenarios, based on the facts of well-known cases, to ascertain the tortious and equitable remedies which might be available against a public authority which fails to adhere to the terms of its soft law. To the extent that the currently available remedies are inadequate, these chapters recommend reforms.

[1] M Aronson and M Groves, *Judicial Review of Administrative Action*, 5th edn (Sydney, Thompson Reuters, 2013) [1.10].

[2] HLA Hart, *The Concept of Law* (Oxford, Clarendon Press, 1961) 97–107; J Raz, 'The Rule of Law and its Virtue', *The Authority of Law: Essays on Law and Morality* (Oxford, Oxford University Press, 1979) 210, 213.

[3] See M Taggart, 'The Province of Administrative Law Determined?' in M Taggart (ed), *The Province of Administrative Law* (Oxford, Hart Publishing, 1997) 1.

[4] PA Keane, 'The Courts and the Academy' (2008) 82 *Australian Law Journal* 623, 633. See also PA Keane, 'Democracy, Participation and Administrative Law' (2012) 68 *Australian Institute of Administrative Law Forum* 1, 13.

5

Remedies Premised on Invalidity: The Province of Judicial Review

THE REASON THAT judicial review is available as a check on governmental power is slightly different in Australia compared to other similar democracies. Many cases over many years have emphasised 'the centrality of section 75(v) [of the Constitution] to the rule of law'.[1] The majority judgment in *Plaintiff S157* noted that section 75(v):[2] 'introduces into the Constitution of the Commonwealth an entrenched minimum provision of judicial review. There was no precise equivalent to section 75(v) in either of the Constitutions of the United States of America or Canada'.

The rule of law, in turn, 'forms an assumptison' upon which the Constitution was framed and which in turn informs the content of judicial review.[3] Therefore, the basis of judicial review as a constitutional fundamental informs the content of the rule of law; the Constitution amounts to a guarantee that judicial review will continue to be available in Australian courts, both at federal and State levels.[4]

The question 'what is judicial review for?' compels the answer, in Australia as elsewhere: 'to restrain the arbitrary exercise of public power, whatever its source and legal form'. This response is in tune with a rule of law analysis but also invites further questions, such as 'what is arbitrariness?' and 'what is public power?'. This chapter addresses these questions.

A helpful starting point is to consider the meaning of 'government'. In its nominal sense, all administrative lawyers generally treat the executive government as being a component of 'the state'. Most modern texts on administrative law now begin with a theory, and some political and historical analysis, of the administrative state, sometimes briefly but often at length.[5] Only a couple offer no background political

[1] M Aronson and M Groves, *Judicial Review of Administrative Action*, 5th edn (Sydney, Thompson Reuters, 2013) [2.120].

[2] *Plaintiff S157 v Commonwealth* (2003) 211 CLR 476, 513 (Gaudron, McHugh, Gummow, Kirby & Hayne JJ). See also J Boughey and G Weeks, '"Officers of the Commonwealth" in the Private Sector' (2013) 36 *University of NSW Law Journal* 316, 320–31.

[3] *Australian Communist Party v Commonwealth* (1951) 83 CLR 1, 193 (Dixon J) ('*The Communist Party Case*'). His Honour's dictum was approved by the majority in *Plaintiff S157* (2003) 211 CLR 476, 513; cf R Sackville, 'The Changing Character of Judicial Review in Australia: The Legacy of *Marbury v Madison*?' (2014) 25 *Public Law Review* 245, 256.

[4] *Kirk v Industrial Relations Commission of New South Wales* (2010) 239 CLR 531.

[5] eg C Harlow and R Rawlings, *Law and Administration*, 3rd edn (Cambridge, Cambridge University Press, 2009) chs 1–2; PP Craig, *Administrative Law*, 7th edn (London, Sweet and Maxwell, 2012) chs 1–4; cf R Creyke and J McMillan, *Control of Government Action*, 3rd edn (Sydney, LexisNexis, 2012) ch 1.

history and no theory of the state.[6] Given that the subject of this book is soft law, which I have defined as any non-legislative but governmental regulatory instrument, this approach to defining government is somewhat inadequate. Rather, I seek to examine 'government' in its use as a verb (an assault on English grammar though that is), since the purpose of soft law is typically to 'do government' other than to act directly through the state. All of administrative law's 'rules and mechanisms are potentially relevant to all the various interactions between "governors" and "the governed"'.[7] This chapter will examine that particular relationship, and the extent to which it is subject to judicial review, in the broadest sense.

Another way of putting this is by differentiating an institutional understanding of the scope of judicial review from a functionalist approach to the same question. Judicial review's principles and remedies have been around for a long time.[8] However, administrative law is a relatively new field of law in Australia. The first Australian text on the subject was not published until 1950.[9] It took a further two decades before the Kerr Report signalled the start of the reforms which would become the 'new administrative law'.[10] It is significant that the High Court is granted jurisdiction by section 75(v) of the Constitution where the constitutional writs of mandamus and prohibition, and the equitable remedy of injunction, are sought against an 'officer of the Commonwealth'.[11] This reflects the reality that, in 1901, seeking a remedy for an ultra vires exercise of public power inevitably meant seeking a remedy against the government or its officers. However, the expansion of the administrative state no longer makes such an institutional approach to judicial review appropriate in all circumstances.

Cane and McDonald put the difference between institutional and functional approaches to the scope of administrative law in these terms:[12]

> The functions which, according to the functional approach, define the scope of administrative law, may be thought of as 'governmental' in the sense that these are functions that would appropriately be performed by organs of government even if they are in fact performed by non-governmental entities. The word 'governance' is apt to capture the idea that

[6] M Aronson and M Groves, *Judicial Review of Administrative Action*, 5th edn (Sydney, Thompson Reuters, 2013) [1.40]; H Woolf et al, *De Smith's Judicial Review*, 7th edn (London, Sweet and Maxwell, 2013).

[7] P Cane and L McDonald, *Principles of Administrative Law: Legal Regulation of Governance*, 2nd edn (Melbourne, Oxford University Press, 2012) 1.

[8] TH Bingham, *The Rule of Law* (London, Penguin, 2010) 60.

[9] W Friedmann, *Principles of Australian Administrative Law* (Melbourne, Melbourne University Press, 1950).

[10] *Kerr Report*, Parliamentary Paper No 144 (1971).

[11] See J Boughey and G Weeks, '"Officers of the Commonwealth" in the Private Sector' (2013) 36 *University of NSW Law Journal* 316; M Aronson and M Groves, *Judicial Review of Administrative Action*, 5th edn (Sydney, Thompson Reuters, 2013) [2.150]. The language of 'prerogative writs' is no longer appropriate: *Re Refugee Review Tribunal; ex parte Aala* (2000) 204 CLR 82, 92–93 (Gaudron & Gummow JJ); 133–34 (Kirby J); 142 (Hayne J); *Bodruddaza v Minister for Immigration and Multicultural Affairs* (2007) 228 CLR 651, 666.

[12] P Cane and L McDonald, *Principles of Administrative Law*, 2nd edn (Melbourne, Oxford University Press 2012) 4.

> government, as well as being a set of institutions, is also a set of activities. Pursuing this line of thinking, we might say that administrative law is about control of governance (certain activities or functions) rather than about the control of government (certain institutions).

Australia has not reached the point, arrived at many years ago in England, where administrative law has a functional, rather than a more limited institutional, scope. Part of the problem is the difficulty in identifying a function of government. Indeed, Cane and McDonald see this form of words as being 'slightly different' to the concept of 'public functions' used in England.[13] Given my broad approach to 'doing government' (that is, where the purpose of an act by a private entity is to govern public behaviour), nothing turns on the distinction for the purposes of this book.

The categorisation of law becomes important when considering what legal status ought to be given to soft law. Creyke and McMillan used a dictionary definition of 'law' to get past the philosophical implications of what that term entails and came to the conclusion that, domestically, positive law must be both enforceable and designed to control.[14] To then discern the legal status of a particular instrument, they stated that three considerations are pre-eminent:[15]

(i) the text of the instrument itself;
(ii) its purpose; and
(iii) whether it has statutory backing or authorisation.

The first of these considerations, I would respectfully suggest, is relevant only to the extent that it casts light upon the second and third considerations.

In regard to the third consideration proposed by Creyke and McMillan, the issues are uncomplicated where the rules or guidelines in question have been specifically authorised or anticipated by the relevant empowering legislation and a court exercising a judicial review function is required only to consider whether the decision-maker acted ultra vires.[16] Guidelines may be reviewable either at common law or under section 39B of the Judiciary Act 1903 (Cth) at Commonwealth level, but they are unreviewable under the Administrative Decisions (Judicial Review) Act 1977 (ADJR Act) because they are not made 'under an enactment'.[17]

Guidelines might be valid but their application invalid. Their application can be challenged on the basis that the policy has been applied inflexibly or without consideration of the merits of the individual case. The purposive element of the definition

[13] ibid, 4–5.

[14] R Creyke and J McMillan, 'Soft Law versus Hard Law' in L Pearson et al (eds), *Administrative Law in a Changing State* (Oxford, Hart Publishing, 2008) 377, 383.

[15] ibid, 393–94.

[16] See eg *Adultshop.com v Members of the Classification Review Board* (2007) 243 ALR 752; R Creyke and J McMillan, 'Soft Law versus Hard Law' in L Pearson et al (eds), *Administrative Law in a Changing State* (Oxford, Hart Publishing, 2008) 377, 395.

[17] Administrative Decisions (Judicial Review) Act 1977 (Cth) s 3(1). See R Creyke and J McMillan, 'Soft Law versus Hard Law' in L Pearson et al (eds), *Administrative Law in a Changing State* (Oxford, Hart Publishing, 2008) 377, 394–96; *Tang* (2005) 221 CLR 99; *White Industries Australia v Federal Commissioner of Taxation* (2007) 160 FCR 298.

by Creyke and McMillan is difficult but central. For example, the Grey-Letter Law Report, which detailed each variety of an 'incentive to comply', stated:[18]

> Guidelines are likely to be quasi-regulation if:
>
> A. they suggest particular actions or procedures not specified in the law itself which businesses should adopt; and
> B. business has a strong incentive to comply.
>
> The incentive to comply can take a number of forms, including:
>
> C. an indication that a business following the guidelines will not be in breach of the relevant legal requirement;[19] …
> D. an indication by a regulator that compliance with the guidelines will be a consideration in its enforcement of regulation, decision making or handling of complaints; … [and]
> E. a perception that adherence to guidelines will help to keep businesses in compliance with the law.

The second of the considerations nominated by Creyke and McMillan in ascertaining the enforceability of a soft law instrument—the purpose of the instrument—is arguably the most important. Creyke and McMillan recognised that the question of purpose may vary from the mechanical, such as when a guidance note indicates the steps that will be taken to implement a certain policy or statute, to the merely aspirational, such as the *Australian Public Service Values*.[20] Where a soft law instrument is intended to have a practical effect, that effect will generally be observable in practice. Consultations undertaken by the Administrative Review Council in preparing the Complex Regulation Report confirmed that:[21]

> despite their non-binding character, soft law 'guidelines', 'practice notes', and so on, developed by government agencies are treated in practice little differently from black letter law. Some of those consulted said that only people with 'deep pockets' would be in a position to mount a legal challenge to the validity of soft law produced by government agencies.

Creyke and McMillan's third element suggests that there is a sense in which the hardness or softness of a legal instrument is an inquiry separate from that as to its legal status. In other words, the legality or legitimacy of an instrument may be decided by its source: acts within power by the legislature and decisions of the courts are law, at least until such time as they are validly overturned.[22] However, if the adjective 'soft' denotes an instrument which a court cannot enforce or otherwise give consequence to, it cuts across some legislation, for example legislation of a wholly aspirational nature. Two examples will suffice.

[18] *Grey-Letter Law Report* (1997), 23–25.

[19] This may fall short of a representation which would be actionable in tort if it were negligently inaccurate; see Chapter 8 of this volume.

[20] APS Commission, *Australian Public Service Values and Code of Conduct in practice: A guide to official conduct for APS employees and agency heads*. R Creyke and J McMillan, 'Soft Law versus Hard Law' in L Pearson et al (eds), *Administrative Law in a Changing State* (Oxford, Hart Publishing, 2008) 377, 380. See also M D'Ascenzo, 'Effectiveness of Administrative Law in the Australian Public Service' (2008) 57 *Australian Institute of Administrative Law Forum* 59.

[21] *Complex Regulation Report* (2008), 14.

[22] See *State of New South Wales v Kable* (2013) 252 CLR 118 ('*Kable (No 2)*').

First, the requirement that tribunals perform their functions in such a way as to provide review which is 'fair, just, economical, informal and quick' appears in several legislative schemes. Hayne, Kiefel and Bell JJ commented that these:[23]

> adjectives … are apt to apply to objectives but not to enforceable requirements, not the least because each pulls the Tribunal in a different direction. It is contended that provisions of this kind do not detract from, but nor do they add to, such obligations, limits or powers as arise from the language of the statute.

Secondly, the Charter of Budget Honesty Act 1998 (Cth) set out the Charter of Budget Honesty as Schedule 1, but stated that 'nothing in the Charter of Budget Honesty creates rights or duties that are enforceable in judicial or other proceedings'.[24] In this sense, the charter was undeniably soft: it sought to regulate behaviour through recommendation rather than by setting a judicially enforceable norm.[25] On the other hand, being an Act of Parliament which had been considered, debated and voted upon, it was undeniably law. Its 'softness' did not make it any less a valid expression of the will of Parliament. In other words, it was certainly 'hard' law in the eyes of the legislature, even if courts could not enforce it. The same point can be made with regard to the 'fair, just, economical, informal and quick' formulation.

McHugh J picked up on this issue in *Plaintiff S157* during argument with Mr John Basten QC (since 2005, Basten JA of the NSW Court of Appeal), who was appearing for the applicants in the case being heard concurrently.[26] His Honour put the following point in relation to reaching a determination whether the relevant section of the Migration Act was a privative clause:[27]

> **McHUGH J**: … It seems to me [the clause] has the dilemma, either it is an ouster clause or, arguably, it runs into various constitutional prohibitions or it is a delegation of power, or it is not even a law. It is not a law in the Austinian sense. Austin's definition of Law may not be exhaustive but in this present context how does one know what the command of the sovereign is?
>
> **MR BASTEN**: Yes, indeed. Your Honour … there is, we say in the submissions, a distinct difference between the circumstance we are now envisaging and the circumstance where the Parliament has simply been silent, as in the *Project Blue Sky*[28] type case, as to the effect of non-compliance, so that we accept …

[23] *Li* (2013) 249 CLR 332, 358. These dicta referred to Migration Act 1958 (Cth) section 353(1), which has since been altered. It once applied to the Migration Review Tribunal, but now applies to the Administrative Appeals Tribunal in its Migration and Refugee Division, into which the MRT was amalgamated in 2015: Migration Act 1958 (Cth) s 336M. The reference to 'providing a mechanism of review that is fair, just, economical, informal and quick' has been removed from the Act, although s 357A still requires that 'the Tribunal must act in a way that is fair and just'.

[24] Charter of Budget Honesty Act 1998 (Cth) s 3(2).

[25] Although some aspects of the Charter regime are more prescriptive than that: see eg Secretary to the Treasury and Secretary to the Department of Finance and Deregulation, '*Charter of Budget Honesty—Policy Costing Guidelines*' (Guidelines, 2012).

[26] *Re Minister for Immigration and Multicultural and Indigenous Affairs; ex parte Applicants S134/2002* (2003) 211 CLR 441.

[27] *Plaintiff S157/2002 v Commonwealth* [2002] HCA Trans 420 (3 September 2002). See also *Offshore Processing Case* (2010) 243 CLR 319, 139; *Plaintiff M79/2012 v Minister for Immigration and Citizenship* (2013) 252 CLR 336, 367 (Hayne J).

[28] *Project Blue Sky v Australian Broadcasting Authority* (1998) 194 CLR 355.

> McHUGH J: I really had in mind cases like *Ex parte Walsh and Johnson*[29] and the *Communist Party Case*,[30] both of which struck down laws which really depended upon the Executive view of the law.

Ultimately the Court was able to 'eviscerate' the privative clause without having to decide this point, although an oblique reference was made to it in the joint judgment.[31] However, Aronson has raised some persuasive doubts about this line of argument, based upon the fact Australia's immigration legislation has gone from being very brief, explicitly racist and full of discretionary power reserved to the Minister to a statutory behemoth full of detail and growing steadily. On what basis can it be suggested that 'an Act without this level of detail is not a real law'?[32]

The question of how the legal system is able to deal with instruments which fall short of being binding law arose in the later High Court case of *Griffith University v Tang*.[33] Both *Tang* and the constitutional requirement of a 'matter', which is relevant to McHugh J's point, are considered in detail below.

A. JUDICIAL REVIEW AND THE RULE OF LAW

If the scope of judicial review is to be broadened to cover all exercises of public power, whether regulated by hard or soft law, there must be some normative justification for that step. One way of reaching this end is to frame as a rule of law issue the expansion of judicial review to cover soft law. This involves casting governance through the mechanism of soft law as an exercise of arbitrary power, to the extent that such governance lacks accountability, which must be made subject to legal safeguards.

The rule of law is frequently defined by its aversion to arbitrariness, although what is meant by that statement can vary.[34] Raz argued that, on a positivist view, the law inherently creates the risk of arbitrary power (power exercised 'either with an indifference as to whether it will serve the purposes which alone can justify the use of that power or with belief that it will not serve them') and that the rule of law serves to minimise this danger.[35] He denied that this occurred through the presence of morality in the rule of law, but took the view that arbitrariness is a subjective

[29] *Re Yates; ex parte Walsh and Johnson* (1925) 37 CLR 36.

[30] *The Communist Party Case* (1951) 83 CLR 1.

[31] *Plaintiff S157* (2003) 211 CLR 476, 512–13 (Gaudron, McHugh, Gummow, Kirby & Hayne JJ). See M Aronson, 'Commentary on "The Entrenched Minimum Provision of Judicial Review and the Rule of Law" by Leighton McDonald' (2010) 21 *Public Law Review* 35.

[32] M Aronson, 'Statutory Interpretation or Judicial Disobedience?' (3 June 2013) *UK Constitutional Law Group Blog*, available at: ukconstitutionallaw.org/2013/06/03/mark-aronson-statutory-interpretation-or-judicial-disobedience/.

[33] *Griffith University v Tang* (2005) 221 CLR 99.

[34] See eg TH Bingham, *Rule of Law* (London, Penguin, 2010) 48–54; M Liston, 'Witnessing Arbitrariness: *Roncarelli v Duplessis* Fifty Years On' (2010) 55 *McGill Law Journal* 689, 691.

[35] J Raz, 'The Rule of Law and its Virtue', *The Authority of Law* (Oxford, Oxford University Press, 1979) 210, 219–24.

concept and that there is no normative basis for the rule of law's opposition to arbitrariness.[36]

Dicey, too, defined the rule of law in opposition to arbitrariness, by which he meant:[37]

> in the first place, that no man is punishable or can be lawfully made to suffer in body or goods except for a distinct breach of law established in the ordinary legal manner before the ordinary courts of the land. In this sense the rule of law is contrasted with every system of government based on the exercise by persons in authority of wide, arbitrary, or discretionary powers of constraint.

Hunt argued that Dicey, in contrast to Raz, in fact used the rule of law in a sense informed by notions of common law constitutionalism.[38] This gave Dicey's view of the rule of law a normative element, since the sovereignty of Parliament was offset by the common law courts which would interpret statutes in accordance with 'fundamental rights' of constitutional standing.[39]

In his controversial paper, *Judicial Activism and the Death of the Rule of Law*, JD Heydon also placed an opposition to arbitrary decision-making at the heart of the rule of law.[40] As others have noted, Heydon J's conception of the rule of law depends on the view that, subject to legislation, *any* failure by a court to adhere strictly to the doctrine of stare decisis (as his Honour formulated it) results in 'arbitrary, whimsical, capricious, unpredictable and autocratic decision making' and may result in 'the citizen ... being at the mercy of an individual mind uncontrolled by due process of law'.[41] The weakness of the historical underpinnings of such a narrow approach to the rule of law were pointed out by Wade, who noted that the attempts of the Stuart monarchs to rule by proclamation were backed by substantial common law precedent.[42]

Heydon J saw the rule of law, in a way not anticipated by Dicey, being violated by unpredictable judges rather than by arbitrary legislation or administration.[43] Dicey saw judges as the heroes of the common law.[44] At least from Hunt's perspective, this view was not altered on Dicey's part by the fact that judges could read down or otherwise influence the implementation of formally impeccable statutes which

[36] cf D Dyzenhaus, 'The Legitimacy of the Rule of Law' in D Dyzenhaus, M Hunt and G Huscroft (eds), *A Simple Common Lawyer* (Oxford, Hart Publishing, 2009) 33, 40.

[37] AV Dicey, *Introduction to the Law of the Constitution*, 10th edn, ECS Wade (ed) (London, Palgrave, 1959) 188.

[38] M Hunt, 'Constitutionalism and the Contractualisation of Government in the United Kingdom' in M Taggart (ed), *The Province of Administrative Law* (Oxford, Hart Publishing, 1997) 21, 24–25.

[39] cf PP Craig, 'Formal and Substantive Conceptions of the Rule of Law: an Analytical Framework' [1997] *PL* 467, 470.

[40] JD Heydon, 'Judicial Activism and the Death of the Rule of Law' (2003) 23 *Australian Bar Review* 110, 132.

[41] ibid; cf AC Hutchinson, '"Heydon" Seek: Looking for Law in All the Wrong Places' (2003) 29 *Monash University Law Review* 85, 90.

[42] ECS Wade, 'Introduction' to AV Dicey, *Introduction to the Law of the Constitution*, 10th edn, ECS Wade (ed) (London, Palgrave, 1959), xcviii–xcix.

[43] See JD Heydon, 'Threats to Judicial Independence: The Enemy Within' (2013) 129 *LQR* 205.

[44] AV Dicey, *Introduction to the Law of the Constitution*, 10th edn, ECS Wade (ed) (London, Palgrave, 1959), 193–94.

interfered with the 'fundamental values' of the common law, and were empowered to protect against the excesses of the administrative state.[45] However, the search for 'fundamental' rights and values has more recently been criticised as lacking utility in the face of parliamentary power, both in Australia and England.[46]

Just as there are different interpretations of the content of the rule of law throughout the last century or more, so too are there different interpretations of its content in different countries today. South Africa is at one end of the spectrum, being a country in which judicial remedies may be based upon nothing more substantive that the court's understanding of the rule of law. Hoexter has written approvingly of the enforceable status of the rule of law in South Africa, and has contended that it was still necessary even after the passage of a Constitution 'fairly bristling with human rights'.[47] Over the past decade, the South African Constitutional Court has taken the same view, to the extent that the rule of law (and specifically the principle of legality) has become directly enforceable. In South Africa, as in Australia and elsewhere, the rule of law exists 'either as a founding value or, if need be, as a doctrine implicit in the Constitution'.[48]

However, the Constitution of the Republic of South Africa 1996 also contains express rights in section 33, such as the right that administrative action be 'procedurally fair'.[49] This scheme of rights was codified in the Promotion of Administrative Justice Act 2000.[50] It is now being subverted by the tendency of courts to apply the principle of legality directly and therefore 'go behind' the difficulties imposed by the terms of the PAJA, despite the official view of the Constitutional Court that constitutionally mandated legislation, such as the PAJA, must be used where it is applicable.[51] The Constitutional Court warned explicitly in *New Clicks* that, where the PAJA applies, it cannot be ignored.[52] However, this has not prevented South African courts (up to and including the Constitutional Court) from avoiding 'the difficult questions' which may sometimes ensue from applying the PAJA rather than the 'generality (and indeed the uncertainty)' of the common law principle of legality.[53]

[45] M Hunt, 'Constitutionalism and Contractualisation' in M Taggart (ed), *The Province of Administrative Law* (Oxford, Hart Publishing, 1997) 21, 25. See also PP Craig, 'Conceptions of the Rule of Law' [1997] *PL* 467, 470–71.

[46] *Malika Holdings Pty Ltd v Streeton* (2001) 204 CLR 290, 298–99 (McHugh J); *R v Secretary of State for the Home Department; ex parte Simms and O'Brien* [2000] 2 AC 115, 131.

[47] C Hoexter, 'The Principle of Legality in South African Administrative Law' (2004) 4 *Macquarie Law Journal* 165, 166.

[48] C Hoexter, 'The Rule of Law and the Principle of Legality in South African Administrative Law Today' in M Carnelley and S Hoctor (eds), *Law, Order and Liberty: Essays in Honour of Tony Mathews* (Pietermaritzburg, UKZN Press, 2011) 9. See n 3 in the Introduction to this chapter, above.

[49] Constitution of the Republic of South Africa 1996 (SA) s 33(1). See generally C Hoexter, *Administrative Law in South Africa*, 2nd edn (Claremont, Juta & Co, 2012) ch 7.

[50] Promotion of Administrative Justice Act 2000 (SA) ('PAJA').

[51] *Minister of Health v New Clicks South Africa (Pty) Ltd* 2006 (2) SA 311 (CC); *Bato Star Fishing (Pty) Ltd v Minister of Environmental Affairs* 2004 (4) SA 490 (CC), [25] (O'Regan J). See C Hoexter, 'Rule of Law and the Principle of Legality' in M Carnelley and S Hoctor (eds), *Law, Order and Liberty* (Pietermaritzburg, UKZN Press, 2011) 10.

[52] *Minister of Health v New Clicks South Africa (Pty) Ltd* 2006 (2) SA 311 (CC), [96] (Chaskalson CJ); [436] (Ngcobo J); [585]–[586] (Sachs J).

[53] C Hoexter, 'The Principle of Legality in South African Administrative Law' (2004) 4 *Macquarie Law Journal* 165, 166. See C Hoexter, 'Rule of Law and the Principle of Legality' in M Carnelley and S Hoctor (eds), *Law, Order and Liberty* (Pietermaritzburg, UKZN Press, 2011) 11–12.

The result is that the principle of legality is the cause of no little unpredictability in South Africa and is 'susceptible of abuse', even though it gives courts an increased capacity to provide administrative justice.[54]

This recent South African jurisprudence is in contrast to the view (articulated above by both Dicey and Heydon) that inconsistency and unpredictability indicate at least possible arbitrariness, the very antithesis to the rule of law. As the Australian AAT discovered in its early years, administrative justice usually calls for a compromise to be struck between consistency and the capacity to do justice in individual cases, with the result that 'you inevitably lose some of the good features from both sides'.[55] Some of the development of South African law may therefore be explicable as a result of that country having no tribunal of broad jurisdiction, equivalent to the Australian AAT, to decide cases on their merits.[56] While there is some scope for administrative decisions to be appealed on their merits, judicial review courts in South Africa bear a greater burden of providing administrative justice than is the case in other comparable jurisdictions, none more so than Australia.[57] The burden is great indeed when one recalls that South African courts need still to respect the doctrines of the separation of powers and legislative supremacy. As the Supreme Court of Appeal has noted (in overturning a decision to enforce an estoppel against a public authority), judges must avoid:[58]

> exempting courts from showing due deference to broad legislative authority, permitting illegality to trump legality and rendering the *ultra vires* doctrine nugatory. None of that would be in the interests of justice. Nor, can it be said, would any of that be sanctioned by the *Constitution*, which is based on the rule of law, and at the heart of which lies the principle of legality.

The principle of legality requires that governmental power be exercised with lawful authority. Judicial review is a component of this, since it has the function of ensuring that the limits to power imposed by law are observed. In this sense, the principle of legality has a more defined meaning than 'the rule of law', which remains indeterminate in its content and scope. A further component of the principle of legality is interpretive, that legislation is to be read such that fundamental rights cannot be abrogated by general or ambiguous words.[59] This is a principle that has been stated in Australian and English cases on numerous occasions, many of them long before the 'principle of legality' became familiar to modern public lawyers.[60] It is possible,

[54] C Hoexter, 'Rule of Law and the Principle of Legality' in M Carnelley and S Hoctor (eds), *Law, Order and Liberty* (Pietermaritzburg, UKZN Press, 2011), 13.

[55] C Hilson, 'Judicial Review, Policies and the Fettering of Discretion' [2002] *PL* 111, 113. See Chapter 2.B.(iv) of this volume above.

[56] See C Hoexter, *Administrative Law in South Africa*, 2nd edn (Claremont, Juta & Co, 2012) 70–72.

[57] ibid, 67–70.

[58] *City of Tshwane Metropolitan Municipality v RPM Bricks (Pty) Ltd* 2008 (3) SA 1 (SCA), [24] (Ponnan JA).

[59] PP Craig, *Administrative Law*, 7th edn (London, Sweet and Maxwell, 2012) 578–79; cf *Malika Holdings* (2001) 204 CLR 290, 298–9 (McHugh J); *Simms* [2000] 2 AC 115, 131 (Lord Hoffmann).

[60] See eg *Plaintiff S157* (2003) 211 CLR 476, 492 (Gleeson CJ); *Simms* [2000] 2 AC 115; *R (Roberts) v Parole Board* [2005] 2 AC 738.

however, for courts to deal with the interpretive aspect of the principle of legality in more than one way.[61]

The first of these is with insouciance bordering on disobedience, as when courts express feigned disbelief that the legislature could have meant to violate a 'fundamental right'. This attitude has a long history. In *Potter v Minahan*, O'Connor J stated that:[62]

> 'It is in the last degree improbable that the legislature would overthrow fundamental principles, infringe rights, or depart from the general system of law, without expressing its intention with irresistible clearness; and to give any such effect to general words, simply because they have that meaning in their widest, or usual, or natural sense, would be to give them a meaning in which they were not really used.'

It is frequently clear that it was precisely the legislature's intention to violate the 'fundamental right' under discussion. A good example may be observed in *Coco v R*, in which the High Court held that, in the absence of express words, a Queensland statute could not confer power on a Supreme Court judge to authorise conduct which would otherwise amount to trespass at common law.[63] This required interpreting the statute such that the power to 'use' a listening device did not carry with it the statutory power to install that device in the face of contrary common law authority.

The House of Lords came to a similar conclusion in *Simms*, in relation to the Home Secretary's policy that journalists would only be allowed to conduct oral interviews with prisoners if they undertook in writing that they would not publish any part of the interviews.[64] Lord Steyn, having referred obliquely to England's sorry recent history of miscarriages of justice in criminal matters, stated that he was 'reasonably confident that once it is accepted that oral interviews with prisoners serve a useful purpose in exposing potential miscarriages of justice the Home Secretary would not wish his present policy to be maintained'.[65] His Lordship went on to declare that the Home Secretary's policy was unlawful, having stated that the principle of legality allowed the Appellate Committee to construe subordinate legislation which gave effect to that policy such that it was not ultra vires because it was presumed to be subject to the 'fundamental and basic rights asserted by the applicants in this case'.[66]

[61] See generally M Groves and G Weeks, 'Substantive (Procedural) Review in Australia' in H Wilberg and M Elliott (eds), *The Scope and Intensity of Substantive Review: Traversing Michael Taggart's Rainbow* (Oxford, Hart Publishing, 2015) 133, 152–61.

[62] *Potter v Minahan* (1908) 7 CLR 277, 304 (O'Connor J), quoting PB Maxwell, *On the Interpretation of Statutes*, 4th edn (1905) 122 (citations omitted). This quotation was later approved in *Bropho v Western Australia* (1990) 171 CLR 1, 18 (Mason CJ, Deane, Dawson, Toohey, Gaudron & McHugh JJ); *Coco v R* (1994) 179 CLR 427, 437 (Mason CJ, Brennan, Gaudron & McHugh JJ). See also *ex parte Walsh and Johnson* (1925) 37 CLR 36, 93 (Isaacs J).

[63] *Coco* (1994) 179 CLR 427, 438 (Mason CJ, Brennan, Gaudron & McHugh JJ).

[64] *R v Secretary of State for the Home Department; ex parte Simms and O'Brien* [2000] 2 AC 115, 119 (Lord Steyn).

[65] ibid, 129 Lords Browne-Wilkinson, Hoffmann and Millett concurred with Lord Steyn's reasoning and proposed orders. Lord Hobhouse concurred as to the invalidity of the regulations but not as to the proposed orders.

[66] ibid, 130. See *Roberts v Parole Board* [2005] 2 AC 738, 784–88; C Harlow and R Rawlings, *Law and Administration*, 3rd edn (Cambridge, Cambridge University Press, 2009) 643.

Lord Hoffmann's reasoning in *Simms* was subtly different, and represents the second method by which courts can deal with the principle of legality. While his Lordship agreed with the reasons given by Lord Steyn, and was prepared to presume the validity of the subordinate legislation on the basis that any legislative instrument expressed in general terms is subject to 'fundamental human rights', his reasons for reaching this conclusion were expressed in slightly different terms.[67] His Lordship stated that the power of the Parliament to legislate contrary to 'fundamental principles of human rights' was subject to restraints which:[68]

> are ultimately political, not legal. But the principle of legality means that Parliament must squarely confront what it is doing and accept the political cost. Fundamental rights cannot be overridden by general or ambiguous words. *This is because there is too great a risk that the full implications of their unqualified meaning may have passed unnoticed in the democratic process.* In the absence of express language or necessary implication to the contrary, the courts therefore presume that even the most general words were intended to be subject to the basic rights of the individual. In this way the courts of the United Kingdom, though acknowledging the sovereignty of Parliament, apply principles of constitutionality little different from those which exist in countries where the power of the legislature is expressly limited by a constitutional document (emphasis added).

This approach requires a Parliament which seeks to override fundamental common law rights to confront what it is doing squarely 'and accept the political cost'.[69] Ensuring that governments say clearly what it is that they want and accept full political responsibility for it has become a common feature of the principle of legality. Sometimes this is implicit in the courts' reasoning on other grounds, such as Laws LJ's finding that the process of consultation required before altering subordinate legislation governing grants of legal aid for public interest litigation was inadequate because it did not reveal that the government's motivation was illegal (namely, to limit embarrassing legal action taken against it).[70] At other times, courts explicitly disapprove of attempts by government to avoid political responsibility for their decisions.

Rarely has such an attempt been as clear as in *Lumba*, in which a senior officer in the Home Office drafted a policy which said in part that, while it was likely the policy in question was unlawful, 'if we were to lose a test case, we could present any change in [foreign national prisoners'] detention practice as having been forced on us by the courts'.[71] Lord Dyson considered this course of action 'deplorable', a conclusion with which it is hard to disagree.[72] At the very least, it demonstrates that the principle of legality will, at least occasionally, have real work to do and cannot simply be categorised, by those so inclined, as the tool of an obstructionist judiciary.

[67] *Simms* [2000] 2 AC 115, 132 (Lord Hoffmann). See Prison Service Standing Order 5 of 1996 (issued by the Secretary of State pursuant to rule 33 of the Prison Rules 1964, under authority conferred by section 47(1) of the Prison Act 1952).

[68] *Simms* [2000] 2 AC 115, 131. See also *Plaintiff S157* (2003) 211 CLR 476, 492 (Gleeson CJ).

[69] PP Craig, *Administrative Law*, 7th edn (London, Sweet and Maxwell, 2012) 579.

[70] *R (on the application of Evans) v The Lord Chancellor and Secretary of State for Justice* [2012] 1 WLR 838, 850 (Stadlen J agreeing).

[71] *Lumba v Home Secretary* [2012] 1 AC 245, 299.

[72] ibid.

To what extent the rule of law ought to be understood as having normative content rather than being merely procedural is beyond the scope of this book. At any rate, the issue is far from settled.[73] It suffices to say that, if courts are opposed to the arbitrary use of power, there is more good to be done by extending the coverage of judicial review to include exercises of soft law than by remaining aloof and thereby legitimating whatever arbitrariness arises.

There are three possible objections to this position, two formal and the other practical. The first formal objection is that, by broadening its jurisdiction to cover applications of soft law, the courts may be acting against the terms of the Bill of Rights 1688 (UK). This argument proceeds on the basis that, by treating soft law as though it has the full force of law, the courts would in effect be saying that soft law derived from the executive branch of government is of the same effect as laws enacted by Parliament.[74] The soft law would thereby be in breach of the second article of the Bill of Rights, which states that:

> the pretended power of dispensing with laws or the execution of laws by regal authority, as it hath been assumed and exercised of late, is illegal.

For such an objection to be upheld would represent a victory of form over substance. The fact of the matter is that the executive *does* regulate behaviour through soft law; this does not become the case only as a result of legal recognition.

As Part I pointed out, soft law is not inherently bad, and has the potential to be beneficial, for example in alerting the public to the executive's view of a statute that has not been interpreted by the courts, or by otherwise bringing predictability to a field of the law by adding a level of detail to a more generally expressed statutory instrument.[75] Soft law is a tool, just as a sharp knife is.[76] The fact that it is sharp means that it is a well-made knife, but it also gives it the potential to be used for ill as well as good, for stabbing people as well as cutting vegetables. What is concerning about soft law is its capacity for misuse: knowing that soft law is followed as though it were hard, and that it can be made without the inconvenience of consulting Parliament, the executive will often be tempted to regulate behaviour through the mechanism of soft law. This is a threat to the spirit of the Bill of Rights, if not to its precise terms. Judicial oversight of the use of soft law by the executive can only serve the better to ensure that it is a tool that is not misused.

The second formal objection is simply that, while soft law would indeed be ultra vires if it were to 'dispense' with laws or their execution, if that is not the case, then soft law is not in fact 'dispensing' with law but *adding* law (of a sort).

The practical objection to extending the scope of judicial review to cover soft law was aptly stated by Aronson, who in commenting on *Datafin*, asked: 'What is the point of supervising the way a body interprets rules which it can change without legal formality? The further a regulatory regime travels from the legal paradigm, the

[73] See PP Craig, 'Conceptions of the Rule of Law' [1997] *PL* 467.

[74] See *Fleming v Ireland* [2013] IEHC 2 (Kearns P) at n 136 below.

[75] RE Megarry, 'Administrative Quasi-Legislation' (1944) 60 *LQR* 125, 126.

[76] This metaphor is borrowed from J Raz, 'The Rule of Law and its Virtue', *The Authority of Law* (Oxford, Oxford University Press, 1979) 210, 226.

less relevant is judicial review as an accountability device'.[77] It is hard to get around this question. To extend the metaphor used above, perhaps judicial review is simply not a tool fit for the purpose of curbing formally extra-legal methods of regulation. To the extent that this is true, Part III below examines various non-judicial methods of dealing with soft law.

The limitations of judicial review in the face of an executive branch capable of altering the rules without parliamentary sanction can be demonstrated by looking at *Quin*, a case involving a judicial review application brought by a former stipendiary magistrate who the government of the day chose not to appoint to a Local Court magistracy when the New South Wales Courts of Petty Sessions were abolished by statute.[78] The government's policy was that stipendiary magistrates would be appointed to the new court unless unfit for judicial office. Quin was one of only five stipendiary magistrates who were not so appointed. The New South Wales Court of Appeal (in *Macrae*) held that these five former stipendiary magistrates had been denied natural justice by the Attorney-General and declared (albeit in a less than clear fashion) that his decision not to recommend their appointment was void.[79] Special leave to appeal was subsequently denied by the High Court. By this time, there had been a change of government in NSW, prior to which the Australian Labor Party had been in power for 12 years and five separate Attorneys-General had held office.[80] The new Attorney-General, John Dowd QC, altered the policy of the previous government to state that, rather than giving preference to former stipendiary magistrates, he would appoint new magistrates to the Local Courts based only on merit. The successful *Macrae* plaintiffs were able to apply on equal terms to any other applicant, and would not have allegations of unsuitability held against them unless they were given an opportunity to respond to such allegations.[81] Quin (along with two other of the *Macrae* plaintiffs, who subsequently withdrew their claims) sought and obtained a declaration from the NSW Court of Appeal that he was entitled to have his original application for appointment considered with procedural fairness, notwithstanding the new policy of the Attorney-General.[82] This was an outcome that the new Attorney-General had evidently anticipated.[83]

By a bare majority, the High Court upheld the Attorney-General's subsequent appeal. The majority judgments of Mason CJ, Brennan J and Dawson J each followed substantially different reasoning, but the basic proposition that can be taken from their combined judgments is that it is not for the courts to compel the executive government to adhere to one policy rather than another.[84] Although it formed no part of

[77] M Aronson, 'A Public Lawyer's Responses to Privatisation and Outsourcing' in M Taggart (ed), *The Province of Administrative Law* (Oxford, Hart Publishing, 1997) 40, 47. See *R v Panel on Take-overs and Mergers; ex parte Datafin plc* [1987] 1 QB 815.

[78] *Attorney General (NSW) v Quin* (1990) 170 CLR 1.

[79] *Macrae v Attorney-General (NSW)* (1987) 9 NSWLR 268.

[80] See www.justice.nsw.gov.au//about-us/history.

[81] *Quin* (1990) 170 CLR 1, 50–51.

[82] *Quin v Attorney-General (NSW)* (1988) 16 ALD 550.

[83] K Mason, *Old Law, New Law: A Second Australian Legal Miscellany* (Sydney, Federation Press, 2014) 136–37.

[84] See Chapter 7 of this volume below.

the Court's formal reasoning, this is true a fortiori where, as in these circumstances, a policy is changed as a result of a change in government. *Quin* is now a quintessential part of the Australian administrative law landscape, and the result reached by the majority was undoubtedly correct. It does, however, point clearly to the fact that judicial review of soft law may be of absolutely no utility without the court having the capacity to enforce previous or existing soft law instruments substantively. While the executive retains the capacity to change soft law without reference to any other body, judicial review's retrospective remedies will likely be of no greater avail than they were to the *Macrae* plaintiffs.

Quin occupies a status of almost unquestionable authority in Australia, making it difficult to argue persuasively that courts should intervene to enforce soft law.[85] There is, however, no equivalent case in England. This chapter therefore examines a recent trio of cases in which the UK's highest court has been faced with soft law issues: *Purdy v DPP*, *Lumba v Home Secretary* and *Kambadzi v Home Secretary*.

(i) *Purdy v DPP*

An additional (although not alternative) method of providing a normative basis for extending the scope of judicial review is through the adoption of legislation which provides for substantive protection of rights, such as the Human Rights Act 1998 (UK). An example of the interaction between the Human Rights Act and soft law was seen in *Purdy*, the last case decided by the judicial branch of the House of Lords.[86] Their Lordships reached what one commentator has described as an 'astonishing' conclusion.[87] The case also showed the difficulties inherent in treating soft law as though it were hard law.

Briefly, the facts of *Purdy* are these. Debbie Purdy suffered from incurable multiple sclerosis and expected that her health would eventually deteriorate to the point that she would wish to end her life. However, she was concerned that, by the time this point were to arrive, she would likely be unable to commit suicide unassisted. Assisting a person to commit suicide is a breach of the Suicide Act 1961:[88]

> A person who aids, abets, counsels or procures the suicide of another, or an attempt by another to commit suicide, shall be liable on conviction on indictment to imprisonment for a term not exceeding fourteen years.

Ms Purdy wished to be able to travel with her husband to Switzerland (where assisted suicide is legal) to commit suicide when she decided that she wished to die, but would not do so if her husband, having helped her in Switzerland, would therefore face criminal liability in England after her death. The Suicide Act confers

[85] See M Groves, 'Federal Constitutional Influences on State Judicial Review' (2011) 39 *Federal Law Review* 399.

[86] *R (on the application of Purdy) v Director of Public Prosecutions* [2009] 1 AC 345.

[87] JM Finnis, 'Invoking the Principle of Legality against the Rule of Law' [2010] *New Zealand Law Review* 601, 603.

[88] Suicide Act 1961 (UK) s 2(1).

upon the Director of Public Prosecutions (DPP) a discretion as to whether s/he will proceed against any person for breach of the sub-section extracted above.[89] The DPP is required by legislation to publish a Code for Crown Prosecutors.[90] The Code is a soft law document providing guidance to Crown Prosecutors about whether a prosecution is justified in various circumstances.[91]

Ms Purdy took action against the DPP to compel him to include specific guidance in the Code about the circumstances in which he would prosecute a person who breached the Suicide Act by travelling with another person to Switzerland to assist the latter person to commit suicide there.[92] She did not seek immunity from criminal prosecution for her husband, nor did she seek to compel the DPP to formulate a policy which stated that he would not prosecute her husband.[93] Indeed, how could she seek either of these outcomes? What she sought, on the face of her claim, was information which would enable her to make an informed choice as to when and how she should commit suicide, based on whether or not she would need to be sufficiently able bodied to do so unassisted. However, Ms Purdy was, in a practical sense, after more than information.[94] After all, the opinion of the DPP about whether he would prosecute a hypothetical crime that had not yet been committed would ordinarily be a thing subject to change in changing circumstances.[95] What Ms Purdy wanted in fact was the promulgation of a detailed policy by the DPP which would thenceforth be treated as though it were hard law. No other outcome would provide any comfort to her husband.

Ms Purdy based her application in article 8 of the European Convention for the Protection of Human Rights and Fundamental Freedoms.[96] A previous case, *Pretty v DPP*, turned on substantially similar facts.[97] However, as Lord Hope pointed out in *Purdy*, there was one very important difference between the two cases:[98]

> Mrs Pretty, who could no longer do anything for herself, was seeking an undertaking that her husband would be immune from prosecution if he assisted her in the very act of committing suicide. Unlike Ms Purdy, she was not contemplating travelling to another country for this purpose. Nor was there any question, in Mrs Pretty's case, of her being forced by lack of information about prosecution policy to choose between ending her life earlier than she would otherwise have wished while she was still able to do this without her husband's assistance. The difference is a subtle one.

In *Pretty v DPP*, the House of Lords had held that the DPP had not breached article 8 by refusing to provide an undertaking that he would not prosecute the husband of

[89] ibid, s 2(4). See Crown Prosecution Service, '*The Code for Crown Prosecutors*' (2010).

[90] Prosecution of Offences Act 1985 (UK) s 10.

[91] Crown Prosecution Service, *Code for Crown Prosecutors* (2010). See *Purdy v DPP* [2009] 1 AC 345, 393 (Lord Hope).

[92] *Purdy v DPP* [2009] 1 AC 345, 391 (Lord Hope). See R Nobles and D Schiff, *Observing Law Through Systems Theory* (Oxford, Hart Publishing, 2012), 82–86.

[93] *Purdy v DPP* [2009] 1 AC 345, 386 (Lord Hope).

[94] cf ibid, 386 (Lord Hope).

[95] ibid, 407 (Lord Neuberger).

[96] The European Convention on Human Rights is included as Schedule 1 to the Human Rights Act 1998 (UK).

[97] *R (Pretty) v Director of Public Prosecutions* [2002] 1 AC 800.

[98] *Purdy v DPP* [2009] 1 AC 345, 390.

a terminally ill woman if he assisted her to commit suicide. Lord Bingham held that article 8 'is expressed in terms directed to protection of personal autonomy while individuals are living their lives, and there is nothing to suggest that the article has reference to the choice to live no longer'.[99] Lord Steyn agreed.[100] However, albeit not in dissent, Lord Hope took the contrary view that:[101]

> respect for a person's 'private life', which is the only part of article 8(1) that is in play here, relates to the way a person lives. The way she chooses to pass the closing moments of her life is part of the act of living, and she has a right to ask that this too must be respected. In that respect Mrs Pretty has a right of self-determination. In that sense, her private life is engaged even where in the face of a terminal illness she seeks to choose death rather than life.

The House of Lords' decision in *Pretty* was overturned by the European Court of Human Rights, which held that Mrs Pretty's decision to end her own life at a time of her choosing engaged article 8 and approved Lord Hope's dictum.[102] His Lordship had, however, immediately gone on to say that:[103]

> it is an entirely different thing to imply into [the words of article 8] a positive obligation to give effect to her wish to end her own life by means of an assisted suicide. I think that to do so would be to stretch the meaning of the words too far.

Finnis criticised *Pretty v UK* on the basis that it remains a criminal offence to aid, abet, counsel or procure the suicide of another person and, if the ECtHR is correct, there is no principled reason why article 8 ought not to cover other crimes.[104] However, in *Purdy*, the House of Lords departed from its earlier decision in *Pretty v DPP* and applied the interpretation of article 8 adopted by the ECtHR in holding that article 8(1) was engaged.[105]

Giving a judgment with which the other members of the Appellate Committee largely concurred, Lord Hope reasoned that, in order to give effect to the stipulation in article 8(2) that the right in article 8(1) could only be interfered with 'in accordance with the law', any such interference would need to be legally justified, expressed with sufficient clarity to enable a person 'to understand its scope and foresee the consequences of his actions so that he can regulate his conduct without breaking the law' and not applied in an 'arbitrary' fashion, for example 'in bad faith or in a way that is not proportionate'.[106] His Lordship stated that 'law' was, in this context, to be understood substantively, rather than formally, with the effect that that term would cover the DPP's soft law Code.[107] Therefore, although section 2(1) of the Suicide Act was drafted such that it could leave Ms Purdy in no

[99] *Pretty v DPP* [2002] 1 AC 800, 821.
[100] ibid, 835.
[101] ibid, 846.
[102] *Pretty v United Kingdom* (2002) ECtHR 427, [64]. See also *Purdy v DPP* [2009] 1 AC 345, 389.
[103] *Pretty v DPP* [2002] 1 AC 800, 846.
[104] JM Finnis, 'Invoking the Principle of Legality against the Rule of Law' [2010] *New Zealand Law Review* 601, 603.
[105] *Purdy v DPP* [2009] 1 AC 345, 390 (Lord Hope).
[106] ibid.
[107] ibid.

doubt that her husband would commit a criminal offence by assisting her to travel to Switzerland for the purpose of committing suicide, Lord Hope accepted the argument put by Lord Pannick QC for Ms Purdy that the rule of law required the DPP to provide guidance as to when he would exercise his discretion to bring a prosecution under section 2(4) of the Suicide Act.[108] Guidelines in regard to when the DPP will exercise his or her power to commence a prosecution against a person who has assisted another person to commit suicide are publicly available in every Australian jurisdiction.[109]

It is important to understand the substantive effect of the existence of the rights in article 8. In Australia, where there is no statutory bill of rights and extremely minimal constitutional protection of rights at a Commonwealth level, it is almost unthinkable that the current High Court would issue an order seeking to confine the scope of a discretion granted to the DPP by Parliament.[110] A person in the position of Ms Purdy's husband would not generally even be able to argue, after the DPP had exercised his statutory discretion to prosecute, that the DPP's decision was *Wednesbury* unreasonable, since, where a discretion is granted in broad terms—and particularly where it calls on the decision-maker to reach a state of satisfaction as 'a matter of opinion or policy or taste'—a court exercising judicial review will never substitute its opinion for that of the decision-maker, even on the clearest evidence.[111] The High Court has stated that the capacity to stop a prosecution in the event of abuse of process means that judicial review is neither required nor available.[112]

Article 8, by contrast, creates a substantive right with which law must comply in order to be valid. Lord Hope followed the Grand Chamber of the European Court of Human Rights in deciding that 'law' includes 'both enactments of lower rank than statutes and unwritten law'.[113] It was on this basis that the House of Lords examined whether the discretion granted by section 2(4) of the Suicide Act was sufficiently certain to allow Ms Purdy's husband to regulate his behaviour without breaking the law.[114]

However, there are a couple of comments which can be made about the way the House of Lords went about this task. First, as Finnis pointed out, there is the misconception that Ms Purdy's husband would have remained 'of a law-abiding persuasion', having committed an act in breach of section 2(1) of the Suicide Act, provided

[108] ibid, 352G; 391.

[109] B White and J Downie, 'Prosecutorial Guidelines for Voluntary Euthanasia and Assisted Suicide: Autonomy, Public Confidence and High Quality Decision Making' (2012) 36 *Melbourne University Law Review* 656, 660–61.

[110] See *Likiardopoulos v The Queen* (2012) 247 CLR 265, 277–81 (Gummow, Hayne, Crennan, Kiefel & Bell JJ).

[111] *Buck v Bavone* (1976) 135 CLR 110, 118–19 (Gibbs J). See generally M Aronson and M Groves, *Judicial Review of Administrative Action*, 5th edn (Sydney, Thompson Reuters, 2013) [6.390]–[6.500].

[112] *Likiardopoulos* (2012) 247 CLR 265, 279–80 (Gummow, Hayne, Crennan, Kiefel & Bell JJ); cf 269–70 (French CJ). See M Aronson and M Groves, *Judicial Review of Administrative Action*, 5th edn (Sydney, Thompson Reuters, 2013) [7.320].

[113] *Purdy v DPP* [2009] 1 AC 345, 390 (Lord Hope). See *Kafkaris v Cyprus* (2008) 25 BHRC 591, [139]–[140].

[114] *Purdy v DPP* [2009] 1 AC 345, 408 (Lord Neuberger).

that he was not prosecuted for that act in the DPP's discretion under section 2(4).[115] Citing Hart, Finnis maintained that there was in fact no question at all of Ms Purdy's husband being able to regulate his behaviour so as to avoid breaking the law; his only interest was in whether, having broken the law, he would be prosecuted for that breach.[116] This brilliant reasoning fails only to deal with the fact the Human Rights Act is capable of overriding pre-existing law, either entirely or merely on a case-by-case basis. Finnis considered that it was at all times entirely clear that Ms Purdy was inviting her husband to commit a criminal act.[117] No judgment by their Lordships could alter the fact that Ms Purdy's husband was proposing to break the law; any such alteration to the law is within the domain of Parliament alone.[118] Nor can a legal system incorporate a right to disobey law.[119] Their Lordships seem to have proceeded on the basis that Ms Purdy's husband would have committed no crime as long as no prosecution was brought against him, an assumption that the DPP was clearly not prepared to make.[120] The House of Lords left to the reader's guesswork the reasoning which led to their Lordships' conclusion rather than setting it out in detail. It may be right, not least in a practical sense, but it nonetheless depends on a view of what it means to be 'law-abiding' which remained unarticulated.

Secondly, the House of Lords' reasoning drew no clear distinction between hard law and the discretion granted to the DPP by the Suicide Act. Even if the concept of 'law' is understood broadly (as this book argues it ought to be), if it is to include what Lord Hope described as 'unwritten law', there are essential differences between legislation and the DPP's Code which must be recognised.[121] This remark does not necessarily betray an exclusively positivist view of 'law'. The difference is not in whether or not the Code is law, but in whether or not it is legitimate in the sense of being representative. The Code is 'harder' than some soft law instruments because it is required by legislation.[122] Nonetheless, it is representative only in the sense that the Parliament has granted discretions to the DPP as to the performance of his function (including under the Suicide Act) and has separately required that he provide guidance as to how those discretions will generally be exercised. Finnis pointed out that this guidance was required by statute to be provided to Crown Prosecutors and was not designed to be directed to people such as Ms Purdy (although the Code

[115] ibid, 397 (Baroness Hale); cf R Nobles and D Schiff, 'Disobedience to Law—Debbie Purdy's Case' (2010) 73 *MLR* 295, 296; JM Finnis, 'Invoking the Principle of Legality against the Rule of Law' [2010] *New Zealand Law Review* 601, 608.

[116] JM Finnis, 'Invoking the Principle of Legality against the Rule of Law' [2010] *New Zealand Law Review* 601, 602.

[117] cf J Waldron, 'Torture, Suicide, and *Determinatio*' (2010) 55 *American Journal of Jurisprudence* 1, 18–19.

[118] *Purdy v DPP* [2009] 1 AC 345, 385 (Lord Hope); *Pretty v DPP* [2002] 1 AC 800, 809 (Lord Bingham). See also Crown Prosecution Service, '*Policy for Prosecutors in Respect of Cases of Encouraging or Assisting Suicide*' (2010), [5].

[119] R Nobles and D Schiff, *Observing Law Through Systems Theory* (Oxford, Hart Publishing, 2012), 58.

[120] Crown Prosecution Service, '*CPS Policy on Assisted Suicide*' (2010), [48].

[121] *Purdy v DPP* [2009] 1 AC 345, 390 (Lord Hope); cf *The Australian Consumer Law* § 20 (Schedule 2 to the Competition and Consumer Act 2010).

[122] Prosecution of Offences Act 1985 (UK) s 10.

is explicitly marked as a 'public document').[123] He queried why 'a duty to give guidance to Crown Prosecutors [should] be converted into a duty to give guidance to prospective offenders about their chances' and concluded that '[i]n holding that the DPP had acted unlawfully in not acceding to Ms Purdy's demand for information, the House of Lords simply substituted its judgment for the DPP's'.[124]

The ECtHR had conceded in *Pretty v UK* that the right to privacy under article 8 could be subordinated to the terms of the Suicide Act.[125] Part of being representative is weighing Ms Purdy's right to privacy against 'the public interest in maintaining a clear and exceptionless prohibition of assisting suicide', which would provide a deterrent effect while remaining flexible enough to deal with particular cases without creating a legitimate expectation that a certain course would be followed.[126] The arguments examined above in favour of limiting discretions with rules lose much of their force when the rule-making is not the result of a democratic process (such as the US Administrative Procedure Act) but at the order of a court which is seeking to delimit the bounds of a statutorily granted discretion. On the other hand, insisting on representativeness as the central factor in the lawfulness of rules amounts to opening a second front against any delegated legislation which is not disallowable in either chamber of the Parliament.

The order ultimately issued by the House of Lords required the DPP to identify in the Code for Crown Prosecutors 'facts and circumstances which he will take into account in deciding ... whether to consent to a prosecution under section 2(1) of the 1961 Act'.[127] The DPP responded by committing to produce an interim policy within two months, which he did in September 2009.[128] This was followed by a public consultation to produce a more detailed permanent policy, assuming 'the continuing absence of any legislative framework'.[129] If this comment was designed to spur Parliament into action, it did not succeed.

In February 2010, the DPP issued his *Policy for Prosecutors in respect of Cases of Encouraging or Assisting Suicide* to stand alongside the Code.[130] It confirmed that it remains against the law in England to end the life of another, even at their express request.[131] This meets some of the concerns expressed by Finnis that Lord

[123] Crown Prosecution Service, '*Code for Crown Prosecutors*' (2010).

[124] JM Finnis, 'Invoking the Principle of Legality against the Rule of Law' [2010] *New Zealand Law Review* 601, 606.

[125] *Pretty v UK* (2002) ECtHR 427, [76]. See JM Finnis, 'Invoking the Principle of Legality against the Rule of Law' [2010] *New Zealand Law Review* 601, 606–7 (fn 20).

[126] JM Finnis, 'Invoking the Principle of Legality against the Rule of Law' [2010] *New Zealand Law Review* 601, 607; cf R Nobles and D Schiff, 'Disobedience to Law—Debbie Purdy's Case' (2010) 73 *MLR* 295, 298.

[127] *Purdy v DPP* [2009] 1 AC 345, 396 (Lord Hope).

[128] Crown Prosecution Service, '*Interim Policy for Prosecutors in Respect of Cases of Assisted Suicide*' (2009).

[129] K Starmer, 'CPS statement on Debbie Purdy' (Press Release, 30 July 2009) www.cps.gov.uk/news/latest_news/debbie_purdy/. See Crown Prosecution Service, *Public Consultation Exercise on the Interim Policy for Prosecutors in respect of Cases of Assisted Suicide Issued by The Director of Public Prosecutions: Summary of Responses*, (2010).

[130] Crown Prosecution Service, '*CPS Policy on Assisted Suicide*' (2010). See B White and J Downie, 'Prosecutorial Guidelines for Assisted Suicide' (2012) 36 *Melbourne University Law Review* 656, 663–71.

[131] Crown Prosecution Service, '*CPS Policy on Assisted Suicide*' (2010), [33]. See R Heywood, 'The DPP's Prosecutorial Policy on Assisted Suicide' (2010) 21 *King's Law Journal* 425, 428.

Brown (with whom Lady Hale and Lord Neuberger agreed) was prepared to recognise 'altruistic' assistance to commit suicide without restricting the ambit of his comments to assistance to travel abroad.[132] The most that anyone can do for a loved one who wishes to commit suicide within England is to stand by while the loved one commits the act of suicide; the law thus remains as it ever was. The Policy is concerned with the potential liability of people in the position in which Ms Purdy's husband expected to find himself (and in which Mrs Pretty's husband did find himself), who may be called upon to assist a person who no longer has the capacity to perform the requisite physical acts to commit suicide. However, as Heywood has noted, the Policy's reference to providing 'minimal assistance' is so general that the Policy may provide little practical guidance:[133]

> Minimal assistance, without any further explanation, is so vague as to be virtually meaningless. Would this include booking a flight to Switzerland, giving the victim a lift to the airport, or accompanying them to Dignitas to provide comfort and help in their last moments?

Heywood commented that the 'Coroners and Justice Act 2009 has now broadened the offence of assisted suicide to potentially include such acts' as would fall within the ambit of 'minimal assistance'.[134]

Interestingly, the Irish High Court declined to follow *Purdy* in *Fleming*, a case which dealt with an identical legislative prohibition.[135] The High Court held that the DPP had no power to issue guidelines, despite the fact that the DPP had already issued a set of general guidelines several years before.[136] It held further that to do so would be unconstitutional since Article 15.2 of the Irish Constitution provides that 'the sole and exclusive power of making laws for the State is hereby vested in the Oireachtas … [and] no other legislative authority has power to make laws for the State'. The DPP would infringe that provision if she issued guidelines which amounted to making a de facto change to the law:[137]

> The plaintiff … accepted that whatever powers the Director might have, they could not have the effect of overriding the intention of the Oireachtas or offending the separation of powers principles inherent in Article 15.2 of the Constitution.

On behalf of the Director it was submitted that the Director would be 'aiding a crime' if she were to grant the plaintiff's request to outline the factors that would be considered when deciding whether or not to prosecute for assisted suicide. Any such guidelines would constitute a 'road map' under which a person might more safely commit a crime and avoid prosecution.

It was argued that the Director has no power to adopt a policy that she will not prosecute in certain cases. The Director was, in effect being asked to legislate in a

[132] *Purdy v DPP* [2009] 1 AC 345, 404 (Lord Brown). See JM Finnis, 'Invoking the Principle of Legality against the Rule of Law' [2010] *New Zealand Law Review* 601, 609.

[133] R Heywood, 'The DPP's Prosecutorial Policy on Assisted Suicide' (2010) 21 *King's Law Journal* 425, 434.

[134] ibid, 434 (fn 39).

[135] *Fleming v Ireland* [2013] IEHC 2.

[136] P Daly, 'Death, Democracy and Delegation' (14 May 2013), *UK Constitutional Law Blog*, available at: ukconstitutionallaw.org/2013/05/14/paul-daly-death-democracy-and-delegation/.

[137] *Fleming* [2013] IEHC 2, [147]–[149] (Kearns P).

way that was quite impermissible under both the Prosecution of Offences Act, 1974 and, more particularly, the Constitution.

Although the case was appealed unsuccessfully to the Supreme Court, this point was not challenged by the appellant.[138] *Fleming* was immediately the subject of some criticism.[139] However, this seems to downplay the constitutional principles relevant to deciding the case, which Kearns P summarised by concluding that 'once guidelines may be characterised as having the effect of outruling a prosecution, they must be seen as altering the existing law and must therefore fall foul of Article 15.2 of the Constitution'.[140] More importantly, criticism of *Fleming* discounts the relevance of the High Court asking what legal consequences would follow from the DPP being compelled to issue guidelines:[141]

> While the plaintiff asserts that she is seeking no more than a statement of factors which would influence the decision of the Director whether or not to prosecute, the reality of course is that, for her own very good reasons, she wishes to know that the Director will not in fact prosecute in her case. Whatever the stated objective of seeking guidelines may be, there can be no doubt but that the intended *effect* of obtaining such relief would be to permit an assisted suicide without fear of prosecution. No amount of forensic legerdemain can alter that fact. For, absent such *effect*, one is driven to ask what practical purpose or value lies in seeking such guidance? There is, in truth, none. It follows therefore that in this context 'effect' is every bit as important as 'object'.

Albeit in a different constitutional context, this is an issue which was all but completely avoided by the House of Lords in *Purdy*. Interestingly, the differences were not only constitutional, since the plaintiff had conceded in *Fleming* that 'even if the [DPP] published fulsome guidelines, there would remain the possibility that the [DPP] could still elect to prosecute any given case'.[142]

In England, while the 'early signs are that the DPP will take a generous approach to what is characterised as minimal assistance', problems will arise when, inevitably, the DPP exercises his or her discretion to prosecute someone who feels that they ought not to have been prosecuted under the Policy or because the prosecution ignores certain considerations of the Policy.[143] Nobles and Schiff have pointed out that if a person who satisfied all of the circumstances which would indicate that a prosecution would be inappropriate under the Policy (which they claim is 'easily foreseeable') were nonetheless prosecuted, it could either amount to an abuse of process

[138] *Fleming v Ireland* [2013] IESC 19.

[139] P Daly, 'Guidelines and Assisted Suicide' (28 April 2013), *Administrative Law Matters*, available at administrativelawmatters.blogspot.com.au/2013/04/guidelines-and-assisted-suicide.html; P Daly, 'Death, Democracy and Delegation' (14 May 2013), *UK Constitutional Law Blog*; cf R Ekins, 'Defying the Law: a Reply to Daly' (23 May 2013) *UK Constitutional Law Group Blog*, available at: ukconstitutionallaw.org/2013/05/23/richard-ekins-defying-the-law-a-reply-to-daly/; L Grolman and G Weeks, 'Guidelines and Assisted Suicide: an Australian Perspective', (7 August 2013) *UK Constitutional Law Group Blog*, available at ukconstitutionallaw.org/2013/08/07/leah-grolman-and-greg-weeks-guidelines-and-assisted-suicide-an-australian-perspective/.

[140] *Fleming* [2013] IEHC 2, [166].

[141] ibid.

[142] ibid, [147].

[143] R Heywood, 'The DPP's Prosecutorial Policy on Assisted Suicide' (2010) 21 *King's Law Journal* 425, 434.

or give rise to judicial review proceedings directed against the DPP.[144] It is hard to imagine a court conducting judicial review of a criminal court, consequent on the disappointment of a legitimate expectation that no prosecution would be launched, given the broad discretion of trial judges to stay proceedings.[145] A court may also have to consider whether it should compel an unwilling DPP to provide formal reasons for his or her decision to prosecute in a certain case.[146] There is no general common law duty to do so.[147]

The real significance of *Purdy* to this book is to show the profound effect that substantively enforceable rights can have. The case was decided on the basis that Ms Purdy had a right to know more about how the DPP might exercise his discretion to prosecute her husband if he assisted her to travel to Switzerland for the purpose of committing suicide. Clearly, in the absence of a bill of rights, the decision in *Purdy* could not have been made in Australia, a jurisdiction which has not yet been required to make decisions necessitating this sort of compromise between doctrinal clarity and the protection of human rights.[148]

(ii) *Lumba v Home Secretary*

The effect of a public authority's failure to adhere to a stated policy, or alternatively to publish its true policy, was at issue in *Lumba*.[149] Two claimants, who had served periods in gaol as a result of having committed criminal offences, challenged the legality of their immigration detention (following the expiry of their prison terms) pending deportation from the United Kingdom, in actions for false imprisonment, and argued successfully at trial that it was unlawful for the Home Secretary to govern their detention through an unpublished policy.[150] That judgment was overturned by the Court of Appeal.

Before the Supreme Court, the claimants were successful in their tort claims for false imprisonment but received only nominal damages. Lord Dyson delivered the lead judgment, with which Lord Hope, Lord Walker, Baroness Hale, Lord Collins and Lord Kerr substantially agreed as to the issue of the unpublished policy's illegality and the consequent finding of false imprisonment. Lord Phillips and Lord Brown (with whom Lord Rodger agreed) each published dissenting judgments as to the result of the case. However, the nine sitting members of the Supreme Court differed

[144] R Nobles and D Schiff, 'Disobedience to Law—Debbie Purdy's Case' (2010) 73 *MLR* 295; cf R Heywood, 'The DPP's Prosecutorial Policy on Assisted Suicide' (2010) 21 *King's Law Journal* 425, 439.

[145] R Nobles and D Schiff, 'Disobedience to Law—Debbie Purdy's Case' (2010) 73 *MLR* 295, 298; *Connolly v Stokes* (Unreported, Queensland Court of Appeal, McPherson, Pincus JJA & Moynihan J, 5 May 1999).

[146] See B White and J Downie, 'Prosecutorial Guidelines for Assisted Suicide' (2012) 36 *Melbourne University Law Review* 656, 696–98.

[147] R Heywood, 'The DPP's Prosecutorial Policy on Assisted Suicide' (2010) 21 *King's Law Journal* 425, 438.

[148] See L Grolman and G Weeks, 'Guidelines and Assisted Suicide: an Australian Perspective' (7 August 2013) *UK Constitutional Law Group Blog*.

[149] *Lumba v Home Secretary* [2012] 1 AC 245.

[150] R Husain, *Joint Case on behalf of the Appellants in R (Walumba Lumba); R (Kadian Mighty) v Secretary of State for the Home Department* (2010), [142]–[189].

from each other on two general bases in the course of eight published judgments. The first was the effect of the Home Office's application of a secret, unpublished 'blanket policy' in preference to the published policy in establishing false imprisonment.[151] The second was the appropriate measure of damages if false imprisonment were made out.

While my focus is mainly on the first of these, it is worth noting that the Court held by a majority that the appropriate measure of damages where the tort of false imprisonment was made out but the claimants had suffered no actual damage (because they would have remained in detention even if the proper policy had been applied) was only the nominal sum of £1 each.[152] Lords Brown and Rodger opposed even nominal damages, and a fortiori vindicatory damages to reflect the seriousness of the tort committed, even though it resulted in no loss to the claimants.[153] Lord Kerr thought that vindicatory damages may be available in a class of cases which is 'very limited indeed' and not on the facts of *Lumba*.[154] By contrast, Lords Hope and Walker and Lady Hale would each have awarded a small, but not merely nominal, sum of vindicatory damages to each claimant in the amount of either £1,000 (Lords Hope and Walker) or £500 (Lady Hale).[155] Lord Hope conceded that the Court had 'no yardstick by which [the sum of vindicatory damages] can be measured to test its accuracy'.[156]

For a period of over two years, the published policy of the Home Office stated that foreign national prisoners (FNPs) would benefit from a 'presumption' in favour of release in most cases, although leaving detention as an available option in some cases. Indeed, Lord Dyson noted that '[t]he "presumption" of release had been entrenched in the Secretary of State's published policies since at least 1991'.[157] The Home Secretary calculated that 'only 1.5% of those who were liable to detention under her immigration powers were actually detained' when this policy was in effect.[158] However, during the same period, an entirely different—and unpublished—policy was in fact being applied by the Home Office, which the Home Secretary advised the Prime Minister amounted to a 'near blanket ban on release, regardless of whether removal can be achieved and the level of risk to the public linked to the nature of the FNP's original offence'.[159]

Lord Dyson's speech discussed the *Hardial Singh* principles at length, which he had earlier summarised as follows:[160]

> (i) The Secretary of State must intend to deport the person and can only use the power to detain for that purpose;

151 *Lumba v Home Secretary* [2012] 1 AC 245, 264 (Lord Dyson).
152 ibid, 281–82 (Lord Dyson); 320–21 (Lord Collins); 351 (Lord Phillips).
153 ibid, 359–60.
154 ibid, 325.
155 ibid, 304 (Lord Hope); 308 (Lord Walker); 315 (Lady Hale).
156 ibid, 304.
157 ibid, 262.
158 ibid, 337 (Lord Phillips).
159 ibid, 261.
160 *R (I) v Secretary of State for the Home Department* [2002] EWCA Civ 888 [46]. See *R v Governor of Durham Prison; ex parte Hardial Singh* [1984] 1 WLR 704 (Woolf J); *Lumba v Home Secretary* [2012] 1 AC 245, 264–65.

(ii) The deportee may only be detained for a period that is reasonable in all the circumstances;
(iii) If, before the expiry of the reasonable period, it becomes apparent that the Secretary of State will not be able to effect deportation within a reasonable period, he should not seek to exercise the power of detention;
(iv) The Secretary of State should act with reasonable diligence and expedition to effect removal.

These common law principles formed the background to the Home Secretary's policy and were not challenged in argument (although Lord Phillips doubted that the first two principles derived from *Hardial Singh*). If *Hardial Singh* is left to one side, the Supreme Court was required to consider the familiar questions of whether the Home Secretary was bound to apply her published policy and the legal status of her unpublished policy.

Lord Dyson held that the unpublished policy, being a blanket policy to which there had been only a handful of exceptions on compassionate grounds, was unlawful as a fetter on the discretion of the decision-makers responsible for assessing whether individual FNPs should be detained.[161] His Lordship further held that the unpublished policy was unlawful on the ground that it conflicted with the Home Office's published policy and cited extensive support for the proposition that a 'policy must be consistently applied', unless there exists a good reason to depart from it.[162] Counsel for the Home Secretary had accepted these propositions in argument.

These two propositions are, however, problematic when considered side by side. There is at once the standard requirement (in both Australia and England) that policy not be applied inflexibly with the largely contrary requirement that policies must be applied consistently unless a 'good reason' exists to depart from that policy. What may qualify as such a reason is likely only to be clear to a decision-maker after it has become the subject of judicial attention. The plot thickens further when one considers that the Home Secretary's unpublished policy *had* been applied consistently, albeit in circumstances which reflected little credit on the Home Secretary herself. Given this emphasis, the real problem was not inconsistency between the decision-making and a policy, but that the Home Office had been consistent in applying the 'bad' policy and not the 'good' one.

Was the unpublished policy a 'bad' policy simply because it had not been published? If that were the case, the Home Office's legal obligation would not really have been one of consistency but one of publication. Ultimately, the position reached by the Supreme Court was simply that an unpublished policy could not legally be applied *if* there was an applicable published policy from which there was no good reason to depart. The principles underlying that conclusion are readily understandable and the Supreme Court need not have gone further to deal with the facts of the case before it.

However, Lord Dyson was prepared to say that policies must be published 'both as a matter of common law and human rights law', albeit in obiter dicta and dealing with a passage of the Court of Appeal's judgment upon which that Court had not

[161] *Lumba v Home Secretary* [2012] 1 AC 245, 264.
[162] ibid, 265.

had the benefit of argument and which counsel for the Home Secretary did not endorse before the Supreme Court.[163] At the heart of his Lordship's reasoning lies the rule of law, which 'calls for a transparent statement by the executive of the circumstances in which … broad statutory criteria will be exercised'.[164] The same principle may also be expressed in the language of procedural fairness by saying that people have a right to know the terms of the policy upon which their cases will be decided.[165] This amounts, I think, to essentially the same thing. Yet, to say that there is a free-standing duty to publish a given policy or soft law instrument rather implies that that instrument carries the force of law. Neither policies nor soft law instruments do so in the way that 'hard law' instruments do, but they nonetheless tend to have much the same effect as hard law, as this book argues throughout. Such a conclusion is implicit in a common law requirement that policies and soft law must be published in order to be valid.

By contrast, the standard Australian position on the legal effect of policies and guidelines is decidedly more equivocal. The orthodox view is that 'such guides are not binding, but they are generally applied unless there are compelling reasons not to do so'.[166] Lord Hope said in *Kambadzi* that '[p]olicy is not law, so it may be departed from if a good reason can be shown'.[167] The similarities between these dicta disguise a very real difference in approach to the enforceability of soft law. The Australian approach simultaneously recognises that soft law has 'general application' in the manner of law, particularly if issued by an authoritative body, but that it can also be ignored by the courts, such as where they conclude that the soft law surpasses its legal limits.

There is an intriguing possibility, which seems to follow from *Lumba*, that the power to issue soft law might be implied from statute.[168] An express power would, on my definition at least, result in an authority making hard, delegated legislation. It may also be implied from statute that persons affected by soft law are obliged to comply with it, as a matter of law rather than only of practicality. If both of these things are true, then an authority which breached its own soft law would have committed an error of law for which judicial review's remedies might be available. Such an approach would certainly bring soft law within judicial review's established conceptual structure by interpreting Parliament's implied intentions as 'hardening' it.[169]

However, this approach is concerning for a number of reasons. The foremost of these is that Parliament generally does not actually intend to authorise soft law. When Parliament expressly authorises sub-parliamentary law-making, what it authorises is the making of delegated legislation. This is a concept which, in Australia, is itself legislated for.[170] To suppose that Parliament also *impliedly* authorises soft law to

[163] ibid, 265–66.
[164] ibid, 268.
[165] See ibid, 268.
[166] *P v Child Support Registrar* [2012] FCA 1398, [3] (Buchanan J).
[167] *R (Kambadzi) v Secretary of State for the Home Department* [2011] 1 WLR 1299, 1315.
[168] I am grateful to Christopher Forsyth for raising this point with me.
[169] See Chapter 4.A of this volume above.
[170] See Legislation Act 2003 s 8(4).

be made, and that soft law can therefore be treated as though it is hard, challenges credulity (or at least raises again the eternally thorny question of what Parliament ever *intends*). Greenberg expressed concern that soft law might in fact be used as tool to make legislation mean whatever the executive later wishes it had invited the Parliament to enact, thereby substituting the current intentions of the executive for the intention which can be ascertained from the text of the enacted legislation.[171]

Another practical concern is that ingenious judicial attempts to 'harden' soft law might result in new soft law appearing wherever previous iterations have changed into hard law. The motivation for regulating through soft law has always been that people will continue to accept regulation even in the absence of time-consuming accountability measures. That motivation, and the effectiveness of the resulting soft law, will remain even if existing soft law is made subject to judicial review. Any criticism of theories seeking to engage the phenomenon of soft law, on the basis that they leave soft law inchoate, fails to account for the fact that such is the very nature of soft law.[172]

Ultimately, there is no significant difference between the English and Australian approaches to the legal effect of policies and guidelines to the extent that they do not apprehend a method of setting aside soft law without judicial participation. Any suggestion that soft law can simply be 'ignored' on the basis that it does not affect a party's legal rights is reminiscent of Lord Diplock's similar statement about the capacity to ignore decisions which are void.[173] What the English approach does have strongly in its favour is that it is prepared both to require public authorities to issue policies and guidelines under certain circumstances, and to bind the public authorities to the terms of the soft law thus issued. The 'hardened' effect of soft law in these circumstances applies symmetrically against both the public authority *and* individuals who are subject to the soft law.

(iii) *Kambadzi v Home Secretary*

The position about government policies outlined in *Lumba* has not been addressed squarely, much less decided, in Australia. A majority of the High Court indicated broad approval, albeit in a fairly Delphic remark that it was 'within the competence' of the Minister for Immigration and Citizenship to issue guidelines which stated in advance whether s/he would be prepared to exercise certain discretionary powers.[174] The footnote to this remark distinguished *Lumba* in saying that '[n]o question arises of the application of an "unpublished" Ministerial policy or guidelines inconsistent with "published" policy or guidelines'. While somewhat unclear, the better view is that the joint judgment in *Kaur* did no more than reserve the question of whether

[171] D Greenberg, 'Dangerous Trends in Modern Legislation' [2015] *PL* 96, 101.

[172] See the introduction to Part I of this volume, above.

[173] *Dunlop v Woollahra* [1982] AC 158, 172.

[174] *Jasvir Kaur and Others v Minister for Immigration and Citizenship* (2012) 246 CLR 636, 665 [91] (Gummow, Hayne, Crennan & Bell JJ).

(and, if so, in what circumstances) the government is bound to publish its policies as a precondition to applying them adversely to a person.

By contrast, *Lumba*'s approach to government policies is now orthodox in England, a point which became clear when the Supreme Court delivered its decision in *Kambadzi v Home Secretary*. Judgment in *Kambadzi* had been delayed until after the Supreme Court had decided *Lumba* and was given the opportunity to hear submissions from counsel in light of that decision. Mr Kambadzi was in a similar position to the *Lumba* claimants, with the exception that the Home Office had not breached the *Hardial Singh* principles in respect of his detention. It had, however, breached its own published guidelines in regard to the frequency with which Mr Kambadzi's detention would be subject to review, the seniority of the officer conducting the review and whether reasons for any continuation of his detention would be provided. Mr Kambadzi argued that these failures caused his detention to be unlawful, grounding his claim for damages for false imprisonment. Because of the way that the case was argued, the Supreme Court did not consider the crucial circumstance from *Lumba*, namely that the Home Office had been applying an unpublished policy which contradicted the terms of its published policy.[175]

Lord Hope, who gave the lead judgment, for substantially the same reasons as those given by Lady Hale and Lord Kerr, started by stating that the statutory power invested in the Home Secretary to detain a person pending his or her deportation was 'not unfettered', but was constrained by the terms of Woolf J's judgment in *Hardial Singh*.[176] Furthermore, the Home Secretary was the repository of a statutory power to make rules for the regulation and management of detention centres, although Lord Hope further opined that the case before the Supreme Court dealt with 'public law duties which are not set out in the statute'.[177]

The legal effect was that the Home Secretary was under a *common law* duty to comply with his department's guidelines unless there existed 'a good reason' to depart from them. What is clear from Lord Hope's judgment is that guidelines published by the Home Office, in this case, and by government more generally, have at least some of the force of law, in that failures of government officers to adhere to the terms of such guidelines are actionable in law and are capable of grounding claims for damages in tort. His Lordship 'sheeted home' the entirety of the responsibility for the relevant breaches to the Home Secretary directly, rather than finding that officers within the Home Department had acted unlawfully by exceeding the terms of their delegated authority, as discerned from the guidelines.

A final interesting point comes from the speech of Lady Hale, with which Lord Hope agreed (presumably including as to Lady Hale's comments about the irrelevance to the case before the Supreme Court of Mr Kambadzi's undeniably bad character).[178] The case had been argued, in light of the previous decision in *Lumba*, on the basis that merely procedural breaches could amount to 'material' public

[175] See *Kambadzi v Home Secretary* [2011] 1 WLR 1299, 1328 (Lady Hale).

[176] ibid, 1306.

[177] ibid, 1308, 1315.

[178] ibid, 1323. Her Ladyship had described the claimant as not being 'the most wicked of men', damning him with the faintest possible praise.

law errors, which would carry as a necessary consequence the unlawfulness of the claimant's detention.[179] Lady Hale reiterated the view she had earlier expressed in *Lumba* that:[180]

> the breach of public law duty must be material to the decision to detain and not to some other aspect of the detention and it must be capable of affecting the result—which is not the same as saying that the result would have been different had there been no breach.

Lady Hale drew a 'distinction between the substantive limitations on the power to detain and the procedural requirements for exercising it'.[181] What is *material* on this view is whether the error leads to invalidity, regardless of whether it was a procedural error. Materiality is not assessed by asking whether the error in question *caused* the adverse decision to be made (that is, by using a 'but for' test).[182]

B. DOES JUDICIAL REVIEW CIVILISE LAW OR POWER?

The system of judicial review as it operates in the common law world is not organised in a 'rational' way, in as much as it does not prescribe a single remedy for breach of any legal norm.[183] This criticism applies a fortiori to the Australian conception of judicial review, which remains firmly 'remedy-oriented'. By comparison, English administrative law looks to the 'public' or 'private' nature of functions to determine their susceptibility to judicial review.[184] However, even if judicial review does not currently give courts the jurisdiction to review the application of soft law on the ground of error of law, that is not to say that it could not do so. The province of judicial review can be broadened to reflect the changing nature of public administration, albeit by a fraught and difficult process which, if driven by the courts, is apt to attract the label of 'judicial activism'.[185] Such an accusation is still considered serious, even if it 'does not necessarily connote bad faith'.[186] Expanding the traditional gamut of judicial review can be justified where it is necessary to make accountable those who exercise public power.[187] Both *Lain* and *CCSU* expanded the scope of judicial review, albeit by 'removing impediments to review, [rather] than with stating

[179] See eg ibid, 1314 (Lord Hope).

[180] ibid, 1325; *Lumba v Home Secretary* [2012] 1 AC 245, 312.

[181] *Kambadzi v Home Secretary* [2011] 1 WLR 1299, 1325.

[182] See *Stead v State Government Insurance Commission* (1986) 161 CLR 141.

[183] S Gageler, 'Administrative Law Judicial Remedies' in M Groves and HP Lee (eds), *Australian Administrative Law: Fundamentals, Principles and Doctrines* (Melbourne, Cambridge University Press, 2007) 368, 368.

[184] P Cane and L McDonald, *Principles of Administrative Law*, 2nd edn (Melbourne, Oxford University Press, 2012) 71.

[185] M Taggart, 'The Province of Administrative Law Determined?' in M Taggart (ed), *The Province of Administrative Law* (Oxford, Hart Publishing, 1997) 1, 2.

[186] J Allan, 'The Three "Rs" of Recent Australian Judicial Activism: *Roach*, *Rowe* and (No) "Riginalism"' (2012) 36 *Melbourne University Law Review* 743, 744; cf JD Heydon, 'Judicial Activism and the Death of the Rule of Law' (2003) 23 *Australian Bar Review* 110.

[187] P Craig, 'Public Law and Control over Private Power' in M Taggart (ed), *The Province of Administrative Law* (Oxford, Hart Publishing, 1997) 196, 216.

positive criteria of reviewability'.[188] As will be seen below, the English Court of Appeal further broadened judicial review's coverage in *Datafin*.[189]

The applicability of judicial review to exercises of soft law poses the fundamental question of whether it is the purpose of judicial review to enforce government adherence to law or to regulate exercises of public power more generally. Judicial review is 'an aspect of the rule of law' in that it is the function whereby the judicial branch says 'what the law is'.[190] However, this is problematic, since failure to comply with the requirements of the rule of law may not equate to illegality, let alone invalidity, which is the standard by which an exercise of statutory or executive power falls foul of judicial review.[191]

Aronson has noted that:[192]

> [P]ublic power is increasingly exercised from places within the private sector, by non-government bodies, and according to rules found in management manuals rather than statute books. If judicial review is about the restraint of public power, it will need to confront these shifts in who exercises public power, and in the rules by which they exercise it.

That is a big 'if', particularly in Australia, where the scope of judicial review is influenced to such a great extent by the constitutional separation of judicial power and, to a lesser extent, by the interpretive approach, associated most strongly with a series of judgments by Sir Gerard Brennan, which holds that the grounds for the exercise of judicial review are to be inferred from statute.[193] It reached its zenith in *Quin*, in which his Honour's judgment included what soon became one of the most frequently quoted passages in Australian public law cases:[194]

> The duty and jurisdiction of the court to review administrative action do not go beyond the declaration and enforcing of the law which determines the limits and governs the exercise of the repository's power. If, in so doing, the court avoids administrative injustice or error, so be it; but the court has no jurisdiction simply to cure administrative injustice or error. The merits of administrative action, to the extent that they can be distinguished from legality, are for the repository of the relevant power and, subject to political control, for the repository alone.

[188] M Aronson and M Groves, *Judicial Review of Administrative Action*, 5th edn (Sydney, Thompson Reuters, 2013) [3.130]. See *R v Criminal Injuries Compensation Board; ex parte Lain* [1967] QB 864; *Council of Civil Service Unions v Minister for the Civil Service* [1985] 1 AC 374 (*CCSU*).

[189] *R v Panel on Take-overs and Mergers; ex parte Datafin plc* [1987] 1 QB 815.

[190] S Gageler, 'The Legitimate Scope of Judicial Review' (2001) 21 *Australian Bar Review* 279, 279. See *Marbury v Madison* 5 US (1 Cranch) 137 (1803), 177; *Quin* (1990) 170 CLR 1, 35–36 (Brennan J).

[191] See eg *New South Wales v Commonwealth*(2006) 229 CLR 1, 175 ('*Work Choices Case*').

[192] M Aronson, 'Soft Law in the High Court' (2007) 35 *Federal Law Review* 1, 4. See also FG Brennan, 'The Review of Commonwealth Administrative Power: Some Current Issues' in P Keyzer and R Creyke (eds), *The Brennan Legacy: Blowing the Winds of Legal Orthodoxy* (Sydney, Federation Press, 2002) 9, 26.

[193] See *FAI Insurances Ltd v Winneke* (1982) 151 CLR 342, 409; *Church of Scientology Inc v Woodward* (1982) 154 CLR 25, 70; *Coutts v The Commonwealth* (1985) 157 CLR 91, 105; *Kioa* (1985) 159 CLR 550, 609–11; *Quin* (1990) 170 CLR 1, 36–37; *Annetts v McCann* (1990) 170 CLR 596, 604; *Ainsworth v Criminal Justice Commission* (1992) 175 CLR 564, 583–86; *Walton v Gardiner* (1993) 177 CLR 378, 408. See also J Basten, 'Judicial Review of Executive Action: Tiers of Scrutiny or Tears of Frustration?' in N Williams (ed), *Key Issues in Judicial Review* (Sydney, Federation Press, 2014) 35.

[194] *Quin* (1990) 170 CLR 1, 35–36.

The consequence is that the scope of judicial review must be defined not in terms of the protection of individual interests but in terms of the extent of power and the legality of its exercise. In Australia, the modern development and expansion of the law of judicial review of administrative action have been achieved by an increasingly sophisticated exposition of implied limitations on the extent or the exercise of statutory power, but those limitations are not calculated to secure judicial scrutiny of the merits of a particular case.

For Brennan J, 'judicial review's primary job was to enforce the statutory limits to the exercise of public power'.[195] Sir Anthony Mason noted in this regard that '[a] careful reading of the judgments reveals that Sir Gerard accepted the doctrine of legislative supremacy as qualified by the Australian Constitution and constantly deferred to the legislative judgment'.[196] He further described Brennan J as subscribing to 'an underlying theory of judicial review which is based on the notion that statute impliedly authorises judicial review for *ultra vires* and nothing else'.[197]

Over the years, much—perhaps too much—has been made of the Mason/Brennan 'debate'.[198] This debate purported to pit a 'common law' interpretation of the law against one of 'legislative intention' (albeit sometimes leading to the same substantive result).[199] In reality, Brennan J's interpretive approach might be seen to amount to 'no more than a principle of statutory construction'.[200] The High Court has latterly been dismissive of the 'false dichotomy' between common law and legislative intention, stating that a debate on those terms (once seen as central to the High Court's approach to public law issues) is 'unproductive' and a distraction.[201] To the extent that it is still seen as being relevant, such a debate is about starting points. Brennan J's view, far from being diametrically opposed to that espoused by Mason J, simply held that a model of judicial interpretation which *starts* with the common law and *then* superimposes values which the legislature clearly never had in mind has the effect of amending Acts, even if only a little.

Aronson suspected Brennan J of dissembling to some extent in his aim, as articulated in *Quin*, noting that the avoidance of administrative injustice was 'a by-product that his Honour's judgments happily produced with remarkable consistency'.[202] Indeed, Brennan J somewhat tempered his views in retirement, stating that:[203]

> Although it has been my view that the exercise or non-exercise of statutory power was the central, if not the exclusive, subject for consideration by a court possessed of judicial

[195] M Aronson, 'Soft Law in the High Court' (2007) 35 *Federal Law Review* 1, 18.

[196] A Mason, 'Judicial Review: the Contribution of Sir Gerard Brennan' in P Keyzer and R Creyke (eds), *The Brennan Legacy* (Sydney, Federation Press, 2002) 38, 43.

[197] ibid, 44. See *Walton v Gardiner* (1993) 177 CLR 378, 408 (Brennan J).

[198] See M Aronson, 'Soft Law in the High Court' (2007) 35 *Federal Law Review* 1, 2.

[199] See eg *Kioa v West* (1985) 159 CLR 550.

[200] W Gummow, 'Rationality and Reasonableness as Grounds for Review' in D Mortimer (ed), *Administrative Justice and its Availability* (Sydney, Federation Press, 2015) 13, 25. See *Kruger v Commonwealth* (1997) 190 CLR 1, 36–37 (Brennan CJ); *Li* (2013) 249 CLR 332, 370–71 (Gageler J).

[201] *Kaur* (2012) 246 CLR 636, 666 (Gummow, Hayne, Crennan & Bell JJ).

[202] M Aronson, 'Process, Quality, and Variable Standards' in D Dyzenhaus et al (eds), *A Simple Common Lawyer* (Oxford, Hart Publishing, 2009) 5, 21.

[203] FG Brennan, 'Commonwealth Administrative Power' in P Keyzer and R Creyke (eds), *The Brennan Legacy* (Oxford, Hart Publishing, 2002) 9, 25 (citations omitted).

review jurisdiction, there is growing judicial opinion that the jurisdiction is not so confined. In those circumstances, the basis for attributing a wider scope to the judicial review jurisdiction should be examined.

> In a free society, the rule of law is incompatible with any unqualified power to create, modify or extinguish rights or liabilities or otherwise to affect the interests of an individual.

Reasoning based on the rule of law led Brennan J to conclude that, in the absence of contrary legislation, and subject to the Constitution, courts could expand their jurisdiction to 'protect the interests of the individual by ensuring that a power which may be exercised in the course of public administration is exercised lawfully, rationally and with procedural fairness'.[204] His Honour cited *Datafin* with apparent approval, and at any rate without criticism.[205]

These comments do not precisely constitute Brennan J 'recanting' the position which he took up in numerous judgments during his tenure on the High Court.[206] Aronson and Groves noted that:[207]

> his Honour's judgments were not all aligned, although his overall suspicion of an autonomous common law theory came across clearly. His judgments in *Kioa*, *Ainsworth* and *Annetts* were careful to reserve for future consideration the possibility of judicial review over prerogative power and power under a Royal Charter, franchise or custom.

His Honour's post-retirement comments do, however, constitute a change in tone. They are consistent with the dicta from *Quin* quoted above in as much as they are expressed as being subject to contrary legislation. Brennan J stated that he was prepared to advance the common law within the confines of the judicial method, but saw the rule of law as depending primarily on the legislature providing laws which 'tend to diminish injustice and establish and maintain a mechanism to redress injustice by application of those laws'.[208]

It is, in a sense, unsurprising that Sir Gerard Brennan appeared to become prepared to extend the scope of judicial review beyond exercises of statutory public power, given that it has always been a weakness of the statutory intent theory of ultra vires that it cannot explain judicial review's coverage of exercises of non-statutory or prerogative power.[209] While *CCSU* has never been expressly approved in its entirety by a High Court majority, Mason J had previously expressed the view that prerogative powers are subject to judicial review.[210] Given that the High Court has since made exercises of executive power under section 61 of the Constitution subject to the remedies in section 75(v), there is no reason to expect that it would not do the

[204] ibid, 32–37.

[205] ibid, 27–28.

[206] See n 193 above; cf M Aronson et al, *Judicial Review of Administrative Action*, 4th edn (Sydney, Thompson Reuters, 2009) 116. Aronson, Dyer and Groves recorded that Brennan J 'virtually recanted' in retirement from the views he had held in office (although this form of words did not appear in their subsequent edition).

[207] M Aronson and M Groves, *Judicial Review of Administrative Action*, 5th edn (Sydney, Thompson Reuters, 2013) [3.110] (fn 83).

[208] FG Brennan, 'Why Be a Judge?' (1996) 14 *Australian Bar Review* 89, 90.

[209] Reviewable in England since *Lain* [1967] QB 864 and *CCSU* [1985] 1 AC 374 respectively.

[210] *R v Toohey; ex parte Northern Land Council* (1981) 151 CLR 170, 219–21.

same for exercises of prerogative power, which is at any rate within the scope of section 61.[211] The statutory intent theory of ultra vires certainly cannot extend to review of private bodies exercising public, non-statutory power.[212] Brennan J acknowledged these limitations frankly.[213]

The limitations of the statutory intent approach, which have been catalogued in detail by both Aronson and Groves and Sir Anthony Mason, at the very least compel the conclusion that statutory intention cannot be a self-sufficient explanation for the capacity of courts to engage in judicial review.[214] Brennan J's remarks subsequent to his retirement from the High Court should be understood as an attempt to shore up the statutory intent theory of ultra vires with principled rule of law foundations. Aronson and Groves noted the difficulty in maintaining that the common law could operate autonomously in an area governed by statute.[215] It would seem to follow that the statutory intent and common law approaches to judicial review are closer than some protagonists in this argument have been prepared to concede. Forsyth, for one, has acknowledged that the common law can and does modify statute.[216]

Notwithstanding his Honour's post-retirement comments, 'bottom-up' concerns with judicial review of soft law can be characterised as belonging to a 'Brennanite approach', whose two broad concerns with extending judicial review to cover exercises of public power stem neither from legislation nor the prerogative. They are:

1. The source of the Court's jurisdiction to review exercises of soft law; and
2. Whether, by reviewing soft law, the Court would effectively be granting legitimacy to a law-making process in which Parliament plays no part.

(i) Can Judicial Review Assert Jurisdiction Over Soft Law?

The first of the Brennanite concerns above seeks only to stretch the coverage of the courts' judicial review jurisdiction as far as *Datafin*, in which the Court of Appeal held that decisions made by the Panel on Take-overs and Mergers were judicially reviewable.[217] The Panel had 'no visible means of legal support' but was a quintessential example of the power of soft law, since it explicitly regulated, without statutory

[211] See *Pape v Commissioner of Taxation* (2009) 238 CLR 1; M Aronson and M Groves, *Judicial Review of Administrative Action*, 5th edn (Sydney, Thompson Reuters, 2013) [3.60].

[212] cf *Datafin* [1987] 1 QB 815. See generally P Cane, *Administrative Law*, 5th edn (Oxford, Oxford University Press, 2011) 14–17.

[213] See R Creyke and J McMillan, *Control of Government Action*, 3rd edn (Sydney, LexisNexis, 2012) 570.

[214] R Creyke and J McMillan, *Control of Government Action*, 3rd edn (Sydney, LexisNexis, 2012) 570. See M Aronson and M Groves, *Judicial Review of Administrative Action*, 5th edn (Sydney, Thompson Reuters, 2013) [3.80]–[3.120]; A Mason, 'Judicial Review' in P Keyzer and R Creyke (eds), *The Brennan Legacy* (Sydney, Federation Press, 2002) 38, 45.

[215] See M Aronson and M Groves, *Judicial Review of Administrative Action*, 5th edn (Sydney, Thompson Reuters, 2013) [3.100].

[216] C Forsyth, 'Of Fig Leaves and Fairy Tales: The Ultra Vires Doctrine, the Sovereignty of Parliament and Judicial Review' in C Forsyth (ed), *Judicial Review and the Constitution* (Oxford, Hart Publishing, 2000) 29.

[217] *Datafin* [1987] 1 QB 815.

support, behaviour which would otherwise have been regulated by government.[218] Donaldson MR remarked that it was 'a body which *de facto* exercises what can only be characterised as powers in the nature of public law powers'.[219] The Panel was responsible for drafting the City Code on Take-overs and Mergers, breach of which led to indirect but real and effective sanctions.[220] By contrast, the Code was not binding on the Panel because it had an unfettered power to change the Code.[221] The Court of Appeal held that the Panel's decisions were subject to judicial review because of the undoubtedly public nature of its power. It was also influenced by the fact that the applicant had no other available cause of action against the Panel in private law.[222]

Put simply, the Court of Appeal in *Datafin* decided that the *provenance* of power which controls behaviour is less important than the *effect* of that power; the fact that the Panel on Take-overs and Mergers had no 'visible means of legal support' was less important than the fact that it was intended to, and did in fact, exercise immense de facto and public power over commercial activities. Lloyd LJ commented that:[223]

> The panel wields enormous power. It has a giant's strength. The fact that it is self-regulating, which means, presumably, that it is not subject to regulation by others, and in particular the Department of Trade and Industry, makes it not less but more appropriate that it should be subject to judicial review by the courts.

The Panel was, at least, *doing* government: its existence and operation were a conscious choice on the part of the Thatcher government and it operated 'wholly in the public domain'.[224] Moreover, it may even have been *part of* the government. Donaldson MR went beyond finding that the Panel was 'without doubt performing a public duty and an important one' to state that the Court should recognise that it also possessed both 'the realities of executive power' and 'the functions of legislator'.[225] In these circumstances, the Court of Appeal thought it right to extend judicial review's coverage to bring accountability to an exercise of public power. It was no more relevant that the power had no statutory basis than if it had been an exercise of prerogative or executive power.

The Australian reception of *Datafin* has been cautious, to put it mildly, although not entirely dismissive. Indeed, Groves has noted a particular fascination with *Datafin* in State Supreme Courts.[226] However, while 'much-discussed' at State level, the *Datafin* principle remains uncertain.[227] Strictly speaking, a State Supreme Court

218 ibid, 824 (Donaldson MR). The Master of the Rolls later noted (at 834) that '[i]nvisible or indirect support there is in abundance'.

219 ibid, 828.

220 ibid, 826.

221 M Aronson, 'Responses to Privatisation and Outsourcing' in M Taggart (ed), *The Province of Administrative Law* (Oxford, Hart Publishing, 1997) 40, 45–46.

222 PP Craig, *Administrative Law*, 7th edn (London, Sweet and Maxwell, 2012) 848.

223 *Datafin* [1987] 1 QB 815, 845.

224 ibid, 835 (Donaldson MR).

225 ibid, 838–39, 841.

226 See eg *MBA Land Holdings Pty Ltd v Gungahlin Development Authority* (2000) 206 FLR 120; *State of Victoria v The Master Builders' Association of Victoria* [1995] 2 VR 121.

227 M Aronson and M Groves, *Judicial Review of Administrative Action*, 5th edn (Sydney, Thompson Reuters, 2013) [3.200].

has granted relief based on the *Datafin* principle in only one case.[228] Cane and McDonald expressed the opinion that the High Court did not give 'serious and direct consideration' to the issues raised in *Datafin* until it decided *NEAT Domestic Trading*, which is a generous assessment of the High Court's approach in that case.[229] The High Court's attitude to *Datafin* is better characterised as one of studious avoidance; indeed, Gummow J once likened dealing with *Datafin* to descending into a pit.[230] In *NEAT Domestic Trading*, only Kirby J even mentioned *Datafin* (although Gleeson CJ's excellent judgment did at least grapple with the possibility that public functions can be exercised by private parties) and the majority concluded that the private sector company in question (AWBI) was amenable to *none* of judicial review's principles at all.

Later, in *Tang*, a differently constituted High Court carried this exercise in problem-avoidance further, to conclude that not only had the appellant University not exercised public power in removing Ms Tang from its PhD programme, but that it had not exercised power at all because its relationship with Ms Tang was entirely consensual.[231] While there was a palpable level of academic disappointment with the result in *Tang*, the result itself was correct.[232] In any case, it was less disappointing than the reasoning of the majority, which set up 'power' and 'consent' as binary opposites in a wholly unconvincing fashion. It is not hard to think of examples of circumstances which are consensual in a formal sense but where one party has little or no power; standard-form contracts for the provision of utility services are an obvious example. The disappointing aspect of *Tang* is truly in the Court's disengagement from examining the possibility of expanding the scope of judicial review in the face of such circumstances. By applying a binary distinction between 'power' on one hand and 'consent' on the other, the majority judges failed to engage with the debate about whether public power can ever be exercised by a private body, which lent their ultimate reasoning a somewhat unreal air. I elaborate on this point and the conclusions drawn in this paragraph in Chapter 5.B.(ii) below.

Aronson and Groves stated frankly that the purpose of judicial review is to curb power (subject to the power in question being justiciable), rather than only *statutory* power.[233] Legal limits and judicial supervision go together in our legal system. On this approach, with which I agree, all that matters is that 'law' is applied through an exercise of public power. This excludes exercises of power which gather their force from private or consensual (usually contractual) arrangements and this is as

[228] *Masu Financial Management Pty Ltd v Financial Industry Complaints Service Ltd and Julie Wong (No 2)* (2004) 50 ACSR 554 (Shaw J).

[229] *NEAT Domestic Trading Pty Ltd v AWB Ltd* (2003) 216 CLR 277. See P Cane and L McDonald, *Principles of Administrative Law*, 2nd edn (Melbourne, Oxford University Press, 2012) 5.

[230] *Gould v Magarey and Others; Albarran v Companies Auditors and Liquidators Disciplinary Board and Anor; Visnic v ASIC* [2007] HCA Trans 5.

[231] *Griffith University v Tang* (2005) 221 CLR 99, 131 (Gummow, Callinan & Heydon JJ).

[232] See the sources cited by M Aronson, 'Soft Law in the High Court' (2007) 35 *Federal Law Review* 1, 2–3 and PA Keane, 'Judicial Review: the Courts and the Academy' (2008) 82 *Autralian Law Journal* 623, 625.

[233] M Aronson and M Groves, *Judicial Review of Administrative Action*, 5th edn (Sydney, Thompson Reuters, 2013) [3.60].

it should be.[234] There is significant overlap between the concepts of law and public power, but their similarities are not absolute. Their key difference, as things stand, from the point of view of judicial accountability is that law is, but power is not necessarily, subject to judicial review. However, what is important from the point of view of accountability is the way that power is exercised in fact, not whether it meets a formalist definition of 'law'. There is no need to characterise soft law as 'real law' in order to impose accountability upon its use.[235] It is enough to say that the common law will allow (and perhaps occasionally compel) the making and application of soft law *on terms set by the common law*, including being subject to judicial review, on the basis that making and applying soft law are, in a sense, common law powers which sit alongside prerogative and executive powers.

(ii) Must Parliament have a Role?

The second of what I have described as Brennanite concerns is that, by performing a review function over exercises of soft law, courts would grant legitimacy to a form of law making which circumvents the authority of Parliament. My response is that this concern is unduly focused on form in preference to substance. As discussed above, the central truth about soft law is that it is frequently used as a regulatory mechanism precisely because people will give it the same respect that they would 'hard' law. Because soft law is easy to make, and change, and requires no debate or compromise in parliamentary proceedings, public entities which use soft law might do so in order to circumvent parliamentary supervision. None of these advantages is lost or diminished by bringing soft law under judicial supervision. On the other hand, those who regulate with soft law will not have circumvented all mechanisms for accountability if the judiciary is able to award judicial review remedies for misuse of power, rather than just for breach of a 'law' in the formal sense.

The capacity of courts exercising a judicial review function to provide 'judicial protection' in the context of relationships governed only by soft law was thrown into doubt by the majority judgment in *Tang*.[236] That case, along with *NEAT Domestic*, provoked a flurry of academic comment, most of it highly critical of the majority's reasoning.[237] The early academic criticism of *Tang* was misguided to the extent that it represented concern with its result. I also disagree with the lament of Kirby J that the both decisions were 'an erosion of one of the most important Australian legal reforms of the last century', referring of course to the ADJR Act.[238] The preferable

[234] See *Tang* (2005) 221 CLR 99. The ADJR Act is notable for restricting review to exercises of statutory power only, and in this regard has failed to keep pace with developments as old as *CCSU* [1985] 1 AC 374. See generally M Aronson, 'Is the *ADJR Act* Hampering the Development of Australian Administrative Law?' (2004) 15 *Public Law Review* 202; M Aronson and M Groves, *Judicial Review of Administrative Action*, 5th edn (Sydney, Thompson Reuters, 2013) [2.520]–[2.640].

[235] *In re McFarland* [2004] 1 WLR 1289, 1299 (Lord Steyn).

[236] M Aronson, 'Soft Law in the High Court' (2007) 35 *Federal Law Review* 1, 2.

[237] See n 232 above.

[238] *Tang* (2005) 221 CLR 99, 133.

view was put in an extra-curial article by Keane J, who argued that *NEAT Domestic* and *Tang* 'faithfully reflect the limits imposed by the legislature upon the scope of judicial review provided by the ADJR Act'.[239] *Tang* in particular was primarily an exercise in construing the ADJR Act's terms, in which regard it is very hard to fault.[240] However, this is not necessarily to express agreement with Keane J's subsequent conclusion that 'this understanding of the limits on judicial review under the ADJR Act is consistent with the historical appreciation of the scope of judicial review of administrative decision-making'.[241]

Keane J focused exclusively on the *outcome* of *Tang*, which was in fact 'entirely predictable'.[242] Additionally, the majority's construction of the disputed ADJR Act phrase, 'under an enactment', was welcome.[243] Part of the reason that the outcome was unsurprising was the way that the case had been argued.[244] The basis upon which the majority allowed the University's appeal was, I venture to think, apparent even to many of those unaccustomed to 'the discipline imposed by the pressures of argument in open court'.[245] However, whether the decision to exclude the respondent from the University's PhD programme was made 'under an enactment' for the purposes of the ADJR Act was important to the outcome of the litigation. To justify the majority's decision based only upon the outcome and the content of the case argued before the High Court is to ignore the most striking aspects of *Tang*.[246] The majority's exclusion of interests conferred under soft law instruments from judicial protection on the basis that they do not amount to a 'matter' in the constitutional sense was one such aspect. The federal judiciary's powers are constitutionally limited to the resolution of 'matters', a term whose meaning is hard to pin down.[247] To point out this thorny doctrinal issue, which became evident in *Tang*, is not to dispute *Tang*'s outcome. Indeed, this disconcerting aspect of *Tang* was not necessary at all for the disposition of the matter on its legal merits by the majority. As a signal of the High Court's general approach to judicial review, *Tang* spoke volumes.

As a concept, soft law tends to expose the inadequacy of traditional categories of legal analysis because it effectively regulates behaviour but is not binding in the manner of primary or delegated legislation. In *Tang*, it was certainly *an* issue that Ms Tang and the University had a relationship which was not governed 'under an enactment'; indeed, this was the decisive legal issue in terms of the outcome of the matter as it was argued before the High Court. However, the fact that this was the central issue presented by the parties for determination by the Court does not alter

[239] PA Keane, 'The Courts and the Academy' (2008) 82 *Australian Law Journal* 623, 625.

[240] See D Stewart, 'Non-Statutory Review of Private Decisions by Public Bodies' (2005) 47 *Australian Institute of Administrative Law Forum* 17, 17. *Tang* in fact considered the Judicial Review Act 1991 (Qld), the relevant terms of which are drafted identically to the ADJR Act 1977 (Cth).

[241] PA Keane, 'The Courts and the Academy' (2008) 82 *Australian Law Journal* 623, 625.

[242] M Aronson, 'Soft Law in the High Court' (2007) 35 *Federal Law Review* 1,13; 23.

[243] ibid.

[244] PA Keane, 'The Courts and the Academy' (2008) 82 *Australian Law Journal* 623, 628.

[245] ibid, 626.

[246] cf ibid, 627.

[247] See n 277 below.

the 'breath-taking' character of the High Court's statement that the relationship between Ms Tang and the University was *no more than* consensual.[248]

It may have been contractual, potentially giving Ms Tang a right to sue for damages for breach of contract. However, this point was not pursued by Ms Tang and the Court made no express findings in this regard. It has been accepted in the Supreme Court of New South Wales that the requirement to provide natural justice in the so-called 'club cases' has its juridical basis in contract.[249] Mere consensus as to Ms Tang's PhD candidacy, on this construction, would not have required Griffith University to provide her with procedural fairness. Regardless, Ms Tang's remedy would have been in damages rather than a judicial review remedy. There is no doubt that the relevant soft law instruments issued by the University (the Policy on Academic Misconduct and the Policy on Student Grievances and Appeals) did *in fact* regulate the interactions between Ms Tang and the University. Likewise, there is no doubt that Ms Tang could have challenged the University's decision on the ground of procedural unfairness, either at common law or under the Judicial Review Act 1991 (Qld), if the relevant soft law instruments had been delegated legislation.[250]

To reiterate, it does not follow from this that *Tang* was wrongly decided. Rather, one is able to make the substantially different criticism that the majority's characterisation of the relationship between Ms Tang and the University was unsatisfying because it considered *only* whether the University's decision was 'under an enactment' and not whether it was public in nature.[251] Aronson argued that the reason why consensual power should not be subject to judicial review is not because it is non-statutory, but because it is not public.[252] To reach the conclusion that the power exercised by the University was consensual without consideration of its publicness is deficient on this reasoning.

Exercises of power by Universities are not inevitably of a public nature, although there are solid arguments in favour of that position.[253] One is that each jurisdiction's Ombudsman has jurisdiction over University decisions and conduct.[254] In Ms Tang's case, this is because the Ombudsman Act 2001 (Qld) empowers the Ombudsman to 'investigate administrative actions of agencies'.[255] Agencies are defined to include public authorities.[256] Public authorities are defined to include:[257]

> an entity, other than an individual, that is:
>
> (i) established for a public purpose under an Act; or
> (ii) established by government for a public purpose under an Act.

[248] M Aronson, 'Soft Law in the High Court' (2007) 35 *Federal Law Review* 1, 23.
[249] *Hinkley v Star City Pty Ltd* [2010] NSWSC 1389, [199]–[200] (Ward J).
[250] M Aronson, 'Soft Law in the High Court' (2007) 35 *Federal Law Review* 1, 15; M Aronson and M Groves, *Judicial Review of Administrative Action*, 5th edn (Sydney, Thompson Reuters, 2013) [2.530].
[251] cf PA Keane, 'The Courts and the Academy' (2008) 82 *Australian Law Journal* 623, 631.
[252] M Aronson, 'Soft Law in the High Court' (2007) 35 *Federal Law Review* 1, 23.
[253] ibid, 14–15.
[254] ibid, 14.
[255] Ombudsman Act 2001 (Qld) s 6(b)(i).
[256] ibid, s 8(1)(c).
[257] ibid, s 9(1)(a).

Ms Tang could have complained to the Ombudsman because Griffith University meets the statutory definition of a 'public authority', having been established under the Griffith University Act 1998 (Qld). However, this (and like considerations) cannot be conclusive of whether a University's use of public power is otherwise legally significant, since the High Court of Australia has largely been slow to embrace foreign innovations which have extended the coverage of judicial review's remedies to exercises of public power generally.

It is commonplace for Australian courts to extend judicial review's *principles*, particularly of procedural fairness, to some private institutions regardless of whether they exercise public power.[258] However, this extended coverage does not include judicial review's *remedies*.[259] The High Court has left open:[260]

> the question whether a party identified as 'an independent contractor' nevertheless may fall within the expression 'an officer of the Commonwealth' in section 75(v) [of the Constitution] in circumstances where some aspect of the exercise of statutory or executive authority of the Commonwealth has been 'contracted out'.

This seems to suggest that the Court is at least open to the possibility that the jurisdiction under section 75(v) attaches to an exercise of power rather than a certain individual.[261]

The extent of judicial review's remedies was at issue in *NEAT Domestic*, whose majority judgment Aronson read as concluding implicitly that AWBI was immune from both judicial review's remedies *and* its grounds.[262] The majority held that the powers and obligations of AWBI were 'to a very great extent' governed by its character as a company limited by shares and incorporated under corporations legislation.[263] While agreeing with the majority's conclusion that the appeal should be dismissed, Gleeson CJ indicated his preference for finding that AWBI's decision to withhold its permission for NEAT to export wheat was a reviewable decision:[264]

> While AWBI is not a statutory authority, it represents and pursues the interests of a large class of primary producers. It holds what amounts, in practical effect, to a virtual or at least potential statutory monopoly in the bulk export of wheat; a monopoly which is seen as being not only in the interests of wheat growers generally, but *also in the national interest*. To describe it as representing purely private interests is inaccurate. It exercises an effective veto over decisions of the statutory authority established to manage the export monopoly in wheat; or, in legal terms, it has power to withhold approval which is a condition precedent to a decision in favour of an applicant for consent (emphasis added).

[258] See eg *Forbes v New South Wales Trotting Club Ltd* (1979) 143 CLR 242; cf *Hinkley v Star City* [2010] NSWSC 1389, [114]–[183] (Ward J).

[259] M Aronson and M Groves, *Judicial Review of Administrative Action*, 5th edn (Sydney, Thompson Reuters, 2013) [7.410].

[260] *Offshore Processing Case* (2010) 243 CLR 319, 345.

[261] See J Boughey and G Weeks, '"Officers of the Commonwealth" in the Private Sector' (2013) 36 *University of NSW Law Journal* 316.

[262] M Aronson, 'Soft Law in the High Court' (2007) 35 *Federal Law Review* 1, 9.

[263] *NEAT Domestic* (2003) 216 CLR 277, 296 (McHugh, Hayne & Callinan JJ).

[264] ibid, 290.

Kirby J appeared to take as established fact that previous exports of wheat by NEAT had been in 'the Australian national interest'.[265]

Notwithstanding that Gleeson CJ's approach has not been adopted by a High Court majority, his Honour's comment that AWBI's interests were not 'purely private' has some application by analogy to soft law. It suggests that the power to regulate conduct must come with some mechanism to ensure accountability for the exercise of that power.

C. THE CONSTITUTIONAL LIMITS TO AUSTRALIAN JUDICIAL REVIEW

Concerns with expanding judicial review to meet the realities described above are now frequently expressed in constitutional terms. In particular, the basis of Australian judicial review in section 75 of the Constitution means that the limitations imposed by constitutional terms cannot be ignored. The restriction of the ADJR Act to decisions made 'under an enactment' means that its jurisdiction is narrower than that provided for under section 75(v) of the Constitution or section 39B of the Judiciary Act 1903 (Cth).

Taggart was responsible for a provocative critique of the Australian High Court's judicial review jurisprudence, which he decried as creating a form of 'Australian exceptionalism' in matters of public law.[266] Spigelman CJ recognised that Taggart did not intend that term as a compliment.[267] Since the publication of Taggart's article, 'Australian exceptionalism' has, if anything, gathered pace, particularly in regard to the importance attached by the High Court of Australia to jurisdictional error as a prerequisite to remedies being available in judicial review proceedings. The centrality of jurisdictional error is justified on constitutional grounds. In his 2010 Garran Oration, Spigelman CJ noted that the process of 'constitutionalising' Australian administrative law had been in train for at least a decade, since the High Court declared that the remedies in section 75(v) of the Constitution were no longer to be known as 'prerogative writs' (as had been common), but as 'constitutional writs'.[268] This distinction was intended to make clear that the Constitution is the source of the power to grant such relief.[269] Since then, the High Court has recognised the constitutional foundations of judicial review at both Commonwealth and State levels, with the result that jurisdictional error has become the 'central unifying principle of administrative law' throughout Australia.[270]

[265] ibid, 301 (Kirby J).

[266] M Taggart, 'Australian Exceptionalism' (2008) 36 *Federal Law Review* 1.

[267] JJ Spigelman, 'Public Law and the Executive' (2010) 34 *Australian Bar Review* 10, 17. See M Aronson, 'Soft Law in the High Court' (2007) 35 *Federal Law Review* 1, 2.

[268] *Re Refugee Review Tribunal; ex parte Aala* (2000) 204 CLR 82, 92–93 (Gaudron & Gummow JJ). See JJ Spigelman, 'Centrality of Jurisdictional Error' (2010) 21 *Public Law Review* 77, 79; S Gageler, 'The Constitutional Dimension' in M Groves (ed), *Modern Administrative Law in Australia: Concepts and Context* (Melbourne, Cambridge University Press, 2014) 165, 172.

[269] JJ Spigelman, 'Public Law and the Executive' (2010) 34 *Australian Bar Review* 10, 15.

[270] *Plaintiff S157* (2003) 211 CLR 476; *Kirk v Industrial Relation Commission of New South Wales* (2010) 239 CLR 531. See JJ Spigelman, 'Public Law and the Executive' (2010) 34 *Australian Bar Review* 10, 16. See also C Finn, 'Constitutionalising Supervisory Review at State Level: The End of *Hickman*?'

The distinction between jurisdictional and non-jurisdictional errors of law has long since ceased to be maintained in many jurisdictions, including England.[271] It is widely believed that England's rejection of non-jurisdictional errors of law began in *Anisminic*, although 'that distinction was critical to the way in which [*Anisminic*] managed to out-manoeuvre a privative clause which the House of Lords took to be a "no certiorari" clause'.[272] In reality, the rejection of jurisdictional error in England was not made official until the decision in *R v Hull University Visitor; ex parte Page*.[273] Although Taggart readily conceded the difficulty of ascribing to a nation's entire jurisprudence the epithet 'exceptionalist' (because such an ascription supposes an external norm against which that jurisprudence can be compared), it is true that the High Court evinces a greater comfort working within established doctrinal categories rather than developing the law afresh.[274] Whether this is an outcome mandated by the Constitution itself, or merely shows 'a tinge of jingoism', is open to doubt.[275]

Both Taggart and Aronson traced the exceptionalism of Australian judicial review to the incrementalist approach of the current High Court, which prefers to change the law in the smallest possible stages from the 'bottom up' rather than in response to normative values.[276]

(i) The Constitutional Requirement of a 'Matter'

The High Court's jurisprudence on the concept of what constitutes a 'matter' has been consistent for almost 90 years. In *Re Judiciary and Navigation Acts*, a High Court majority held that the original jurisdiction of the High Court was limited by the requirement in sections 75 and 76 of the Constitution that there be a 'matter':[277]

> It was suggested in argument that 'matter' meant no more than legal proceeding, and that Parliament might at its discretion create or invent a legal proceeding in which this Court might be called on to interpret the Constitution by a declaration at large. We do not accept this contention; we do not think that the word 'matter' in section 76 means a legal proceeding, but rather the subject matter for determination in a legal proceeding. In our opinion

(2010) 21 *Public Law Review* 92; JJ Spigelman, 'Centrality of Jurisdictional Error' (2010) 21 *Public Law Review* 77; M Groves, 'Federal Constitutional Influences on State Judicial Review' (2011) 39 *Federal Law Review* 399; S Gageler, 'The Constitutional Dimension' in M Groves (ed), *Modern Administrative Law in Australia* (Melbourne, Cambridge University Press, 2014) 165, 172–75.

271 *Cart v Upper Tribunal* [2012] 1 AC 663. See M Aronson and M Groves, *Judicial Review of Administrative Action*, 5th edn (Sydney, Thompson Reuters, 2013) [1.120].

272 M Aronson and M Groves, *Judicial Review of Administrative Action*, 5th edn (Sydney, Thompson Reuters, 2013) [4.290]. See *Anisminic Ltd v Foreign Compensation Commission* [1969] 2 AC 147.

273 *R v Lord President of the Privy Council; ex parte Page* [1993] AC 682 ('*R v Hull University Visitor; ex parte Page*').

274 M Taggart, 'Australian Exceptionalism' (2008) 36 *Federal Law Review* 1, 2; 9.

275 ibid, 27.

276 cf K Mason, 'What is Wrong With Top-Down Legal Reasoning?' in N Perram and R Pepper (eds), *The Byers Lectures 2000–2012* (Sydney, Federation Press, 2012) 69.

277 *Re Judiciary and Navigation Acts* (1921) 29 CLR 257, 265 (Knox CJ, Gavan Duffy, Powers, Rich & Starke JJ).

> there can be no matter within the meaning of the section unless there is *some immediate right, duty or liability to be established by the determination of the Court* (emphasis added).

In *Tang*, it was held by majority that the respondent could not compel the University to provide her with procedural fairness, even though its academic misconduct code promised that it would. Aronson argued that this conclusion was based not on considerations of whether the University was exercising public power, but on whether the University's decision to exclude the respondent created or altered any legal right or obligation between the parties.[278] The majority said that a PhD candidacy created no legal right or obligation between the parties and that the misconduct code made no difference. This was a necessity imposed by the terms of Queensland's Judicial Review Act, but the majority stated expressly that the same conclusion would have applied if the respondent had been a federal body and a constitutional writ had been sought. In that scenario, the Court said that there would have been no 'matter'.[279]

The *Tang* majority's application of *Lam*'s conclusion that Australian courts will not substantively enforce legitimate expectations is considered in detail in Chapter seven. The point that I wish to make here draws upon both *Tang* and the previous comments of McHugh J during argument before the High Court in *S157*: there is a disjuncture between the concept of 'law' on one hand, as it is understood either in purely Austinian terms or through the High Court's 'matter' jurisprudence, and instruments which have a legal *effect* on the other.[280] Aronson alluded to this notion in remarking that:[281]

> classical imagery can sometimes be misleading. Some government contracts are in reality rules, and the same is true of some non-contractual relationships adopting a seemingly consensual form. The characterisation of Ms Tang's relationship with her former university as merely consensual is nothing short of breath-taking.

The distinction which I have drawn should not be confused with whether or not an instrument has a legal consequence, in the sense that it confers a right or imposes an obligation; the High Court's interpretation of Constitutional 'matters' has consistently stated that the courts are not interested in any controversy which falls short of this standard. A 'matter' therefore requires that an instrument have binding effect. On the other hand, judicial review is only ever about acts and omissions. The immediate relevance of this is that the real issue before a court will be to assess whether certain acts or omissions need to conform to soft law instruments.

The discussion above demonstrates that soft law has a level of 'practical legality', particularly where it constitutes the basis for action by an administrative decision-maker. In other words, rules and soft law can be binding in a practical sense, even if they are not legally binding.[282] There is, however, an asymmetrical effect to soft law,

[278] M Aronson, 'Soft Law in the High Court' (2007) 35 *Federal Law Review* 1, 15.

[279] *Tang* (2005) 221 CLR 99, 131 (Gummow, Callinan & Heydon JJ).

[280] *Plaintiff S157/2002 v Commonwealth* [2002] HCA Trans 420 (3 September 2002). See the text accompanying n 27 above.

[281] M Aronson, 'Soft Law in the High Court' (2007) 35 *Federal Law Review* 1, 23; cf PA Keane, 'The Courts and the Academy' (2008) 82 *Australian Law Journal* 623, 629.

[282] RA Anthony, 'Interpretive Rules, Policy Statements, Guidances, Manuals, and the Like' (1992) 41 *Duke Law Journal* 1311, 1327–29.

as *Tang* demonstrates. This stems from the difference between law having an effect and that effect being binding on both the law-maker *and* those subject to the law. The rule of law requirement that laws be predictable is not satisfied by soft law for this reason. The legislation nominated by McHugh J in the extracts from argument in *S157* reproduced above may fail to meet an Austinian standard of law, but such legislation can be relied on for its effect and is *binding* upon both the parties subject to it and the state. This stands in contrast to the academic misconduct code in *Tang*, which had the practical effect of guiding the behaviour of the parties, but which could not be enforced by the respondent.

A further point that arises in Australia relates to the powers reposed in the Commonwealth executive by section 61 of the Constitution, which provides that:

> The executive power of the Commonwealth is vested in the Queen and is exercisable by the Governor-General as the Queen's representative, and extends to the execution and maintenance of this Constitution, and of the laws of the Commonwealth.

The powers of the executive which are covered by section 61 include prerogatives of the Crown, such as the powers to enter into treaties and to declare war, and the 'capacities' which may be held by any person other than the Crown.[283] In *Pape*, French CJ stated that 'such powers as may be conferred upon the Executive by statutes made under the Constitution are plainly included' but that these powers taken together are not exhaustive of the content of section 61.[284] To the same end, Gummow, Crennan and Bell JJ commented that:[285]

> the phrase 'maintenance of this Constitution' in section 61 imports more than a species of what is identified as 'the prerogative' in constitutional theory. It conveys the idea of the protection of the body politic or nation of Australia.

What has long been uncertain is the extent to which section 61 of the Constitution provides scope for the executive government to operate independently of the Commonwealth Parliament. In *Pape*, a majority of the High Court was prepared to allow some level of independent operation to the executive. In this respect, the Court continues to move away from the approach to section 61 advocated by Winterton, who argued that the power of the executive to 'maintain' the Constitution should be limited to the prerogative powers traditionally vested in the Crown.[286] Winterton believed that history—including the Watergate scandal which brought down the Nixon administration in the USA—provides ample warning against giving the executive government a field of authority independent from parliamentary control.[287]

Furthermore, the *Pape* majority's interpretation of the extent of executive power under section 61 leaves a much smaller scope for judicial review, since there are no

[283] *Pape v Federal Commissioner of Taxation* (2009) 238 CLR 1, 60. See also *Williams v The Commonwealth* (2012) 248 CLR 156 ('*Williams (No 1)*').

[284] *Pape* (2009) 238 CLR 1, 60.

[285] ibid, 83.

[286] G Winterton, *Parliament, the Executive and the Governor-General: a Constitutional Analysis* (Melbourne, Melbourne University Press, 1983) 33.

[287] ibid. See *The Communist Party Case* (1951) 83 CLR 1, 287 (Dixon J).

statutory boundaries for the courts to police.[288] While *CCSU* stands for the proposition that power of this kind is subject to judicial review, it also shows the limitations of the courts' oversight. The House of Lords held in *CCSU* that national security implications excused the Minister for the Civil Service (who was also the Prime Minister, Mrs Thatcher) from the necessity of observing procedural fairness.[289] The current ubiquity of 'national security' issues means that action independent of Parliament under section 61 may often be similarly protected.[290] However, this was not relevant in *Pape*.

After *Pape*, the High Court handed down a decision which has served to limit the operation of section 61. *Williams (No 1)* concerned a challenge to the National School Chaplaincy and Student Welfare Program (NSCP), under which the Commonwealth government provided funds to allow school chaplains to be placed in public schools. The plaintiff's primary legal argument—that the arrangement was contrary to the limited prohibition in section 116 of the Constitution on the Commonwealth involving itself in religious matters—failed comprehensively. However, he succeeded on another basis, the Court rejecting the Commonwealth's arguments that it had contractual power equivalent to its legislative capacities under section 51 of the Constitution and that it had all the powers of a natural person.[291] It held invalid the arrangements under which the Commonwealth entered into contracts for the provision of chaplaincy services and spent money to perform its obligations under those contracts. In this sense, the Court's statements about the scope of section 61 were obiter dicta, but were no less significant for that.[292]

The High Court confirmed in *Williams (No 1)* that, aside from exercises of prerogative power, the Commonwealth's capacity to enter into and perform under contracts is always limited by statute. Further, the Court's finding that the Commonwealth's power under section 61 is not co-extensive with that of a natural person sets Australia's jurisprudence on this issue apart from England's, although by reasoning which is not restricted to the Australian constitutional setting.[293] The so-called 'Ram doctrine' has been interpreted in England as allowing the state and its individual departments to do whatever a natural person can, subject to statutory limitations.[294]

[288] See C Horan, 'Judicial Review of Non-Statutory Executive Powers' (2003) 31 *Federal Law Review* 551.

[289] *CCSU* [1985] 1 AC 374.

[290] See eg B Saul, 'The Kafka-esque Case of Sheikh Mansour Leghaei: The Denial of the International Human Right to a Fair Hearing in National Security Assessments and Migration Proceedings in Australia' (2010) 33 *University of NSW Law Journal* 629.

[291] M Aronson and M Groves, *Judicial Review of Administrative Action*, 5th edn (Sydney, Thompson Reuters, 2013) [6.310].

[292] See P Gerangelos, 'The Executive Power of the Commonwealth of Australia: Section 61 of the Commonwealth Constitution, "Nationhood" and the Future of the Prerogative' (2012) 12 *Oxford University Commonwealth Law Journal* 97, 128.

[293] See M Taggart, 'The Nature and Functions of the State' in P Cane and M Tushnet (eds), *The Oxford Handbook of Legal Studies* (Oxford, Oxford University Press, 2005) 101, 117.

[294] See H Woolf et al, *De Smith's Judicial Review*, 6th edn (London, Sweet and Maxwell, 2007) 236; J McLean, *Searching for the State in British Legal Thought: Competing Conceptions of the Public Sphere* (Cambridge, Cambridge University Press, 2012) 161–62.

The correctness of this doctrine has been assumed in recent English litigation, although it has otherwise been subject to some debate.[295]

Especially by contrast with section 51, the power granted by section 61 is vaguely articulated, with the result that for many years it was often discussed 'but never defined'.[296] It is intriguing that, although consistent with much of the High Court's constitutional jurisprudence, the definition which is starting to develop as to the grant of power to the executive under section 61 is peculiar to Australia, even though that result has not specifically been 'sheeted home' to the Constitutional text.[297] This development could also lead to further difficulties which may require legislative intervention to the extent that principles of statutory interpretation do not allow any resort to the natural person powers once statutory authority runs out.[298]

An example of this type of problem led to the litigation in *ABC v Redmore*, in which the High Court was obliged to interpret whether failure to comply with legislation which required the Australian Broadcasting Corporation (ABC) to obtain Ministerial approval for expenditure over a certain sum rendered the ABC's act invalid or merely unlawful.[299] The answer was crucial to Redmore, which had rented premises to the ABC for a sum of rent over the statutory limit for reporting imposed upon the ABC. Redmore would not have been able to obtain an order compelling the ABC to pay the rent if the ABC's entry into the lease contract was invalid. By a bare majority, the High Court held that the ABC's failure did not lead to invalidity. However, the dissenting judgment was very strong and a case on similar facts would not lead to a certain outcome, notwithstanding subsequent consideration of the subject by the High Court.[300]

There is a rich field of scholarship and many authoritative statements from the High Court with respect to section 61 of the Constitution, a source of executive power that has expanded significantly following the *Tampa* litigation.[301] Subject to the limitations imposed by *Pape* and *Williams (No 1)*, an increased scope of operation for section 61 will likely remain, particularly in regard to arguments based on the 'nationhood power', which have not traditionally met with great success.[302] However, those limitations are significant.

French CJ commented in *Pape*:[303]

> Section 61 is an important element of a written constitution for the government of an independent nation. While history and the common law inform its content, it is not a locked display cabinet in a constitutional museum. It is not limited to statutory powers and the prerogative. It has to be capable of serving the proper purposes of a national government.

[295] M Aronson and M Groves, *Judicial Review of Administrative Action*, 5th edn (Sydney, Thompson Reuters, 2013) [3.250] (fn 299).

[296] *Davis v The Commonwealth* (1988) 166 CLR 79, 92 (Mason CJ, Deane & Gaudron JJ).

[297] See M Taggart, 'Australian Exceptionalism' (2008) 36 *Federal Law Review* 1.

[298] See M Aronson and M Groves, *Judicial Review of Administrative Action*, 5th edn (Sydney, Thompson Reuters, 2013) [6.130].

[299] *Australian Broadcasting Corporation v Redmore Pty Ltd* (1989) 166 CLR 454.

[300] *Project Blue Sky* (1998) 194 CLR 355.

[301] *Ruddock v Vadarlis (The Tampa)* (2001) 110 FCR 491.

[302] See G Williams, S Brennan and A Lynch, *Blackshield and Williams' Australian Constitutional Law and Theory: Commentary and Materials*, 6th edn (Sydney, Federation Press, 2014) 388.

[303] *Pape* (2009) 238 CLR 1, 60.

Full acceptance of this view could allow the executive government in Australia a law-making role differing substantially from the traditional Diceyan conception of 'law', although this is not to say that all Executive Orders are 'law'. Furthermore, acceptance of French CJ's proposition amounts to an implicit rejection of the warning sounded by Winterton.[304] However, both *Pape* and *Williams (No 1)* indicated that the High Court was prepared to impose limits on the Commonwealth's powers under section 61.

In particular, both *Pape* and *Williams (No 1)* indicated that expenditures in reliance on the 'appropriations power' will be invalid. This is especially interesting given that the response of the Commonwealth government to *Williams (No 1)* was to rush through legislation to protect schemes which it believed to be threatened by the result in that case.[305] The amending legislation was clearly intended to allow the government to continue much as it always had, with several sections specifically 'reserved' for grants yet to be made. Otherwise, it simply listed grants and schemes, with the intention of putting them beyond the scope of *Williams (No 1)* by placing what were previously executive schemes on a legislative footing, rather than simply making the necessary payments following the passage of an Appropriations Act.[306]

The results in *Pape* and *Williams (No 1)* were reaffirmed by the High Court in *Williams (No 2)*. The plaintiff from *Williams (No 1)* was again granted standing to challenge the NSCP, this time in its legislative form, albeit he was not granted standing to argue that the amending legislation was wholly invalid.[307] He succeeded on the basis that the legislation which purported to provide funding to the NSCP was not supported by a constitutional head of power. This case is examined in detail in Chapter 12.B below.

D. THE INFLUENCE OF SOFT LAW ON JUDICIAL REVIEW PROCEEDINGS

There have been indications in recent cases that courts exercising a judicial review function are prepared to give considerable weight to soft law instruments in some circumstances. I will consider two such cases in detail and seek to draw some general conclusions. I will also consider a third case which indicates that there remains significant risk in relying on soft law.

(i) *Plaintiff M61 v Commonwealth* (*'The Offshore Processing Case'*)

The High Court clarified that executive power needs to be controlled by law for constitutional reasons in the *Offshore Processing Case*, which involved a challenge by two Sri Lankan citizens who had been detained under statute after arriving at

[304] See n 287 above.

[305] Financial Framework Legislation Amendment Bill (No 3) 2012 (Cth). The Act also took care to amend the ADJR Act in order to ensure that it would not apply.

[306] See M Aronson and M Groves, *Judicial Review of Administrative Action*, 5th edn (Sydney, Thompson Reuters, 2013) [2.640].

[307] *Williams v The Commonwealth* (2014) 252 CLR 416, 455 ('*Williams (No 2)*').

Christmas Island claiming refugee status. That status was to be determined under Australia's 'offshore processing regime' for asylum-seekers. The Court rejected the submissions made on behalf of the respondent Minister that departmental assessment officers were able to hold persons who arrived in an 'offshore' location in administrative detention, with no obligation to bring that detention to an end while there was a reasonable possibility that the Minister might exercise his powers under the Migration Act 1958 (Cth).[308] In response to that submission, the Court stated that 'it is not readily to be supposed that a statutory power to detain a person permits continuation of that detention at the unconstrained discretion of the Executive'.[309] This comment must be understood as referring solely to discretionary extension of a period of detention as opposed to circumstances in which, provided that a purpose of detention is the eventual removal of unlawful non-citizens, an indefinite period of detention is not prohibited by the Constitution.[310]

In response to the government's attempts to justify both detention and determinations of asylum seekers' refugee status as being exercises of power authorised under section 61 of the Constitution, the Court held that the Minister had in fact exercised his statutory powers:[311]

> constituted by two distinct steps: first, the decision to consider exercising the power to lift the bar or grant a visa and second, the decision whether to lift the bar or grant a visa. The Minister is not obliged to take either step.

An interesting point implicit in this reasoning, but which the Court did not confront directly, is what might happen in the event that an asylum seeker were held offshore and her claim for refugee status were assessed without reference either to the Migration Act or Australia's treaty obligations. Her detention may be illegal (in which case she would be able to get habeas corpus) but it is arguable that her status assessment would not have contained jurisdictional error of law on the basis that there would be no applicable law.[312] A Full Federal Court bench of five was evidently discomforted by such a line of argument.[313]

In the *Offshore Processing Case*, the High Court expressly declined to decide the really interesting question which arose on the facts. This was whether a remedy—*any* remedy—was available against a contractor to whom executive power had been outsourced.[314] It nonetheless articulated what was capable of constituting an error of law in determining whether Australia owed protection obligations to the plaintiffs by saying that, although the contractors had made errors of law in relying on soft law instruments which both misstated certain statutory requirements and

[308] *Plaintiff M61/2010E v Commonwealth* ('*Offshore Processing Case*') (2010) 243 CLR 319, 348–49.
[309] ibid.
[310] *Al-Kateb v Godwin* (2004) 219 CLR 562.
[311] *Offshore Processing Case* (2010) 243 CLR 319, 350–51.
[312] M Aronson and M Groves, *Judicial Review of Administrative Action*, 5th edn (Sydney, Thompson Reuters, 2013) [14.40]–[14.50].
[313] See *Minister for Immigration and Citizenship v SZQRB* [2013] FCAFC 33, [349]–[391] (Flick J).
[314] *Offshore Processing Case* (2010) 243 CLR 319, 345. See M Groves, 'Outsourcing and s 75(v) of the Constitution' (2011) 22 *Public Law Review* 3; J Boughey and G Weeks, '"Officers of the Commonwealth" in the Private Sector' (2013) 36 *University of NSW Law Journal* 316, 317.

erroneously indicated that Australian case law could and should be ignored, these errors were in fact the Minister's errors because the Minister had, in effect, decided to consider exercising his statutory powers in *every* case where an offshore entry person claimed to be owed protection obligations.[315]

There were two soft law manuals provided to the outsourced decision-makers. The High Court held that each contained legal errors and any decision made in reliance on either one would also be legally wrong. The 'Refugee Status Assessment Procedures Manual' (RSA Manual) stated that 'the Migration Act, the Migration Regulations 1994 … and Australian case law on the interpretations of the definition of a refugee and "protection obligations" do not apply' to assessments of whether Australia owes obligations to 'offshore entry persons', although it stated that they should nonetheless be followed as a matter of policy. This statement was echoed in the 'Guidelines for the Independent Merits Review of Refugee Status Assessments' (IMR Manual). The High Court dealt with the significance of the manuals decisively and clearly by holding that the reviewers had erred in law by not treating Australian legislation and relevant case law as binding upon their decisions. The Court's reasoning was expressly on the basis that any decision by the Minister to use section 46A of the Migration Act to allow the plaintiffs to make valid applications for protection visas would be 'pointless' unless it was made consistently with the terms of the legislation as construed by Australian courts. However, it would have been a remarkable result if the Court had held that it was valid for the executive to use soft law to authorise decisions which could be inconsistent with Australian legislation and case law.

The two soft law manuals:[316]

> were cast in terms that made plain that the processes for which each provided were to be applied to *all* unlawful non-citizens who entered Australia at an excised offshore place and who, as the RSA Manual said, raised 'claims or information which *prima facie* may engage Australia's protection obligations'.

The adoption of the procedures set out in the Manuals and their application to the plaintiffs could therefore 'only be understood as implementing' the Minister's policy announcements.[317] These had the effect of stating that the Minister would consider exercising his statutory powers 'in every case in which an offshore entry person claimed that Australia owed that person protection obligations'.[318]

In regard to an available remedy, the Court held that the assessment and review inquiries commenced under the Manuals directly affected the plaintiffs' rights and interests by prolonging their detention 'for so long as the assessment and any necessary review took to complete'.[319] The Court thereby gave an expansive reading of what triggers an obligation to provide procedural fairness, although this ought not to have been at all complicated since, for example, the members of the plaintiff's

[315] *Offshore Processing Case* (2010) 243 CLR 319, 351.
[316] ibid, 342.
[317] ibid.
[318] ibid, 350–51.
[319] ibid, 352–53.

family in *Kioa* had no rights whatsoever.[320] Those contracted to make the inquiries on the Minister's behalf were therefore bound by the common law obligation to afford procedural fairness to the plaintiffs. This was not an obligation with any substantive element, since the plaintiffs had 'no right to have the Minister decide to exercise the power or, if the assessment or review were favourable, to have the Minister exercise one of the relevant powers in his or her favour'.[321] The Court held that neither of the plaintiffs had been afforded procedural fairness by the contractors who had undertaken internal merits review of the decisions that they were not parties to whom Australia owed obligations under the Refugees Convention.[322]

Nothing hard-edged can be taken from the *Offshore Processing Case* for the purposes of this book. However, it must be relevant that the High Court was prepared to recognise that the two soft law manuals did not exist in a legal void; rather, they meant *something*. This may become important as a step towards the High Court extending judicial review under section 75(v) to providers of contractually outsourced government services by holding them to be 'officers of the Commonwealth', particularly in circumstances where the party to whom power has been outsourced operates in a milieu of soft law—an issue that the *Offshore Processing Case* raised, but did not resolve.

This chapter has posited that a more expansive approach to the application of judicial review to exercises of public power, typified in England by *Datafin*, may lead courts to recognise and exercise supervisory control over governance through soft law. There is, however, much more to be done before a court could, for example, require a private repository of public power to adhere to a soft law instrument by which it governed the behaviour of members of the public. Consideration of the role of Independent Merits Reviewers (IMRs) in the Federal Court since the *Offshore Processing Case* has referred to IMRs themselves (rather than the Minister who has the statutory power to act upon an IMR's recommendation) committing jurisdictional errors.[323] In *SZQOT*, Marshall J held that the Court below had erred in finding that an IMR had committed a jurisdictional error in the circumstances but assumed that it could properly have done so in the appropriate circumstances.[324] It seems that the Federal Court is saying that the IMRs are *themselves* exercising statutory functions (removing any need to consider *Datafin*), on the basis that the Minister has already made decisions which trigger his or her dealing with certain matters. If that reading of the Federal Court's decisions is correct, there remains an 'officer of the Commonwealth' issue.[325] This might be avoided by simply joining the Minister and/or somebody from the Department as parties to any litigation.

[320] *Kioa* (1985) 159 CLR 550.
[321] *Offshore Processing Case* (2010) 243 CLR 319, 353.
[322] ibid, 356, 358.
[323] See eg *MZYPW v Minister for Immigration and Citizenship* (2012) 289 ALR 541, 547–48 (Flick & Jagot JJ); *MZYPO v Minister for Immigration and Citizenship* [2013] FCAFC 1 [59] (Lander & Middleton JJ). See also *SZQDZ v Minister for Immigration and Citizenship* (2012) 200 FCR 207, 210–11 (Keane CJ, Rares & Perram JJ).
[324] *Minister for Immigration and Citizenship v SZQOT* [2012] FCAFC 141 [22].
[325] See M Groves, 'Outsourcing' (2011) 22 *Public Law Review* 3; J Boughey and G Weeks, '"Officers of the Commonwealth" in the Private Sector' (2013) 36 *University of NSW Law Journal* 316.

By way of contrast to the *Offshore Processing Case*, in *Kaur* the High Court heard applications from four individual plaintiffs who were each non-citizens and had been refused visas which would have allowed them to remain in Australia. In circumstances where the Minister had issued ministerial guidelines in the form of directions to departmental officers setting out the circumstances in which the Minister might wish to consider exercising certain discretionary statutory powers, the applicants argued that the guidelines amounted to a decision by the Minister to consider exercising his powers and that the exercise of the relevant statutory powers 'is conditioned upon compliance with the requirements of procedural fairness'.[326] These propositions were rejected.

At its broadest, *Kaur* can be interpreted as the High Court distinguishing the decision in the *Offshore Processing Case*, each judgment having pointed out that the specific statutory scheme which was considered in the *Offshore Processing Case* did not apply to the plaintiffs in *Kaur*, none of whom was an 'offshore entry person'. French CJ and Kiefel J additionally noted that:[327]

> there has not been, in relation to the cases presently before the Court, any ministerial announcement of the kind which applied to the assessment and review processes considered in the *Offshore Processing Case*. The function of the guidelines in issue in these cases was significantly different from the function of the assessment and review procedures under consideration in the *Offshore Processing Case*. Those were procedures which were undertaken as an incident of the exercise of a statutory power which the Minister had effectively announced was to be undertaken, namely, the power to consider whether to exercise the substantive [statutory] powers.

Kaur also gave strong indications that the guidelines in question simply did not apply to the applicants. The ministerial guidelines were issued 'from time to time' in order to inform the exercise of the Minister's statutory powers.[328] French CJ and Kiefel J noted that some were 'cast in the first person as instructions from the Minister', who remained personally responsible to Parliament in respect of certain statutory powers.[329] Gummow, Hayne, Crennan and Bell JJ expressed this point in a slightly different way, stating that '[t]he term "guidelines" is apt to mislead; their content is in the form of directions by the Minister'.[330] Each of the statutory powers had as a prerequisite to its exercise that the non-citizen applicant had previously had a visa application determined by a body other than the Minister.[331]

Further, none of the judgments was prepared to find that the plaintiffs were owed procedural fairness. Their expressions of reasons supporting that conclusion differed. French CJ and Kiefel J said that the statutory powers were exceptional in nature and should not be encumbered with obligations of procedural fairness.[332]

[326] *Kaur and Others v Minister for Immigration and Citizenship* (2012) 246 CLR 636, 641.
[327] ibid, 653.
[328] ibid, 649.
[329] ibid, 649–50.
[330] ibid, 664.
[331] See ibid, 669–70.
[332] ibid, 649.

Gummow, Hayne, Crennan and Bell JJ interpreted the statute as excluding procedural fairness altogether. Heydon J put the matter with great clarity:[333]

> The [four disputed] provisions create only powers to soften the rigours an adverse outcome of the former regime might create—powers depending on much vaguer and more impressionistic criteria, which are to be invoked when all else has failed. The terms in which [those] provisions are cast and the circumstances in which the Minister's powers are to be exercised, when compared to … the provisions giving merits review, suggest that no rights to procedural fairness exist in relation to either the Minister's powers or to the activities of officials of the Minister's Department in advising the Minister whether to consider to exercise those powers, or to exercise those powers.

The contrast between the plaintiffs in *Kaur* and those in the *Offshore Processing Case* is obvious once the respective statutory schemes and their attendant soft law instruments are compared. Each of the three judgments in the High Court in *Kaur* addressed (at greater or lesser length) and rejected the analogy between the cases which the plaintiffs sought to draw.[334] The guidelines in the *Offshore Processing Case* were construed as part of a process intended to trigger the applicability of the Migration Act in a context where the Minister's intention was determinative, which is to say that he was not required to think about exercising his special powers. The guidelines in *Kaur*, on the other hand, were not interpreted as the Minister agreeing to engage in further consideration, pursuant to powers that carried duties only if he *chose* to trigger those powers into operation. Hence, the purpose and effect of the guidelines in *Kaur* was also different to those considered in the *Offshore Processing Case*, although a detailed consideration of the effect of publishing soft law was expressly deferred by a majority of the Court.[335]

(ii) *Khan v Minister for Immigration and Citizenship*

Mr Khan was a Bangladeshi citizen who arrived in Australia on a student visa and was subsequently sponsored for a Business (Long Stay) visa of four years' duration by his employer at an Indian restaurant. A manager employed by Mr Khan's employer wrote to the Department of Immigration and Citizenship (DIAC) and alleged that Mr Khan had engaged in 'fraudulent behaviour' which would disentitle him from holding a visa. The manager requested that the DIAC cancel his employer's sponsorship of Mr Khan and that the DIAC not reveal to Mr Khan that the manager had made any allegations against him. About a month later, the DIAC wrote to Mr Khan to inform him that the DIAC was considering the cancellation of his visa and that 'the grounds for cancellation of your visa appear to exist because the Department received advice from your sponsor … indicating that you had ceased employment'.[336]

333 ibid, 672–73.

334 ibid, 652–53 (French CJ & Kiefel J); 656–57, 662–63 (Gummow, Hayne, Crennan & Bell JJ); 673–74 (Heydon J).

335 ibid, 665 (Gummow, Hayne, Crennan & Bell JJ).

336 *Khan v Minister for Immigration and Citizenship* (2011) 192 FCR 173, 176.

A delegate of the Minister informed Mr Khan that his visa had been cancelled because he had ceased to be employed by his sponsor, but did not mention the accusations made against Mr Khan by the manager, meaning that 'Mr Khan was misinformed about the nature (and impliedly the content) of the advice received by [the DIAC]'.[337] The Migration Review Tribunal (MRT) affirmed the delegate's decision but noted (contrary to the implication contained in the delegate's reasons for decision) that it was not mandatory for Mr Khan's visa to be cancelled. Rather, the remit of the MRT was to consider whether or not to cancel Mr Khan's visa 'considering the circumstances as a whole'.[338]

The Minister's discretion to cancel a visa arises, inter alia, if s/he is satisfied that 'any circumstances which permitted the grant of the visa no longer exist'.[339] The relevant circumstances were, in part, defined by the DIAC's 'Procedures Advice Manual' (Manual), which set out guidelines to assist DIAC officers in assessing visa applications. Flick J noted that the Manual was 'available to at least some migration agents'.[340] Relevant to the cancellation of Mr Khan's visa, the Manual listed the following matters that could be considered by officers:[341]

— If cancellation is being considered because of a breach of visa condition (and cancellation is not mandatory)—the reason for, and extent of, the breach. As a rule, a visa should not be cancelled where the breach of a visa condition occurred in circumstances beyond the visa holder's control;
— The circumstances in which the ground for cancellation arose (for example, whether extenuating or compassionate circumstances outweigh the grounds for cancelling the visa); and
— The visa holder's past and present behaviour towards the department (for example, whether they have been truthful in statements or applications made to the department or have previously complied with visa conditions).

Mr Khan's appeal on the merits was unsuccessful before the MRT. That decision was upheld by the Federal Magistrates' Court but, in the Full Federal Court, Buchanan J (with whom Flick and Yates JJ agreed) held that, because the MRT had not disclosed the substance of the manager's allegations against Mr Khan, it had breached section 359A of the Migration Act.[342] However, the Division of the Migration Act in which section 359A appears 'is taken to be an exhaustive statement of the requirements of the natural justice hearing rule in relation to the matters it deals with'.[343] There was therefore no question of any breach of a common law duty of natural justice toward Mr Khan, in as much as disclosure of the existence and contents of the manager's letters were 'matters' dealt with by the relevant Division of the Migration Act.[344]

337 ibid, 177 (Buchanan J).
338 ibid, 178.
339 Migration Act 1958 (Cth) s 116(1)(a). See ibid, 191.
340 *Khan* (2011) 192 FCR 173, 191.
341 ibid, 178.
342 ibid, 186–89.
343 Migration Act 1958 (Cth) s 357A(1).
344 *Saeed v Minister for Immigration and Citizenship* (2010) 241 CLR 252, 266–67.

The statutory discretion to cancel Mr Khan's visa was not mandatory unless there existed 'circumstances in which a visa must be cancelled', which were prescribed in the Migration Regulations.[345] The MRT found that there were no such prescribed circumstances.[346] Nonetheless, the Court held that the MRT was 'bound to consider' the 'circumstances in which the ground for cancellation arose (for example, whether extenuating or compassionate circumstances outweigh the grounds for cancelling the visa)'.[347] This was a matter listed as relevant in the Manual but it did not bear the status of a mandatory matter which had been prescribed in subordinate legislation.

I take no issue with the finding of Buchanan J that the 'circumstances in which the ground for cancellation *arose*' have an entirely different import from the matters which explain the MRT's decision.[348] There is no doubt that the MRT failed to review the matter whose relevance was indicated by the Manual, namely *why* Mr Khan was no longer employed by his sponsor, rather than the mere fact that he was not. This reasoning certainly supports Buchanan J's earlier finding that common law procedural fairness would have demanded that the existence and contents of the manager's letters be revealed to Mr Khan. However, it does not establish that the manager's letters and the reasons for which they reveal that Mr Khan lost his job were considerations that were *mandatory* for the MRT to take into account; nor does the fact that these documents were evidently viewed as 'relevant' by the DIAC.[349]

As Chapter 6.A.(iii) explains in detail, the 'relevancy grounds' of review do not require that a decision-maker consider every matter which is objectively relevant to his or her decision.[350] Rather, jurisdictional error results when a decision-maker:[351]

> disregards ... some matter in circumstances where the statute or other instrument establishing it and conferring its jurisdiction requires that that particular matter be taken into account ... as a pre-condition of the existence of any authority to make [a] ... decision in the circumstances of the particular case (emphasis added).

This is a point that has been made repeatedly by the High Court, most notably by Mason J, who said in *Minister for Aboriginal Affairs v Peko-Wallsend Ltd* that the 'ground of failure to take into account a relevant consideration can only be made out if a decision-maker fails to take into account a consideration which he is *bound* to take into account in making that decision'.[352] As I discuss below, there is nonetheless frequent slippage between what is mandatory and what is merely relevant.

Whether or not a decision-maker is *bound* to take a certain matter into account is a matter of statutory construction and most legislation is properly construed as

[345] Migration Act 1958 (Cth) s 116(3).
[346] *Khan* (2011) 192 FCR 173, 189.
[347] ibid, 189–90 (Buchanan J); 191 (Flick J). Counsel for the Minister conceded this point at the appellate hearing.
[348] ibid, 189.
[349] ibid, 190.
[350] See M Aronson and M Groves, *Judicial Review of Administrative Action*, 5th edn (Sydney, Thompson Reuters, 2013) [5.20].
[351] *Craig* (1995) 184 CLR 163, 177. See *Khan* (2011) 192 FCR 173, 189.
[352] *Minister for Aboriginal Affairs v Peko-Wallsend Ltd* (1986) 162 CLR 24, 39.

requiring very few things from those on whom it confers a power or discretion.[353] Section 116 of the Migration Act certainly cannot be read as *requiring* the decision-maker to take account of the terms of the Manual. The better view, as put by Flick J, was that, 'when exercising the discretionary power conferred by section 116, the delegate and the [MRT] were *entitled* to take into account government policy and such other matters as are set forth in the Manual' (emphasis added).[354] To the extent that Flick J's analysis of this issue modified that of Buchanan J, his Honour was in the minority.[355]

Flick J cited *Peko-Wallsend* to the effect that the matters which a decision-maker is bound to take into account 'remain to be determined by reference to the objects and purposes' of the legislation which confers power on the decision-maker.[356] The requirement to look to the circumstances in which the cancellation arose was, on this approach, sourced to the Migration Act, rather than to the Manual.[357] Flick J read section 116 to require a consideration of the circumstances in which cancellation arose, on the basis that one cannot consider whether the visa conditions no longer exist unless one first considers whether those conditions had ceased to exist at the time of cancellation. If cancellation of Mr Khan's visa was wrong at the time, then the visa should be restored (and perhaps re-cancelled if the conditions subsequently cease to exist). Flick J reached this conclusion regardless of the Manual.[358]

In his concluding remarks, Flick J nonetheless indicated concern with the submissions made on behalf of the Minister 'as to the limited consequences of a delegate or the [MRT] not taking into account those matters which are apparently set forth with some considerable detail in the Manual'. While those issues were left to be argued another day, his Honour said that the Manual amounts to:[359]

> *a formal guide as to how the power conferred by section 116 is to be administered as a matter of practice.* Where such guidance has been provided and where matters are there identified as matters that should be taken into account, it is not self-evidently correct to further conclude that a failure on the part of the [MRT] to properly apply the guidance provided has such limited consequences as was contended by the Minister. Consistency in the administration of provisions such as section 116 would not appear to be promoted if such consideration as is required to be given to the matters identified in the Manual is satisfied by the oblique or ambiguous references as made by the [MRT] in the present proceeding (emphasis added).

This is a remarkable passage, referring as it does to the Manual as a 'formal' guide and leaving open the question of whether a failure to apply the terms of the Manual consistently with other similar decisions opens a ground of judicial review. Flick J therefore stepped away from the orthodoxy of the position in *Peko-Wallsend* to

353 M Aronson and M Groves, *Judicial Review of Administrative Action*, 5th edn (Sydney, Thompson Reuters, 2013) [5.30].

354 *Khan* (2011) 192 FCR 173, 191. See also *Hneidi v Minister for Immigration and Citizenship* (2010) 182 FCR 115 (Spender, Emmett & Jacobson JJ).

355 Yates J had agreed with the reasons of Buchanan J in full: *Khan* (2011) 192 FCR 173, 195–96.

356 ibid, 192; see *Peko-Wallsend* (1986) 162 CLR 24, 39–40 (Mason J).

357 *Khan* (2011) 192 FCR 173, 194–95.

358 ibid, 192–93.

359 ibid, 195.

recognise, as the High Court did in the *Offshore Processing Case*, that soft law (particularly at this level of sophistication) must mean *something*. It is unnecessary to determine whether the Manual's terms are mandatory considerations (whether because they are sourced directly from the Migration Act itself or are sourced to procedural fairness obligations). A public authority cannot depart from a 'promise' of the sort contained in the Manual without first providing a warning. If a warning is needed, it follows that the authority's decision-maker has to think about it and therefore *consideration* must be given to the terms of the Manual.

(iii) *Davies v HMRC*

The UK Supreme Court's decisions on appeal from the Court of Appeal in favour of Her Majesty's Revenue and Customs Commissioners (the Revenue) in *Davies v HMRC* were long awaited, particularly amongst tax advisors, yet were not received with unbridled satisfaction. Each appeal had broadly similar facts: the first appellants (Davies and James) and second appellant (Gaines-Cooper) were each British citizens who were born and had worked in the UK; each purchased residential property outside the UK in which they lived for some months every year; each appellant nonetheless maintained ties to the UK and returned every year. The appellants did not wish to have the status of being 'resident' in the UK since they would then have been required to pay taxes—such as income tax and capital gains tax—to which they would not have been subject if they were 'resident' abroad (in Belgium and the Seychelles respectively).

Between 1999 and 2009, the Revenue published a soft law instrument called IR20 which, amongst other things, purported to offer guidance as to when a person could be said to be 'resident' in the UK.[360] The appellants' contentions were twofold. The first was that, properly construed, IR20:[361]

> contained a more benevolent interpretation of the circumstances in which an individual becomes non-resident and not ordinarily resident in the UK than is reflected in the ordinary law and that the appellants had a legitimate expectation … that the more benevolent interpretation would be applied to the determination of their status for tax purposes.

The second was that, regardless of the construction of IR20:[362]

> it was the settled *practice* of the Revenue to adopt [a more benevolent interpretation than is reflected in the ordinary law] and that the practice was such as to give rise to a legitimate expectation … that the interpretation would be applied to the determination of their status.

The Revenue did not contest that, if one were to exist, a legitimate expectation on either basis should be given substantive effect, a point on which this case is already at odds with Australian precedent and practice, as Chapter seven will discuss.

[360] IR20 had existed 'in various guises' since 1973. It was replaced by a new guidance document in 2009: M Spinney, 'Case Comment: *R (Davies and Anor) v HMRC; R (Gaines-Cooper) v HMRC* [2011] UKSC 47' (30 October 2011), *UKSC Blog*, available at: ukscblog.com/r-on-the-application-of-davies-and-anotherappellants-v-the-commissioners-for-her-majestys-revenue-customs-respondents-and-r-on-the-application-of-gaines-cooper-appellant-v-the-com/.

[361] *Davies v HM Revenue & Customs* [2011] 1 WLR 2625, 2629.

[362] ibid.

The parties agreed on certain points: that 'residence' was not a concept which the statute defined (although the government subsequently indicated that it planned to change this state of affairs); and that the case law was neither clear nor of easy application.[363] These circumstances left a gap on a matter of some practical importance which IR20 sought to fill in quite specific terms.[364] The appellants therefore invited the Supreme Court, and the Court of Appeal before it, to construe IR20 as though it were a legislative instrument. The appellants clearly hoped that this approach would steer them around the troublesome, contentious and uncertain case law which held that a person only ceases to be ordinarily resident in the UK if s/he makes 'a distinct break'.[365] This was not a requirement that was given clear expression in IR20, a circumstance of which Lord Mance made much in his dissenting speech.[366] Lord Wilson accorded it much less importance, saying that 'if invited to summarise what [IR20] required, [the ordinarily sophisticated taxpayer] might reasonably have done so in three words: a distinct break'.[367]

The appellants' claimed reliance on IR20, rather than the case law, was not necessarily a cynical manipulation of the tax system. Their submissions to the Court of Appeal indicated genuine dismay that the Revenue refused to apply the terms of IR20 as the appellants understood them. The Revenue's approach had been characterised as a 'betrayal of trust'.[368] In this vein, Moses LJ commented that:[369]

> from time to time in the meandering course of these proceedings, it has appeared that the appellants, their advisers and the taxation profession have doubted whether IR20 can be relied upon at all; they harbour the suspicion that the Revenue regards itself as free to apply or to disapply its guidance, as it chooses. They describe IR20 as misleading and a trap.

Ward LJ delivered a concurring judgment in the Court of Appeal, but 'not without considerable hesitation' as a result of his sympathy for the circumstances in which the appellants (particularly the first appellants) found themselves.[370] Furthermore, there is much to support the conclusion that, despite the appellants' relative sophistication and that of their advisors, they had every reason to rely upon IR20 rather than to reach their own views as to the requirements of the law. Lord Mance noted that the first appellants were advised by 'accountants rather than lawyers, and correspondingly [were] interested in HMRC's understanding and practice rather than prepared to attempt exhaustive analysis of legal authority'.[371]

This is an excellent example of the power and danger of soft law. The appellants were unsuccessful before a united Court of Appeal and ultimately had their appeals dismissed by majority in the Supreme Court. This outcome was due in large measure

[363] *Davies v HM Revenue & Customs* [2011] 1 WLR 2625, 2632; see M Spinney, 'Case Comment: *Davies*' (30 October 2011), *UKSC Blog*.

[364] See *R (Davies) v Commissioners for Her Majesty's Revenue & Customs* [2010] EWCA Civ 83 [38] (Moses LJ).

[365] *Davies v HMRC* [2011] 1 WLR 2625, 2633–35.

[366] ibid, 2662 (Lord Mance), cf 2648 (Lord Hope).

[367] ibid, 2644.

[368] *R (Davies) v Commissioners for Her Majesty's Revenue & Customs* [2010] EWCA Civ 83 [2].

[369] ibid, [20].

[370] ibid, [122]; cf *Davies v HMRC* [2011] 1 WLR 2625, 2648 (Lord Walker).

[371] *Davies v HMRC* [2011] 1 WLR 2625, 2663; cf 2647 (Lord Wilson).

to the fact that IR20 was expressed as providing 'general guidance only'.[372] This disclaimer and its effect are reminiscent of the result in *Hedley Byrne*.[373] The crucial issue in this litigation might accurately be expressed as whether, having issued guidance in the form of a soft law instrument, the Revenue could argue that those who followed the guidance so issued had erred in doing so on the basis that the guidance was only 'general' and support its conclusions by pointing to inconsistent and contested case law.

The Revenue stated throughout that it would submit to an order to give substantive effect to any legitimate expectation it could be held to have created in the appellants, although there is long-standing precedent that the Revenue *can* exercise its discretion not to enforce the law to the full.[374] In the end, the point was not central to the outcome of the case because Lord Wilson held that the relevant paragraphs of IR20 were 'very poorly drafted', and expressed doubt that they were sufficiently precise to generate a legitimate expectation in the first place.[375]

More than the result in *Davies*, this specific outcome is a cause for significant concern. Where people, indeed sophisticated businessmen with professional advisors, read and rely upon soft law, how can it be any kind of response to say that nothing can be done to aid them because the soft law was so badly drafted in the first place? This finding must be distinguished from examples of badly drafted legislation, which are legion; these primarily become the problem of lawyers, who are trained to deal with legislative drafting, be it good, bad or indifferent.[376] Soft law, on the other hand, is presented as an accessible guide to the requirements of government and is therefore more likely to be relied upon by people who would never dream of attempting to extract meaning from legislation. The Supreme Court's approach places the risk attached to poor drafting of soft law upon the claimant—who, after all, was sufficiently able to understand the soft law to rely upon it—rather than the public authority responsible for the poor drafting. Put more briefly, it is akin to saying that soft law means nothing; the authority which issues soft law can avoid its effects with careful disclaimers or careless drafting. A poorly drafted statute cannot be dismissed in this way. While England is still far ahead of Australia in its capacity to enforce the terms of soft law, *Davies* contains some worrisome elements which suggest that soft law remains a dangerously one-sided phenomenon.

[372] ibid, 2639 (Lord Wilson); 2648 (Lord Hope); 2649 (Lord Walker).

[373] *Hedley Byrne* [1964] AC 465; cf *R v Board of Inland Revenue, ex parte MFK Underwriting Agencies Ltd* [1990] 1 WLR 1545, 1569 (Bingham LJ and Judge J); cited in *Davies v HMRC* [2011] 1 WLR 2625, 2637–38 (Lord Wilson).

[374] See *R v Inland Revenue Commissioners; ex parte National Federation of Self-Employed and Small Businesses Limited* [1982] AC 617 ('*Fleet Street Casuals Case*').

[375] *Davies v HMRC* [2011] 1 WLR 2625, 2641–42.

[376] cf *Day v Harness Racing New South Wales* [2014] NSWCA 423, [79] (Leeming JA).

6

Procedural Judicial Review Remedies

THIS CHAPTER AND the one following proceed on the assumption that exercises of power pursuant to a soft law instrument are within the scope of common law judicial review, albeit not of the Commonwealth ADJR Act (or equivalent State and Territorial legislation) which cover only decisions made 'under an enactment'.[1] If that assumption is correct, there are three possible outcomes:

1. that a party is able to obtain a judicial review remedy, all of which are axiomatically procedural in their effect, by establishing that a decision made in relation to soft law has breached one or more grounds of judicial review; or
2. that a court will take account of the legitimate expectation entertained by a party who has relied on the terms of a soft law instrument and require either that any departure not be *Wednesbury* unreasonable or that the opportunity for consultation be given 'unless there is an overriding reason to resile from it';[2] or
3. that, where the legitimate expectation is of a substantive benefit, the frustration of the legitimate expectation will be prevented if it is 'so unfair that to take a new and different course will amount to an abuse of power'.[3]

The third outcome, substantive enforcement of a legitimate expectation of a benefit, will be examined in Chapter 7.B. At this point, it suffices to say that the weight of Australian authority is against this doctrine as it has developed in England.[4]

The first and second outcomes are considered in this chapter, which looks at the grounds upon which traditional judicial review remedies may be available where a public authority fails to adhere to a soft law instrument. Some courts have been prepared to allow judicial review of decisions made under soft law, although they still fall short of having the status of hard law.[5] Evans JA succinctly noted in this regard that, 'although not legally binding on a decision-maker in the sense that it may be an error of law to misinterpret or misapply them, guidelines may validly

[1] Administrative Decisions (Judicial Review) Act 1977 (Cth) s 3(1).

[2] *R v North and East Devon Health Authority, ex parte Coughlan* [2001] QB 213, 242. See *Attorney-General (Hong Kong) v Ng Yuen Shiu* [1983] 2 AC 629; M Groves, 'Substantive Legitimate Expectations in Australian Administrative Law' (2008) 32 *Melbourne University Law Review* 470, 478–79.

[3] *Coughlan* [2001] QB 213, 242; subject to the comments of the Court of Appeal in *R (Bibi) v Newham London Borough Council* [2002] 1 WLR 237.

[4] See *Attorney General (NSW) v Quin* (1990) 170 CLR 1; *Re Minister for Immigration and Multicultural Affairs, ex parte Lam* (2003) 214 CLR 1.

[5] *Gillick* [1986] AC 112, 163 (Lord Fraser); 177–78 (Lord Scarman); *Bristol-Myers Squibb Australia Pty Ltd v Minister for Health and Family Services* (1997) 49 ALD 240, 258 (Wilcox, O'Loughlin & Lindgren JJ).

influence a decision-maker's conduct'.[6] This chapter will also examine the ways in which guidelines might assist a court in concluding that a decision-maker has fallen into reviewable error.

A. POSSIBLE GROUNDS OF JUDICIAL REVIEW

(i) Improper Fettering of Discretion

This ground of review is essentially the inverse of the argument that a person has a legitimate expectation that a decision-maker will adhere to a rule or policy from which s/he seeks to depart.[7] Classically, a decision-maker who applies rules or policies inflexibly without listening to submissions that an exception be made, commits a jurisdictional error.[8] As I discuss below, the same principle forms the basis of the common law prohibition on future exercises of discretion being fettered by estoppels.[9] I also noted in Part I of this volume that the 'no fettering' rule as expressed in *British Oxygen* is usually justified on the basis that it is generally preferable for the potential breadth of statutory discretions granted to public decision-makers not to be fettered, even by their own representations, in reaching the decision which is most beneficial for the public at large.[10] However, the rule has more recently been subject to criticism, on the basis that it 'should no longer be regarded as almost universally applicable'.[11]

Usually, the no-fettering principle is invoked where a decision-maker imposes restraints on himself or herself by adhering to the terms of a soft law instrument which impermissibly narrows the scope of his or her discretion such that s/he does not take account of the merits of an individual applicant's case.[12] However, this principle cuts both ways. A decision-maker will not commit a jurisdictional error under this ground by disappointing an applicant's expectation that the terms of a soft law instrument would be adhered to in all circumstances; nor is a jurisdictional error committed by the mere fact of having a policy or rule. Jurisdictional error is caused by a rule applied consistently but without regard to the merits of an individual case.[13]

[6] *Thamotharem v Canada* [2008] 1 FCR 385, [59].

[7] C Hilson, 'Policies and Fettering' [2002] *PL* 111. The terms 'rule' and 'policy' are often used interchangeably; see eg PP Craig, *Administrative Law*, 7th edn (London, Sweet and Maxwell, 2012) 542. They sometimes indicate a different level of flexibility; see eg M Aronson and M Groves, *Judicial Review of Administrative Action*, 5th edn (Sydney, Thompson Reuters, 2013) [5.270].

[8] See *British Oxygen Co Ltd v Ministry of Technology* [1971] AC 610, 625 (Lord Reid).

[9] Chapter 7.A.(i) of this volume below. See M Aronson and M Groves, *Judicial Review of Administrative Action*, 5th edn (Sydney, Thompson Reuters, 2013) [5.280].

[10] See P Cane and L McDonald, *Principles of Administrative Law*, 2nd edn (Melbourne, Oxford University Press, 2012) 144.

[11] M Aronson and M Groves, *Judicial Review of Administrative Action*, 5th edn (Sydney, Thompson Reuters, 2013) [5.260].

[12] *Green v Daniels* (1977) 13 ALR 1; *R v London County Council; ex parte Corrie* [1918] 1 KB 68.

[13] *R v Secretary of State for the Home Department; ex parte Venables* [1998] AC 407, 496–97 (Lord Browne-Wilkinson); *MLC Investments Ltd v Commissioner of Taxation* (2003) 137 FCR 288, 300–302 (Lindgren J).

There have been numerous cases which have recognised that soft law is necessary, particularly in relation to high-volume decision-making.[14] From such judicial acceptance, it follows that soft law must be *intra vires*, subject to the prohibition on fettering. Indeed, the tendency of decision-makers in high-volume areas, such as migration and social security, to fetter exercises of discretion according to publicly unavailable soft law instruments led to a legislative response.[15] This does not provide a bright-line test, since the entire point of soft law is that it will guide decision-makers into making decisions which are at least broadly consistent with each other. Brennan J dealt with this issue when he said that there is a balance which needs to be struck between ensuring that each case is decided on its merits and not giving the impression of arbitrariness by allowing different results in cases which are substantially alike.[16]

Aronson and Groves have suggested that the rule against fettering be modified:[17]

> If the courts were to acknowledge the intolerable pressures produced by prohibiting the fettering of discretions in agencies handling high-volume caseloads, they could modify the rule against fettering so as to allow the development of a requirement that discretionary powers be exercised consistently. In developing 'inconsistency' as a ground of judicial review, the courts could then explore the possibilities of giving more force to non-statutory guidelines.

This suggestion is persuasive, albeit not without difficulty since it challenges the 'judicial review mantra' that decisions ought to be based on the individual merits of each case.[18] Aronson and Groves pointed out that the prohibition on fettering is what prevents soft law from being treated in exactly the same way as hard law in court proceedings, but regarded it as being at odds with 'the requirement (in certain circumstances) that those deciding like cases should treat subjects consistently'.[19]

In some situations, consistency and the rule against fettering are in direct tension.[20] Take for example the case of *MLC Investments v Commissioner of Taxation*, in which the Commissioner's delegate had a broad statutory discretion to allow a company to end its accounting period on a date other than 30 June (the end of the Australian financial year) in any given year. The delegate treated as decisive two taxation rulings which had been issued by the Commissioner which severely curtailed this discretion to circumstances, inter alia, in which there was a 'substantial business need', where the change was not for mere administrative convenience or competitive advantage, or 'where the most exceptional circumstances exist'.[21]

[14] See M Aronson and M Groves, *Judicial Review of Administrative Action*, 5th edn (Sydney, Thompson Reuters, 2013) [3.250]–[3.290]; W Gummow, 'Rationality and Reasonableness as Grounds for Review' in D Mortimer (ed), *Administrative Justice and its Availability* (Sydney, Federation Press, 2015) 13, 18.

[15] Aronson and Groves, *Judicial Review of Administrative Action*, 5th edn (2013) [5.250]. See fns 87–88 in Chapter 4.B of this volume above.

[16] *Drake v Minister for Immigration and Ethnic Affairs* ('*Drake (No 2)*') (1979) 2 ALD 634, 639–40.

[17] M Aronson and M Groves, *Judicial Review of Administrative Action*, 5th edn (Sydney, Thompson Reuters, 2013) [3.280].

[18] See R Creyke and J McMillan, *Control of Government Action*, 3rd edn (Sydney, LexisNexis, 2012) 827.

[19] M Aronson and M Groves, *Judicial Review of Administrative Action*, 5th edn (Sydney, Thompson Reuters, 2013) [5.270].

[20] See ibid, [3.280] (fn 334), [5.270] (fn 115).

[21] *MLC Investments* (2003) 137 FCR 288, 295–97.

Lindgren J held that the delegate fell into error by purporting to make a decision which was consistent with current ATO policy rather than exercising the full discretion available to him under statute.[22] With respect, this decision must be correct; otherwise the Court would have been taken as applying the interpretation of the statute contained in the rulings rather than reaching its own view.[23]

However, there is nothing in this decision which would prevent courts from accepting *explicitly* that soft law, once issued, cannot simply be ignored. There is already plenty of implicit suggestion from courts that soft law must mean something.[24] To the extent that courts and tribunals are concerned that decision-makers ought not to look as though their decisions are made arbitrarily, this would be an important step, since failing to adhere to soft law issued by the public authority in which a decision-maker works looks very arbitrary indeed. The question then becomes in what way courts are able to enforce consideration of soft law. The weight of case law (discussed below) suggests that this is most likely to occur by viewing policies as mandatory, relevant considerations in some circumstances.

There are indications that, subject to limits, soft law can be a tool of statutory interpretation. In *Cheng*, Cowdroy J heard an appeal from members of a Chinese family who claimed that they were entitled to residence visas on the basis that they ran a business with an annual turnover over a certain threshold.[25] There was a dispute over the meaning of the word 'turnover', a term which appeared in the requirements for receiving a visa in Subclass 892 of Schedule 2 to the Migration Regulations 1991 (Cth) but was undefined by either the Migration Act 1958 or the Regulations. The MRT was called upon to construe a word which bore its ordinary English meaning, thereby making its construction a question of fact, provided its construction was within a reasonable 'either-way' margin.[26] In the course of its decision, the Migration Review Tribunal (MRT) referred to the Procedures Advice Manual (PAM3) of the Department of Immigration, which set out guidelines for the determination of visa applications and included guidance on the meaning of 'turnover'. The MRT found against the applicants. Its approach in doing so was upheld by the Federal Magistrate in review proceedings.

On appeal to Cowdroy J, the appellants submitted that the MRT erred in its construction of the word 'turnover' and that the PAM3 should not have been considered in preference to established authorities from English courts since it was not binding on the MRT. His Honour cited both *Drake (No 2)* and the statement of French and Drummond JJ in *Gray* that the 'proposition that government policy cannot bind the [MRT] does not imply that the policy can be ignored'.[27] Cowdroy J held that the MRT had a discretionary power to seek out a construction of 'turnover' that would

[22] Here in relation to ADJR Act 1977 (Cth) s 5(2)(f). The result would have been the same at common law.

[23] See *Corporation of the City of Enfield v Development Assessment Comission* (2000) 199 CLR 135, 151–54.

[24] See eg *Plaintiff M61/2010E v Commonwealth* ('*Offshore Processing Case*') (2010) 243 CLR 319.

[25] *Cheng v Minister for Immigration and Citizenship* (2013) 213 FCR 362.

[26] *Collector of Customs v Agfa-Geveart Ltd* (1996) 186 CLR 389, 395. See M Aronson and M Groves, *Judicial Review of Administrative Action*, 5th edn (Sydney, Thompson Reuters, 2013) [4.260].

[27] *Minister for Immigration, Local Government and Ethnic Affairs v Gray* (1994) 50 FCR 189, 206.

be consistent with other cases.[28] It was therefore permissible for the MRT to be *guided* by the relevant soft law (PAM3), provided that the MRT did not allow the soft law to *dictate* the outcome of the hearing.

The rule against fettering administrative discretion is not demanding, even on decision-makers in high-volume areas of government. All that it requires is that a decision-maker have regard to the merits of each individual case rather than applying a soft law exegesis of his or her statutory discretion mechanically.[29] As Deane J noted, while consistency in decision-making is generally desirable, it is an ingredient, rather than a hallmark, of justice.[30] Where a statutory discretion is the subject of soft law, exercises of that discretion will largely be consistent with each other. The rule against fettering requires no more than that the elegance of this consistency be put aside where justice so demands.[31]

The 'no fettering' rule does not provide any protection to the party whose concern is that a public authority *has not* adhered to a soft law instrument in exercising a discretion; indeed, where the relevant body is not sufficiently 'public', an applicant may struggle to prove that the matter is justiciable in the first place.[32] Aside from circumstances creating an obligation to provide procedural fairness before the terms of a soft law instrument are departed from, the existence of soft law is all but legally irrelevant.[33] The suggestion from Aronson and Groves that courts 'explore the possibilities of giving more force to non-statutory guidelines' is interesting in as much as it foreshadows the possibility that soft law may be required to adhere to the presumption that it either applies symmetrically or not at all.[34] Once one recognises exceptions to the prohibition on fettering, then there is room for consistency to operate as more than just a procedural restraint.

It is unclear exactly how a court would bring about this end. The *British Oxygen* formulation of the 'no fettering' rule only purports to handle the tension between the competing needs for decision-making to be both flexible and consistent. Aronson and Groves were critical of this position:[35]

> Any requirement for consistency must limit the requirement that each case be decided on its individual merits. Indeed, that concern touches on a large debate as to the style of the rules or policies themselves. If one conceives for the moment of 'rules' as being rigid, and 'policies' as being flexible, it should be obvious that some situations call for rules, some for policies, and some for neither. And yet the current law as traditionally expounded allows for policies to shape the application of discretionary power, provided they are flexible, without indicating the degree of requisite flexibility.

[28] *Cheng* (2013) 213 FCR 362, 367.

[29] See *British Oxygen* [1971] AC 610; cf M Aronson and M Groves, *Judicial Review of Administrative Action*, 5th edn (2013) [5.240]–[5.330].

[30] *Nevistic v Minister for Immigration and Ethnic Affairs* (1981) 51 FLR 325, 334 (Deane J). See also *Drake* (1979) 46 FLR 409, 420–21 (Bowen CJ & Deane J).

[31] See *Drake (No 2)* (1979) 2 ALD 634, 639.

[32] See eg *Jackson v Bitar* [2011] VSC 11; *Cameron v Hogan* (1934) 51 CLR 358.

[33] cf PP Craig, *Administrative Law*, 7th edn (London, Sweet and Maxwell, 2012) 545–47.

[34] M Aronson and M Groves, *Judicial Review of Administrative Action*, 5th edn (Sydney, Thompson Reuters, 2013) [3.280].

[35] ibid, [5.270].

The tenuous current place of consistency in judicial review is an aspect of *Wednesbury* unreasonableness.[36] That fact necessarily calls to attention the fact that the *Wednesbury* ground has very rarely been argued with success in Australia. Another way of giving greater substance to soft law may be to interpret each soft law instrument as an implied undertaking that the public authority who issued it undertakes to be bound by its terms unless or until the instrument is terminated. Yet another may be to give no evidentiary weight to any soft law instrument which does not apply symmetrically. What is clear is that it is difficult to create a solution in legal terms where the very potency of soft law comes from the fact that it is treated by so many individuals as having legal effect although it does not. It may be that the best response simply does not lie within the purview of the courts.[37]

(ii) **Procedural Fairness**

Procedural fairness may offer the best opportunity of subjecting decisions made subject to a soft law scheme to judicial review, since '[i]t is trite law that promises and undertakings can generate obligations to observe the rules of natural justice'.[38] Soft law may create procedural obligations on the part of bodies which use it as a regulatory tool, although Australian courts will not give substantive effect to legitimate expectations which are generated by representations made in soft law instruments.[39]

Procedural obligations will most obviously be created where there has been a specific representation that the terms of a soft law instrument will be applied to a particular case. For example, consider a public authority which has the statutory power to grant a licence. Through soft law, it lists a series of requirements which need to be met by every licence application, amounting to a representation as to how the decision-maker will exercise his or her discretion.[40] It then states that it will grant a licence to every 'complying application'. If a person makes an application which meets all the requirements for obtaining a licence which are contained in the soft law instrument (and therefore 'complies'), then s/he has at least a legitimate expectation that s/he will be heard before any decision is made not to grant the licence.[41]

In Australia, even the procedural consequences of such a legitimate expectation are quite limited. *Lam* stands as authority for the proposition that the authority with the power to grant the licence could satisfy the requirements of procedural fairness by either publicly withdrawing the soft law instrument or warning individuals that they ought not to rely on it. Indeed, Gleeson CJ stated explicitly that, in order for a

[36] See eg *Sunshine Coast Broadcasters Ltd v Duncan* (1988) 83 ALR 121, 131–32 (Pincus J).

[37] See J McMillan, 'Re-thinking the Separation of Powers' (2010) 38 *Federal Law Review* 423. This issue is explored at length in Part III.

[38] M Aronson and M Groves, *Judicial Review of Administrative Action*, 5th edn (Sydney, Thompson Reuters, 2013) [3.260]. See *Haoucher v Minister for Immigration and Ethnic Affairs* (1990) 169 CLR 648; *Re Minister for Immigration and Multicultural Affairs, ex parte Lam* (2003) 214 CLR 1.

[39] See Chapter 7 below.

[40] See M Aronson and M Groves, *Judicial Review of Administrative Action*, 5th edn (Sydney, Thompson Reuters, 2013) [7.200].

[41] *Gerah Imports Pty Ltd v Minister for Industry, Technology and Commerce* (1987) 17 FCR 1.

judicial review remedy to be available for breaching the requirements of procedural fairness, 'what must be demonstrated is unfairness, not merely departure from a representation'.[42] This was an opinion with which the rest of the Court concurred, each identifying the lack of detrimental reliance on the part of Mr Lam as indicating that procedural fairness had been satisfied.[43] In other words, substantive unfairness may be relevant to judicial review in Australian courts, although the remedy is only ever procedural and never substantive.

It will not, however, arise merely from the failure to adhere to a stated procedure where the breach was immaterial. Gleeson CJ stated expressly that:[44]

> the content of the requirements of fairness may be affected by what is said or done during the process of decision-making, and by developments in the course of that process, including representations made as to the procedure to be followed.

Mr Lam *had* suffered a breach of procedural fairness (by not having been warned that the decision-maker responsible for cancelling his visa no longer proposed to seek comment from the woman who was caring for his children as to the effect of the cancellation on them), but it was accepted that he had lost nothing as a result of that breach because she had already given her statement to the authorities and would not have said anything different or new had they approached her again. Common law judicial review does not require that remedies be provided where to do so would be futile.[45] This is to be contrasted with the situation where the content of the procedural fairness hearing rule is determined entirely by statute.[46]

Lam had the effect of inhibiting the use to which the concept of legitimate expectations can be put in Australian judicial review, but judicial review of representations or policy statements made by public authorities need not rely on that concept.[47] One case in which a public authority was held to its own soft law guidelines was *Applicants M16*, in which Gray J considered 'gender guidelines' (draft guidelines issued by the respondent Minister for dealing with gender-related claims by asylum seekers).[48] His Honour found a want of procedural fairness in the failure of the Refugee Review Tribunal (RRT) to apply the gender guidelines in the case of a female Tamil asylum-seeker from Sri Lanka who had suffered a brutal assault while pregnant.[49] She had indicated unequivocally that she was prepared to discuss these

[42] *Lam* (2003) 214 CLR 1, 12.
[43] ibid, 34 (McHugh & Gummow JJ); 35–36 (Hayne J); 48–49 (Callinan J).
[44] ibid, 12.
[45] *Stead v State Government Insurance Commission* (1986) 161 CLR 141, 145.
[46] See *SAAP v Minister for Immigration and Multicultural and Indigenous Affairs* (2005) 228 CLR 294; G Weeks, 'Expanding Role of Process' (2008) 15 *Australian Journal of Administrative Law* 100, 105.
[47] *Darling Casino Ltd v NSW Casino Control Authority* (1997) 191 CLR 602, 609 (Brennan CJ, Dawson & Toohey JJ). See eg *Applicant NAFF of 2002 v Minister for Immigration and Multicultural and Indigenous Affairs* (2004) 221 CLR 1; *Stewart v Deputy Commissioner of Taxation* (2011) 194 FCR 194, 203. See also M Aronson and M Groves, *Judicial Review of Administrative Action*, 5th edn (Sydney, Thompson Reuters, 2013) [7.200].
[48] *Applicants M16 of 2004 v Minister for Immigration and Multicultural and Indigenous Affairs* (2005) 148 FCR 46; applied in *MZXFJ v Minister for Immigration and Multicultural Affairs* [2006] FMCA 1465. See also *Khawar v Minister for Immigration and Multicultural Affairs* (1999) 168 ALR 190, 199.
[49] *Applicants M16* (2005) 148 FCR 46, 50–51.

aspects of her case only with a female case officer.[50] The gender guidelines had been put in place in order to ensure a 'sensitive and fair process' for persons who claimed refugee status based on 'gender-related claims' and recognised the specific difficulties faced by female asylum-seekers, particularly those who had been subjected to sexual violence.[51] Gray J hinted that the procedural safeguards implemented by the gender guidelines may in any case have been required as a matter of common law since:[52]

> [t]he willingness, and often the very ability, of people to talk about their experiences are affected by what are described as 'gender issues', and by cultural norms. This is now so well understood that it hardly seems necessary to state it.

The gender guidelines supplemented the common law hearing rule of procedural fairness by establishing appropriate procedures for women to argue their claims for refugee status in circumstances where they may face 'social and cultural barriers' to articulating the details of those claims.

The failure of the RRT to follow the gender guidelines was a breach of the requirements of procedural fairness only in as much as it resulted in the RRT failing to give the first applicant a proper hearing.[53] This is to say that the gender guidelines did not assume the status of a hard legal requirement. They merely indicated what steps needed to be taken to lead to a procedurally fair outcome. Gray J was not prepared to accept on the facts, as the High Court had in *Lam*, that the breach of procedural fairness had had no substantive effect.[54] The RRT had therefore been obliged to follow the gender guidelines unless it had previously warned the first applicant that it would not do so (which would be most unlikely in circumstances where the gender guidelines were issued by the Minister). It is important to realise that courts have held that no reviewable error follows from the failure to consider other guidelines relating to refugee hearings.[55]

The effect of *Lam* can be seen in *Stewart v Deputy Commissioner of Taxation*, in which Perram J considered seizure of documents relating to the taxation affairs of the second and third applicants (Mr Hogan and Mr Cornell) and their accountant (Mr Stewart) by the Australian Crime Commission (ACC) under a compulsory statutory process.[56] The ACC subsequently provided the documents to the Australian Tax Office (ATO), which decided to allow the documents relevant to the respective applicants to be seen by the ATO officers who were auditing each applicant. These decisions were made in circumstances where the Commissioner of Taxation had publicly issued *Guidelines to Accessing Professional Accounting Advisors' Papers* (the Guidelines) which applied to Mr Stewart and Mr Cornell (but not, as Perram J ultimately held, to Mr Hogan).[57] The Guidelines stated that advices prepared for taxpayers by their accountants should 'in all but exceptional circumstances' remain

[50] ibid, 51.
[51] ibid, 56.
[52] ibid, 56.
[53] See also *Stewart v DCT* (2011) 194 FCR 194, 208; cf *R (BAPIO Action Limited) v Secretary of State for the Home Department* [2008] 1 AC 1003.
[54] *Applicants M16* (2005) 148 FCR 46, 60.
[55] *SZTGV v Minister for Immigration and Border Protection* (2015) 229 FCR 90, 112–13.
[56] *Stewart v DCT* (2011) 194 FCR 194.
[57] ibid, 212.

confidential, and set out how such circumstances were to be identified. They included, relevantly, that there was a scheme or arrangement within the meaning of Part IVA of the Income Tax Assessment Act 1936 (the Act's anti-avoidance provisions) or that there were reasonable grounds to believe that fraud or evasion had taken place. Mr Stewart and Mr Cornell alleged that they were denied procedural fairness because the Guidelines were misapplied by the ATO. This argument was rejected by Perram J on the facts in relation to Mr Cornell:[58]

> [I]t is clear that … [the second respondent] had twice called for submissions on whether there were exceptional circumstances by reason of a Part IVA scheme or the existence of reasonable grounds to suspect fraud or evasion. Further, Mr Cornell had, in fact, made submissions about those issues.
>
> It was in that context that [the second respondent] then made the decision to allow access to the documents … He concluded that there were exceptional circumstances justifying access. I do not see how this could be procedurally unfair. Submissions were called for on whether there were exceptional circumstances and Mr Cornell's particular attention was twice drawn to the fact that [the second respondent] was considering whether such circumstances existed by reason of a Part IVA scheme or fraud or evasion. Mr Cornell made submissions on that issue. [The second respondent] did not accept them. There was no procedural unfairness.

His Honour applied the same reasoning to Mr Stewart.[59] By contrast, he found that the ATO had not represented to Mr Hogan's solicitors that the Guidelines applied to their client.[60] This was because, although a decision was made to give them access, the audit teams had not seen the documents in the case of Mr Stewart and Mr Cornell. In Mr Hogan's case, however, 'the audit team had already had access to the documents and the decision in his case was, in effect, that there was no reason to change that state of affairs'.[61] The Guidelines were not capable of applying to a situation in which a third party already had possession of the disputed documents, even if that circumstance arose as a result of some compulsory process.[62] That put Mr Hogan in a different position to the other applicants because the ATO team conducting the audit of his affairs had already obtained access to the documents to which the Guidelines might otherwise have applied.

The ATO took the view that Mr Hogan had waived the benefit of the Guidelines because his solicitors had asked the ATO to 'obtain all documentation relating to Mr Hogan from the ACC'.[63] Perram J rightly considered that failing to apply the Guidelines without first giving Mr Hogan an opportunity to be heard on that course of action would have been a breach of procedural fairness, if the Guidelines in fact applied to Mr Hogan. If they had not, 'there was nothing procedurally unfair about departing from the [Guidelines] because there was nothing within them from which

[58] ibid, 201.
[59] ibid, 207.
[60] ibid, 207–8.
[61] ibid, 196.
[62] ibid, 211.
[63] ibid, 208.

it was possible to depart (their having no application)'.[64] His Honour's interpretation of the Guidelines was that they could not apply to documents held by third parties, such as the ACC.[65] The point is that, even if they did apply to him, the fullest extent to which Mr Hogan could ever have compelled the ATO to adhere to the Guidelines was to allow him to be heard before deciding not to apply them. The rights which are provided by procedural fairness in relation to soft law are limited indeed.

(iii) Mandatory and Forbidden Considerations

The prohibition on taking account of irrelevant and forbidden considerations is a ground of review that is unlikely to affect cases involving soft law. It would be most unusual for a court to construe legislation such that certain material was *forbidden* from consideration because of a soft law instrument to which the legislation itself did not refer.

Review for failing to take into account a mandatory relevant consideration has been substantially discussed above in regard to *Khan*.[66] In *Peko-Wallsend*, the High Court extended the process of statutory interpretation involved in determining the issues mandatory for consideration by the decision-maker beyond the express terms of the Act to implications which could justifiably be drawn from them.[67] There is no reason why *Peko-Wallsend*'s logic cannot be applied symmetrically, although not every implication will be justifiably able to be drawn from legislative instruments such that it would make the terms of a soft law instrument binding upon a decision-maker.[68] If, as the High Court held in *Peko-Wallsend*, there is a requirement on a decision-maker to consider the case that an applicant brings to the table, why ought the decision-maker not also be required to take account of what s/he brings to the table (such as any applicable soft law)?

Subsequent to *Peko-Wallsend*, Davies J stated that:[69]

> even if non-statutory rules do not, of themselves, have binding effect, the failure of a decision-maker to have regard to them or his failure to interpret them correctly may amount to an error of law justifying an order of judicial review.

Courts have been prepared to view decisions involving disregard or misconstruction of soft law as judicially reviewable on the basis that the decision-maker has failed to take account of a mandatory relevant consideration.[70] This may particularly be

[64] ibid.

[65] ibid, 209–11.

[66] *Khan* (2011) 192 FCR 173. See the text accompanying Chapter 5.D.(ii) above.

[67] *Minister for Aboriginal Affairs v Peko-Wallsend Ltd* (1986) 162 CLR 24, 39–40 (Mason J). See M Aronson and M Groves, *Judicial Review of Administrative Action*, 5th edn (Sydney, Thompson Reuters, 2013) [5.40].

[68] See *Dunkerley v Comcare* (2012) 58 AAR 287; cf *Attorney General of New South Wales v Chiew Seng Liew* [2012] NSWSC 1223, [71].

[69] *Gerah Imports* (1987) 17 FCR 1, 15.

[70] *Holden Ltd v Chief Executive Officer of Customs* (2005) 141 FCR 571, 583; cf *Minister for Immigration and Ethnic Affairs v Conyngham* (1986) 11 FCR 528.

so where there is an available inference that a discretion is to be guided by soft law. French J commented:[71]

> Where the parliament has conferred wide discretions on an official decision-maker, particularly in relation to high-volume decision-making, it is entirely consistent with the legislative intention in conferring such a discretion that its exercise will be guided by administrative policies. Indeed, it may be inferred that the creation of such policies is contemplated by the legislature when it confers such discretions.

Such an inference may be drawn either as a matter of statutory interpretation or by evidence of a:[72]

> commitment on the part of the [decision-maker] to a particular approach to the law in those cases to which [the relevant soft law] applies … [which] will necessarily be qualified by the extent to which the [soft law] itself embodies qualifications and conditions in its own terms.

The Full Federal Court had previously commented that a public ruling issued by the Federal Commissioner of Taxation 'operates as if it is the *statutory* basis upon which tax is to be levied. No question arises as to whether it is or is not relied upon' (emphasis added).[73] A 'commitment' of the type to which French J referred must, of course, fall short of fettering or estoppel.[74] It is therefore difficult to know exactly what kind of commitment his Honour had in mind.

The high-water mark of judicial acceptance that sufficiently serious misconstruction of soft law could amount to jurisdictional error came in *Gray*. In that case, French and Drummond JJ stated (over a dissenting judgment by Neaves J) that Ministerial policy statements regarding deportation of non-citizens convicted of criminal offences 'were relevant factors which the [decision-maker] was *bound to consider* although not bound to apply so as to prejudice its independent assessment of the merits of the case' (emphasis added).[75] Their Honours had previously stated that:[76]

> where the existence and content of such a policy is to be regarded as a relevant fact which the Tribunal is bound to consider, a serious misconstruction of its terms or misunderstanding of its purposes in the course of decision-making may constitute a failure to take into account a relevant factor and for that reason may result in an improper exercise of the statutory power. If a decision-maker, not bound to apply policy, purports to apply it as a proper basis for disposing of the case in hand but misconstrues or misunderstands it so that what is applied is not the policy but something else, then there may be reviewable error.

[71] *BHP Billiton Direct Reduced Iron Pty Ltd v Duffus, Deputy Commissioner of Taxation* (2007) 99 ALD 149, 171 (French J).
[72] ibid, 171.
[73] *Bellinz v Commissioner of Taxation* (1998) 84 FCR 154, 169.
[74] See Chapter 8 of this volume below.
[75] *Minister of State for Immigration, Local Government and Ethnic Affairs v Gray* (1994) 50 FCR 189, 211.
[76] ibid, 208.

Aronson and Groves suggested that subsequent Federal Court authority may require that *Gray* be reconsidered.[77] For example, in *AB*, Tracey J said that the passage quoted above:[78]

> cannot be understood as supporting an unqualified proposition that an error in construing and applying a policy or an unincorporated treaty, which the decision-maker is not bound to apply, will amount to jurisdictional error. This will only be so if the misconstruction is 'serious' such that 'what is applied is not the policy but something else'. Moreover, their Honours' reasoning assumes that the tribunal was bound to give consideration to the ministerial policy.

These comments, although consistent with what was said by French and Drummond JJ in *Gray*, draw attention to the fact that it remains unclear what their Honours conceived of being a 'serious' misconstruction of a policy. It appears that a 'serious' misconstruction is one which results in jurisdictional error, although this is unhelpful in as much as it states a conclusion rather than a test by which that conclusion may be reached.[79] While it is now widely accepted that the term 'jurisdictional error' is no worse for being conclusory, some have resiled from that view.[80] Tracey J was prepared to distinguish *Gray* in order to find that an international treaty which had not been incorporated into Australian domestic legislation could not form the basis of a mandatory relevant consideration.[81] French J had himself reached the same conclusion in an earlier case.[82] This departure from *Gray* is explicable, particularly after the High Court in *Lam* rejected much of the reasoning underlying *Teoh* as relying on the difference between, on one hand, a treaty of which a decision-maker is able but not obliged to take note and, on the other hand, soft law which amounts to a representation, binding on the decision-maker at least to consider, if not to apply.[83] Indeed, Taggart commented that the Court in *Lam* had 'done about as much as judges can by way of *obiter dicta* in a case where the point was not argued to overrule' *Teoh*.[84] However, the precedent value of *Teoh* and *Lam* must now be understood in light of the High Court's view that 'seriously considered dicta of a majority of this Court' ought not to be overruled by intermediate appellate courts.[85]

Treaties and soft law are both non-statutory and courts will not elevate obligations assumed under either type of instrument above 'hard' domestic law.[86] There must, however, be a difference between the many hundreds of treaties to which

[77] M Aronson and M Groves, *Judicial Review of Administrative Action*, 5th edn (Sydney, Thompson Reuters, 2013) [3.270].

[78] *AB v Minister for Immigration and Citizenship* (2007) 96 ALD 53, 62.

[79] See M Aronson, 'Jurisdictional Error and Beyond' in M Groves (ed), *Modern Administrative Law in Australia: Concepts and Context* (Melbourne, Cambridge University Press, 2014), 248.

[80] See eg J Basten, 'Judicial Review of Executive Action: Tiers of Scrutiny or Tears of Frustration?' in N Williams (ed), *Key Issues in Judicial Review* (Sydney, Federation Press, 2014) 35, 41–42.

[81] *AB* (2007) 96 ALD 53, 63.

[82] *Le v Minister for Immigration and Multicultural and Indigenous Affairs* [2004] FCA 875, [61]–[66].

[83] See *Minister of State for Immigration and Ethnic Affairs v Teoh* (1995) 183 CLR 273; *Lam* (2003) 214 CLR 1.

[84] M Taggart, '"Australian Exceptionalism" in Judicial Review' (2008) 36 *Federal Law Review* 1, 17.

[85] *Farah Constructions Pty Ltd v Say-Dee Pty Ltd* (2007) 230 CLR 89, 151.

[86] Regarding treaties, see *CPCF v Minister for Immigration and Border Protection* (2015) 89 ALJR 207, 219 (French CJ); 229 (Hayne & Bell JJ); 273 (Gageler J); 286 (Keane J).

Australia is party and policies and guidelines issued by the same public authority which is then to make a decision to which that soft law applies. In other words, it is the creation of the soft law by the public authority which makes it assume importance in comparison to the enormous wealth of treaties to which Australia is party but the bulk of which will be unfamiliar to individual decision-makers.[87]

The possibilities for giving greater application to soft law by presuming that it amounts to a mandatory relevant consideration may be easier to achieve than any attempt to do away with the prohibition of fettering. On the other hand, and as I will discuss below, this would be a process which would serve to exacerbate the damage that has already been done to the doctrine of relevant considerations as an exercise in statutory construction. An (overly) expansive interpretation of what constitutes, or can be inferred from the governing statute to be, a mandatory consideration has a long history, going back at least to *Peko-Wallsend* itself. Although it was found as a fact in that case that Peko had not intended to mislead the Aboriginal Land Commissioner, the High Court's conclusion that the appellant Minister was obliged to consider the 'most recent and accurate information … at hand' in effect made a mockery of the process of public consultation that had preceded the Commissioner's recommendation to the Minister that land be granted to Aborigines. This was because Peko only revealed important information about the location of certain valuable uranium deposits after the Commissioner had reported, which had earlier led the Full Federal Court to characterise Peko's evidence as 'vague, inaccurate and misleading'.[88] How can the implied mandatory consideration of the most recent information be reconciled with the statutory powers and duties of the Commissioner when the result is that Peko was allowed to withhold evidence to be presented to the Minister alone?[89]

There are significant potential pitfalls to inferring that soft law constitutes a mandatory consideration, a point that may be illustrated by reference to two cases.[90] In *Nikac*, Wilcox J considered applications from three persons who were not citizens of Australia and who had committed certain criminal acts. The respondent Minister's predecessor in office (Mr Mick Young) decided that they should be deported, against the advice of the AAT. The government had a Criminal Deportation Policy which had been tabled in the Commonwealth Parliament and which said, at paragraph 4, that the Minister ought to overturn recommendations of the AAT in respect of deporting criminals 'only in exceptional circumstances and only when strong evidence can be produced to justify the decision'.[91] Wilcox J noted that the Minister's understanding of the word 'exceptional' owed much to the interpretive techniques of Humpty Dumpty: 'When I use a word, it means just what I choose it

[87] See *Teoh* (1995) 183 CLR 273, 316 (McHugh J); *Project Blue Sky Inc v Australian Broadcasting Authority* (1998) 194 CLR 355, 392 (McHugh, Gummow, Kirby & Hayne JJ).

[88] *Peko-Wallsend* (1986) 162 CLR 24, 34 (Mason J); see *Peko-Wallsend Ltd v Minister for Aboriginal Affairs* (1985) 5 FCR 532, 542 (Bowen CJ); 553 (Sheppard J); 566–69 (Wilcox J).

[89] See M Aronson and M Groves, *Judicial Review of Administrative Action*, 5th edn (Sydney, Thompson Reuters, 2013) [5.100].

[90] *Nikac v Minister for Immigration, Local Government and Ethnic Affairs* (1988) 20 FCR 65; *Re Tracey* (2011) 80 NSWLR 261.

[91] *Nikac* (1988) 20 FCR 65, 70.

to mean—neither more nor less'.[92] His Honour conceded however that the Minister was 'not bound by the terms of para 4 of the Criminal Deportation Policy, in the sense that he [was] free to depart from that policy if he [saw] fit'.[93] Nor could the Minister's misconstruction of the policy have amounted to jurisdictional error.[94] This finding has since been approved on the basis that '[w]here the instrument concerned is an unincorporated international treaty which is subject to interpretation by a potentially wide range of international bodies it will be harder to make good an allegation of error much less jurisdictional error'.[95] In any event, the Minister had considered the terms of the Criminal Deportation Policy and this was determinative of the first two applicants' cases.

The third applicant (Mr Sorenson) was a convicted murderer. However, unlike the first two applicants, who had been born in Yugoslavia and Turkey respectively, he had been born in Scotland and the Migration Act 1958 had only recently been amended (with effect from 1984) to allow for the deportation of a British subject in Mr Sorenson's circumstances. But for that legislative change, he could not have been deported. At the time that the Act was amended, the then Minister had approved the following policy recommendation, described in *Nikac* as the 'Transition Policy':[96]

> It is recommended that as a general policy the following persons not be considered for criminal deportation under section 12 of the Migration Amendment Act 1983:
>
> Non-citizens convicted of offences committed prior to the date of proclamation of the amended Act and who, although liable for deportation under the amended Act are not liable under present legislation [as it stood prior to amendment]; but excluding cases which come to notice involving very serious crimes and/or where special circumstances exist which warrant your personal consideration.

Minister Young did not take the Transition Policy into account in exercising his discretion to deport Mr Sorenson. Wilcox J held that this failure 'vitiated the Minister's decision' because:[97]

> Although a non-statutory policy is not binding upon a decision-maker, in the sense that he or she may decide in the particular case not to act in accordance with that policy, a policy applicable to the case is *always a relevant consideration* in the making of a decision (emphasis added).

This is, on the face of it, an odd conclusion. Wilcox J did not indicate the basis for his finding that the Transition Policy was a consideration that the Minister was bound to take into account other than to say that the Transition Policy was

[92] Lewis Carroll, *Alice Through the Looking Glass*, cited at *Nikac* (1988) 20 FCR 65, 77. The most notorious use of this quotation was in *Liversidge v Sir John Anderson* [1942] AC 206, 245 (Lord Atkin). See K Barlow SC, 'Alice, Humpty Dumpty and the Law' (2011) 85 *Australian Law Journal* 365, 366–68; K Mason, *Lawyers Then and Now: An Australian Legal Miscellany* (Sydney, Federation Press, 2012) 188, 200–201.

[93] *Nikac* (1988) 20 FCR 65, 78.

[94] ibid, 77–78.

[95] *AB* (2007) 96 ALD 53, 63.

[96] *Nikac* (1988) 20 FCR 65, 75.

[97] ibid, 81.

'directly applicable'. His Honour accepted that the Minister could revoke the Transition Policy 'at any time' but stated that it seemed:[98]

> likely that any Minister with a sense of fairness, confronted with this policy and considering its rationale, would have been extremely reluctant to deport Mr Sorensen for offences committed by him before the amendments took effect.

I disagree with his Honour's reasoning. It cannot be right to say that, simply because a court finds that a Minister would likely have decided to exercise a discretion differently had s/he considered a policy, therefore consideration of that policy was mandatory. Unless the requirement to take account of a policy appears on the face of, or could justifiably be implied from, applicable legislation, the conclusion drawn by Wilcox J was irrelevant.[99] His Honour's reasoning did not provide any principled basis for reaching the conclusion that a *directly applicable* policy is therefore a mandatory consideration.

More recently, in *Re Tracey*, Spigelman CJ found that the trial judge in the District Court had fallen into jurisdictional error by failing to treat the United Nations Convention on the Rights of the Child 1989 (CROC) as 'capable of being relevant to the exercise of the discretion to make the relevant order sought by the appellant'.[100] Specifically, the trial judge had said that the CROC was irrelevant to the matter before her, in which sense it is clear that she did not see CROC as being a mandatory (as opposed to relevant) consideration. One might therefore conclude that her use of the word 'irrelevant' was an expression of this finding: the CROC was simply *other than mandatory*. However, Spigelman CJ 'identif[ied] error on the part of the primary judge in rejecting as impermissible (or prohibited) reliance upon any provision of the [CROC] ... [since] reliance on provisions in the [CROC] might be permissible in particular circumstances'.[101] Such a result is a further example of the confusion caused by using the terms 'relevant' and 'irrelevant' in relation to grounds of review which have no connection to those terms as they are used by people other than administrative lawyers.[102]

Spigelman CJ expressly denied that the Court had been presented with any evidence which compelled the conclusion that the relevant legislation included 'obligations' under the CROC.[103] Indeed, his Honour cited French J's statement that the 'provisions of an international treaty to which Australia is a party may be a relevant consideration in the exercise of statutory discretions. Such considerations do not thereby become mandatory'.[104] Basten JA thought it unlikely, in these circumstances, that Spigelman CJ had used the term 'relevant consideration' in its usual sense of

[98] ibid, 82.

[99] See *Peko-Wallsend* (1986) 162 CLR 24, 39–40 (Mason J).

[100] *Re Tracey* (2011) 80 NSWLR 261, 272 (Beazley JA agreeing; Giles JA declining to decide this point).

[101] *Re Henry; JL v Secretary, Department of Family and Community Services* [2015] NSWCA 89, [266] (Basten JA).

[102] See M Aronson and M Groves, *Judicial Review of Administrative Action*, 5th edn (Sydney, Thompson Reuters, 2013) [5.20]; G Weeks, 'Holding Government to its Word' in M Groves (ed), *Modern Administrative Law in Australia* (Melbourne, Cambridge University Press, 2014) 224, 228.

[103] *Re Tracey* (2011) 80 NSWLR 261, 267.

[104] *Le* [2004] FCA 875, [59] (citation omitted).

'mandatory consideration'.[105] Spigelman CJ's statement that the CROC was at least relevant to the exercise of a statutory discretion, because the applicable legislation had been drafted to reflect provisions of the CROC, therefore supported the finding that the trial judge had committed a jurisdictional error by stating that the CROC was an *irrelevant* consideration (in the sense that it was forbidden).[106]

Certainly, not every failure to refer to the CROC will attract a judicial review remedy.[107] The effect of the Chief Justice's reasoning therefore seems to be that there is a difference between a decision-maker forgetting something which s/he is under no obligation to remember on one hand and, on the other, making the incorrect statement that s/he is *not allowed* to take that thing into account. If consideration of the CROC was not mandatory, it follows from the approach of Spigelman CJ that the trial judge would not have fallen into jurisdictional error by ignoring the CROC but *would* do so by stating explicitly that the CROC was 'irrelevant'. Subsequent cases have seemed to limit the applicability of *Re Tracey* to circumstances in which the trial judge has 'explicitly' made a 'positive statement' that the CROC is irrelevant.[108] Likewise, a trial judge does not fall into jurisdictional error by not considering the CROC if it has not been raised by the parties.[109]

Re Tracey remains a worrisome case in the sense that it contains slippage between consideration of the CROC being mandatory in the sense expressed by Mason J in *Peko-Wallsend* and being merely 'permissible', with its provisions '*capable* of being relevant to the exercise' of the statutory discretion exercised by the trial judge (emphasis added).[110] The former approach would continue the tendency of judges to declare certain issues to be mandatory considerations ex post facto, based on requirements inferred from legislation rather than stated explicitly in its terms. Such inferences may involve a greater or lesser degree of alchemy. Basten JA drew attention to this issue, and also warned that:[111]

> The fact that Australia has entered into an international convention on a particular subject is not, of itself, likely to be relevant. Rather, relevance must derive from the particular provisions of the convention which may be relied upon in the circumstances of the particular case. If provisions add nothing to domestic law, it is unlikely that they will be material to the outcome in the domestic court. If the provisions are inconsistent with domestic law, they should be disregarded. Between those positions, it is possible that the provisions of a convention may affect the weight to be given to a permissible (or even a mandatory) consideration under domestic law; they may also assist in construing domestic law.

[105] *Re Henry; JL v Department of Family and Community Services* [2015] NSWCA 89, [266].

[106] *Re Tracey* (2011) 80 NSWLR 261, 268–70. It is arguable that the trial judge had, at worst, made an error of law within jurisdiction: see ibid, 272 (Giles JA). An order in the nature of certiorari would regardless have been available to remedy an error of law on the face of the record, which includes the reasons of a District Court judge: Supreme Court Act 1970 (NSW) s 69(4).

[107] *Re Henry* [2015] NSWCA 89, [217] (McColl JA).

[108] ibid, [265] (Basten JA); *Re Kerry (No 2)* [2012] NSWCA 127, [36] (Barrett JA). See *Re Tracey* (2011) 80 NSWLR 261, 268–69.

[109] *JL v Secretary, Department of Family and Community Services* [2015] NSWCA 88, [188] (McColl JA).

[110] *Re Tracey* (2011) 80 NSWLR 261, 267; 272.

[111] *Re Henry* [2015] NSWCA 89, [266]–[267].

Such an approach must be correct, since it connects the relevance of an instrument such as the CROC to domestic legislation. To the extent that the principle of relevant considerations in Australian administrative law is taken to have been expressed by Mason J in *Peko-Wallsend*, the interpretation of domestic legislation is essential to any finding that consideration of a convention is mandatory.

Given the prevalence of such an inclusive approach to what constitutes a mandatory consideration, development of this ground of review to compel decision-makers to take account of their own soft law or policies is not, on the face of it, too much to ask. No issue arises as to the separation of powers, since applicable soft law would regardless need to be consistent with any relevant statute.[112] In any case, mandatory considerations require only 'proper, genuine and realistic consideration', not a substantive result.[113] An extension of this ground to cover soft law could mean that the certainty of the current ground of review is reduced, since the practical issue will be whether a given instrument is sufficiently 'law-like' to compel consideration by a decision-maker. I suggest that this will usually be an issue determinable on the facts of each case.

Basten JA noted, in a passage quoted with evident approval by a unanimous High Court, that the language of 'proper, genuine and realistic consideration' calls for a proper consideration of 'the merits of the case'.[114] His Honour warned that:[115]

> Taken out of context and without understanding their original provenance, these epithets are apt to encourage a slide into impermissible merit review. If it is demonstrated in a particular case that an administrative decision-maker has failed to address a claim properly made, or has failed to identify the statutory power under which the claim should properly be disposed of, there will be a constructive failure to exercise jurisdiction. Relief will be available accordingly. Thus, 'to fail to respond to a substantial, clearly articulated argument relying on established facts was at least to fail to accord [the applicant] natural justice'. Where a decision-maker does address the claim, by reference to the correct power, asking whether he or she did so 'properly' or 'genuinely', or 'realistically' may be taken, inappropriately, as an invitation to assess the correctness of the result, rather than the legality of the process.

It is evident from these dicta, and from the High Court's decisions in *NAIS*, *SZJSS* and *Li*, that there is considerable overlap between the considerations grounds of review and those for unreasonableness and irrationality.[116] Indeed, the overlap between these grounds of review and procedural fairness can be observed in the fact that it is now almost ritual for the reasoning of courts to state that the merits of a matter are off-limits (a point illustrated by the frequency with which judgments cite

[112] *Green v Daniels* (1977) 13 ALR 1; cf D Greenberg, 'Dangerous Trends in Modern Legislation' [2015] *PL* 96.

[113] *Khan v Minister for Immigration and Ethnic Affairs* (1987) 14 ALD 291, 292 (Gummow J); *Minister for Immigration and Citizenship v SZJSS* (2010) 243 CLR 164, 312–14.

[114] See *SZJSS* (2010) 243 CLR 164, 313.

[115] *Swift v SAS Trustee Corporation* (2010) 6 ASTLR 339, 351–52 (citations omitted).

[116] See M Aronson and M Groves, *Judicial Review of Administrative Action*, 5th edn (Sydney, Thompson Reuters, 2013) [5.10]. See *NAIS v Minister for Immigration and Multicultural and Indigenous Affairs* (2005) 228 CLR 470; *SZJSS* (2010) 243 CLR 164; *Minister for Immigration and Citizenship v Li* (2013) 249 CLR 332, 350–51 (French CJ); 365–66, 366, 369 (Hayne, Kiefel & Bell JJ); 376–77 (Gageler J).

the celebrated dicta of Brennan J in *Quin*).[117] Such a conclusion is often implicit in courts' reasoning.[118] It is sometimes explicit.[119]

Without seeking to oversimplify the reasons for this phenomenon, it is fair to say that where grounds of review take account of qualitative issues, courts are often sufficiently concerned not to 'slide into impermissible merit review' that they take especial care to ensure that their reasoning relates only to procedural issues.[120] This confirms the point made above that it is *more* likely that any successful judicial review application involving soft law will be on the ground that procedural fairness was owed and denied. However, there are sufficient grounds for developing a requirement to consider soft law outside the limits of procedural fairness simply by applying the (also procedural) mandatory considerations ground in a symmetrical fashion.

(iv) Unreasonableness and Irrationality

The *Wednesbury* unreasonableness ground of review is a 'stringent' ground of procedural judicial review rather than a substantive ground of review in Australia and, for this reason, was often traditionally understood as the last resort of desperate counsel.[121] The same became true of review for serious illogicality or irrationality in fact-finding after *S20*.[122] These grounds of review have been difficult to establish because they straddle the boundary between merits review and judicial review. They exist to remedy poor quality decisions (usually a question of fact) but only on the basis that they were so bad as not to be proper exercises of the decision-makers' jurisdiction (a question of law). This is not a judicial function which was created by the *Wednesbury* case itself, but one that had been long understood by judges.[123] After *S20* separated the standard for review in regard to poor quality fact-finding from *Wednesbury* unreasonableness, the rump of the *Wednesbury* ground became confined to really bad discretionary choices. The High Court's decision in *Li* has now

[117] *Quin* (1990) 170 CLR 1, 35–36.

[118] See G Weeks, 'Expanding Role of Process' (2008) 15 *Australian Journal of Administrative Law* 100, 107–11.

[119] *Swift* (2010) 6 ASTLR 339, 352 (Basten JA).

[120] *Kindimindi Investments Pty Ltd v Lane Cove Council* (2006) 143 LGERA 277, 298 (Basten JA); *Swift* (2010) 6 ASTLR 339, 351–52 (Basten JA). See M Aronson and M Groves, *Judicial Review of Administrative Action*, 5th edn (Sydney, Thompson Reuters, 2013) [6.440]; G Weeks, 'Litigating Questions of Quality' (2007) 14 *Australian Journal of Administrative Law* 76.

[121] *A v Pelekanakis* (1999) 91 FCR 70, 89 (Weinberg J); *Taveli v Minister for Immigration, Local Government and Ethnic Affairs* (1989) 86 ALR 435, 453 (Wilcox J).

[122] *Minister for Immigration and Multicultural Affairs; ex parte Applicant S20/2002* (2003) 198 ALR 59. See M Aronson and M Groves, *Judicial Review of Administrative Action*, 5th edn (Sydney, Thompson Reuters, 2013) [4.690]–[4.760].

[123] See eg *Sharp v Wakefield* [1891] AC 173; *Kruse v Johnson* [1898] 2 QB 91; *Moreau v Commissioner of Taxation (Cth)* (1926) 39 CLR 65, 68 (Isaacs J); *R v Connell; ex parte Hetton Bellbird Collieries Ltd* (1944) 69 CLR 407, 432 (Latham CJ); *Associated Provincial Picture Houses Ltd v Wednesbury Corporation* [1948] 1 KB 223. This history was emphasised by the different judgments in *Li* (2013) 249 CLR 332.

effectively run the unreasonableness and irrationality standards back together.[124] It appears that these standards will hereafter be less demanding than they had been.

On the other hand, it has become practically more difficult than it once was to establish that a decision is unreasonable in the *Wednesbury* sense. Courts used to be able to conclude, following a line of reasoning developed by Sir Owen Dixon, that a decision was unreasonable if no good reason was provided for it and none could be observed.[125] However, since most modern decisions come with a statement of reasons, courts now generally have little scope to infer that there cannot have been a reasonable basis for the challenged decision.[126] On the other hand, the High Court has indicated that it now prefers a less restrictive approach to the *Wednesbury* 'absurdity' standard than has been assumed over the last two decades.[127] In *Li*, Gageler J held that the 'stringency' of the *Wednesbury* standard would be unchanged and that the frequency with which it falls for judicial determination would not be increased, but his Honour's prediction in this regard seems at odds with the reasons of the other members of the Court.[128]

Li saw a unanimous High Court hold that the Migration Review Tribunal (MRT) was unreasonable to refuse a further adjournment to Ms Li's hearing in order to allow her to organise proper evidence of her professional qualifications. While the MRT had a statutory power to grant or refuse Ms Li's request for an adjournment, the statute did not indicate how that power should be exercised. The majority judgment held that the statute did not therefore displace the MRT's common law obligation to act reasonably, and that the reasonableness standard could include consideration of:[129]

> whether the Tribunal gave excessive weight—more than was reasonably necessary—to the fact that Ms Li had had an opportunity to present her case. So understood, an obviously disproportionate response is one path by which a conclusion of unreasonableness may be reached.

Introducing proportionality reasoning into *Wednesbury* looks decidedly as though the High Court means for that ground to move further than ever before beyond the 'porous' boundary between legality and the merits and into substantive review.[130]

[124] *Li* (2013) 249 CLR 332, 351–52 (French CJ); 367–68 (Hayne, Kiefel & Bell JJ).

[125] *House v The King* (1936) 55 CLR 499, 505 (Dixon, Evatt & McTiernan JJ); *Avon Downs Pty Ltd v Federal Commissioner of Taxation* (1949) 78 CLR 353, 360 (Dixon J); *Klein v Domus Pty Ltd* (1963) 109 CLR 467, 473 (Dixon CJ). See M Groves and G Weeks, 'Substantive (Procedural) Review in Australia' in H Wilberg and M Elliott (eds), *The Scope and Intensity of Substantive Review: Traversing Taggart's Rainbow* (Oxford, Hart Publishing 2015) 133, 145–47; W Gummow, 'Rationality and Reasonableness as Grounds for Review' in D Mortimer (ed), *Administrative Justice and its Availability* (Sydney, Federation Press, 2015) 13, 20–21.

[126] See J Basten, 'Judicial Review of Executive Action: Tiers of Scrutiny or Tears of Frustration?' in N Williams (ed), *Key Issues in Judicial Review* (Sydney, Federation Press, 2014), 35.

[127] *Li* (2013) 249 CLR 332, 364, 365–66 (Hayne, Kiefel & Bell JJ). See M Aronson and M Groves, *Judicial Review of Administrative Action*, 5th edn (Sydney, Thompson Reuters, 2013) [6.460].

[128] *Li* (2013) 249 CLR 332, 377–78.

[129] ibid, 639 (Hayne, Kiefel & Bell JJ).

[130] JJ Spigelman, 'The Integrity Branch of Government' (2004) 78 *Australian Law Journal* 724, 732.

It remains unclear what this will mean on a practical level.[131] At least one commentator saw nothing in *Li*'s result beyond 'conventional *Avon Downs*' reasoning.[132]

One way in which there may be scope for a court to find jurisdictional error is if a decision-maker reaches a decision which is completely at odds with soft law guidance issued by the decision-maker's public authority. Keyes noted that 'administrative guidelines may be "of great help" in determining the reasonableness of administrative action'.[133] In *Taveli*, Wilcox J explained that his previous decision in *Prasad* was a case in which there was 'an illogicality in, or misapplication of, the reasoning adopted by the decision-maker; so that the factual result is perverse, by *the decision-maker's own criteria*' (emphasis added).[134] Wilcox J was referring to internal inconsistencies which revealed a want of rationality or logic *within* a decision.[135] However, his Honour's reasoning could extend to cover *external* soft law, where the decision is at odds with the terms of that soft law and the decision-maker has given no indication why s/he has not applied it.

This sounds very much like review for breach of procedural fairness where an applicant had a legitimate expectation that the soft law would be applied. The High Court has recently noted that there is significant overlap between concepts of procedural fairness, rationality and reasonableness; indeed, *Li* treated unreasonableness as an indicator of breach of procedural fairness.[136] Since *Lam*, legitimate expectations are only relevant for actual expectations generated by government action, such as promises. However, they are not the major determinant of whether procedural fairness applies. Procedural fairness can apply based upon the existence of a policy about which the subject had not known, a proposition which is not incongruous with the comment by McHugh J in dissent in *Teoh* that it is very hard to speak of a legitimate expectation being disappointed when it was not subjectively held by the applicant for judicial review.[137] The application of procedural fairness in such circumstances requires at least that soft law be considered before a decision-maker is able to reach a decision contrary to it, and supplements the broader position that soft law is a common law creature which is able to be made and applied on terms set by the common law, including being subject to judicial review.

Take, for example, facts similar to those in *Teoh* and *Lam*. Suppose that the Department of Immigration and Border Protection published a Ministerial policy which stated that the Minister would consider the interests of any related children before

[131] See Chapter 7.A.(ii) of this volume below.

[132] JT Gleeson, 'Taking Stock after *Li*' in D Mortimer (ed), *Administrative Justice and its Availability* (Sydney, Federation Press, 2015) 33, 43. See *Avon Downs* (1949) 78 CLR 353.

[133] JM Keyes, *Executive Legislation*, 2nd edn (New South Wales, Butterworths, 2010) 53. See *Baker v Canada (Minister of Citizenship and Immigration)* [1999] 2 SCR 817, [72] (L'Heureux-Dubé J).

[134] *Taveli* (1989) 86 ALR 435, 453. See *Prasad v Minister for Immigration and Ethnic Affairs* (1985) 6 FCR 155. Wilcox J referred also to *Parramatta City Council v Pestell* (1972) 128 CLR 305. See M Aronson and M Groves, *Judicial Review of Administrative Action*, 5th edn (Sydney, Thompson Reuters, 2013) [5.200] (fn 88).

[135] *Prasad* would have been decided on the basis of revealing irrationality or illogicality after the High Court's decision in *Applicant S20* (2003) 198 ALR 59.

[136] *Li* (2013) 249 CLR 332, 360–62 (Hayne, Kiefel & Bell JJ); 373–74 (Gageler J).

[137] *Teoh* (1995) 183 CLR 273, 312–14 (McHugh J). See also C Hoexter, *Administrative Law in South Africa*, 2nd edn (Claremont, Juta & Co, 2012) 427.

exercising his statutory power to deport any person who has failed the 'character test' under the Migration Act. Specifically, the policy says that any decision to deport will only be made after inquiring into the circumstances of any dependent children of the person who would be subject to deportation. Further suppose that Mr X, the father of two infant children, has been convicted of being knowingly concerned in the importation of heroin and of being in possession of heroin (and is therefore undoubtedly of 'bad character'). Presumptively, the Ministerial policy would apply. However, let us suppose that the Minister exercises his statutory power to deport Mr X without having made the promised inquiries after the circumstances of his children.

Lam tells us that this is a breach of procedural fairness, but that no remedy will follow where there cannot have been any material unfairness.[138] The result in *Lam* was peculiar in as much as neither side contended that Mr Lam would have received any benefit to the merits of his case if the promised inquiries had been made, *because* the children's carer had nothing more to say. That outcome does not necessarily follow from the hypothetical facts in the paragraph above. If it did, it would be impossible to argue that the decision was unreasonable in the *Wednesbury* sense.[139] If *Australian Pork* was correct to hold that reaching a scientific conclusion, albeit a complicated one, on the basis of a guess is not necessarily an irrational process of fact-finding, it follows that the grounds of unreasonableness and irrationality will rarely be established absent other imperatives.[140] Another, perhaps more persuasive approach to *Australian Pork* is that the appellant's officers were called upon to make not only a scientific judgement but also an economic and political judgement which was risk-based. The fact that science is, of its nature, uncertain explains the fact that the officers' process of reasoning involved some guesswork, in circumstances where the economic and political considerations required certainty.[141] In any case, it is very difficult to persuade a court that persons with relevant expertise have acted in a manner which is *Wednesbury* unreasonable.[142]

Is there a basis on which unreasonableness could be made out on the facts above? One way in which unreasonableness might be demonstrated is through the so-called common law duty to make inquiries. There had been some doubt as to whether such a duty was properly an aspect of reasonableness or of procedural fairness or was a mandatory consideration.[143] That debate was settled by the High Court in *SZIAI*, in which a majority held that '[i]t is difficult to see any basis upon which a failure to inquire could constitute a breach of the requirements of procedural fairness at

[138] See *Stead* (1986) 161 CLR 141; cf L Pearson, 'Procedural Fairness: the Hearing Rule' in M Groves and HP Lee (eds), *Australian Administrative Law: Fundamentals, Principles and Doctrines* (Melbourne, Cambridge University Press, 2007) 265.

[139] See *Minister for Immigration and Citizenship v SZIAI* (2009) 83 ALJR 1123, 1129.

[140] *Director of Animal and Plant Quarantine v Australian Pork Ltd* (2005) 146 FCR 368, 382–83 (Heerey & Lander JJ).

[141] I am indebted to Elizabeth Fisher for this point.

[142] See *Australian Retailers* (2005) 148 FCR 446; G Weeks, 'Litigating Questions of Quality' (2007) 14 *Australian Journal of Administrative Law* 76.

[143] See *Abebe v Commonwealth* (1999) 197 CLR 510, 578 (Gummow & Hayne JJ); *Prasad* (1985) 6 FCR 155, 167–70 (Wilcox J); M Aronson and M Groves, *Judicial Review of Administrative Action*, 5th edn (Sydney, Thompson Reuters, 2013) [5.210]–[5.230].

common law'.[144] The Court in that case found that in the circumstances there was no need for the Refugee Review Tribunal to make its own inquiries in order to avoid jurisdictional error but commented that:[145]

> The duty imposed upon the [Refugee Review] Tribunal by the *Migration Act* is a duty to review. It may be that a failure to make an obvious inquiry about a critical fact, the existence of which is easily ascertained, could, in some circumstances, supply a sufficient link to the outcome to constitute a failure to review. If so, such a failure could give rise to jurisdictional error by constructive failure to exercise jurisdiction. It may be that failure to make such an inquiry results in a decision being affected in some other way that manifests itself as jurisdictional error.

In essence, the Court held that there is no general duty to inquire, although a duty to inquire may occasionally arise in specific circumstances, for example as an incident to the duty to 'review' that is imposed on most merits review tribunals. Another example is that it may be unreasonable *not* to make further inquiries. This is probably not a separate consideration to the one to which Wilcox J referred in *Taveli*. Rather, it expresses the result that, where it is unreasonable not to 'make an obvious inquiry about a critical fact, the existence of which is easily ascertained', the result of that unreasonableness is jurisdictional error. A decision-maker's failure to adhere to his or her 'own criteria' is simply one example of unreasonableness.

Returning, then, to the hypothetical facts above concerning Mr X, the Minister *might* act unreasonably in failing to apply the terms of his policy. To make that out would require Mr X to establish that the Minister was under a common law duty to make inquiries about whether Mr X has dependent children, a duty which would not be created simply by the terms of the policy itself. It would need to be found that, in all the circumstances, the Minister was unreasonable not to make those inquiries.[146] In the event that the matter subsequently came before the Administrative Appeals Tribunal (AAT) for review on the merits, the AAT's statutory duty to inquire would further bolster that position. It follows that Mr X could enforce the Ministerial policy that decision-makers inquire after his children's welfare before exercising the statutory power to deport him, as a matter of reasonableness rather than of procedural fairness per se, if a failure to do so was so unreasonable that no reasonable decision-maker could have failed to do so. This outcome, which treats unreasonableness as an indicator of breach of procedural fairness, follows from the High Court's analysis in *Li*.

At present, there are clear indications that an authority's failure to attend to its own soft law will not without more amount to unreasonableness. Take the example of *SZTGV*, in which the appellant challenged before the Full Federal Court the decision of the RRT to deny him a protection visa.[147] He had lied when seeking a tourist visa upon his initial arrival in Australia by claiming that he had a female de facto partner. When this deception was exposed, the appellant claimed to be unable to return to his native Namibia because he feared persecution on the basis of his homosexuality. One argument that the appellant raised before the Full Federal Court

[144] *SZIAI* (2009) 83 ALJR 1123, 1129.
[145] ibid, 1129 (citation omitted).
[146] cf *Prasad* (1985) 6 FCR 155.
[147] *SZTGV v Minister for Immigration and Border Protection* (2015) 229 FCR 90.

was that the Tribunal member had committed a jurisdictional error by failing to apply the RRT's *Guidance on Vulnerable Persons* ('Guidance'), including by failing to request a report on the appellant's mental health.[148] The appellant's history of sexual abuse caused him to stutter when anxious and the Court noted that the RRT's adverse credit findings could be 'readily explained by the appellant's stutter'.[149]

The hearing was also unsatisfactory in certain procedural aspects. The RRT member asked questions:[150]

> based on stereotypes about gay male behaviour and, at times, bordered on the offensive (such as the question whether the appellant had done anything else 'of a gay nature' in Canada). The Tribunal's reasoning about the appellant's evidence of his conduct in Canada was not based on the Guidelines and in light of the appellant's obvious difficulties in giving evidence. For example, the Tribunal relied, unreasonably, on the appellant wrongly locating a gay bar in Toronto half a block away from its true location.

It is at least clear that the appellant would have better able to respond to the RRT member's inquiries had the Guidance, which called inter alia for 'questioning in a sensitive and respectful manner and in a way the person understands', been applied. However, the RRT member's reasons made no suggestion that the Guidance had been considered at all.[151]

The Court concluded that the Guidance had not necessarily been engaged on its terms but, if it had been, it would not have been mandatory for the RRT member to take it into account.[152] This is a finding entirely in keeping with Australian orthodoxy since *Quin*. The Court heard argument on the application of *Li*, but considered that case only briefly before holding that it did not apply on the facts. Any suggestion that *Li* has sufficiently broadened the application of the unreasonableness ground to allow a greater chance of success in proceedings where it is alleged that a public body has neglected to apply its own soft law must be treated with caution. It is not yet supported by case law.

B. JUDICIAL REVIEW'S TRADITIONAL REMEDIAL SCOPE

Judicial review's traditional remedial scope is implicitly procedural. The orders available in public law are restricted to:

- compelling the performance of an unperformed public duty;[153]
- quashing an invalid decision;[154]
- declaring the law;[155] and
- preventing the commencement or continuation of an action which is either invalid or unlawful.[156]

148 ibid, 110.
149 ibid, 111.
150 ibid.
151 ibid, 110.
152 ibid, 112.
153 Known as mandamus or, in England, a 'mandatory order'.
154 Known as certiorari or, in England, a 'quashing order'.
155 Known as a declaration.
156 Known respectively as prohibition (or, in England, a 'prohibiting order') and injunction.

Statutory reforms have not altered the substance of these remedies, tending merely to replace 'writs' with 'orders' of the same name and effect.[157] Statutory judicial review schemes also tend to adhere to the model of procedural remedies.[158] The system of administrative law judicial remedies has not changed substantially from its ancient origins. As a result, judicial review remedies are problematic for a party which has relied on a soft law instrument on at least two bases: they may not be available at all and, even if they are, they may be of limited utility.

Mandamus does not lie against every public officer (for example, State and Territorial Supreme Court judges). In practice, judges of the Federal Court are also rarely subject to an order for mandamus. In *Edwards v Santos*, the Federal Court and its judges had filed an appearance submitting to any order the High Court might make. Heydon J did not elaborate on his reasons for not ordering mandamus beyond stating that it was 'not necessary in this case', but it is fair to assume that the High Court did not think it appropriate for mandamus to issue against a court and its judicial officers which had already undertaken to act in accordance with the High Court's orders.[159]

Mandamus does have the benefit of being available against private persons who have public duties.[160] Mandamus enforces the obligation to perform public duties, but not mere powers. Soft law will not generally be able to *create* a public law duty and, for that reason, mandamus will not generally lie to compel a public official to comply with a soft law instrument. As we have seen above in relation to *Purdy* and *Lumba*, there is now judicial recognition in England that public officers may come under an obligation to make and publish soft law. It is conceivable that mandamus may be sought in order to compel a public officer to issue guidelines in certain circumstances.

To the extent that mandamus will lie to compel a decision-maker to perform his or her duty to exercise a discretion but will not compel that decision-maker to make a specific choice where multiple valid options exist, it is probably inapplicable to soft law. One of the key purposes of soft law is to indicate—both to the delegates who will exercise the power in fact and to those who will be subject to such exercises of power—how the recipient of a statutory grant of power intends to exercise that power. However, mandamus will not lie to compel a decision which is inconsistent with parent legislation, nor will it compel a certain decision where the proper interpretation of the statute is that the decision-maker is intended to retain a discretion.[161]

The orders based upon prerogative writs—mandamus, certiorari and prohibition—all require a finding that the challenged administrative action is a nullity. As

[157] See eg Supreme Court Act 1970 (NSW) s 69; Administration of Justice (Miscellaneous Provisions) Act 1933 (UK); Civil Procedure Rules (UK) RSC Ord 53 r 1 (now Part 54). For the history of the various remedies, see S Gageler, 'Judicial Remedies' in M Groves and HP Lee (eds), *Australian Administrative Law* (Melbourne, Cambridge University Press, 2007) 368.

[158] See eg ADJR Act 1977 (Cth) s 16(1).

[159] *Edwards v Santos* (2011) 242 CLR 421, 441.

[160] See M Aronson and M Groves, *Judicial Review of Administrative Action*, 5th edn (Sydney, Thompson Reuters, 2013) [13.30] (fn 22).

[161] See ibid, [13.110].

Aronson and Groves have noted, this is a task which contains some implicit difficulties:[162]

> Nullification involves the court in overturning some of the effects of the impugned act or decision. In a sense, it involves the court in rewriting history. The further back in time the object of challenge, the more difficult it is for the court surgically to separate the impugned part of history from its ramifications and interconnections.

The availability of certiorari relies on establishing that a decision is invalid, but the time travel alluded to above is not the only difficulty created by a system based on nullification of administrative acts. The very point of soft law is that it is not susceptible to ultra vires review—those subject to soft law do not generally inquire into its *vires* but comply because its legal standing is assumed. It is likely that certiorari will apply only when soft law is inconsistent with the legislative obligations of the decision-maker. This will not assist a person who has *relied* on soft law with which the decision-maker subsequently refuses to comply.

Injunctive relief is more flexible, not being restricted to invalid decisions but focusing instead on acts which would be unlawful and therefore not requiring that a jurisdictional error be proved.[163] This flexibility does not, however, cause the injunction to have the same level of utility as would the equitable jurisdiction to enforce estoppels against government parties.[164] Aronson and Groves noted that 'government parties are frequent users' of injunctions, reflecting the fact that, unlike the remedies which originated as writs, the purpose of the injunction is not specifically to prevent public authorities from acting outside their jurisdiction.[165]

The injunction has developed several specific applications.[166] It is best known for its capacity to forbid certain acts (although this is only an example of what an injunction may do and is therefore accurate only in a general sense which, while sufficient for the purposes of this book, is certainly inadequate as a definition of the injunction).[167] As such, the injunction suffers extensively from the same limitations as certiorari and prohibition, in as much as those remedies cannot compel a decision-maker to adhere to a soft law instrument but merely have the possibility of striking down decisions made under such an instrument. Injunctions are able to issue to compel a party to act, although courts have traditionally been highly reluctant to issue mandatory injunctions. In public law, too, the mandatory injunction is notable for the few occasions on which it has issued and the general dearth of judicial exposition on the subject.[168] On the whole, it is unlikely that an injunction will be of greater utility than certiorari or prohibition to a person who has relied on soft law.

162 ibid, [10.370].

163 See ibid, [3.350].

164 See Chapter 7 of this volume below.

165 M Aronson and M Groves, *Judicial Review of Administrative Action*, 5th edn (Sydney, Thompson Reuters, 2013) [16.10].

166 See JD Heydon, MJ Leeming and PG Turner, *Meagher, Gummow and Lehane's Equity: Doctrines and Remedies*, 5th edn (New South Wales, LexisNexis, 2015) Ch 21.

167 ibid, 698–99. See also M Aronson and M Groves, *Judicial Review of Administrative Action*, 5th edn (Sydney, Thompson Reuters, 2013) [16.10].

168 See M Aronson and M Groves, *Judicial Review of Administrative Action*, 5th edn (Sydney, Thompson Reuters, 2013) [16.200].

That the declaration is the remedy most likely to assist such a person is indicative of the limits of judicial review's traditional remedies. Declaratory relief is a relative newcomer to public law and has long been subject to doubts as to its true utility.[169] Megarry VC expressed his conclusion that:[170]

> there is a real difference between a declaration of right, on the one hand, and an order to pay on the other; and a declaration of obligation (i.e. that the Crown ought to pay something) seems to me to be in essence an order to pay, put in a somewhat pallid, or perhaps I should say respectful, form. At the very least it is morally coercive in effect. It may be that some case will emerge in which it is proper to make such an order: but I do not think that this case is that case.

Aronson and Groves cited this dictum in making the point that, while injunctive and declaratory relief lie against Crown officers, it appears that they do not lie against emanations of the Crown itself, such as State Governors.[171] The matter has for many years been—and still remains—uncertain.[172] For example, whereas Hogg and his co-authors concluded that declaratory relief is now available against the Crown because it is non-coercive, Aronson and Groves read the precedents as reaching the opposite conclusion.[173]

Even if only used in respect of officers of the Crown, the declaration might sometimes affect rights, but might also be available 'even where it grants no new rights, imposes no new obligations, and quashes no adverse decision'.[174] This was the case in *Ainsworth*, in which a declaration was considered desirable by the plaintiff because it had the effect, even if only a limited effect, of removing the stain to the plaintiff's reputation which had been placed there by the respondent.[175] However, while a court may have cause to declare that a certain soft law instrument is legally incorrect (although, in practice, there is probably no reason why a plaintiff would not seek an injunction in such a case), it would not, for example, have the power to declare that the plaintiff should have had a certain decision made in his or her case, consistent with the soft law instrument. Aronson and Groves described the boundaries of the declaratory jurisdiction as being 'the boundaries to judicial power more generally'.[176] If the complaint about a soft law instrument is that it has not been applied as expected, rather than that it is unlawful or invalid, it is not within the jurisdiction of the court to intervene with regard to the instrument's application as the law stands. Guidance through soft law is not unlawful per se; on the contrary,

[169] For a good history of the declaration as a public law remedy, see ibid, [15.10]–[15.90].

[170] *Tito v Waddell (No 2)* [1977] Ch 106, 259.

[171] M Aronson and M Groves, *Judicial Review of Administrative Action*, 5th edn (Sydney, Thompson Reuters, 2013) [16.60]. See *FAI Insurances Ltd v Winneke* (1982) 151 CLR 342.

[172] PW Hogg et al, *Liability of the Crown*, 4th edn (Toronto, Carswell, 2011) 6.

[173] ibid, 37–38; cf M Aronson and M Groves, *Judicial Review of Administrative Action*, 5th edn (Sydney, Thompson Reuters, 2013) [16.60] (fn 28).

[174] M Aronson and M Groves, *Judicial Review of Administrative Action*, 5th edn (Sydney, Thompson Reuters, 2013) [15.50].

[175] *Ainsworth v Criminal Justice Commission* (1992) 175 CLR 564; cf *Castle v Director General, State Emergency Service* [2008] NSWCA 231; *Castle v Director General, State Emergency Service* (2007) 98 ALD 78.

[176] M Aronson and M Groves, *Judicial Review of Administrative Action*, 5th edn (Sydney, Thompson Reuters, 2013) [15.70]; see the *Offshore Processing Case* (2010) 243 CLR 319, 359.

it is usually seen as desirable and is certainly permitted.[177] Courts will generally only uphold challenges to soft law on jurisdictional bases.

Judicial review's traditional remedies were not developed with the modern phenomenon of soft law in mind and this explains why, on the whole, they are inadequate to deal with the specific problems thrown up by soft law. Much of this has to do with the procedural limitations of the existing remedies. The following chapters consider whether remedies could be developed which will better allow courts to intervene to prevent the misuse of soft law.

[177] M Aronson and M Groves, *Judicial Review of Administrative Action*, 5th edn (Sydney, Thompson Reuters, 2013) [5.310].

7

Substantive Judicial Review Remedies

IF THE TRADITIONAL role of judicial review can be typified as employing a 'light touch' to review of administrative decision-making, this chapter deals with 'Judicial Review Heavy'. The Justice/All Souls Committee recommended in 1988 that:[1]

> where erroneous advice or misleading assurance is given by a public official and loss is thereby caused to a person who reasonably acts on the advice or assurance, that person should have a remedy for his loss without having to prove that the official acted negligently.

The Committee recommended that compensation should lie as a remedy for the effects of a person being misled to his or her cost by the representative of a public authority. Relevantly to this book, the Committee apparently did not consider it sufficient for public authorities to be bound to their undertakings or bad advice, even where they were under no statutory duty, but recommended substantive protection.[2]

A. CONTRASTING REMEDIAL MECHANISMS

There are several methods by which substantial remedies might be awarded in public law. Section A considers three contrasting mechanisms: public law estoppel, which is based upon reasoning directly transplanted from private law; proportionality, which has developed in public law under the influence of rights-based approaches; and consistency, which may develop as a ground of review within the law of judicial review of administrative action.

(i) Public Law Estoppel

The greater use of estoppel in public law matters was a development almost entirely driven by Lord Denning in cases decided over a period of more than 30 years.[3] It was

[1] JUSTICE—All Souls, *Administrative Justice: Some Necessary Reforms—The Report of the Committee of the Justice-All Souls Review of Administrative Law in the United Kingdom* (P Neill (ed), Oxford, Clarendon Press, 1988) 176 (ch 7, Rec 1).

[2] ibid, 174. See *Attorney General of Hong Kong v Ng Yuen Shiu* [1983] 2 AC 629; cf *Western Fish Products Ltd v Penwith District Council* [1981] 2 All ER 204.

[3] *Robertson v Minister of Pensions* [1949] 1 KB 227; *Wells v Minister of Housing and Local Government* [1967] 1 WLR 1000; *Lever (Finance) Ltd v Westminster Corp* [1971] 1 QB 222; *HTV Ltd v Price Commission* [1976] ICR 170. See G Weeks, 'Estoppel and Public Authorities' (2010) 4 *Journal of Equity* 247; G Weeks, 'Holding Government to its Word' in M Groves (ed), *Modern Administrative Law in Australia* (Melbourne, Cambridge University Press, 2014) 224; JD Heydon et al, *Meagher, Gummow and Lehane's Equity*, 5th edn (New South Wales, LexisNexis, 2015) 513–14.

ultimately accepted by the House of Lords after Lord Denning's retirement.[4] There has not been a role for estoppel in English public law since the House of Lords' subsequent decision in *Reprotech*, at which point the substantive protection of interests generated by government promises was transferred to the public law doctrine of substantive legitimate expectations.[5]

Lord Denning's role as the driving force behind these legal developments is notable because it is indicative of his Lordship's 'credo … "I must do justice, whatever the law may be"'.[6] In applying this judicial doctrine, he was untrammelled by the requirements of legal precedent which generally constrain even the most noted 'judicial activists' (although that term, once very much in vogue, is now rightly seen as both conclusory and unhelpful).[7] His Lordship is usually acknowledged as the source of the phrase 'legitimate expectation' in English law.[8] Additionally, given that he disclaimed any continental influence in developing it, Lord Denning has also been credited with giving 'the name "legitimate expectations" to the similar, but not identical, principle that operates in European Law'.[9] Lord Denning was frank about the fact that doing justice in a case was the only way he could 'sleep at nights' and his view that this subjective view of 'justice' was disappointingly absent from 'some of the judges'.[10] His Lordship further stated that justice was superior as a guide to the meaning of legislation to any other interpretive technique and hinted at both regret and indifference that the House of Lords did not 'think that way'.[11]

Lord Denning had a steadfast belief that he knew the just outcome in any given case, although his views were not universally consistent with those of society at large, as evidenced by his Lordship's comments about the unsuitability for teaching work of unmarried but sexually active women.[12] His views were for a long time still less consonant with those of the Appellate Committee of the House of Lords. *Robertson v Minister for Pensions* was overturned by the House of Lords in *Howell v Falmouth Boat Construction* shortly after Denning J handed it down.[13] A marked general preference for the dissent of Russell LJ has caused the majority position in *Wells v Housing Minister* to be now considered 'highly dubious'.[14] Lord Denning's judgment in *Lever Finance* scantly justified his disapproval of the earlier decision in

[4] *R v Inland Revenue Commissioners; ex parte Preston* [1985] AC 835, 866–67 (Lord Templeman).

[5] *Reprotech (Pebsham) Ltd v East Sussex County Council* [2003] 1 WLR 348.

[6] C Stephens, *The Jurisprudence of Lord Denning: a Study in Legal History* (Newcastle upon Tyne, Cambridge Scholars Publishing, 2009) vol 3—'Freedom Under the Law: Lord Denning as Master of the Rolls, 1962–1982', 5.

[7] See M Aronson, 'Process, Quality, and Variable Standards' in D Dyzenhaus et al (eds), *A Simple Common Lawyer* (Oxford, Hart Publishing, 2009) 5, 23–28; cf JD Heydon, 'Judicial Activism' (2003) XLVII *Quadrant* 9.

[8] *Schmidt v Secretary of State for Home Affairs* [1969] 2 Ch 149, 170–71.

[9] C Forsyth, 'Lord Denning and Modern Administrative Law' (1999) 14 *Denning Law Journal* 57, 62.

[10] J Mortimer, *In Character: Interviews with Some of the Most Influential and Remarkable Men and Women of Our Time* (London, Penguin, 1983) 13.

[11] ibid.

[12] *Ward v Bradford Corporation* (1971) 70 LGR 27.

[13] *Robertson* [1949] 1 KB 227; *Howell v Falmouth Boat Construction Co Ltd* [1951] AC 837.

[14] M Aronson and M Groves, *Judicial Review of Administrative Action*, 5th edn (Sydney, Thompson Reuters, 2013) [6.630] (fn 386).

Southend-on-Sea which, along with *Maritime Electric*, nonetheless still represents the orthodox view of the law in Australia.[15] Brown has further commented that in 'neither *Lever Finance* nor *Western Fish* is the result satisfactory', concluding that the ombudsman's involvement in each case would have provided an appropriate 'middle road'.[16] Even the best-intentioned quests for justice cause more harm than good if they proceed contrary to law and the doctrine of stare decisis.

The concept of 'heavy' judicial review might also be said to include any review process in which the judiciary is doing more than merely assessing the legality of the challenged decision. It is trite to observe that judicial review on this basis is deeply heterodox in Australia, but it is nonetheless worth noting that the argument is likely to continue regardless of disapprobation from the judiciary. The reason for this is the singular capacity of soft law to create reliance.[17]

(ii) Proportionality

Proportionality is a ground of review associated with bills of rights and, to some extent, overlaps with the variable intensity unreasonableness ground (with which I do not propose to deal here) championed by Taggart.[18] In countries with statutory or constitutional rights instruments, such as England, South Africa, Canada and New Zealand, the literature on proportionality is voluminous.[19] Such is not the case in Australia;[20] it remains formally in a much criticised, pre-*CCSU* state in which *Wednesbury* unreasonableness is the only ground upon which courts will interfere with poor quality decision-making.[21] The Australian High Court has never adopted the passage in *CCSU* in which Lord Diplock referred to the possibility of adopting a proportionality standard, perhaps reflecting the fact that such a standard in Australia would not 'embrace a fully structured proportionality analysis' as

[15] *Maritime Electric Co Ltd v General Dairies Ltd* [1937] AC 610; *Southend-on-Sea Corporation v Hodgson (Wickford) Ltd* [1962] 1 QB 416.

[16] P Brown, 'The Ombudsmen: Remedies for Misinformation' in G Richardson and H Genn (eds), *Administrative Law and Government Action: the Courts and Alternative Mechanisms of Review* (Oxford, Clarendon Press, 1994) 309, 319.

[17] JM Keyes, *Executive Legislation*, 2nd edn (New South Wales, Butterworths, 2010) 61–63.

[18] See eg M Taggart, 'Australian Exceptionalism' (2008) 36 *Federal Law Review* 1, 11–16; M Aronson, 'Process, Quality, and Variable Standards' in D Dyzenhaus et al (eds), *A Simple Common Lawyer* (Oxford, Hart Publishing, 2009) 5, 11–16, 28–30; and the essays collected in H Wilberg and M Elliott (eds), *The Scope and Intensity of Substantive Review: Traversing Taggart's Rainbow* (Oxford, Hart Publishing, 2015).

[19] See P Sales, 'Rationality, Proportionality and the Development of the Law' (2013) 129 *LQR* 223; *New Clicks* 2006 (2) SA 311 (CC), [637] (Sachs J); C Hoexter, *Administrative Law in SA*, 2nd edn (Claremont, Juta & Co, 2012) 381–90; M Taggart, 'Australian Exceptionalism' (2008) 36 *Federal Law Review* 1, 25–26. Canada and New Zealand have adopted proportionality *only* in regard to rights and not in their administrative law generally.

[20] J Boughey, 'The Reasonableness of Proportionality in the Australian Administrative Law Context' (2015) 43 *Federal Law Review* 59, 61.

[21] See eg M Taggart, 'Proportionality, Deference, *Wednesbury*' [2008] *New Zealand Law Review* 423, 424–25; M Taggart, 'Australian Exceptionalism' (2008) 36 *Federal Law Review* 1, 24–26; cf S Kiefel, 'Proportionality: A Rule of Reason' (2012) 23 *Public Law Review* 85, 86. See *Council of Civil Service Unions v Minister for the Civil Service (CCSU)* [1985] AC 374.

used elsewhere.[22] The High Court has, however, recently lowered the standard of the *Wednesbury* ground from one of absurdity to one which could be met by an 'an obviously disproportionate response'.[23] Previous changes to the common law unreasonableness ground, following the decision in *Applicant S20*, were considered to be essentially superficial and there are signs that the High Court now sees significant overlap between what is 'unreasonable' and what is 'irrational'.[24] *Li* may yet prove to be no more than another example of the High Court manipulating labels.[25] However, the High Court seems at least to be prepared to discuss proportionality in relation not only to legislative acts which infringe upon constitutional rights but to administrative action.[26]

There has been a series of explicit indications from several members of the Court that they are prepared to adopt proportionality reasoning. Kiefel J has been the foremost judicial proponent of adopting of a proportionality standard which is appropriate to Australia's constitutional arrangements.[27] In *Li*, neither party made a submission to the High Court about proportionality but the majority judgment to which Kiefel J contributed addressed the issue regardless.[28] There are also indications that, along with the *Li* majority, French CJ might be prepared to entertain proportionality reasoning.[29] Crennan J had also joined with Kiefel J in a lengthy consideration of proportionality in *Momcilovic*. That would have constituted a majority of the Court, although Hayne and Crennan JJ have since retired and the possible views of the newly-appointed Nettle and Gordon JJ are as yet unknown on this subject. By contrast, Gageler J's judgment in *Li* stayed closer to the traditional conception of *Wednesbury* unreasonableness, although Basten JA has noted extra-curially that Gageler J nonetheless 'sought to establish a grand unifying theory based on … "the framework of rationality"'.[30]

[22] JT Gleeson, 'Taking Stock after *Li*' in D Mortimer (ed), *Administrative Justice and its Availability* (2015) 33, 43; see also K Walker, 'Judicial Review for Unreasonableness or Irrationality: The Role of Proportionality' in D Mortimer (ed), *Administrative Justice and its Availability* (Sydney, Federation Press, 2015) 45, 47–48; cf *Bank Mellat v Her Majesty's Treasury (No 2)* [2014] 1 AC 700, 770–71 (Lord Sumption).

[23] *Li* (2013) 249 CLR 332, 366 (Hayne, Kiefel and Bell JJ); cf *Hetton Bellbird Collieries* (1944) 69 CLR 407 (Latham CJ); M Aronson and M Groves, *Judicial Review of Administrative Action*, 5th edn (Sydney, Thompson Reuters, 2013) [6.460]. See *CCSU* [1985] AC 374.

[24] *Li* (2013) 249 CLR 332, 350–52 (French CJ); 364, 365–66 (Hayne, Kiefel and Bell JJ). See M Aronson, 'Process, Quality, and Variable Standards' in D Dyzenhaus et al (eds), *A Simple Common Lawyer* (Oxford, Hart Publishing, 2009) 5, 11–12.

[25] See eg *Re Minister for Immigration and Multicultural Affairs; ex parte Applicant S20/2002* (2003) 198 ALR 59; *Minister for Immigration and Multicultural Affairs v Yusuf* (2001) 206 CLR 323, 349–52 (McHugh, Gummow and Hayne JJ).

[26] See *McCloy v New South Wales* [2015] HCA 34, [3] (French CJ, Kiefel, Bell and Keane JJ).

[27] *Rowe v Electoral Commissioner* (2010) 243 CLR 1, 131–42; *Momcilovic v R* (2011) 245 CLR 1, 209–17 (Crennan and Kiefel JJ); S Kiefel, 'Proportionality' (2012) 23 *Public Law Review* 85. See M Aronson and M Groves, *Judicial Review of Administrative Action*, 5th edn (Sydney, Thompson Reuters, 2013) [6.510]–[6.560].

[28] See W Gummow, 'Rationality and Reasonableness as Grounds for Review' in D Mortimer (ed), *Administrative Justice and its Availability* (Sydney, Federation Press, 2015) 13, 31.

[29] *Li* (2013) 249 CLR 332, 351–52.

[30] J Basten, 'Judicial Review of Executive Action: Tiers of Scrutiny or Tears of Frustration?' in N Williams (ed), *Key Issues in Judicial Review* (Sydney, Federation Press, 2014), 35.

In *Li*, the High Court unanimously dismissed an appeal from a finding that the Migration Review Tribunal (MRT) had been unreasonable in the *Wednesbury* sense not to allow an adjournment of proceedings so that Ms Li could arrange for proper evidence of her employment qualifications. The majority of judges in the High Court used the consequent dispute as an opportunity explicitly to discuss proportionality reasoning. French CJ stated:[31]

> A distinction may arguably be drawn between rationality and reasonableness on the basis that not every rational decision is reasonable. It is not necessary for present purposes to undertake a general consideration of that distinction which might be thought to invite a kind of proportionality analysis to bridge a propounded gap between the two concepts. Be that as it may, a disproportionate exercise of an administrative discretion, taking a sledgehammer to crack a nut, may be characterised as irrational and also as unreasonable simply on the basis that it exceeds what, on any view, is necessary for the purpose it serves. That approach is an application of the principles discussed above and within the limitations they would impose on curial review of administrative discretions.

The majority decision also made specific reference to proportionality reasoning:[32]

> Whether a decision-maker be regarded, by reference to the scope and purpose of the statute, as having committed a particular error in reasoning, given disproportionate weight to some factor or reasoned illogically or irrationally, the final conclusion will in each case be that the decision-maker has been unreasonable in a legal sense.

Their Honours referred to Allars' 'third paradigm' of unreasonableness, which employed a 'proportionality analysis by reference to the scope of the power', but noted that 'the submissions in this case do not draw upon such an analysis'.[33] The majority decision stated, however, that on the facts of the matter:[34]

> consideration could be given to whether the Tribunal gave excessive weight—more than was reasonably necessary—to the fact that Ms Li had had an opportunity to present her case. So understood, an obviously disproportionate response is one path by which a conclusion of unreasonableness may be reached.

Gageler J did not deal expressly with proportionality but did comment that:[35] 'the stringency of the [*Wednesbury*] test remains. Judicial determination of *Wednesbury* unreasonableness in Australia has in practice been rare. Nothing in these reasons should be taken as encouragement to greater frequency. This is a rare case'.

His Honour's *dictum* was an accurate expression of the law before *Li*, but that case must be seen as having wrought some changes to the application of *Wednesbury*. A majority of the Court widened the test significantly from the previous 'lunacy' standard by linking disproportionality to unreasonableness and has, as a result,

[31] *Li* (2013) 249 CLR 332, 351–52 (citations omitted).

[32] ibid, 365–66 (Hayne, Kiefel & Bell JJ).

[33] M Allars, *Introduction to Australian Administrative Law* (Sydney, Butterworths, 1990) 190–91; approved in *Fares Rural Meat and Livestock Co Pty Ltd v Australian Meat and Livestock Corporation* (1990) 96 ALR 153, 167–68 (Gummow J). See *Minister for Immigration and Citizenship v Li* (2013) 249 CLR 332, 366.

[34] *Li* (2013) 249 CLR 332, 366.

[35] ibid, 377–78.

'lower[ed] ... the barrier to judicial review of administrative decisions'.[36] The joint judgment explicitly stated that the former standard no longer applies:[37]

> The legal standard of unreasonableness should not be considered as limited to what is in effect an irrational, if not bizarre, decision—which is to say one that is so unreasonable that no reasonable person could have arrived at it—nor should Lord Greene MR be taken to have limited unreasonableness in this way in his judgment in *Wednesbury*. This aspect of his Lordship's judgment may more sensibly be taken to recognise that an inference of unreasonableness may in some cases be objectively drawn even where a particular error in reasoning cannot be identified.

This represents a startling change of gear for the High Court.[38] Aronson has noted that the outcome in *Li* 'has pushed the High Court into frankly substantive review. This might be only at the margins, but it was something the Court had previously denied doing'.[39] Even Kirby J characterised judicial review for illogicality or irrationality as looking at a process of reasoning rather than at the quality of the decision.[40]

The long-term orthodoxy in Australia has been, to adopt the phrase employed by French CJ, that a decision-maker may crack a nut with a sledgehammer or anything else s/he pleases, provided that s/he is still exercising her statutory power for its authorised purpose.[41] It is not for a court to tell the decision-maker how to crack the nut simply because the court would have done so differently. The fact that 'a complete lack of proportion between the consequences of a decision and the conduct upon which it operates may manifest [*Wednesbury*] unreasonableness' does not mean that all disproportionate decision-making *will* do so.[42] For the High Court to start applying the unreasonableness ground for anything short of a decision-maker no longer being able to be characterised as performing his or her statutory function amounts to an admission that the decision-maker's discretion can now be over-ridden on judicial review in circumstances which would not previously have given rise to jurisdictional error. Australian courts have long been concerned that review for unreasonableness is merely 'merits review in drag'.[43] There is now some substance to that concern, since 'proportionality is plainly more susceptible of permitting a court to trammel upon the merits of a decision than *Wednesbury* unreasonableness'.[44] If his limitation of proportionality to circumstances in which the decision-maker 'exceeds [the exercise of administrative discretion which], *on any view*, is necessary

[36] J Basten, 'Judicial Review of Executive Action: Tiers of Scrutiny or Tears of Frustration?' in N Williams (ed), *Key Issues in Judicial Review* (Sydney, Federation Press, 2014), 35.

[37] *Li* (2013) 249 CLR 332, 364.

[38] J Boughey, 'The Reasonableness of Proportionality in the Australian Administrative Law Context' (2015) 43 *Federal Law Review* 59, 74–77.

[39] M Aronson, 'Statutory Interpretation or Judicial Disobedience?' (3 June 2013) *UK Constitutional Law Group Blog*.

[40] ibid; see *Applicant S20* (2003) 198 ALR 59, 88.

[41] See n 31 above.

[42] *Bruce v Cole* (1998) 45 NSWLR 163, 185 (Spigelman CJ).

[43] This phrase appears to have originated in New Zealand: *Powerco Ltd v The Commerce Commission* [2006] NZHC 662, [24]. Like so many good things from that country, it has since been adopted in Australia: *Real Estate and Business Agents Supervisory Board v Carey* [2010] WASCA 109, [58] (Owen JA).

[44] *Bruce v Cole* (1998) 45 NSWLR 163, 185 (Spigelman CJ). See J Boughey, 'The Reasonableness of Proportionality in the Australian Administrative Law Context' (2015) 43 *Federal Law Review* 59, 87.

for the purpose it serves' was intended to prevent such an outcome, it is unclear what French CJ thought that this might add to traditional *Wednesbury* reasoning (emphasis added).[45]

The decision to replace *Wednesbury* with a proportionality standard for rights protected by the European Convention for the Protection of Human Rights was imposed on English courts from without when the European Court of Human Rights declared that *Wednesbury* was an inadequate standard for protecting Convention rights.[46] However, the more generous proportionality standard appears since to have been broadly accepted in regard to matters under the Human Rights Act.[47] The authors of *de Smith* went so far as to note that proportionality can be observed within English law as far back as *Magna Carta*.[48] What has remained uncertain is whether the proportionality standard is to be applied only where Convention rights are affected or whether proportionality is now part of English domestic law.[49] The *ABCIFER Case* is sometimes cited to the effect that it remains orthodox that 'proportionality is not strictly part of English law', or possibly that proportionality is not yet part of English law and will not be until the Supreme Court addresses the issue.[50] However, the decision of the House of Lords in *Daly* indicates that 'the principle of proportionality is a principle of public law' applicable at least in human rights cases.[51] Lord Bingham explained extra-judicially that the specific text of Article 8(2) of the Convention compels a proportionality approach since it asks courts to compare the right to respect for family and private life to the benefits which may accrue to the wider community if such rights are infringed in individual cases.[52] The history of proportionality is, of course, much older than the Convention.[53]

Lord Steyn's speech in *Daly* stated that proportionality is 'more precise and more sophisticated than the traditional grounds of review'.[54] His Lordship

[45] *Li* (2013) 249 CLR 332, 351–52. See J Boughey, 'The Reasonableness of Proportionality in the Australian Administrative Law Context' (2015) 43 *Federal Law Review* 59, 77.

[46] M Aronson and M Groves, *Judicial Review of Administrative Action*, 5th edn (Sydney, Thompson Reuters, 2013) [6.390], [6.510].

[47] H Woolf et al, *De Smith's Judicial Review*, 6th edn (London, Sweet and Maxwell, 2007) 590–91.

[48] ibid, 586.

[49] See PP Craig, 'Proportionality, Rationality and Review' [2010] *New Zealand Law Review* 265, 266; D Mullan, 'Proportionality: A Proportionate Response to an Emerging Crisis in Canadian Judicial Review Law?' [2010] *New Zealand Law Review* 233; M Hunt, 'Against Bifurcation' in D Dyzenhaus, M Hunt and G Huscroft (eds), *A Simple Common Lawyer* (Oxford, Hart Publishing, 2009) 99; PA Joseph, *Constitutional and Administrative Law in New Zealand*, 3rd edn (Wellington, Thomson Brookers, 2007); cf P Sales, 'Rationality, Proportionality and the Development of the Law' (2013) 129 *LQR* 223, 226.

[50] *R (Association of British Civilian Internees: Far East Region) v Secretary of State for Defence* [2003] QB 1397. See C Hoexter, *Administrative Law in SA*, 2nd edn (Claremont, Juta & Co, 2012) 344 (fn 117); H Woolf et al, *De Smith's Judicial Review*, 6th edn (London, Sweet and Maxwell, 2007) 590; P Sales, 'Rationality, Proportionality and the Development of the Law' (2013) 129 *LQR* 223, 224.

[51] *R (Daly) v Secretary of State for the Home Department* [2001] 2 AC 532. See T Hickman, *Public Law after the Human Rights Act* (Oxford, Hart Publishing, 2010) 173.

[52] TH Bingham, *Rule of Law* (London, Penguin, 2010) 74–76.

[53] A Barak, *Proportionality: Constitutional Rights and their Limitations* (Cambridge, Cambridge University Press, 2012) 175–86.

[54] *Daly* [2001] 2 AC 532, 547.

was referring specifically to criteria set out in the Privy Council by Lord Clyde in *de Freitas*:[55]

> In determining whether a limitation is arbitrary or excessive he said that the court would ask itself:
>
> 'whether: (i) the legislative objective is sufficiently important to justify limiting a fundamental right; (ii) the measures designed to meet the legislative objective are rationally connected to it; and (iii) the means used to impair the right or freedom are no more than is necessary to accomplish the objective.'

This pretence of sophistication does not entirely convince. Harlow and Rawlings have noted that, although not co-extensive in their capacity to do so, both proportionality and unreasonableness can open the way to judicial review, but that the real issue is the intensity of the consequent review.[56] One suspects that the basis on which Lord Steyn was able to describe this proportionality test as having greater 'sophistication' than *Wednesbury* might equally support an opposing claim that it gives much greater scope for the judiciary to impose its views on the executive. Sales regarded the proportionality standard thus articulated as 'clearly contemplat[ing] a more intensive form of judicial review than the rationality/*Wednesbury* reasonableness standard' but was concerned rather than impressed by this 'divergence'.[57]

Denunciation of the *Wednesbury* standard's descriptive inarticulacy is nothing new.[58] Lord Diplock's attempt in his speech in *CCSU* at reworking the standard made famous by Lord Greene MR was scarcely an improvement on that front.[59] The real, and 'more contentious', issue that the English judiciary had with *Wednesbury* was its restrictiveness.[60] Lord Diplock felt that whether a decision should be held invalid for unreasonableness was 'a question that judges by their training and experience should be well equipped to answer, or else there would be something badly wrong with our judicial system'.[61] Lord Steyn denied that the use of proportionality reasoning would precipitate 'a shift to merits review', since 'the respective roles of judges and administrators are fundamentally distinct and will remain so'.[62] One senses some of this feeling in the Australian High Court decision in *Li*.[63]

This approach to proportionality is reminiscent of the English treatment of *Wednesbury* in the 1980s. The English courts started to take a far more permissive approach to *Wednesbury* than had previously been the case or, one might add,

55 *de Freitas v Permanent Secretary of Ministry of Agriculture, Fisheries, Lands and Housing* [1999] 1 AC 69, 80; citing *Nyambirai v National Social Security Authority* [1996] 1 LRC 64, 75 (Gubbay CJ). See P Sales, 'Rationality, Proportionality and the Development of the Law' (2013) 129 *LQR* 223, 226.

56 C Harlow and R Rawlings, *Law and Administration*, 3rd edn (Cambridge, Cambridge University Press, 2009) 120–26.

57 P Sales, 'Rationality, Proportionality and the Development of the Law' (2013) 129 *LQR* 223, 226.

58 *Daly* [2001] 2 AC 532, 549 (Lord Cooke). See generally M Aronson and M Groves, *Judicial Review of Administrative Action*, 5th edn (Sydney, Thompson Reuters, 2013) [6.440].

59 *CCSU* [1985] 1 AC 374, 410. See T Poole, 'The Reformation of English Administrative Law' (2009) 68 *Cambridge Law Journal* 142, 143; P Sales, 'Rationality, Proportionality and the Development of the Law' (2013) 129 *LQR* 223, 223.

60 M Aronson and M Groves, *Judicial Review of Administrative Action*, 5th edn (Sydney, Thompson Reuters, 2013) [6.440].

61 *CCSU* [1985] 1 AC 374, 410.

62 *Daly* [2001] 2 AC 532, 548.

63 See the text accompanying n 43 above.

could be justified by Lord Greene's dicta.[64] Although Australian courts initially followed this approach, the High Court soon made it clear that it preferred a restrictive interpretation of the *Wednesbury* ground.[65] Its approach in this regard was consistent with Latham CJ's pre-*Wednesbury* judgment in *Hetton Bellbird Collieries*.[66] It was generally expected that the response of Australian courts to the claim that proportionality review has no effect on the roles of judges and administrators would be similarly restrictive.[67] However, as noted above, the decision in *Li* has made such expectations less certain.

One aspect of the test of proportionality in England that remains unlikely to be emulated in Australia is the involvement of courts in weighing competing interests to reach a decision. Lord Steyn conceived his preferred approach as follows:[68]

> First, the doctrine of proportionality may require the reviewing court to assess the balance which the decision maker has struck, not merely whether it is within the range of rational or reasonable decisions. Secondly, the proportionality test may go further than the traditional grounds of review inasmuch as it may require attention to be directed to the relative weight accorded to interests and considerations.

Hickman argued that this reasoning results inevitably in courts substituting their decisions for those of administrators and thereby engaging in merits review.[69] This observation foreshadows the likely Australian judicial response, which one might expect to be substantially the same in effect, if not vehemence, as it was to the notion of judicial balancing of interests raised in *Coughlan*.[70] Even a suggestion that *Coughlan*'s reasoning would be applied only in extreme cases, and therefore on a basis almost the same as *Wednesbury*, would be unlikely to mollify Australian courts.[71] Notwithstanding the more relaxed approach demonstrated in *Li*, which was premised on treating the existing unreasonableness ground with greater permissiveness, Australia's far more rigid doctrine of the separation of judicial power is likely to be determinative of this issue.[72]

I do not propose to deal here with the many persuasive arguments in favour of adopting a proportionality review standard.[73] The High Court's gesture in *Li* towards developing proportionality within the ground of unreasonableness is more than anyone outside the Court had expected. It is hard to predict how the issue will develop past this point and whether Australia will see the creation of a free-standing proportionality ground of review in the absence of statutory or constitutional

[64] See M Aronson and M Groves, *Judicial Review of Administrative Action*, 5th edn (Sydney, Thompson Reuters, 2013) [6.440]. See also W Gummow, 'Rationality and Reasonableness as Grounds for Review' in D Mortimer (ed), *Administrative Justice and its Availability* (Sydney, Federation Press, 2015) 13, 27–29.

[65] See eg *Minister for Immigration v Eshetu* (1999) 197 CLR 611; *Applicant S20* (2003) 198 ALR 59.

[66] *R v Connell; ex parte Hetton Bellbird Collieries Ltd* (1944) 69 CLR 407.

[67] See eg T Hickman, *Public Law after the Human Rights Act* (Oxford, Hart Publishing, 2010) 175.

[68] *Daly* [2001] 2 AC 532, 547.

[69] T Hickman, *Public Law after the Human Rights Act* (Oxford, Hart Publishing, 2010) 175. See Administrative Review Council, *Federal Judicial Review in Australia*, Report No 50, (2012) 135 [7.42].

[70] See *Lam* (2003) 214 CLR 1. *R v North and East Devon Health Authority; ex parte Coughlan* [2001] QB 213.

[71] M Aronson and M Groves, *Judicial Review of Administrative Action*, 5th edn (Sydney, Thompson Reuters, 2013) [6.650].

[72] cf J Boughey, 'The Reasonableness of Proportionality in the Australian Administrative Law Context' (2015) 43 *Federal Law Review* 59, 65–66.

[73] See generally ibid.

rights protection. One issue in this regard is that, unlike jurisdictions like England, New Zealand, South Africa and Canada, an Australian proportionality ground would lack the anchor of starting with the breach of a person's rights and would therefore also lack even the relatively weak level of objectivity that proportionality can claim in those jurisdictions.[74] The Administrative Review Council's examination of *Federal Judicial Review in Australia* dedicated very little space to considering whether it was desirable for Australia to move to a proportionality standard, noting baldly that:[75]

> Australia does not have a statutory list of human rights, meaning that proportionality would not have the same certainty in terms of what rights, interests or freedoms would give rise to a consideration of the proportionality of an executive action.

This dismissive remark suggests that, whatever arguments may be made against the adoption of proportionality review in Australia, the entire debate is somewhat premature in the absence of an instrument setting out rights, such as exists in every other common law country. On the other hand, Boughey pointed out that *Li* 'did not involve any obvious human rights interest', indicating that proportionality might not be based on human rights violations alone.[76] It remains unclear exactly on what basis the High Court intends that proportionality might be adopted or would operate in Australian administrative law.

(iii) Consistency

Consistency is generally seen as a desirable attribute of judicial or executive decision-making where similar cases are being considered. This principle is often put on the basis that inconsistency tends to indicate arbitrariness, which is at the least 'inelegant' or a bad look.[77] The New South Wales Court of Appeal conceded as much in *Segal*, although it held regardless that the two decision-makers in question were able to reach opposite, but nonetheless valid, results in circumstances which were so similar as to be virtually identical.[78] A more serious way of seeing inconsistency is as an affront to the rule of law.

However, consistency is not an absolute good: the secret policy in *Lumba* was no less obnoxious for having been applied with almost total consistency. Therefore, consistency has generally been seen as an antidote to another long-standing administrative law principle, that each decision must be made on its merits. Like the principle in favour of consistency, the requirement that every decision be made on the merits of the case before the decision-maker cannot and ought not to be applied as it reads. The greatest reason for this is that decisions made by multiple decision-makers in high-volume areas (such as immigration and taxation) are likely

[74] ibid, 69–74, 88.
[75] ibid, 135 [7.44].
[76] J Boughey, 'The Reasonableness of Proportionality in the Australian Administrative Law Context' (2015) 43 *Federal Law Review* 59, 86.
[77] *Drake v Minister for Immigration and Ethnic Affairs* ('*Drake (No 2)*') (1979) 2 ALD 634, 639 (Brennan J).
[78] *Segal v Waverley Council* (2005) 64 NSWLR 177.

to be wildly inconsistent with each other if they are not fettered (or guided) to some degree.[79]

There is a need to strike a balance between the principles of consistency and merits-based decision-making.[80] This dichotomy is not universally applied: in *Drake (No 2)*, Brennan J placed consistency *within* the merits.[81] One of the issues most apparent in regard to balancing consistency and the merits when considering soft law is that the requirement to have regard to the merits of every case is a stand-alone ground of judicial review, whereas the principle in favour of consistency is not.[82] Submissions to the Administrative Review Council (ARC)'s inquiry into *Federal Judicial Review in Australia* argued that the ADJR Act should be amended to include reference to the principles of consistency. Aronson made a recommendation, with which I agreed, that the current text of ADJR Act section 5(2)(f) be replaced with the words 'applying a rule or policy that invalidly purports to narrow the breadth or content of an applicable discretionary power'.[83] My submission further stated that:[84]

> published soft law and policies must mean *something*; in other words, that those who use them as a regulatory tool ought not lightly to be able to apply any other standard. On the other hand, soft law cannot be applied as though it were hard law. The problem, in essence, is not simply regulation with soft law but the fact that the soft law applies asymmetrically: it operates as *de facto* hard law on those who are being regulated but is decidedly soft in its effect on the regulators.

The ARC was not sufficiently persuaded that it needed to recommend the advocated amendment to the ADJR Act, noting instead that 'the courts are currently dealing with these issues'.[85]

I do not share the ARC's confidence in this regard. Most of the attempts to deal with the issues thrown up by the tension between consistency and decision-making on the merits of each case have emerged from the academy rather than the courts. Bringing compromise between the two principles within the list of judicial review's grounds has not been easy.[86] Others have preferred to see compromise reached outside judicial review.[87] What is clear is that attempts to compel an Australian public authority to act consistently with its soft law will, for the time being, succeed only where failure to do so is in breach of one or more other grounds of review.

[79] See W Gummow, 'Rationality and Reasonableness as Grounds for Review' in D Mortimer (ed), *Administrative Justice and its Availability* (Sydney, Federation Press, 2015) 13, 18.

[80] See E Johnson, '"Inconsistency" of Administrative Decisions' (2013) 72 *Australian Institute of Administrative Law Forum* 50.

[81] *Drake (No 2)* (1979) 2 ALD 634, 639.

[82] See eg *Green v Daniels* (1977) 13 ALR 1; Admistrative Decisions (Judicial Review) Act 1977 (Cth) (ADJR Act) s 5(2)(f).

[83] M Aronson, *Submission No 1 to Administrative Review Council Consultation Paper Judicial Review in Australia* (2011).

[84] G Weeks, *Submission No 8 to Administrative Review Council Consultation Paper Judicial Review in Australia* (2011).

[85] Administrative Review Council, *Federal Judicial Review in Australia* (2012) 139.

[86] See eg L Zelenak, 'Should Courts Require the Internal Revenue Service to be Consistent?' (1985) 40 *Tax Law Review* 411; R Clayton, 'Legitimate Expectations, Policy and the Principle of Consistency' (2003) 62 *Cambridge Law Journal* 93.

[87] See eg HJ Krent, 'Reviewing Agency Action for Inconsistency with Prior Rules and Regulations' (1997) 72 *Chicago Kent Law Review* 1187.

The readiness of English courts to direct the publication of guidelines and prevent departure from their terms, demonstrated in *Purdy* and *Lumba*, is yet to be followed in Australia.[88] It is unlikely that consistency will develop as a ground of review in Australia on that basis, given the generally minimalist approach of Australian courts to interfering in administrative decision-making. However, the decision of the High Court in *Li* may present a glimmer of hope in this regard.

B. SUBSTANTIVE ENFORCEMENT OF LEGITIMATE EXPECTATIONS

Lord Denning MR first coined the term 'legitimate expectation' in *Schmidt*.[89] Brennan J subsequently noted, drily, that 'this seed ... has grown luxuriantly in the literature of administrative law.[90] *Schmidt* came at a time when English courts 'were developing the modern law with respect to standing and the range of circumstances which attracted the rules of natural justice'.[91] His Lordship's purpose was to extend the coverage of procedural fairness to a deportee with an unexpired visa (which was not then a legal entitlement which amounted to a 'right or interest' in respect of which procedural fairness was owed), although Aronson has noted that *Kioa* has long since extended procedural fairness to putative deportees, even if they have expired visas.[92] As a concept which confers merely procedural rights, 'legitimate expectation' now has little work to do, since the threshold test of the duty to accord procedural fairness is extremely broad.[93] Indeed, sometimes in relation to domestic bodies and in the so-called 'club cases' it is broader than the coverage of judicial review's remedies.[94]

The term 'legitimate expectation' has itself been judicially criticised as a 'fiction'.[95] Aronson commented that usually:[96]

> the subject could more accurately be said to have 'naturally' or 'reasonably' assumed a certain course of conduct on the decision-maker's part or taken it for granted. It is submitted that in such cases, it might be more straightforward to talk of 'reasonable assumptions'.

[88] See Administrative Review Council, *Federal Judicial Review in Australia* (2012), 139.

[89] *Schmidt v Home Secretary* [1969] 2 Ch 149, 170–71.

[90] *Kioa v West* (1985) 159 CLR 550, 617; cf A Mason, 'Judicial Review' in P Keyzer and R Creyke (eds), *The Brennan Legacy* (Sydney, Federation Press, 2002) 38, 49.

[91] *Lam* (2003) 214 CLR 1, 16 (McHugh and Gummow JJ). See also A Mason, 'Procedural Fairness: its Development and Continuing Role of Legitimate Expectation' (2005) 12 *Australian Journal of Administrative Law* 103, 106.

[92] M Aronson, 'Soft Law in the High Court' (2007) 35 *Federal Law Review* 1, 5. See also *Minister of State for Immigration and Ethnic Affairs v Teoh* (1995) 183 CLR 273, 311–12 (McHugh J).

[93] *Applicant NAFF of 2002 v Minister for Immigration and Multicultural and Indigenous Affairs* (2004) 221 CLR 1, 23 (Kirby J); *Lam* (2003) 214 CLR 1, 16; 27–28 (McHugh & Gummow JJ); 45–46 (Callinan J); cf A Mason, 'Continuing Role of Legitimate Expectation' (2005) 12 *Australian Journal of Administrative Law* 103, 106; Administrative Law Act 1978 (Vic) s 2 (definition of 'Tribunal'); M Groves, 'Should the *Administrative Law Act 1978* (Vic) be Repealed?' (2010) 34 *Melbourne University Law Review* 451, 460–66.

[94] JRS Forbes, *Justice in Tribunals*, 4th edn (Sydney, Federation Press, 2014) Ch 3; M Aronson and M Groves, *Judicial Review of Administrative Action*, 5th edn (Sydney, Thompson Reuters, 2013) [7.410].

[95] *Teoh* (1995) 183 CLR 273, 310–14 (McHugh J); cf *NAFF v Minister for Immigration and Multicultural and Indigenous Affairs* (2004) 221 CLR 1, 22 (Kirby J).

[96] M Aronson, 'Soft Law in the High Court' (2007) 35 *Federal Law Review* 1, 5 (citations omitted). See *Lam* (2003) 214 CLR 1, 30–32 (McHugh & Gummow JJ); 45–47 (Callinan J); *Kioa* (1985) 159 CLR 550, 563 (Gibbs CJ).

Therefore, the 'legitimacy' of the expectation is not relevant and the 'focus should be on whether the decision-maker's conduct in making and then breaching the expectation was fair in the circumstances'.[97] In Australia, 'there will usually be no unfairness if the subject was adequately forewarned of the decision-maker's change of course' and sometimes even where no warning is given.[98]

Even prior to this modern criticism, Barwick CJ had indicated his strong disapproval for the legal purpose of 'legitimate expectation'. He stated that, while it was an 'eloquent phrase', he appreciated 'its literary quality better' than he perceived 'its precise meaning and the perimeter of its application'.[99] In the Privy Council, which did not share the critical approach of Barwick CJ, Lord Fraser said that '"legitimate expectations" in this context are capable of including expectations which go beyond enforceable legal rights, provided they have some reasonable basis'.[100] Gibbs CJ appeared to accept this reasoning in *Kioa v West* when he stated simply that 'the expression "legitimate expectation" means "reasonable expectation"'.[101] However, Brennan J adopted a similar approach to Barwick CJ, concluding that the term 'legitimate expectation' added nothing to the concepts of rights and interests for the purposes of determining to whom a duty of procedural fairness is owed.[102] His Honour noted that the appellant's infant child could scarcely be said to have any 'expectation' of a particular outcome. Perhaps it is this very awkwardness of expression which has seen the public law doctrine in England for *enforcing* 'legitimate expectations' often described as considering 'substantive unfairness'. It is certainly fair to say that whatever controversy remains around the term 'legitimate expectation' is now focused on the suitability of giving such expectations substantive effect—or of giving 'some usages of soft law a harder edge'.[103] It is not focused on whether the term is a suitable guide to the circumstances in which procedural fairness is owed.[104]

The following sections will analyse the approach to the substantive enforcement of legitimate expectations in several different jurisdictions. These are by no means the only jurisdictions in which the concept of legitimate expectations has been influential.[105]

[97] M Aronson, 'Soft Law in the High Court' (2007) 35 *Federal Law Review* 1, 5.

[98] ibid; see eg *Attorney General (NSW) v Quin* (1990) 170 CLR 1; *Lam* (2003) 214 CLR 1, 9–14 (Gleeson CJ).

[99] *Salemi v Mackellar (No 2)* (1977) 137 CLR 396, 404.

[100] *Attorney General of Hong Kong v Ng Yuen Shiu* [1983] 2 AC 629, 636.

[101] *Kioa* (1985) 159 CLR 550, 563.

[102] ibid, 617–22.

[103] R Rawlings, 'Soft Law Never Dies' in D Feldman and M Elliott (eds), *The Cambridge Companion to Public Law* (Cambridge, Cambridge University Press, 2015) 215, 223.

[104] See *Kaur and Others v Minister for Immigration and Citizenship* (2012) 246 CLR 636, 658.

[105] See eg A Brown, 'Justifying Compensation for Frustrated Legitimate Expectations' (2011) 30 *Law and Philosophy* 699, 700–701; M Cohn, 'Pure or Mixed? The Evolution of Three Grounds of Judicial Review of the Administration in British and Israeli Administrative Law' (2012) 6 *Journal of Comparative Law* 86, 99; G Quinot, 'Substantive Legitimate Expectations in South African and European Administrative Law' (2004) 5 *German Law Journal* 65, 68; S Schønberg, *Legitimate Expectations in Administrative Law* (2000); R Flanagan, 'Legitimate Expectation and Applications: An Outdated and Unneeded Distinction' (2011) 17 *Canterbury Law Review* 283.

(i) English Developments

Going beyond the genesis of 'legitimate expectation' to define when a duty of procedural fairness is owed, the English public law doctrine of legitimate expectations has developed a substantive element, but nonetheless features a substantial conceptual overlap with the private law doctrine of estoppel as it applies to public authorities. The development of this body of law was driven in England by migration, revenue and planning cases. In regard to the last of these, it contradicts the warning of Lord Scarman that:[106]

> In the field of property law, equity is a potent protection of private rights, operating on the conscience of those who have notice of their existence. But this is no reason for extending it into the public law of planning control, which binds everyone.

Harlow and Rawlings characterised the development of a substantive element within the doctrine of legitimate expectations as 'procedure plus', in which procedural failures were corrected by courts with 'the implication that the new decision must be favourable'.[107] In *Reprotech*, Lord Hoffmann made the enigmatic statement that 'public law has already absorbed whatever is useful from the moral values which underlie the private law concept of estoppel and the time has come for it to stand upon its own two feet'.[108] Furthermore, English cases have argued that it should do so, since the doctrine of substantive unfairness is more sensitive, and tailored, to the particular context of public law.[109] Such a claim is, however, difficult to reconcile with the dictum of Lord Wilson that, if a public authority makes representations which lack clarity and are confusing, those representations may thereby fail to trigger the doctrine of legitimate expectations at all, regardless of whether or not they are relied upon.[110]

It seems that, in England where a doctrine of substantive unfairness evolved from the procedurally-focused legitimate expectation, the two doctrines will henceforth develop along essentially different paths.[111] By contrast, in Australia the doctrine of substantive legitimate expectations has been conclusively rejected by the High Court, which probably makes this question moot since at least one (and perhaps both)

[106] *Newbury DC* [1981] AC 578, 616. See A Mason, 'The Place of Estoppel in Public Law' in M Groves (ed), *Law and Government in Australia: Essays in Honour of Enid Campbell* (Sydney, Federation Press, 2005) 160, 178.

[107] C Harlow and R Rawlings, *Law and Administration*, 3rd edn (Cambridge, Cambridge University Press, 2009) 224.

[108] *Reprotech (Pebsham) Ltd v East Sussex County Council* [2003] 1 WLR 348, 66.

[109] *R (on the application of Bhatt Murphy (a firm)) v The Independent Assessor* [2008] EWCA Civ 755, [40]; *Reprotech* [2003] 1 WLR 348, 351 (Lord Mackay); 356–58 (Lord Hoffmann).

[110] *Davies v HM Revenue & Customs* [2011] 1 WLR 2625, 2642.

[111] M Aronson and M Groves, *Judicial Review of Administrative Action*, 5th edn (Sydney, Thompson Reuters, 2013) [7.150]. See M Groves, 'Substantive Legitimate Expectations in Australian Administrative Law' (2008) 32 *Melbourne University Law Review* 470; C Stewart, 'The Doctrine of Substantive Unfairness and the Review of Substantive Legitimate Expectations' in M Groves and HP Lee (eds), *Australian Administrative Law: Fundamentals, Principles and Doctrines* (Melbourne, Cambridge University Press, 2007) 280; K Stern, 'Substantive Fairness' (2007) 29 *Australian Bar Review* 266.

of those doctrines is not developing in Australia at all.[112] Sir Anthony Mason commented that Lord Hoffmann's dictum in *Reprotech*:[113]

> suggests that the role of private law estoppel in English public law, to the extent to which a private law estoppel would not be *ultra vires* the statute, is now subsumed in the doctrine of legitimate expectation, notably in the substantive protection of legitimate expectation, a concept which has no counterpart in Australian public law.

That there is common ground between the doctrines of equitable estoppel and substantive legitimate expectations is nonetheless implicit in Lord Hoffmann's approach. Most notably, substantive effect can only be given to either an estoppel or a legitimate expectation if to do so would neither be ultra vires the relevant legislation nor impinge on the scope of a statutory discretion.[114] Lord Templeman's speech in *Preston* stated that, in special circumstances, it would be open to a court to hold that a tax authority could not collect revenue if it would be unfair or unjust to enforce that duty.[115]

The watershed case for recognition in England that the holder of a legitimate expectation may sometimes be entitled to substantive protection of that expectation was *Coughlan*.[116] The doctrine of substantive legitimate expectations has since been considered repeatedly in the Court of Appeal.[117] Although it has not been expressly approved by the House of Lords or the Supreme Court, it has at least been impliedly approved.[118]

Ms Coughlan was a severely disabled patient who agreed to be moved from Newcourt Hospital, a facility which it was planned to close. Along with seven similarly disabled patients, she was moved to Mardon House, a purpose-built facility run by the National Health Service (NHS). These patients were told by the respondent's predecessor authority that this would be their home for life or as long as they chose. However, within five years, the North and East Devon Health Authority had made the policy decision that it would close Mardon House and instead transfer the care of Ms Coughlan to the local authority as a social service for which she would ordinarily be obliged to pay. Prior to making this decision, the health authority had engaged in a process of public consultation and had allowed the patients to voice their opposition to the proposed change. When the health authority decided to close Mardon House, Ms Coughlan sought judicial review of the decision and was successful at first instance in obtaining an order of certiorari to quash the decision to close Mardon House.

[112] See *Lam* (2003) 214 CLR 1, 20, 27–28 (McHugh & Gummow J); 36–38 (Hayne J); 45–48 (Callinan J); *Kaur* (2012) 246 CLR 636, 658.

[113] A Mason, 'Estoppel in Public Law' in M Groves (ed), *Law and Government in Australia* (Sydney, Federation Press, 2005) 160, 179.

[114] See A Mason, 'Continuing Role of Legitimate Expectation' (2005) 12 *Australian Journal of Administrative Law* 103, 108.

[115] *R v Inland Revenue Commissioners; ex parte Preston* [1985] AC 835, 339. See M Groves, 'Substantive Legitimate Expectations in Australian Administrative Law' (2008) 32 *Melbourne University Law Review* 470, 476.

[116] *Coughlan* [2001] QB 213.

[117] R Moules, *Actions Against Public Officials: Legitimate Expectations, Misstatements and Misconduct* (London, Sweet and Maxwell, 2009), 44 (fn 6).

[118] *Lumba v Home Secretary* [2012] 1 AC 245, 275 (Lord Dyson).

On behalf of a unanimous Court of Appeal, Lord Woolf dismissed the appeal brought by the health authority. In doing so, his Lordship outlined three 'categories' of case in which a court exercising a judicial review function is able to provide a remedy for the disappointment of a legitimate expectation.[119] The first two of these categories—the court either having the capacity to require a public authority to reconsider its previous policy on the *Wednesbury* ground or ordering that there be an opportunity for consultation where the policy in question has created a legitimate expectation—are not controversial.[120] The Court held, however, that *Coughlan* fell into the third category:[121]

> Where the court considers that a lawful promise or practice has induced a legitimate expectation of a *benefit which is substantive*, not simply procedural, authority now establishes that here too the court will in a proper case decide whether to frustrate the expectation is so unfair that to take a new and different course will amount to an abuse of power. Here, once the legitimacy of the expectation is established, the court will have the task of weighing the requirements of fairness against any overriding interest relied upon for the change of policy.

The 'unjustified breach of a clear promise given by the health authority's predecessor to [Ms] Coughlan that she should have a home for life at Mardon House' was held to constitute 'unfairness amounting to an abuse of power by the health authority'.[122] The Court upheld the order of certiorari granted in the court below on this basis and thereby remedied the 'unfairness' to Ms Coughlan by substantively enforcing her legitimate expectation that Mardon House would be her home for life.

In the years since, English courts have refined and modified the principles expressed by the Court of Appeal in *Coughlan* by further conditioning any substantive enforcement of a legitimate expectation. The principles articulated in *Coughlan*—which, as they related to 'substantive expectations of service delivery', proved 'particularly troublesome for public administration because of an inchoate jurisprudence'—have in some respects been wound back.[123] However, the basic principle remains that public law remedies will be available, albeit very occasionally, where a public authority reneges on a representation in a way that is so unfair as to amount to an abuse of power.[124] Laws LJ attempted an exposition of what constitutes an abuse of power in any given circumstance, but the matter remains less than clear.[125] Although a helpful starting point, maladministration is not itself a ground for judicial review: the question is only 'has the public body acted unlawfully?'[126] Identifying reviewable

[119] *Coughlan* [2001] QB 213, 241–42.

[120] M Groves, 'Substantive Legitimate Expectations in Australian Administrative Law' (2008) 32 *Melbourne University Law Review* 470, 478.

[121] *Coughlan* [2001] QB 213, 242.

[122] ibid, 260.

[123] R Rawlings, 'Soft Law Never Dies' in D Feldman and M Elliott (eds), *The Cambridge Companion to Public Law* (Cambridge, Cambridge University Press, 2015) 215, 223. See now *R (Patel) v General Medical Council* [2013] 1 WLR 2801.

[124] See eg *R (Grimsby Institute) v Chief Executive of Skills Funding* [2010] EWHC 2134 (Admin) [89]. See M Aronson and M Groves, *Judicial Review of Administrative Action*, 5th edn (Sydney, Thompson Reuters, 2013) [1.160].

[125] *R (on the application of Nadarajah) v Home Secretary* [2005] EWCA Civ 1363, [67].

[126] *Grimsby Institute* [2010] EWHC 2134 (Admin) [111]. See also M Groves, 'Substantive Legitimate Expectations in Australian Administrative Law' (2008) 32 *Melbourne University Law Review* 470, 487–89.

error based on maladministration is doubly difficult in Australia, since the High Court's 'constitutional [judicial review] jurisdiction does not exist for the purpose of enabling the judicial branch of government to impose upon the executive branch its ideas of good administration'.[127] The amorphous nature of 'abuse of power' forms a large part of the reason why the term is treated with such suspicion—or outright hostility—in Australia.[128] However, the 'abuse of power' concept has also endured plenty of criticism within England.[129]

Prior to the Court of Appeal's decision in *Coughlan*, English cases had been edging towards allowing public law enforcement of legitimate expectations, a process in which Lord Denning had been prominent.[130] *Coughlan* represented a leap, with the Court recognising a substantively unfair outcome as a ground of judicial review. Stewart remarked that the facts of *Coughlan* were 'perfect' for developing the nascent doctrine of substantive unfairness.[131] I do not argue with that assessment; Ms Coughlan was certainly a more sympathetic claimant than the applicant in *Lam*. Seen from another angle, however, *Coughlan*'s facts also demonstrate the shortcomings of using unfairness of a particular outcome as a determinant of whether there has been abuse of power sufficient for the decision of a public authority to be invalid. Groves described English cases which use the concept of abuse of power as a determinant of validity as reaching a 'result in search of a principle'.[132]

Endicott examined this issue in the context of the related doctrine of proportionality, which is a required feature of English judicial reasoning at least in regard to human rights matters.[133] He considered circumstances where courts are called upon to reconcile issues which are 'incommensurable'; for example, whether rules issued by the Home Office with the purpose of reducing incidences of forced marriage by restricting the issue of visas to married couples unless both are over the age of 21 result in acts which are invalid for breach of the Human Rights Act, or whether a broken promise to a few people should prevent administrative changes which are intended to benefit the community as a whole.[134] Where they are called

[127] *Re Minister for Immigration and Multicultural Affairs; ex parte Lam* (2003) 214 CLR 1, 12 (Gleeson CJ); see also *NEAT Domestic* (2003) 216 CLR 277, 288 (Gleeson CJ).

[128] See *Lam* (2003) 214 CLR 1, 23–24 (McHugh and Gummow JJ); M Aronson and M Groves, *Judicial Review of Administrative Action*, 5th edn (Sydney, Thompson Reuters, 2013) [3.100], [5.330], [6.650].

[129] See eg T Poole, 'Between the Devil and the Deep Blue Sea' in L Pearson et al (eds), *Administrative Law in a Changing State* (Oxford, Hart Publishing, 2008) 15, 39–40; T Hickman, *Public Law after the Human Rights Act* (Oxford, Hart Publishing, 2010) 279–81; cf Lord Phillips' ringing endorsement in *Lumba v Home Secretary* [2012] 1 AC 245, 344–45.

[130] See the text accompanying nn 6–16 above; and M Aronson and M Groves, *Judicial Review of Administrative Action*, 5th edn (Sydney, Thompson Reuters, 2013) [6.630].

[131] C Stewart, 'Substantive Unfairness' in M Groves and HP Lee (eds), *Australian Administrative Law* (Melbourne, Cambridge University Press, 2007) 280, 286.

[132] M Groves, 'The Surrogacy Principle and Motherhood Statements in Administrative Law' in L Pearson et al (eds), *Administrative Law in a Changing State* (Oxford, Hart Publishing, 2008) 71, 92.

[133] T Endicott, 'Proportionality and Incommensurability' in G Huscroft, BW Miller and G Webber (eds), *Proportionality and the Rule of Law: Rights, Justification, Reasoning* (Cambridge, Cambridge University Press, 2014) 311, 320–23. See *Daly* [2001] 2 AC 532, 546 and the text accompanying nn 46–72 above.

[134] The first example refers to *R (Aguilar Quila) v Secretary of State for the Home Department* [2012] 1 AC 621, where the breach alleged (and found) was of Article 8 of the *European Convention on Human Rights*. The second example refers broadly to the facts of *Coughlan* [2001] QB 213.

upon to reconcile incommensurable issues, Endicott argued that the courts are not truly engaged in a process of *balancing* the interests of the greater number against the damage done to the rights of the few because the material that would be placed on either side of the scales cannot effectively be compared.[135]

Some things which Endicott classified as incommensurable can *never* be compared (because they are essentially different, or *radically* incommensurable) and some can be compared *sometimes* but it is often unclear in such cases what result a balancing exercise will reach (these are classified as *vaguely* incommensurable).[136] Some comparisons are easy to reconcile (for example, there is no public benefit that can justify acts of torture on individuals), others much more difficult or even impossible. The point is that judicial attempts to reconcile the loss suffered by an individual as against the benefit to society caused by the same conduct is generally fraught with uncertainty because, even if the two are not incommensurable, it is always difficult to *measure* one against the other.[137] This reality was not obvious on the face of Lord Steyn's unadorned statement in *Daly* that 'the intensity of review is somewhat greater under the proportionality approach' than under the traditional grounds of judicial review.[138] His Lordship noted the fundamental differences between proportionality reasoning and the common law *Wednesbury* ground.[139] These differences had kept proportionality out of English law altogether until the passage of the Human Rights Act 1998.

There is no doubt that Ms Coughlan had every reason to feel that she had been treated rather shabbily by the health authority, which had reneged on the offer of a 'home for life' within five short years. In other circumstances, she may have been able to argue successfully that she was entitled to an equitable remedy, although on the facts she would not have been able to demonstrate detrimental reliance on the relevant representation, since she had not altered her position on the faith of it. This was held to be the position of the applicant in *Kurtovic*, in which the Full Federal Court of Australia rejected the respondent's argument that the appellant Minister had, in effect, promised not to deport him if he was convicted of no further criminal offences.[140] The High Court has since confirmed that equitable estoppel requires actual, rather than imputed or presumed, detrimental reliance.[141] Despite Lord Woolf's finding to the contrary, it is not clear from the facts that Ms Coughlan

[135] T Endicott, 'Proportionality and Incommensurability' in G Huscroft, BW Miller and G Webber (eds), *Proportionality and the Rule of Law* (Cambridge, Cambridge University Press, 2014) 311, 315–19; cf A Barak, *Proportionality* (Cambridge, Cambridge University Press, 2012) ch 12.

[136] T Endicott, 'Proportionality and Incommensurability' in G Huscroft, BW Miller and G Webber (eds), *Proportionality and the Rule of Law* (Cambridge, Cambridge University Press, 2014) 311, 319–20.

[137] C Harlow and R Rawlings, *Law and Administration*, 3rd edn (Cambridge, Cambridge University Press, 2009) 226.

[138] *Daly* [2001] 2 AC 532, 547.

[139] See A Barak, *Proportionality* (Cambridge, Cambridge University Press, 2012) 192–93; cf *Li* (2013) 249 CLR 332 (see Chapter 7.A.(ii) above).

[140] *Minister for Immigration, Local Government and Ethnic Affairs v Kurtovic* (1990) 21 FCR 193, 196 (Neaves J); 218 (Gummow J). See G Weeks, 'Estoppel and Public Authorities' (2010) 4 *Journal of Equity* 247, 252–59.

[141] *Sidhu v Van Dyke* (2014) 251 CLR 505, 522.

had any genuine alternative to the course of action which she in fact adopted on the faith of the representation of the health authority's predecessor.[142]

Ms Coughlan sought substantive redress through judicial review for the disappointment of her legitimate expectation, which meant that her interests needed to be 'weighed' by the Court of Appeal against the public interest more generally.[143] The Court held that this could be done by assessing the fairness of the *outcome* to Ms Coughlan against the public interest.[144] Necessarily, however, such a process pits the immediately apparent disappointment of a severely disabled woman against the somewhat more abstract interest that the public had in the health system being run efficiently and cost effectively, a point acknowledged in *Bibi*:[145]

> Where one is dealing with a promise made by an authority a major part of the problem is that it is often not adequate to look at the situation purely from the point of view of the disappointed promisee who comes to the court with a perfectly natural grievance.

It is scarcely surprising that when a comparison of that sort is made, it becomes more difficult to find an 'overriding public interest' to justify the breach of the 'home for life' promise.[146] Endicott pointed out that making difficult or impossible comparisons (in the sense of a court having trouble 'finding rational grounds for choosing between two alternatives') is not necessarily the same as incommensurability, which describes a situation where two considerations do not belong in the same 'set of scales'.[147]

Where there is no clear guidance about the elements which will ground a finding of abuse of power, there is always a chance that such a finding is not made upon only objective considerations, but Endicott argued that 'we actually need a system that authorises judges to balance the unbalanceable'.[148] Indeed, we have a judicial system which does not spare judges from the duty of reaching a decision where finding an answer is beyond the capacity of science or medicine.[149] Judges must also reach a decision even where there is no rational basis for doing so.[150] The concept of 'legal certainty' is entirely different from objective certainty, a legal fiction which has been appreciated at the highest level of the Australian judiciary for many decades. In the *Bank Nationalisation Case*, Dixon J stated in this regard that:[151]

> There are few, if any, questions of fact that courts cannot undertake to inquire into. In fact it may be said that under the maxim *res iudicata pro veritate accipitur* [a thing adjudged

[142] *Coughlan* [2001] QB 213, 253; cf M Aronson and M Groves, *Judicial Review of Administrative Action*, 5th edn (Sydney, Thompson Reuters, 2013) [6.640].

[143] See T Endicott, 'Proportionality and Incommensurability' in G Huscroft, BW Miller and G Webber (eds), *Proportionality and the Rule of Law* (Cambridge, Cambridge University Press, 2014) 311.

[144] *Coughlan* [2001] QB 213, 247.

[145] *R (on the application of Bibi) v Newham London Borough Council* [2002] 1 WLR 237, 247 (Schiemann LJ).

[146] *Coughlan* [2001] QB 213, 254.

[147] T Endicott, 'Proportionality and Incommensurability' in G Huscroft, BW Miller and G Webber (eds), *Proportionality and the Rule of Law* (Cambridge, Cambridge University Press, 2014) 311, 322–23.

[148] ibid, 324.

[149] *Amaca Pty Ltd v Ellis* (2010) 240 CLR 111, 121–22.

[150] *Howe v Teefy* (1927) 27 SR (NSW) 301. Damages in this case were assessed by a jury but the principle that they must be assessed regardless of the difficulty of doing so has long been accepted as applying to judges.

[151] *Bank of New South Wales v The Commonwealth* (1948) 76 CLR 1, 340.

must be taken as true] courts have an advantage over other seekers after truth. For by their judgment they can reduce to legal certainty questions to which no other conclusive answer can be given.

Dixon J went on to point out that '[it] would, I should imagine, be necessary completely to satisfy a court of the legal, factual and economic considerations which made it inevitable' that a certain proposition should be reduced to legal certainty. Endicott argued that allowing the judiciary sufficient flexibility to decide difficult matters is something we ought to celebrate.[152]

To the extent that he is positing these matters should be left to the courts, Endicott makes a sound case. The opposing case, however, is one with which he does not engage: must this be the job of the courts at all? To put the problem another way, why should government *not* legitimately be able to put in place rules which exercise its discretion to prosecute a certain policy goal which it has decided is of greater importance than the infringements upon the rights of a smaller group of people? Does the fact that a choice has been made deliberately by our elected representatives count for something when reconciling the (largely abstract) public interest against an (immediate and apparent) breach to the rights of an individual?

A final point worth making in relation to *Coughlan* is that the English recognition of 'substantive unfairness' as a form of maladministration deserving of a judicial review remedy has not led to the recognition of a tort of frustrating legitimate expectations.[153] The fact that there has been maladministration—or even an 'abuse of power'—is yet to translate reliably into a right to compensation for the losses incurred thereby. Given the immense capacity for the 'substantive unfairness' ground as it has developed in England to result in expense for the defendant public authority, it is arguable that both parties would often be better served by a remedy in compensation.[154] At any rate, courts ought to be given the option of choosing the most efficacious remedy for the applicant, given the relative costs to the public authority, from ordering compensation or 'allowing the representation to bind'.[155]

(ii) Responses in Canada and South Africa

(a) Canada

The Supreme Court of Canada rejected *Coughlan*'s variation of the legitimate expectation doctrine in *Mount Sinai*.[156] It did so neither as forcefully nor as completely as the High Court of Australia was later to do in *Lam*, leading the High Court to indicate a suspicion that the Canadian Supreme Court had not sufficiently refuted *Coughlan*.[157] What the Supreme Court did in *Mount Sinai* was specifically to reject

[152] T Endicott, 'Proportionality and Incommensurability' in G Huscroft, BW Miller and G Webber (eds), *Proportionality and the Rule of Law* (Cambridge, Cambridge University Press, 2014) 311, 341.

[153] A Brown, 'Frustrated Legitimate Expectations' (2011) 30 *Law and Philosophy* 699, 700 (fn 2).

[154] PP Craig, *Administrative Law*, 7th edn (London, Sweet and Maxwell, 2012) 715.

[155] ibid, 716.

[156] *Mount Sinai Hospital Centre v Quebec (Minister of Health and Social Services)* [2001] 2 SCR 281.

[157] *Lam* (2003) 214 CLR 1, 22 (fn 49) (McHugh & Gummow JJ).

the notion that it should be the judiciary, rather than the Minister, which determines whether the public interest overrides substantive enforcement of a legitimate expectation.

The Mount Sinai Hospital Centre was originally established as a facility treating patients suffering from tuberculosis but, in the 1950s, it changed the nature of its services to encompass general respiratory care and began to provide both long-term and short-term care facilities. The government, which provided the Centre's funding, was aware throughout of the facilities and services which were being offered. By 1984, when the Centre was involved in negotiations with the Ministry of Health and Social Services to move to Montreal, it held a permit to provide 107 long-term care beds, but had for 10 years instead provided 57 long-term care beds and 50 intermediary or short-term care beds. The Minister promised the Centre that, once it moved to Montreal, its permit would be altered to reflect the reality of its practice. However, once the Centre had moved to Montreal in 1991, the Minister responded to its formal request to have its permit altered by stating that the Centre would have to continue to operate under the old, unaltered permit. The Centre was not given a further chance to make submissions before this decision was communicated. The government continued to fund the Centre's short-term services, even though they fell outside the scope of the permit. The Centre challenged the government's decision not to issue the promised permit and, although unsuccessful at first instance, it succeeded on appeal.

The majority judgment in the Supreme Court was given by Bastarache J, who relied essentially upon the interpretation that the Minister's statutory discretion had already been exercised, and consideration of whether that exercise of discretion had been validly reversed, therefore making it unnecessary to decide whether the doctrines of substantive unfairness or public law estoppel had any application.[158] Binnie J, whose judgment was also delivered on behalf of McLachlin CJ, preferred to view the relationship (and, crucially, the communications) between the Minister and the respondent Centre as the vital issue.[159] Like Bastarache J, his Honour found for the Centre and joined in dismissing the Minister's appeal, leaving in place the order of mandamus issued by the Court of Appeal for Quebec which required the Minister to issue the permit which had been promised to the Hospital Centre. Binnie J reached this conclusion without resort to the reasoning used in *Coughlan*, although his Honour did rely on the ground of *Wednesbury* unreasonableness, finding that the Minister's decision 'was patently unreasonable in terms of the public interest'.[160] This ground has traditionally been very nearly as contentious in Australia as the substantive enforcement of legitimate expectations.[161] Upon closer inspection it becomes clear that Binnie J was still prepared for the courts to intervene to correct executive decision-making.[162] The difference between *Mount Sinai* and *Coughlan*

[158] *Mount Sinai* [2001] 2 SCR 281, [101]–[114].

[159] ibid, [4].

[160] ibid, [64].

[161] See G Weeks, 'Expanding Role of Process' (2008) 15 *Australian Journal of Administrative Law* 100, 107–11.

[162] See G Huscroft, 'From Natural Justice to Fairness: Thresholds, Content, and the Role of Judicial Review' in C Flood and L Sossin (eds), *Administrative Law in Context*, 2nd edn (Toronto, Emond Montgomery, 2012) 147, 169–70.

was that the Supreme Court's intervention depended not on the existence of a legitimate expectation but on the Court finding that the decision of the Minister or other executive officer was patently unreasonable (which is to say unreasonable in the *Wednesbury* sense).

Binnie J denied this, stating that 'where Canadian law parts company with the developing English law is the assertion, which lies at the heart of the *Coughlan* treatment of *substantive* fairness, of the centrality of the judicial role in regulating government policy'.[163] His Honour quoted Lord Woolf's dictum from *Coughlan* that the doctrine of legitimate expectation would only sound in substantive relief 'if there is an overriding public interest. Whether there is an overriding public interest is a question for the court'.[164] Binnie J continued:[165]

> In Canada, at least to date, the courts have taken the view that it is generally the Minister who determines whether the public interest overrides or not. The courts will intervene only if it is established that the Minister's decision is patently unreasonable in the sense of irrational or perverse or (in language adopted in *Coughlan*) 'so gratuitous and oppressive that no reasonable person could think [it] justified'.

Binnie J rejected the explicit language and overtly interventionist approach of *Coughlan* but at the same time allowed for judicial intervention into executive decision-making under another process. His Honour rejected a system under which the courts could enforce promises which it was rational to break, settling for the established *Wednesbury* ground, which allows courts to intervene only when a decision-maker has made a decision so bad that his or her jurisdiction is not engaged at all.

This was immensely clever, because it did not look like Binnie J was rending Canada's constitutional principles asunder in order to garner ever more power to the courts. His Honour was swift to note that:[166]

> [a]t the high end [the English cases on legitimate expectations] represent a level of judicial intervention in government policy that our courts, to date, have considered inappropriate in the absence of a successful challenge under the *Canadian Charter of Rights and Freedoms*.

Binnie J did not argue for intervention in these terms but ensured that a court following his decision in *Mount Sinai* could nonetheless use the flexibility of the *Wednesbury* unreasonableness doctrine to intervene on principled grounds where the court thought it appropriate to do so.

Could Australia follow this reasoning to allow for a level of judicial intervention notwithstanding the constitutional problems identified in *Lam*? As with so many innovations, it has been assumed that the High Court might but probably will not do so. This assumption would explain the High Court's hostility to *Mount Sinai*, demonstrated in the disapproving comment of McHugh and Gummow JJ that, in that case, Canada 'appears to have gone further in allowing … a doctrine [of substantive legitimate expectations]' than either Australia or the United States.[167] Many of the

[163] *Mount Sinai* [2001] 2 SCR 281, [62].
[164] *Coughlan* [2001] QB 213, 249.
[165] *Mount Sinai* [2001] 2 SCR 281, [63].
[166] ibid, [27].
[167] *Lam* (2003) 214 CLR 1, 22 (n 49); cf *Duncan v Minister of Environmental Affairs and Tourism* 2010 (6) SA 374 (SCA) [13].

same constitutional considerations which caused the High Court to conclude that it is impossible for Australia to adopt the doctrine of substantive unfairness have also led it to adopt a highly restrictive approach to *Wednesbury* unreasonableness, which was only applicable to 'absurd' decisions and, in practice, had virtually ceased to be applied at all.[168] This position might now change following *Li*, which saw the High Court apply a much broader conception of the *Wednesbury* ground of review. If the breadth of *Wednesbury*'s coverage is more elastic than had been believed, there is no reason why it should not be used in Australia to support reasoning of the sort advanced by Binnie J in *Mount Sinai*.

(b) South Africa

The doctrine of legitimate expectations was officially adopted into South African law in *Administrator, Transvaal v Traub*.[169] However, the doctrine has since been advanced, particularly by the more recent creation of rights under the 1996 Constitution and the constitutionally mandated PAJA,[170] an Act to:

> give effect to the right to administrative action that is lawful, reasonable and procedurally fair and to the right to written reasons for administrative action as contemplated in section 33 of the Constitution of the Republic of South Africa 1996.

Section 3(1) of the PAJA expressly requires that 'administrative action which materially and adversely affects the rights or legitimate expectations of any person must be procedurally fair', which would seem to guarantee the role of legitimate expectations in South African law. It does not follow that South African courts will give *substantive*, rather than merely procedural, protection to legitimate expectations. Hoexter noted that they have done so on a number of occasions, but suggested that these instances seem to have been unconscious.[171]

A judicial exposition of the current state of South African law in this regard had been awaited.[172] It was summarised in the Supreme Court of Appeal's decision in *Duncan*.[173] In that case, the appellant, who had operated as a line fisherman since 1995, had his application for a long-term licence to undertake commercial fishing for traditional line fish rejected in 2005 by the Chief Director of the Department of Environmental Affairs and Tourism (the second respondent), a decision which was later affirmed by the Minister (the first respondent). These decisions were made on the basis that his vessel, *MFV Endeavour*, was not a 'suitable line fish vessel' as that term was defined in guidelines issued by the Department.

[168] See G Weeks, 'Litigating Questions of Quality' (2007) 14 *Australian Journal of Administrative Law* 76.

[169] *Administrator of the Traansvaal v Traub* [1989] 4 All SA 924 (AD). See C Hoexter, *Administrative Law in South Africa*, 2nd edn (Claremont, Juta & Co, 2012) 363, 394–95.

[170] Promotion of Administrative Justice Act 2000 (SA).

[171] C Hoexter, *Administrative Law in South Africa*, 2nd edn (Claremont, Juta & Co, 2012) 421, 432.

[172] See *Residents of Joe Slovo Community, Western Cape v Thubelisha Homes* 2010 (3) SA 454 (CC), [306] (O'Regan J); C Hoexter, *Administrative Law in SA*, 2nd edn (Claremont, Juta & Co, 2012) 432–36.

[173] *Duncan v Minister of Environmental Affairs and Tourism* 2010 (6) SA 374.

Before the Supreme Court of Appeal, the appellant argued that he had a legitimate expectation that he should continue to have a fishing licence granted to him based upon several circumstances. Giving the judgment of the Court, Brand JA remarked that the time would presumably come, in an appropriate case, 'for our courts to cut the Gordian knot' regarding whether the recognition of legitimate expectations in *Traub* and the PAJA would allow for such expectations to be enforced substantively:[174]

> But this is not that case. Even if substantive protection of legitimate expectations were to be recognised as part of our law, the appellant has in my view failed to lay the foundation for his claim of a legitimate expectation to acquire a long term licence in respect of the *Endeavour*.

His Honour rejected each of the appellant's contentions. The first was that, having held a licence since 1995 to fish both for line fish and squid, he was obliged in 2001 to choose between having a chance to obtain a licence to fish for line fish or for squid but not both. Brand JA held that the appellant's application for a medium-term line fishing licence, which was granted for a period ending in December 2005, did not include:[175]

> any intimation by the Department that if he gave up squid he could expect to acquire a right to catch line fish. Giving up squid was a precondition for his application in 2001, not a guarantee that the application would be granted. Hence the appellant gave up squid at his own risk and because he thought that line fish would be more profitable.

Brand JA rejected the view that the earlier grant of a medium-term fishing licence created a reasonably-held legitimate expectation that a long-term licence would subsequently be granted, noting that the appellant 'knew that the concept of a medium term licence had been introduced as a precursor to long term licences and to provide the Department with a window of observation and research' to assess the extent and consequences of over-fishing off the South African coast.[176] Additionally, any legitimate expectation that the medium-term licence would automatically be converted into a long-term licence would be in direct conflict with the applicable statute, which stated that a licence 'shall be valid for the period determined by the Minister … whereafter it shall automatically terminate and revert back to the State to be reallocated'.[177]

The appellant argued that he had been led to believe that the guidelines as to what would be a 'suitable vessel' would be applied flexibly and that, therefore, the fact that the 16-metre-long *Endeavour* was substantially longer than the guideline 10 metres ought not to prevent it from being considered 'suitable'. The 'flexible' application of the guidelines was always subject to the fact that the Chief Director had a discretionary power to grant long-term licences which was not fettered by the guidelines and was able to be exercised with regard to departmental policy. By 2005, the Department's policy with regard to granting long-term line fishing licences

174 ibid, [14].
175 ibid, [18].
176 ibid, [17].
177 ibid, [19].

took into account the pressure placed on fish stocks by vessels with the range of the *Endeavour* and had the objective of allowing fish stocks to replenish beyond the range of ski-boats and 'chukkies'.[178] To enforce a substantive legitimate expectation that the appellant would be granted a long-term line fishing licence would amount to the court overturning that policy and removing that discretion from the executive. *Duncan* represents a fairly traditional approach to the possibility that legitimate expectations might be substantively enforced, although this conclusion owes much to the fact that the facts were scarcely likely to tempt the court to intervene.[179]

The appellant further alleged that his treatment was inconsistent with the fact that the operator of the *Kowie*, a vessel over 13 metres long, had been granted a long-term line fishing licence. This contention fell apart once the specifications and capabilities of the respective vessels, and those that were presumptively 'suitable' under the guidelines, were considered. The *Endeavour* was a 'freezer boat', with significantly larger gross tonnage, hold capacity and crew than either ski-boats or traditional wooden deck boats (or 'chukkies'), like the *Kowie*.[180] Whereas ski-boats and chukkies need to return to shore each night and therefore have a maximum range of 80 kilometres, freezer boats can stay at sea for up to two weeks, with a maximum range of 2,000 kilometres.[181] Any inconsistency in the treatment of the *Endeavour* in comparison to the *Kowie* was therefore explicable by the fact that they were very different vessels.

The appellant's fallback argument was that, having held a licence for the *Endeavour* since 2001, he was entitled to be heard prior to any finding that that vessel was no longer 'suitable', notwithstanding the fact that it did not strictly comply with the guidelines.[182] For Australians, this is immediately reminiscent of the successful argument made by the appellant in *FAI v Winneke*.[183] However, this argument was rejected by Brand JA on the basis that 'any legitimate expectation of an opportunity to persuade the respondents that the *Endeavour* was a suitable vessel, had been satisfied' when the Chief Director considered the appellant's submissions that the criteria within the guidelines ought not to be applied to the *Endeavour*.[184]

South African courts have so far treated the doctrine of substantive legitimate expectations 'cautiously'.[185] It nonetheless seems likely that South Africa will sooner or later accept that legitimate expectations are capable of substantive enforcement, probably as a result of the express constitutional recognition of legitimate expectations.[186] This view was supported by the way in which a majority of the Constitutional Court of South Africa expressed its agreement with *Duncan*. It cited *Duncan* in a footnote which stated that:[187]

[178] ibid, [10].
[179] cf *Coughlan* [2001] QB 213.
[180] *Duncan* 2010 (6) SA 374, [4]; [11].
[181] ibid, [9].
[182] ibid, [21].
[183] *FAI Insurances Ltd v Winneke* (1982) 151 CLR 342.
[184] *Duncan* 2010 (6) SA 374, [22].
[185] C Hoexter, *Administrative Law in SA*, 2nd edn (Claremont, Juta & Co, 2012), 432.
[186] ibid, 431; G Quinot, 'Substantive Legitimate Expectations in South African and European Administrative Law' (2004) 5 *German Law Journal* 65, 66.
[187] *KwaZulu-Natal Joint Liaison Committee v MEC Department of Education, Kwazulu-Natal* 2013 (4) SA 262 (CC), [31] (Cameron J).

> The current position in our law is that where a party has a legitimate expectation he or she is entitled to procedural fairness. That is, an opportunity to be heard before an adverse decision is made. Our courts have expressly left open the question whether a legitimate expectation may give rise to a substantive benefit.

Strangely, however, that footnote was appended to a sentence which read:[188]

> Courts *enforce* undertakings when parties agree by contract to be bound by their terms; *when the undertaking gives rise to a legitimate expectation and administrative fairness requires some measure of their enforcement*; or when any other legal principle or rule requires enforcement (emphasis added).

This expresses a view somewhat closer to what was decided in *Coughlan* than to the 'current position' expressed in *Duncan*, given that Cameron J expressly compared the actions of a court in enforcing a legitimate expectation and enforcing the terms of a contract. Any move to such an approach will cause South African law to need to deal with a variety of consequential legal problems.[189] Australian courts have avoided (and will likely continue to avoid) these problems altogether due to an emphatic rejection of substantively enforceable legitimate expectations, also for constitutional reasons.

(iii) Australian Resistance to the Development of Substantive Fairness

It seems most unlikely that an Australian court could agree with the proposition that 'the requirements for legitimate expectation in public law [should] stand separately from private law doctrines such as estoppel … being more sensitive, and tailored to, the particular context of public law'.[190] Indeed, for the reasons stated by the High Court in *Lam*, it is impossible for an Australian court to weigh substantive unfairness done to an individual against an 'overriding interest' in a public authority being able to disappoint a legitimate expectation as a matter of public law, at least without a 'revolution in Australian judicial thinking'.[191] The English courts, by contrast, see issues like:

— whether the decision challenged is in the macro-political field;[192] and/or
— whether the decision challenged involves social or political value judgements as to priority of expenditure;[193] and/or
— the nature and clarity of the promise or prior practice in question;[194]

[188] ibid.
[189] J Campbell, 'Legitimate Expectations: The Potential and Limits of Substantive Protection in South Africa' (2003) 120 *South African Law Journal* 292, 294–95.
[190] *Grimsby Institute* [2010] EWHC 2134 (Admin) [90]; cf K Stern, 'Substantive Fairness' (2007) 29 *Australian Bar Review* 266. Dr Stern appeared as junior counsel for the intervening Royal College of Nursing in *Coughlan* [2001] QB 213.
[191] A Mason, 'Continuing Role of Legitimate Expectation' (2005) 12 *Australian Journal of Administrative Law* 103, 108.
[192] *Bibi* [2002] 1 WLR 237, 244; *R (on the application of Begbie) v Department Of Education and Employment* [2000] 1 WLR 1115, 1131.
[193] *Bibi* [2002] 1 WLR 237, 252.
[194] *R (Bancoult) v Secretary of State for Foreign and Commonwealth Affairs (No 2)* [2009] 1 AC 453, 533.

as factors shaping the discretion to grant relief, rather than a bar to jurisdiction. One may well ask whether a public law remedy for disappointment of a legitimate expectation is necessary at all, particularly if alternative remedies are available, for example in equity.[195]

There is a tension between the doctrine of substantive enforcement of legitimate expectations and the rule against fettering discretions, which is essentially the same as the tension between an estoppel and a statutory discretion of a public character.[196] The *Southend-on-Sea* principle prevents a court from enforcing an estoppel so as to fetter a statutory discretion. It is difficult to see, as a matter of principle, why the equivalent position in public law should be otherwise. The factor that is conclusive of this issue in Australia is the constitutional entrenchment of the separation of powers doctrine, which defines and confines judicial power in equal measure.[197]

The classic modern exposition of the legal principle involved is that of Brennan J in *Quin*, extracted above.[198] In that case, his Honour further stated that:[199]

> if an express promise be given or a regular practice be adopted by a public authority, and the promise or practice is the source of a legitimate expectation, the repository is bound to have regard to the promise or practice in exercising the power, and it is unnecessary to enquire whether those factors give rise to a legitimate expectation. But the court *must stop short of compelling fulfilment* of the promise or practice unless the statute so requires or the statute permits the repository of the power to bind itself as to the manner of the future exercise of the power (emphasis added).

Brennan J's reasoning is fundamentally at odds with the proposition in *Coughlan* that a court can weigh 'the requirements of fairness against any overriding interest relied upon for [a] change of policy'.[200] Rather, on this orthodox view, an Australian court exercising judicial review cannot simply 'cure administrative injustice', regardless of whether it outweighs the benefits of valid administrative action, because the merits of a decision fall outside its jurisdiction.[201] This reasoning was not applied directly to the issue of substantive unfairness as a ground of judicial review in *Lam*. Rather, it was held that the constitutional issues did not arise because of the limited scope of legitimate expectations.[202]

In 1990, judgments by the Full Federal Court in *Kurtovic* and the High Court in *Quin* rejected cases brought by two very different applicants who each sought to have a public authority estopped from resiling from a representation it had made to them.[203] Those cases, and particularly the judgments of Gummow J (in *Kurtovic*)

[195] See G Weeks, 'Estoppel and Public Authorities' (2010) 4 *Journal of Equity* 247.

[196] P Sales and K Steyn, 'Legitimate Expectations in English Public Law: An Analysis' [2004] *Li* 564. See *Southend-on-Sea* [1962] 1 QB 416, 423 (Lord Parker CJ).

[197] M Groves, 'Substantive Legitimate Expectations in Australian Administrative Law' (2008) 32 *Melbourne University Law Review* 470, 507.

[198] *Quin* (1990) 170 CLR 1, 35–36. See fn 194 in Chapter 5.B of this volume above.

[199] ibid, 40. See *Lam* (2003) 214 CLR 1, 16–17.

[200] *Coughlan* [2001] QB 213, 242.

[201] See M Groves, 'Substantive Legitimate Expectations in Australian Administrative Law' (2008) 32 *Melbourne University Law Review* 470, 507.

[202] *Lam* (2003) 214 CLR 1, 21.

[203] *Kurtovic* (1990) 21 FCR 193; *Quin* (1990) 170 CLR 1.

and Mason CJ (in *Quin*), are the last of any note to have considered the concept of public law estoppel in Australia and they are generally viewed as standing against its availability.[204] However, neither case in fact rejected out of hand the possibility of an estoppel being raised against a public authority.

Allars argued that the 'clear message of *Kurtovic* and *Quin* is a judicial discomfort' with the principle that an estoppel can *never* be 'raised to prevent the performance of a statutory duty or hinder the exercise of a statutory discretion'.[205] She argued that 'both Gummow J and Mason CJ sought to preserve the separation of powers', whose protection is inherent in the principle that an estoppel cannot be enforced such as to require the performance of an ultra vires act, 'but to leave the door open to do individual justice'.[206] While the quarter of a century since the decisions in *Kurtovic* and *Quin* has not seen an Australian case which explores the possibility of a residual jurisdiction to raise an estoppel against a public authority in regard to the exercise of a statutory power, nor has there been a case which shuts the door that was left open in *Kurtovic* and *Quin*. French CJ noted that the 'possibility that estoppels may apply in public law is not foreclosed by the current state of authority in Australia'.[207] In appropriate circumstances, a court is still able to provide a remedy where an equitable estoppel has been raised against a public authority.

The same cannot be said of the substantive enforcement of legitimate expectations in Australian courts as a matter of public law: the High Court in *Lam* slammed that particular door very firmly indeed. Finn J subsequently held in the Federal Court that it was not open to him even to entertain any cause of action based on a claim that a substantive legitimate expectation was not satisfied.[208] The vehemence with which *Coughlan* was denounced in *Lam* was emphasised by the fact that Mr Lam had not attempted explicitly to rely on *Coughlan*.[209] The High Court's disapproval of the doctrine of substantive enforcement of legitimate expectations has not changed in the decade since *Lam*; indeed, recent judicial statements of the subject have been even sterner, in tone if not in substance.[210]

If the High Court adopts proportionality reasoning or develops the *Wednesbury* ground to cover instances of massive injustice, it will still not be able to substitute its decision for that of the holder of the statutory or prerogative discretion under consideration.[211] It is arguable that, unless the Court has heard argument to the effect that it should give substantive effect to a legitimate expectation, the point is now sufficiently clear that further judicial exposition serves only as a distraction from the

[204] G Weeks, 'Estoppel and Public Authorities' (2010) 4 *Journal of Equity* 247, 254.

[205] M Allars, 'Tort and Equity Claims Against the State' in PD Finn (ed), *Essays on Law and Government—Volume 2: The Citizen and the State in the Courts* (Sydney, LBC Information Services, 1996) vol 2, 49, 93; 86.

[206] ibid, 93.

[207] RS French, 'The Equitable Geist in the Machinery of Administrative Justice' (2003) 39 *Australian Institute of Administrative Law Forum* 1, 11.

[208] *Rush v Commissioner of Police* (2006) 150 FCR 165, 185.

[209] *Lam* (2003) 214 CLR 1, 9–10.

[210] See *Kaur* (2012) 246 CLR 636, 658; cf *Offshore Processing Case* (2010) 243 CLR 319, 352.

[211] *Li* (2013) 249 CLR 332, 363.

real issues.[212] While the courts may still have some scope to provide an equitable remedy where an estoppel has been raised against a public authority, *Lam* means that the parallel remedial jurisdiction in judicial review is definitively off the table in Australia, at least for the foreseeable future.

One basis upon which the Court rejected Mr Lam's application for certiorari quashing the decision to cancel his visa was that, simply because he had a legitimate expectation that the respondent Minister's delegate would contact the carer of Mr Lam's children and this expectation was disappointed, it did not follow that he had suffered procedural unfairness. Mr Lam had a right to a fair hearing before the decision to cancel his visa was made.[213] This he received, notwithstanding the disappointment of his expectation that the delegate would contact his children's carer. As Gleeson CJ noted, there was no suggestion that Mr Lam was deprived of the opportunity to put his full case and, therefore, no practical injustice had resulted from the disappointment of his expectation.[214]

Additionally, the joint judgment of McHugh and Gummow JJ noted explicitly the nature of the Australian Constitution in comparison to English constitutional arrangements. Their Honours considered the comment of Laws LJ in *Begbie* that:[215]

> Abuse of power has become, or is fast becoming, the root concept which governs and conditions our general principles of public law. It may be said to be the rationale of the doctrines enshrined in the *Wednesbury* and *Padfield* [*v Minister of Agriculture, Fisheries and Food* [1968] AC 997] cases, of illegality as a ground of challenge, of the requirement of proportionality, and of the court's insistence on procedural fairness. It informs all three categories of legitimate expectation cases as they have been expounded … in *Coughlan.*

McHugh and Gummow JJ commented:[216]

> The notion of 'abuse of power' applied in *Coughlan* appears to be concerned with the judicial supervision of administrative decision-making by the application of certain minimum standards now identified by the English common law. These standards fix upon the quality of the decision-making and thus the merits of the outcome.

This dictum should not be taken to express any doubt about the validity of 'qualitative' grounds of review, such as *Wednesbury* unreasonableness and *S20* illogical fact-finding.[217]

Their Honours expressly contrasted the English and French public law systems with that which exists under the Australian Constitution and held that the 'distinction between jurisdictional and non-jurisdictional error which informs section 75(v)' provides a further reason why the role of Australian courts 'does not extend to the performance of the legislative function of translating policy into statutory form or

[212] See *Kaur* (2012) 246 CLR 636, 642.
[213] *Ng Yuen Shiu* [1983] 2 AC 629, 636.
[214] *Lam* (2003) 214 CLR 1, 13–14.
[215] *R (Begbie) v Department Of Education and Employment* [2000] 1 WLR 1115, 1123.
[216] *Lam* (2003) 214 CLR 1, 23.
[217] See G Weeks, 'Litigating Questions of Quality' (2007) 14 *Australian Journal of Administrative Law* 76, 81. *Minister for Immigration and Multicultural Affairs; ex parte Applicant S20/2002* (2003) 198 ALR 59.

the executive function of administration'.[218] By way of contrast, Kirby J had in an earlier dissent floated the idea of judicial review for 'serious administrative injustice', which would operate as a minimum normative standard, in the manner of 'abuse of power'.[219] Groves has argued convincingly, however, that this suggestion, although 'interesting', cannot be applied in Australia while the doctrine of jurisdictional error is so firmly embedded in the jurisprudence of the High Court.[220] That is a process which shows no signs of imminent reversal.[221] *Lam*'s reasoning cannot co-exist with a ground of review such as that proposed by Kirby J.

The best understanding of the approach to substantive unfairness expressed by the High Court in *Lam* should therefore be seen as twofold. First, 'legitimate expectations' may have a role to play in determining when a duty of procedural fairness is owed but, in that case, the focus of the court will be on the fairness of the procedure and not on the legitimacy of the expectation or the substantive fairness of the outcome.[222] Secondly, the Constitution restricts the availability of remedies under section 75(v) to occurrences of jurisdictional error, meaning that courts lack the jurisdiction to grant a remedy in respect of a legally valid exercise of power, even if it results in substantive unfairness. The door to relief in public law for the disappointment of a legitimate expectation is firmly closed in Australia for the immediate future.

However, as Taggart argued, this conclusion rests on conclusions about the influence of the Constitution on judicial review that need not be as permanent as currently assumed. He took the view that Australia's insistence that section 75(v) demands a division of errors of law into jurisdictional and non-jurisdictional piles is a leading contributor to what he saw as Australia's 'exceptionalist' status:[223]

> Retention of jurisdictional error contributes, I think, to the often-Byzantine quality of much of the Australian judicial and academic analysis. Moreover, it means Australian courts are not speaking the new international language of judicial review and that sets its jurisprudence apart, and over time may create something of a 'time warp' effect.

Taggart was unconvinced that the constitutional entrenchment of section 75(v)'s remedies meant that the 'historical baggage' would be difficult to dispense with, reasoning that all that is enshrined in the Constitution are the remedies, not the grounds of review.[224] To adopt an argument from Poole, might Australian courts start by working substantive interests into judgments under cover of procedural issues, and from there achieve normative purchase and greater honesty in judicial reasoning?[225]

[218] *Lam* (2003) 214 CLR 1, 24–25.

[219] *Applicant S20* (2003) 198 ALR 59, 91–93; 98.

[220] M Groves, 'Substantive Legitimate Expectations in Australian Administrative Law' (2008) 32 *Melbourne University Law Review* 470, 512.

[221] See *Kirk v Industrial Relation Commission of New South Wales* (2010) 239 CLR 531, 581.

[222] *Lam* (2003) 214 CLR 1, 36.

[223] M Taggart, 'Australian Exceptionalism' (2008) 36 *Federal Law Review* 1, 9.

[224] ibid, cf P Cane, 'The Making of Australian Administrative Law' (2003) 24 *Australian Bar Review* 114, 116.

[225] T Poole, 'Reformation' (2009) 68 *CLJ* 142, 143–44.

Some might argue that this would be nothing new.[226] As a method of securing long-term development of Australian administrative law, such an approach would rely on some flexibility in the application of the grounds of judicial review. Australia may rightly be accused of having a 'judicial reluctance to explore principle', despite the availability of broad (but largely unused) catch-all statutory grounds within the ADJR Act.[227] Nonetheless, the history of administrative law in England contains examples of 'structural and fundamental' changes.[228] Poole cited two examples in this regard. The first was the 'holy trinity' of cases which constituted a 'fairness revolution'.[229] The second was Dicey tempering his hostility to administrative law, which he had dismissed as a French notion and had hitherto not even been able to refer to other than as *droit administratif*.[230]

Poole expressed elsewhere his concerns about the High Court's 'formalism', with the implication that this cast of mind stands between Australian administrative law and changes of the sort that he has discussed.[231] However, Aronson argued (albeit not in direct response to Poole's arguments) that the 'vague' charge of formalism is in essence simply a complaint that the High Court lacks 'style and transparency', followed by a demand that the Court develop 'judicial review grounds [which are] more directly normative or principles-based'.[232] On this analysis, as Poole acknowledged, there is every chance that the development he described may in fact look in Australia like a regression into 'formalism' before the High Court achieves 'normative purchase'.

The possibility of development under a written constitution was Taggart's central point:[233]

> [M]y point here is simply that the Australian *Constitution* is not a conversation stopper. Simply citing the 'memorable words' in the venerable US Supreme Court decision of *Marbury v Madison* [5 US (1 Cranch) 137 (1803)]—that '[i]t is, emphatically, the province and duty of the judicial department to say what the law is'—is too simplistic.

In response to Gageler's claim that the Brennan J's '*ultra vires* approach' now holds sway in the High Court, Taggart remarked '*Marbury v Madison*, of course, has not

[226] G Weeks, 'The Expanding Role of Process in Judicial Review' (2008) 15 *Australian Journal of Administrative Law* 100, 107–16; M Aronson, 'Process, Quality, and Variable Standards' in D Dyzenhaus et al (eds), *A Simple Common Lawyer* (Oxford, Hart Publishing, 2009) 5, 21.

[227] M Aronson and M Groves, *Judicial Review of Administrative Action*, 5th edn (Sydney, Thompson Reuters, 2013) [1.170]. See ibid, [4.750]; Administrative Review Council, *Federal Judicial Review in Australia* (2012), 137.

[228] See T Poole, 'Reformation' (2009) 68 *CLJ* 142, 142.

[229] *Ridge v Baldwin* [1964] AC 40; *Padfield* [1968] AC 997; and *Anisminic Ltd v Foreign Compensation Commission* [1969] 2 AC 147.

[230] AV Dicey, 'The Development of Administrative Law in England' (1915) 31 *LQR* 148. See HW Arthurs, 'Rethinking Administrative Law: a Slightly Dicey Business' (1979) 17 *Osgoode Hall Law Journal* 1.

[231] T Poole, 'Between the Devil and the Deep Blue Sea' in L Pearson et al (eds), *Administrative Law in a Changing State* (Oxford, Hart Publishing, 2008) 15; cf J Boughey and G Weeks, '"Officers of the Commonwealth" in the Private Sector: Can the High Court Review Outsourced Exercises of Power?' (2013) 36 *University of NSW Law Journal* 316, 329–30.

[232] M Aronson, 'Process, Quality, and Variable Standards' in D Dyzenhaus et al (eds), *A Simple Common Lawyer* (Oxford, Hart Publishing, 2009) 5, 23–24.

[233] M Taggart, 'Australian Exceptionalism' (2008) 36 *Federal Law Review* 1, 11 (citations omitted).

prevented the US courts adopting a version of the deference doctrine in their administrative law'.[234]

The High Court appears to be reconsidering its 'absurdity' (or 'bizarreness') standard of *Wednesbury* unreasonableness and may have taken early steps towards embracing proportionality review.[235] Whether this will lead to an acceptance of variable intensity unreasonableness review, or the doctrine of substantive enforcement of legitimate expectations, or to Australia developing a doctrine of deference, or making any of the other changes which would supposedly bring Australia into conformity with the rest of the 'common law world' is to a large extent beside the point. Taggart used these examples but they are essentially no more than emblematic; different jurisdictions can legitimately come to different conclusions on all these points, which Aronson and Groves recognised when they remarked:[236]

> Exaggerations can be useful. It is an exaggeration to say that Australia's judicial review cases are long on rules but short on principles, and that England's judicial review cases have reversed that order. To the extent that these exaggerations are true, each system is defective.

What Taggart opposed was Australians figuratively shrugging their shoulders and stating that nothing could be other than the way it is because the Constitution demands that it be that way. He believed that there was greater scope for change provided that the High Court would accept that it was, at least, constitutionally possible.

Is it possible? Aronson and Groves remarked that 'Australia's judicial review arrangements *intersect* with the Constitution' and pointed out that while the 'constitutional writs are tethered to those judicial review grounds which constitute jurisdictional error … section 75(v)'s injunction is not' (emphasis added).[237] In regard to retaining the concept of jurisdictional error, they said:[238]

> We think that *by itself*, the English answer [of making all errors of law jurisdictional] solved nothing. It assumes the equal importance of all questions of law. It further assumes that all doubts, all genuine questions of law, need resolution at superior court level. Further again, it assumes that unresolved differences of legal interpretation within an authoritative hierarchy are always intolerable, with the consequent need for all questions of law to bear the same answer. And finally, it assumes that there can be only one right answer to every question of law.

Their point was that, if a legal system defines *all* legal errors as deserving judicial review, it must necessarily develop filters to distinguish the important from the trivial. Australia does this through a number of mechanisms, including reserving judicial review for errors of law going to jurisdiction.[239] It is commonly accepted

[234] ibid, 11 (and see 23); cf S Gageler, 'Sir Gerard Brennan and Some Themes in Judicial Review' in P Keyzer and R Creyke (eds), *The Brennan Legacy* (Sydney, Federation Press, 2002), 62, 62–67. See *Chevron* 467 US 837 (1984).

[235] *Li* (2013) 249 CLR 332, 364 (Hayne, Kiefel and Bell JJ); cf 377–78 (Gageler J). See the text accompanying n 43 above.

[236] M Aronson and M Groves, *Judicial Review of Administrative Action*, 5th edn (Sydney, Thompson Reuters, 2013) [1.170].

[237] ibid, [1.50].

[238] ibid, [1.120].

[239] See ibid, [1.130]–[1.150].

that jurisdiction 'is a slippery term with different meanings according to the context' but it serves a purpose.[240] If nothing else, the concept that some errors of law can be made within jurisdiction has given Australian courts greater facility in dealing with privative clauses.[241] That purpose also needs to be served in England but is dealt with there as a matter of judicial discretion.[242] Not *every* error of law needs to be corrected; the 'need' in any given case is instead balanced against the 'functionality' of the court or tribunal.[243] Therefore, Lord Bingham's dictum that 'it would require very potent considerations of public policy … to override the rule of public policy which has first claim on the loyalty of the law: that wrongs should be remedied' cannot be literally true, if it ever was.[244] Lord Hoffmann doubted it, finding Lord Bingham's dictum to be 'as question-begging a statement as you could find'.[245]

On the orthodox Australian view, it is one thing for English courts to recognise that there is some flexibility in the way that they apply discretion to the question of which matters receive judicial review. In is quite another for Australian courts to exercise a similar discretion, given that it is commonly understood to be minimal under Australia's written Constitution. However, it is beyond the scope of this book to settle that question; the point is that there is something to gain by the High Court *considering* these questions and not treating the Constitution as automatically negating every argument for change. Doing so will not necessarily see Australian courts engaged in 'outcome review' as courts in England are.[246]

C. MONEY REMEDIES FOR INVALIDITY

There is a remaining possibility, albeit one that this book will not consider in any depth, and that is that invalidity might be remedied with monetary compensation. There are two main possibilities in this regard.

The first is either through the creation of a public law damages remedy, or alternatively to create tort liability for invalid administrative action. Even in England, this is considered a remedy beyond the proper scope of judicial review, as the responses (ranging from merely sceptical to highly antagonistic) to the Law Commission's *Administrative Redress* consultation paper demonstrated.[247] In Australia, too, the case against public law damages is very strong, not least because it would be highly likely to make the existing judicial review remedies otiose.[248]

240 ibid, [3.350].
241 See ibid, [17.40], [17.140]; cf HWR Wade and C Forsyth, *Administrative Law*, 11th edn (Oxford, Oxford University Press, 2014) 613–14.
242 M Aronson and M Groves, *Judicial Review of Administrative Action*, 5th edn (Sydney, Thompson Reuters, 2013) [1.120].
243 *Cart v Upper Tribunal* [2012] 1 AC 663, 688–89.
244 *X v Bedfordshire County Council* [1995] 2 AC 633, 663.
245 Lord Hoffmann, 'Reforming the Law of Public Authority Negligence' at the Bar Council Law Reform Lecture (17 November 2009), [20].
246 M Aronson and M Groves, *Judicial Review of Administrative Action*, 5th edn (Sydney, Thompson Reuters, 2013) [1.160].
247 Law Commission, *Administrative Redress: Public Bodies and the Citizen*, Report No 322, (2010).
248 See *New South Wales v Paige* (2002) 60 NSWLR 371.

The second possible monetary remedy, which I have analysed more fully elsewhere, is restitution for unjust enrichment where a public authority has made an ultra vires demand through the mechanism of a soft law instrument.[249] Consideration of such a remedy is inevitably driven by the English case of *Woolwich*.[250] Working through the elements of a claim for restitution, it is open for an Australian court to conclude that an ultra vires demand from a public authority is a public event to which public law can respond and that *Woolwich* should be followed.[251] Such a conclusion does not require that Australia should follow the Canadian model, which links the 'public law of restitution' directly to the Constitution.[252] Australian courts have not yet taken this step.[253] However, Australian litigants can nonetheless be confident that restitution will be an effective remedy where a public authority is unjustly enriched due to payment on an ultra vires demand, albeit probably not in a wide range of cases.

[249] G Weeks, 'The Public Law of Restitution' (2014) 38 *Melbourne University Law Review* 198.

[250] *Woolwich Equitable Building Society v Inland Revenue Commissioners* [1993] AC 70. See the essays in S Elliott, B Häcker and C Mitchell (eds), *Restitution of Overpaid Tax* (Oxford, Hart Publishing, 2013).

[251] See R Williams, *Unjust Enrichment and Public Law: a Comparative Study of England, France and the EU* (Oxford, Hart Publishing, 2010); R Williams, 'Overpaid Taxes: A Hybrid Public and Private Approach' in S Elliott, B Häcker and C Mitchell (eds), *Restitution of Overpaid Tax* (Oxford, Hart Publishing, 2013) 23.

[252] *Kingstreet Investments Ltd v New Brunswick (Finance)* [2007] 1 SCR 3. See R Chambers, 'Restitution of Overpaid Tax in Canada' in S Elliott, B Häcker and C Mitchell (eds), *Restitution of Overpaid Tax* (Oxford, Hart Publishing, 2013) 303, 303.

[253] cf PW Hogg, PJ Monahan and WK Wright, *Liability of the Crown*, 4th edn (Toronto, Carswell, 2011) 353 (fn 61).

8

Court-based Remedies: Compensation not Premised on Invalidity

Threshold Issues

GOVERNMENTS AND PUBLIC authorities have immense practical influence over the decision-making of individuals. People generally are apt to act on the faith of representations or guidance from public authorities without necessarily exercising the same caution that they would (or should) in dealings with purely commercial entities. This is true where the representations in question take the form of soft law; it is arguable that this circumstance also carries particular risks. Provided that such reliance is reasonable and that the other requisite elements of each cause of action are made out, it may be possible to obtain damages in negligence or compensation in equity. These remedies are, however, available against public authorities on a somewhat narrower basis than as against private actors.

The starting point for any analysis of state liability is dependent on one's conception of the state. McLean has commented that 'the law contains no single concept of the state. The way that different areas of law conceive of the government as a legal person can be manipulated to achieve different results'.[1] She argued that some legal contexts have no need to conceptualise the state and that, in others, the state may not have *all* of the characteristics of a natural person.[2] However, in general, governments and public authorities are able to act in the same manner as private individuals: they are able to enter into contractual relationships, including contracts of employment; pursue commercial goals; and enter into litigation, either to vindicate their own rights or to defend an action instigated by another party. They are subject to equitable remedies, including estoppel.[3] Each of these statements is equally true of government bodies and natural persons. Public authorities may also be liable in tort, either directly or vicariously in all Australian jurisdictions except Victoria, but vicariously only in New Zealand and England.[4]

[1] J McLean, 'The Transformation from Government to State: Globalisation and Governments as Legal Persons' (2003) 10 *Indiana Journal of Global Legal Studies* 173, 196. See also J McLean, 'The Crown in the Courts: Can Political Theory Help?' in L Pearson et al (eds), *Administrative Law in a Changing State* (Oxford, Hart Publishing, 2008) 161, 174–78.

[2] J McLean, *Searching for the State in British Legal Thought* (Cambridge, Cambridge University Press, 2012), 165–66; cf AV Dicey, *Introduction to the Law of the Constitution*, 10th edn (ECS Wade (ed) (London, Palgrave, 1959)) 187–88.

[3] eg *Commonwealth v Verwayen* (1990) 170 CLR 394.

[4] See Crown Proceedings Act 1950 (NZ) s 6(1); Crown Proceedings Act 1947 (UK) s 2(1).

However, it is in the very nature of governments and public authorities that they are also able to act in ways that private individuals cannot. Specifically, they may be given special powers by statute which are able to be used for the benefit of the public generally, or a subset thereof, rather than in their own interest. Public authorities may be empowered or compelled by legislation to act in certain circumstances, although a statutory power to act does not mean that the authority is necessarily under a common law duty of care to undertake a positive act.[5] Alternatively, they may have a broader general discretion to perform certain acts. Indeed, Jaffe noted that one of the issues which confused the common understanding of the doctrine of sovereign immunity is the tendency to misinterpret the liability of the sovereign, on the basis that litigation was not truly on the same terms as between subject and subject. Procedural means had developed which enabled subjects to litigate against the King, but:[6]

> [a]t the same time, many of the circumstances were already manifest which have always made litigating against public officials very different from litigating against private persons. The desire of the King to supervise his own officials, to protect their discretion, to follow different policies than the courts approved, all appeared, with their counterparts in opposition, shaping the extent to which relief was in fact available against public officials.

Any failure by public authorities to act within the limits of their statutory powers is remediable using judicial review.[7] An act having been performed ultra vires may also create a 'private law' liability, for example in tort, although the fact that an act has been performed ultra vires is not alone sufficient for this purpose.[8] For example, an ultra vires act does not constitute a per se breach of a duty of care in negligence, and the fact that an act is *intra vires* provides no defence to a negligence action. Harlow made this point as follows:[9]

> The *ultra vires* test did not *replace* negligence as a test of legality; on the contrary, it has always been the test of administrative legality in English law. Nor has the *ultra vires* test, except in Lord Diplock's mind, ever replaced negligence as a test of administrative liability; negligence has always been, and still remains, the test of *liability*, as the *Dorset Yacht* case itself establishes.

Therefore, obtaining a compensatory remedy from a public authority in either tort or equity requires first that the plaintiff satisfy the threshold requirement of establishing that the public authority's conduct is susceptible to litigation in the circumstances. Before considering the legal outcomes of two example problems in Chapters nine and ten, I will first address in this chapter four important threshold issues which determine whether litigation can proceed against public authorities: the extent of public authorities' capacity to be held liable in tort; whether public authorities can ever be liable in circumstances where a private individual would not be; the extent

[5] *Stuart v Kirkland-Veenstra* (2009) 237 CLR 215.

[6] LL Jaffe, 'Suits against Governments and Officers: Sovereign Immunity' (1963) 77 *Harvard Law Review* 1, 3.

[7] See Chapters 5 and 6 of this volume above.

[8] See eg *Cooper v Wandsworth Board of Works* (1863) 14 CBNS 180.

[9] C Harlow, '"Public" and "Private" Law: Definition without Distinction' (1980) 43 *MLR* 241, 243.

to which public authorities owe a common law duty in respect to both acts and omissions; and the availability of equitable remedies where an estoppel is raised against a public authority.

A. CAN PUBLIC AUTHORITIES EVER BE LIABLE IN TORT?

The short answer to this question is 'of course' but the history which leads to this now obvious response is revealing. The doctrine of sovereign immunity from suit has a long history in England.[10] That is also true of the republics of France and the United States of America.[11] Indeed, the doctrine survived in America long after it had been abandoned in England, leading Schwartz and Wade to comment:[12]

> It is a source of wonder to an English lawyer that American law should cling so tenaciously to the doctrine of sovereign immunity, battered though it is by statutory inroads, by judicial hostility, and by almost universal disapproval. It seems quite incapable of justification, yet it casts a kind of spell which can produce quite irrational arguments from the greatest American judges.

This was a specific reference to an opinion delivered by Holmes J for the Supreme Court.[13]

Traditionally, the English monarch was immune from tort action, supposedly on the basis that, as a matter of procedure, a feudal lord could not be sued in his own court and, therefore, as a feudal lord himself, the King could not be sued at all.[14] The monarch was, however, able to consent to a suit being brought personally against the Crown. The procedural requirement for suing the Crown by name was therefore to bring a petition of right. The early history of this procedure remains 'obscure' but the essence of it was that if the Chancellor, having made inquiries as to the facts of the case, concluded that the plaintiff had a 'right' against the Crown in fact, then 'the King would plead to the questions of law' and the petition would be endorsed with the King's fiat, 'let right be done'.[15] This process was ultimately simplified by statute.[16] Jaffe cites historical authority that the monarch's consent was determined as a matter of law and not subject to regal whim. The somewhat tortured procedural requirement that the King give his consent to a suit being brought against him by name was based on the notion that the Crown 'could not refuse to redress wrongs'. Hence 'the expression "the King can do no wrong" originally meant precisely the

[10] See generally PW Hogg et al, *Liability of the Crown*, 4th edn (Toronto, Carswell, 2011) 4–11; M Aronson and H Whitmore, *Public Torts and Contracts* (Sydney, Law Book Co, 1982) 1–2.

[11] See J McLean, 'The Crown in the Courts' in L Pearson et al (eds), *Administrative Law in a Changing State* (Oxford, Hart Publishing, 2008) 161, 175.

[12] B Schwartz and HWR Wade, *Legal Control of Government: Administrative Law in Britain and the United States* (Oxford, Oxford University Press, 1972) 185.

[13] *Kawananakoa v Polyblank* 205 US 349 (1907).

[14] LL Jaffe, 'Suits against Governments and Officers' (1963) 77 *Harvard Law Review* 1, 18. See PW Hogg et al, *Liability of the Crown*, 4th edn (Toronto, Carswell, 2011) 5; C Harlow, *Compensation and Government Torts* (London, Sweet and Maxwell, 1982) 17.

[15] PW Hogg et al, *Liability of the Crown*, 4th edn (Toronto, Carswell, 2011) 5.

[16] Petitions of Right Act 1860 (UK) 23 & 24 Vict c 34. See *Mulcahy v Ministry of Defence* [1996] QB 732, 740.

contrary to what it later came to mean. "[I]t meant that the king must not, was not allowed, not entitled, to do wrong"'.[17]

On this understanding, the King was under a legal or equitable obligation to remove the procedural barrier to a petitioner bringing suit against the Crown. Further support for this position can be found in an early High Court decision in which Griffith CJ recorded that Sir Edward Coke had referred to the maxim 'the King can do no wrong' in the *Magdalen College Case* to mean that the King:[18]

> is the fountain of justice and common right, and the King being God's lieutenant cannot do a wrong: *solum Rex hoc non potest facere, quod non potest injuste agere*. ... And although a right was remediless, yet the Act which provides a necessary and profitable remedy for the preservation of it, and to suppress wrong, shall bind the King.

The maxim was misunderstood throughout the nineteenth century, during which influential English judges held that the constitutional independence of the Crown required that it not be held liable in tort.[19] Ultimately, petitions of right were used to enforce rights against the Crown for breach of contract.[20] However, while the procedural expedient of a petition of right allowed an individual to seek legal redress against the Crown, it was held not to do so for torts committed by Crown servants.[21] This approach was ultimately recognised as a misapplication of the doctrine, not least because of its consequences for actions against Crown servants for their tortious acts.[22] In Australia, several respected sources have concurred with earlier authority that the understanding that the sovereign had a common law 'immunity' from suit is misconceived. The issue was settled in *Mewett*, where it was held that the immunity was procedural rather than substantive.[23]

The widespread tendency to elide the issues of sovereign immunity from suit and the capacity of the sovereign to violate the law was able to be avoided in England under the approach taken, most famously, by AV Dicey.[24] Dicey insisted that government officials should be accountable for their tortious acts in the same way as any other private individual, through actions brought by private individuals against them *personally* in the 'ordinary courts' of law, on the basis that, by acting unlawfully,

[17] LL Jaffe, 'Suits against Governments and Officers' (1963) 77 *Harvard Law Review* 1, 3–4 (footnotes omitted). See also S Gageler, 'Judicial Remedies' in M Groves and HP Lee (eds), *Australian Administrative Law* (Melbourne, Cambridge University Press, 2007) 368, 369; PW Hogg et al, *Liability of the Crown*, 4th edn (Toronto, Carswell, 2011) 5 (fn 17).

[18] *Sydney Harbour Trust Commissioners v Ryan* (1911) 13 CLR 358, 365. See *Magdalen College* (1615) 11 Co Rep 66, 72a; A Gray, 'Options for the Doctrine of Crown Immunity in 21st Century Australia' (2009) 16 *Australian Journal of Administrative Law* 200, 201.

[19] See eg *Tobin v The Queen* (1864) 16 CB (NS) 310.

[20] *Thomas v The Queen (No 1)* (1874) LR 10 QB 31.

[21] *Feather v The Queen* (1865) 6 B&S 257. See generally C Harlow, *Compensation and Government Torts* (London, Sweet and Maxwell, 1982) 22–23.

[22] See *Mulcahy* [1996] QB 732, 740.

[23] *Commonwealth v Mewett* (1997) 191 CLR 471, 502 (Dawson J); 513 (Toohey J); 532 (McHugh J); 550–51 (Gummow & Kirby JJ). See also G Hill, 'Private Law Actions Against the Government (Part 1)—Removing the Government's Immunity from Suit in Federal Cases' (2007) 30 *Melbourne University Law Review* 716, 725; M Leeming, 'The Liability of the Government under the Constitution' (1998) 17 *Australian Bar Review* 215, 216.

[24] LL Jaffe, 'Suits against Governments and Officers' (1963) 77 *Harvard Law Review* 1, 4.

their actions were in fact unofficial.[25] This insistence reflects more the old-fashioned nature of the common law than of Dicey's views themselves, at least in England, where Allison argued that Dicey's analysis of the rule of law perpetuated a common law tradition, started by Austin, in which the concept of the state was doctrinally neglected.[26] Dicey was not prepared to exclude public authorities from his general principle that individual tortfeasors be liable for their wrongs as a matter of 'private law', a view which may now rightly be regarded as old-fashioned. The position was stated by Sedley LJ:[27]

> [T]he English common law has no knowledge of the state. Public law recognises the Crown as the repository of a range of prerogative and statutory powers. By the prerogative writs and orders, it has for centuries called ministers to account if they abuse the latter, and in recent years if they misuse the former. But the State has no tortious liability at common law for wrongs done by its servants, from ministers down. In England at least (Scottish law has historically differed) either the Crown's servants are personally liable or there is no redress. It was to change this anomalous situation that the Crown Proceedings Act 1947 was passed. But the 1947 Act does not work by making the state a potential tortfeasor: it works by making the Crown vicariously liable for the torts of its servants. It has only been with the enactment of the Human Rights Act 1998 that the Crown, in the form of a 'public authority', has acquired a primary liability for violating certain rights. Where, of course, a limb of the state has corporate legal personality—a local authority, for example, or the Bank of England—no such problem arises.

Dicey's approach therefore had no need of the common law maxim that 'the King can do wrong' because public officials were unable to use their public status as a defence to a private law damages action.[28]

Statutory reform had already replaced the Diceyan approach in Australia, where the Crown's specially protected position was removed by statute under a series of Australian Crown Proceedings Acts from the 1850s.[29] The first Crown Proceedings Act was passed in South Australia in 1853, followed by New South Wales and Queensland.[30] Finn stated that the early colonial legislation was not drafted with the intention that it would provide for liability in tort.[31] Nonetheless, the Privy Council

[25] See PW Hogg and PJ Monahan, *Liability of the Crown*, 3rd edn (Toronto, Carswell Thomson Professional Publishing, 2000) 1–4.

[26] JWF Allison, 'Theoretical and Institutional Underpinnings of a Separate Administrative Law' in M Taggart (ed), *The Province of Administrative Law* (Oxford, Hart Publishing, 1997) 71, 75.

[27] *Chagos Islanders v Attorney General and Another* [2004] EWCA Civ 997, [20]; see also J McLean, *Searching for the State in British Legal Thought* (Cambridge, Cambridge University Press, 2012) 226–32.

[28] M Aronson and M Groves, *Judicial Review of Administrative Action*, 5th edn (Sydney, Thompson Reuters, 2013) [10.50].

[29] See now Crown Suits Act 1947 (WA); Crown Proceedings Act 1958 (Vic); Crown Proceedings Act 1980 (Qld); Crown Proceedings Act 1988 (NSW); Crown Proceedings Act 1992 (ACT); Crown Proceedings Act 1992 (SA); Crown Proceedings Act 1993 (Tas); Crown Proceedings Act 1993 (NT).

[30] See M Aronson, 'Government Liability' (2008) 32 *Mebourne University Law Review* 44, 44; M Leeming, 'The Liability of the Government under the Constitution' (1998) 17 *Australian Bar Review* 215, 217–19; N Seddon, 'The Crown' (2000) 28 *Federal Law Review* 245, 257; M Aronson and H Whitmore, *Public Torts and Contracts* (Sydney, Law Book Co, 1982) 3–8.

[31] PD Finn, *Law and Government in Colonial Australia* (1987) 143. See also M Leeming, 'The Liability of the Government under the Constitution' (1998) 17 *Australian Bar Review* 215, 218.

held that the terms of the legislation were sufficiently broad to cover claims in tort.[32] Most subsequent colonial legislation was ultimately drafted expressly to cover tort claims (although the terms of the Victorian and Western Australian legislation were somewhat narrower than was the case in other jurisdictions).[33]

The legislation required that suits between a private individual and the Crown be conducted on the 'same' basis as suits between private individuals. Following Federation, this language was replicated at Commonwealth level, with the result that the same rights were covered federally as had been the subject of the Privy Council's advice in *Farnell v Bowman*.[34] Therefore the Commonwealth was 'in the same position as the colonies had been in prior to Federation'.[35] The relevant provision of the Judiciary Act reads:[36]

> In any suit to which the Commonwealth or a State is a party, the rights of parties shall *as nearly as possible be the same*, and judgment may be given and costs awarded on either side, as in a suit between subject and subject (emphasis added).

The precise effect of this provision was unclear. It was argued, on the one hand, that liability precedes the statute, which simply removes immunity. On the other hand, it was argued that the statute itself was the *source* of the liability. This argument was settled in *Commonwealth v Mewett*, in which a majority of the High Court held that the Commonwealth government had a common law liability in tort, but was unable to take advantage of any common law immunity from such liability. This was because sovereign immunity had only ever been a procedural bar, which was removed by section 75(iii) of the Constitution. For the reasons given above, the Constitution is not wholly compatible with the common law maxim that 'the King can do no wrong' in any case.

Consequently, the majority in *Mewett* took the view that section 64 of the Judiciary Act does not *impose* a liability and define its extent but merely recognises the existence of the Commonwealth's liability in tort. Selway argued that this changed the law in theory but brought it into line with how it had long been applied in practice and was therefore desirable regardless of the persuasiveness of the constitutional considerations applied by the majority.[37] Hill, by contrast, indicated a greater level of concern that the majority's approach had unduly disturbed the common law doctrine of government immunity from suit, arguing that the plurality should have modified the common law doctrine to make it compatible with Australia's Constitution rather than abolishing it altogether.[38]

Contrary to the view of the majority, Dawson J (with whom Toohey and McHugh JJ agreed in separate judgments) dissented on the basis that the Crown's common

[32] *Farnell v Bowman* (1887) 12 App Cas 643. See also *Sydney Harbour Trust Commissioners v Ryan* (1911) 13 CLR 358, 370 (Barton J).

[33] See M Leeming, 'The Liability of the Government under the Constitution' (1998) 17 *Australian Bar Review* 215, 218.

[34] *Asiatic Steam Navigation Co Ltd v The Commonwealth* (1956) 96 CLR 397, 427 (Kitto J).

[35] M Leeming, 'The Liability of the Government under the Constitution' (1998) 17 *Australian Bar Review* 215, 221; *Baume v Commonwealth* (1906) 4 CLR 97.

[36] Judiciary Act 1903 (Cth) s 64.

[37] B Selway, 'Liability in Tort of Australian Governments' (2002) 10 *Tort Law Review* 14, 22.

[38] G Hill, 'Private Law Actions Against the Government (Part 1)' (2007) 30 *Melbourne University Law Review* 716, 725.

law immunity in Australia had been removed by the various Crown Proceedings Acts and that these statutes were in turn the source of government liability in tort.[39] At Commonwealth level, therefore, liability was *imposed* by section 64. Further, the minority held that section 75(iii) of the Constitution does not affect the issue of immunity from suit per se, nor impose liability in private law actions, but simply confers jurisdiction on the High Court to hear such matters.

Since *Mewett*, the majority view that government liability in tort is not conferred by statute has become orthodox and has been applied without comment in numerous cases, including the subsequent High Court case of *British American Tobacco v Western Australia*.[40] In an article published prior to this line of authority developing, Leeming stated the view that judicial support for the majority position in *Mewett* had been 'only relatively slight'.[41] On either view, government immunity from suit in federal matters is not constitutionally entrenched, and it can therefore be modified or overturned by statute, subject to the Constitution.[42]

Selway argued convincingly that there is no constitutional imperative for the Commonwealth to be liable in tort under section 75(iii) of the Constitution and that the *Mewett* majority's attempt to base its conclusion on constitutional reasoning was 'not altogether satisfactory'.[43] Nonetheless, he approved of the *result* reached by the majority because the common law doctrine of immunity from suit 'was based on a misunderstanding' (by which he was referring to the arguments surveyed above in relation to the maxim 'the King shall do no wrong') and ought not, in any case, to be extended vicariously to every agent of the Commonwealth.[44] With respect, this must be correct, since *Mewett*'s result was the only one which is practical. Crown liability in tort had been a practical reality long before the High Court decided *Mewett*.[45] This goes some way to explaining the minimalist position adopted by the majority, which viewed liability as being imposed by the common law and special exemptions for government made by statute where required.

B. CAN PUBLIC AUTHORITIES EVER BE LIABLE IN TORT WHERE INDIVIDUALS WOULD NOT BE?

Most current Australian iterations of Crown proceedings legislation continue to qualify the proposition that governments are to be liable to subjects in tort

[39] *Mewett* (1997) 191 CLR 471, 496 (Dawson J).

[40] *British American Tobacco v Western Australia* (2003) 217 CLR 30, 57–58 (McHugh, Gummow & Hayne JJ). See G Hill, 'Private Law Actions Against the Government (Part 1)' (2007) 30 *Melbourne University Law Review* 716, 721.

[41] M Leeming, 'The Liability of the Government under the Constitution' (1998) 17 *Australian Bar Review* 215, 223.

[42] *Mewett* (1997) 191 CLR 471, 531 (Gaudron J). See M Leeming, 'The Liability of the Government under the Constitution' (1998) 17 *Australian Bar Review* 215, 229; G Hill, 'Private Law Actions Against the Government (Part 1)' (2007) 30 *Melbourne University Law Review* 716, 721; N Seddon, 'The Crown' (2000) 28 *Federal Law Review* 245, 257–58.

[43] B Selway, 'Liability in Tort of Australian Governments' (2002) 10 *Tort Law Review* 14, 34.

[44] ibid, 34–35.

[45] ibid, 35.

in the same way as in any action between subjects, by stating that suits between individuals and government are to be conducted *as nearly as possible* on the same basis as between subjects. This form of words is not precisely consistent across every Australian jurisdiction.[46] The NSW, Queensland and Victorian legislation each uses the words 'as nearly as possible', as does section 64 of the Judiciary Act. These qualifying words are not found in the relevant sections of the legislation in the other Australian jurisdictions. However, the effect of the respective sections is the same in each jurisdiction regardless of whether the same formulation of words is used because the 'qualification flows not from statute but from substantive principles of the common law'.[47]

The qualification 'as nearly as possible' recognises implicitly that governments cannot be dealt with on *exactly* the 'same' basis as private individuals and that their responsibilities *do* make them different to individuals in some important senses. Gleeson CJ noted that:[48]

> That formula reflects an aspiration to equality before the law, embracing governments and citizens, and also a recognition that perfect equality is not attainable. Although the first principle is that the tortious liability of governments is, as completely as possible, assimilated to that of citizens, there are limits to the extent to which that is possible. They arise from the nature and responsibilities of governments. In determining the existence and content of a duty of care, there are differences between the concerns and obligations of governments, and those of citizens.

On this view, the qualification 'as nearly as possible' is an aspiration that cannot be realised completely. It is, however, worth noting Cane's admonition that, to the extent that it cannot, we should not let our focus remain on mere equality but on 'the "right" mix of similar and dissimilar treatment'.[49]

The equality principle expressed by Dicey is subject to the reality of limitation expressed by Gleeson CJ, which affects the extent of governments' liability in tort and, more specifically, in the law of negligence, which has been the battleground for testing the extent of the differences between government and private actors since the decision of the House of Lords in *Dorset Yacht*.[50] The problem with this 'is that while most people have a sense that governments occasionally warrant different treatment, the commentators have difficulty agreeing on a set of principles to

[46] Compare Judiciary Act 1903 (Cth) s 64; Crown Proceedings Act 1992 (ACT) s 5(1); Crown Proceedings Act 1988 (NSW) s 5(2); Crown Proceedings Act 1993 (NT) s 5(1); Crown Proceedings Act 1980 (Qld) s 9(2); Crown Proceedings Act 1992 (SA) s 5(1); Crown Proceedings Act 1993 (Tas) s 5(1); Crown Proceedings Act 1958 (Vic) s 25; Crown Suits Act 1947 (WA) s 5(1); Crown Proceedings Act 1950 (NZ) s 6. See generally S Kneebone, 'Claims Against the Commonwealth and States and Their Instrumentalities in Federal Jurisdiction: Section 64 of the *Judiciary Act*' (1996) 24 *Federal Law Review* 93; B Selway, 'The Source and Nature of the Liability in Tort of Australian Governments' (2002) 10 *Tort Law Review* 14, 19–20; M Aronson and H Whitmore, *Public Torts and Contracts* (Sydney, Law Book Co, 1982) 9–12.

[47] M Aronson, 'Government Liability' (2008) 32 *Melbourne University Law Review* 44, 45.

[48] *Graham Barclay Oysters Pty Ltd v Ryan* (2002) 211 CLR 540, 556 (citation omitted). His Honour was discussing the Crown Proceedings Act 1988 (NSW) s 5.

[49] P Cane, 'Damages' (1999) 9 *Otago Law Review* 489, 490–91.

[50] See *Home Office v Dorset Yacht Co Ltd* [1970] AC 1004.

determine when that is the case'.[51] Stevens, for example, espoused the view that public authorities should always be treated in the same manner as private actors, absent some statutory duty or privilege being imposed to alter that state of equality.[52] Where public authorities are held to a lesser standard than private individuals, that is now a consequence of legislation in Australia.[53] The real difficulties lie where there is an argument that public authorities should be held to some *greater* standard.

Government can be liable for the negligent performance of acts which are never performed by private individuals. In *Indian Towing*, Frankfurter J asked whether there was:[54]

> a rational ground, one that would carry conviction to minds not in the grip of technical obscurities, why there should be any difference in result ... [depending] ... on such a completely fortuitous circumstance—the presence or absence of identical private activity.

This point is obvious once one realises that 'otherwise, all sorts of governmental activities—such as police, prisons, fire fighters, air traffic control and licensing—would [be] free of any duty of care'.[55] Courts have additionally held over the course of the last 40 years (since *Dorset Yacht* and, particularly, *Anns*) that public authorities may in some circumstances have a common law duty to perform a *positive* act in order to prevent loss or damage to an individual, even without that individual having any subjective expectation of, or express reliance on, such action.[56]

This development has not been met with universal approbation; Harlow noted that '*Dorset Yacht* set the state squarely in the liability frame'.[57] This remark reflected Harlow's long-held low opinion of that case.[58] She quoted Atiyah to the effect that a belief by the public 'that ultimately the government is responsible for everything that happens in society' will result in government and other public bodies getting sued, 'whatever they do or fail to do', because it creates a 'blame culture'.[59] Lord Reid had earlier made an infamous, chest-beating rejection of concerns that the decision in *Dorset Yacht* would lead to an opening of the 'floodgates':[60]

> It may be that public servants of the State of New York are so apprehensive, easily dissuaded from doing their duty and intent on preserving public funds from costly claims that they could be influenced in this way [ie into 'defensive' procedures in correctional facilities]. But my experience leads me to believe that Her Majesty's servants are made of sterner stuff. So I have no hesitation in rejecting this argument. I can see no good ground in public policy for giving this immunity to a government department.

[51] M Aronson, 'Government Liability' (2008) 32 *Melbourne University Law Review* 44, 46.
[52] R Stevens, *Torts and Rights* (Oxford, Oxford University Press, 2007) 218–19.
[53] See eg Civil Liability Act 2002 (NSW) Part 5.
[54] *Indian Towing Co Inc v United States* 350 US 61 (1955), 66–67.
[55] M Aronson and H Whitmore, *Public Torts and Contracts* (Sydney, Law Book Co, 1982) 42.
[56] *Dorset Yacht* [1970] AC 1004; *Anns v Merton Borough Council* [1978] AC 728.
[57] C Harlow, *State Liability* (Oxford, Oxford University Press, 2004) 22.
[58] See C Harlow, *Compensation and Government Torts* (London, Sweet and Maxwell, 1982) 47–50.
[59] C Harlow, *State Liability* (Oxford, Oxford University Press, 2004) 22; citing PS Atiyah, *The Damages Lottery* (Oxford, Hart Publishing, 1997) 139.
[60] *Dorset Yacht* [1970] AC 1004, 1033.

Harlow stated that, contrary to Lord Reid's confidence, 'the floodgates were, however, soon to open' in cases like *Sharp*, *Dutton v Bognor Regis* and *Anns*.[61]

However, this response did not entirely square with his Lordship's point, made immediately before the statement extracted above:[62]

> The basic question is: who shall bear the loss caused by that carelessness [ie that of the Home Office's employees to control the Borstal boys effectively]—the innocent respondents or the Home Office, who are vicariously liable for the conduct of their careless officers?

A similar point had been made 50 years previously by Lord Moulton.[63] It was ultimately approved by Lord Reid, who said that:[64]

> the feeling that it was equitable that burdens borne for the good of the nation should be distributed over the whole nation and should not be allowed to fall on particular individuals has grown to be a national sentiment.

In *Dorset Yacht*, the burden suffered by the respondents was not specifically 'for the good of the nation', but it was a burden which it was within the power of the nation (through its employees) to prevent. Just as a 'national sentiment' had developed by 1920 that war damage caused by the nation should not be borne by unfortunate individuals alone, so too by 1970 the House of Lords was able to conclude that it was improper for 'innocent respondents' to bear alone the cost of the damage caused by boys over whom the state was supposed to exercise control. That is an entirely satisfactory response to Lord Reid's 'basic question', which is not to say that issues of state liability which flow from it will ever be easy.

In any case, it is unarguable that public authorities, by their very nature, will sometimes have a greater level of responsibility than a private actor in the same circumstances and ought to take positive action to exercise that responsibility because 'government is different from its citizens in having power which they do not have, and in having responsibilities to the community as a whole which they do not have'.[65] Aronson has noted that:[66]

> the starting point in most cases involving government defendants is to ask why their status should entitle them to any special dispensation. In other words, the government's civil liability should be judged by the same standards that govern private sector defendants. It is commonplace, however, that people expect positive action from government that they would not demand of a private person or firm,[67] and some of the leading negligence cases have tried to turn that expectation into a common law duty.

[61] C Harlow, *State Liability* (Oxford, Oxford University Press, 2004) 19. See *Ministry of Housing and Local Government v Sharp* [1970] 2 QB 223; *Dutton v Bognor Regis Urban District Council* [1972] 1 QB 373; *Anns* [1978] AC 728. See also C Harlow, *Compensation and Government Torts* (London, Sweet and Maxwell, 1982) 49–50.

[62] *Dorset Yacht* [1970] AC 1004, 1032.

[63] *Attorney-General v De Keyser's Royal Hotel Ltd* [1920] AC 508, 553.

[64] *Burmah Oil Co Ltd v Lord Advocate* [1965] AC 75, 104. See also C Harlow, *Compensation and Government Torts* (London, Sweet and Maxwell, 1982) 107.

[65] P Cane, 'Damages' (1999) 9 *Otago Law Review* 489, 490.

[66] M Aronson, 'Government Liability' (2008) 32 *Melbourne University Law Review* 44, 68.

[67] See eg *Graham Barclay Oysters* (2002) 211 CLR 540, 553.

In *Stuart*, Crennan and Kiefel JJ were the only members of the Court to consider this possibility. Their Honours stated that:[68]

> In principle a public authority exercising statutory powers should not be regarded by the common law any differently from a citizen. It should not be considered to have an obligation to act. *But the position of a public authority is not the same as that of a citizen and the rule of equality is not regarded as wholly applicable. It has public functions and it has statutory powers which the citizen does not.* Some powers might be effective to avert or minimise a risk of harm to particular persons or their property, but the statute might not oblige their use. The relevant concern of the common law is whether a public authority might nevertheless be considered to be under a duty of care which obliges it to exercise its powers in a particular way (emphasis added).

In other words, there is more than one sense in which public authorities and private actors are not 'the same'. I have referred above to the fact that legislation which enshrines the Diceyan concept that a public authority ought not to be exempted from liability merely due to its 'public' status, is qualified by the legislative statement that public and private actors shall be treated only 'as nearly as possible … the same'.[69] This qualification is generally seen as recognising that the liability of public authorities may properly be less than that of private actors in some circumstances, due to the greater demands under which they operate. Crennan and Kiefel JJ commenced their analysis in *Stuart* with the converse proposition, that *more* might sometimes be expected of public authorities where they have a capacity to prevent harm which is not possessed by individuals. This is, however, not a position that has yet found majority support in the High Court.

C. CAN PUBLIC AUTHORITIES BE LIABLE FOR BOTH ACTS AND OMISSIONS IN BREACH OF COMMON LAW DUTY?

Public authorities have long been subject to tortious liability at common law for negligently failing to act in circumstances where a duty of care exists to take positive action, despite the 'fundamental' distinction between misfeasance and nonfeasance.[70] This is because liability for negligent omissions is one area in which public authorities are sometimes held to a higher standard than a private individual, although the proposition that public authorities may owe a duty of care in respect of failures to act is qualified in certain circumstances by statute.[71] Claims of this sort are sometimes cast in terms of a negligent failure to exercise a statutory power (rather than a duty), an issue with which I deal in relation to the scenario in Chapter nine.

[68] *Stuart v Kirkland-Veenstra* (2009) 237 CLR 215, 259 (Crennan & Kiefel JJ) (citations omitted).

[69] eg Judiciary Act 1903 (Cth) s 64.

[70] RP Balkin and JLR Davis, *Law of Torts*, 5th edn (New South Wales, LexisNexis Butterworths, 2013) 207.

[71] See eg Civil Liability Act 2002 (NSW) s 44.

There is no *general* common law duty to act to prevent another from being harmed, either on a private actor or on a public authority.[72] As Crennan and Kiefel JJ noted in *Stuart*, this is a separate consideration to a *statutory* duty to act which may fall upon a public authority.[73] Common law duty of care in respect of omissions is limited to a few sets of circumstances. First, there is a general common law duty owed by any person or authority to take positive action where he, she or it *creates* a risk.[74] Such an omission to take care of others exposed to a risk created by the defendant is contrasted to 'pure' or 'mere' omissions. The line of authority started in England by the decision of the House of Lords in *Anns* extended the liability of public authorities by holding, in essence, that not only was a public authority under an obligation not to cause or increase danger or risk, but that it may be exposed to liability in respect of a 'pure' omission if a court held that it owed a common law duty of care to exercise statutory powers available to it which would have reduced or prevented the plaintiff's loss. This line of reasoning was subsequently rejected by the House of Lords in *Stovin*.[75] It was not followed by the High Court in *Pyrenees*, which in turn has since been applied in both *Crimmins* and *Brodie*.[76]

Secondly, any person or authority may come under a duty to take positive action by undertaking 'some task which leads another to rely on its being performed'.[77] A number of cases have supported the proposition that a public authority may owe a duty to act where it 'has undertaken to do so or induced a person to rely on [it] doing so'.[78] Specifically, a duty of care may be owed by a public authority in circumstances where it has conducted itself in such a way that others have relied on it to exercise its statutory powers.[79] This doctrine has been described as 'specific reliance' and may apply to a public authority which excites an expectation in individuals that it will exercise a statutory power or discretion. Lord Toulson has warned against allowing the circumstances in which a defendant can be said to have assumed responsibility for the plaintiff to be 'expanded artificially', such as by making the test whether a court has imposed responsibility upon the defendant.[80]

The first and second qualifications above apply in the same manner to public authorities as to any private individual. A third circumstance is applicable only to public actors, even in the absence of specific reliance, and liability is on a fundamentally different basis from the first two qualifications, since private actors will not generally be invested with statutory powers. A common law duty to act may arise as

[72] *Smith v Leurs* (1945) 70 CLR 256, 262 (Dixon J); *Hargrave v Goldman* (1963) 110 CLR 40, 66 (Windeyer J); *Council of the Shire of Sutherland v Heyman* (1985) 157 CLR 424, 444 (Gibbs CJ); 459–60 (Mason J); *Stovin v Wise* [1996] AC 923, 943 (Lord Hoffmann); *Stuart* (2009) 237 CLR 215, 258 (Crennan & Kiefel JJ).

[73] *Stuart* (2009) 237 CLR 215, 259.

[74] See S Wotherspoon, 'Translating the Public Law "May" into the Common Law "Ought": the Case for a Unique Common Law Cause of Action for Statutory Negligence' (2009) 83 *Australia Law Journal* 331, 334.

[75] *Stovin v Wise* [1996] AC 923.

[76] *Pyrenees Shire Council v Day* (1998) 192 CLR 330. See *Crimmins v Stevedoring Industry Finance Committee* (1999) 200 CLR 1; *Brodie v Singleton Shire Council* (2001) 206 CLR 512.

[77] *Heyman* (1985) 157 CLR 424, 479 (Brennan J).

[78] *Stovin* [1996] AC 923, 944 (Lord Hoffmann).

[79] See *Heyman* (1985) 157 CLR 424, 459–60 (Mason J).

[80] *Michael v Chief Constable of South Wales Police* [2015] 2 WLR 343, 366.

a result of interaction between a public authority and another party, taking account of their relative strengths and weaknesses. This may be because they have a relationship of a kind in which it is accepted that the public authority owes the other party a duty to take positive action. In *Stuart*, Crennan and Kiefel JJ gave examples of such relationships including 'employer and employee, teacher and pupil, carrier and passenger, shipmaster and crew'.[81] To describe the interaction between parties as a 'relationship' often strains the limits of that particular appellation. More generally, a duty of care may arise due either to the control that one party has over the circumstances, or to the vulnerability of the other party in those circumstances.[82] This was Gould's understanding of *East Suffolk v Kent*.[83]

Hence, the result in *Crimmins* may be understood as deriving from a situation in which the Stevedoring Authority had and exerted immense practical control over the circumstances and conditions in which stevedores, vulnerable to exposure to asbestos fibres, were required to work. McHugh J saw the relevant breach of duty to be in the fact that the Authority had directed Mr Crimmins, and others like him, to work in circumstances where it knew that he would be exposed to danger in the form of asbestos fibres.[84] With respect, this is the approach that best reflects the reality of the relationship between Mr Crimmins and the Authority, which had both the power to direct Mr Crimmins where to work and the power to cancel or suspend his registration to work as a stevedore if he did not comply with the Authority's directions, although Gaudron J viewed this only as a circumstance going to Mr Crimmins' vulnerability.[85] In their judgment in *Stuart*, Gummow, Hayne and Heydon JJ seemed prepared to accept that the Authority had, at least, done something positive; it had 'put the workers at risk of harm because it was the Authority that assigned the workers to particular stevedores'.[86] However, this was expressed as a factor indicating 'control' rather than that the Authority's duty of care was based in the fact that it had directed Mr Crimmins into danger. Importantly, once the relevant breach of duty is characterised as a positive act (a direction) on the part of the Authority, questions of whether and how the liability of public authorities should be limited become moot.[87]

The potential relevance of a positive duty to act on the part of a public authority can be demonstrated using the example of *East Suffolk v Kent*.[88] The plaintiff suffered flooding to his land as the result of a breach in a sea wall. This was not caused by any positive act of the defendant authority. Rather, Mr Kent sought compensation from the defendant because it had exercised its statutory power to repair the

[81] *Stuart* (2009) 237 CLR 215, 259.

[82] *Crimmins* (1999) 200 CLR 1, 24–25 (Gaudron J); 40–41 (McHugh J); 85 (Kirby J); *Pyrenees* (1998) 192 CLR 330, 361 (Toohey J); 372–73 (McHugh J); *Stuart* (2009) 237 CLR 215, 260–61 (Crennan & Kiefel JJ); cf *Brodie* (2001) 206 CLR 512, 627 (Hayne J).

[83] *East Suffolk Rivers Catchment Board v Kent* [1941] AC 74. See BC Gould, 'Damages in Administrative Law' (1972) 5 *New Zealand Universities Law Review* 105, 109–10.

[84] *Crimmins* (1999) 200 CLR 1, 28.

[85] ibid, 24–25.

[86] *Stuart* (2009) 237 CLR 215, 255.

[87] See eg *Heyman* (1985) 157 CLR 424; *Graham Barclay Oysters* (2002) 211 CLR 540; *Pyrenees* (1998) 192 CLR 330; *Stovin* [1996] AC 923.

[88] [1941] AC 74.

wall in such an inefficient manner that Mr Kent's farm land remained flooded for longer than it would have done if the Board had exercised its powers with due care and skill. Stevens categorised this as nothing more than a failure of the Board to confer a benefit to which Mr Kent had no enforceable right.[89] This reasoning would be incontestable, in the absence of an undertaking to the contrary on which the plaintiff had relied, if the party who failed to confer the benefit of repairing the sea wall was merely Mr Kent's neighbour.[90] Regardless, Stevens' statement of the law relating to public authorities is accurate in England following *Gorringe*.[91]

If we assume, however, that repairing sea walls was a substantial purpose of the defendant Board and that the plaintiff either elected not to take action to help himself in the expectation that the Board would, or was unable to help himself in any case, then the Board's failure to prosecute its statutory purpose with reasonable skill and expedition breaches, at the very least, a moral duty on the part of the Board, even if it cannot *create* a common law duty of care per se. The starting point for liability in negligence has always been articulated in terms of the existence of a moral duty.[92] The absence of a right to the benefit which it was the purpose of the Board to confer does not on its own provide a satisfactory basis for denying the existence of such a duty of care. Stevens has noted that the fact that 'we do not have a right good against the rest of the world not to suffer economic harm was firmly established in the 1890s in a trio of decisions in the House of Lords'.[93] In response to this, Priel said that 'such statements … suggest that at times Stevens' argument is about legal rights. Whatever one may think of these cases, they do not "establish", definitely not "firmly", what *moral* rights we have'.[94] Upon this reasoning, the fact that economic harm has been inflicted due to the negligent failure of a public authority to intervene may well form the legal basis for the payment of damages where the entire purpose of the public authority was to prevent the harm from occurring.

Lord Atkin's dissent in *East Suffolk v Kent* provides, at best, a vague basis on which to extend a duty of care to public authorities which have a statutory power, but not a statutory duty, to act. His Lordship said that the Board in *East Suffolk v Kent* should have been liable to Mr Kent for the period after which its failure to relieve the flooding of his land became 'unreasonable'.[95] This begs the question, which is not answered by his Lordship's analogy to a case of contractual duty.[96] A court charged with interpreting the meaning of an express contractual term that a party 'should proceed without unreasonable delay' is engaged in an entirely different process to one which imposes upon that party a common law duty to the same effect, primarily because in the latter case the defendant has not consented to the

[89] R Stevens, *Torts and Rights* (Oxford, Oxford University Press, 2007) 221; cf T Cornford, *Towards a Public Law of Tort* (Aldershot, Ashgate, 2008) 131.

[90] BC Gould, 'Damages in Administrative Law' (1972) 5 *New Zealand Universities Law Review* 105, 109.

[91] *Gorringe v Calderdale Metropolitan Borough Council* [2004] WLR 1057.

[92] *Donoghue v Stevenson* [1932] AC 562, 580.

[93] R Stevens, *Torts and Rights* (2007) 21–22. See *Mogul Steamship Co v McGregor Gow & Co* [1892] AC 25; *Bradford v Pickles* [1895] AC 587; *Allen v Flood* [1898] AC 1.

[94] D Priel, 'Review of *Torts and Rights*' (2011) 2 *Jurisprudence* 227, 234.

[95] *East Suffolk v Kent* [1941] AC 74, 92.

[96] ibid, 93.

imposition of a legal duty. What is the source of the common law duty that action be undertaken within a reasonable time? A court obliged to ascertain at what point such a duty has been breached has no principles of statutory or contractual construction to fall back on. Lord Atkin's point was that principles of *causation* of damage are the same in contract and tort. Nonetheless, the analogy pursued by his Lordship provides no assistance in determining the *existence* of a duty of care.

D. CAN PUBLIC AUTHORITIES BE LIABLE IN EQUITY WHERE AN ESTOPPEL IS RAISED?

Equity is sometimes—erroneously—viewed as having little to contribute to public law issues.[97] Additionally, in regard to equity's application to decision-making by public authorities, as in regard to tort liability, there is no prima facie reason why equitable remedies should not be available against public authorities.[98] Indeed, the power of the High Court to grant injunctive relief against an officer of the Commonwealth is enshrined in section 75(v) of the Constitution, and declaratory relief is a remedy inherently available from superior courts on judicial review applications.[99] It must be remembered, however, that the declaration was historically, and remains only, a statutory remedy, albeit one which could only be granted by Chancery. Courts nonetheless can and do 'borrow equitable principles when exercising the discretion to grant or refuse the remedy'.[100] While there is no difficulty per se with equitable remedies being available in litigation against the government, difficulties arise because private law remedies are inapt to certain government functions.

There is no specific doctrine of public law estoppel.[101] It is connected to the doctrine of legitimate expectations in judicial review but the differences between the two doctrines have long been noted.[102] The fact that public authorities are not truly the same as private individuals means that consideration must be given to the impact on the public at large of enforcing a promise to an individual. The differences between equity's application to individuals and public entities also arise in other contexts. For example, Mason J expressly noted the importance of public interest considerations in applying 'private law' causes of action to public authorities.[103] Equity is sometimes capable of raising an estoppel to create a cause of action where an individual is misled to his or her detriment by a government entity which is exercising powers

[97] cf JJ Spigelman, 'The Equitable Origins of the Improper Purpose Ground' in L Pearson et al (eds), *Administrative Law in a Changing State* (Oxford, Hart Publishing, 2008) 147.

[98] See Judiciary Act 1903 (Cth) s 64 and the legislation cited in n 29 above.

[99] *Ainsworth v Criminal Justice Commission* (1992) 175 CLR 564, 581.

[100] M Aronson and M Groves, *Judicial Review of Administrative Action*, 5th edn (Sydney, Thompson Reuters, 2013) [15.20].

[101] *Annetts v McCann* (1990) 170 CLR 596, 605 (Brennan J).

[102] See eg *Haoucher v Minister for Immigration and Ethnic Affairs* (1990) 169 CLR 648, 669–70 (Toohey J); *Minister of State for Immigration and Ethnic Affairs v Teoh* (1995) 183 CLR 273, 301 (Toohey J); *Mount Sinai Hospital Centre v Quebec (Minister of Health and Social Services)* [2001] 2 SCR 281, [30] (Binnie J); H Woolf and J Jowell, *De Smith's Judicial Review*, 5th edn (London, Sweet and Maxwell, 1995) 426.

[103] *Commonwealth v John Fairfax & Sons Ltd* (1980) 147 CLR 39, 51–52.

held in common with natural persons.[104] As with liability in tort, this occurs on the same basis as an estoppel against any other party, subject to some additional considerations peculiar to public authorities. As Stevens J, writing for the Supreme Court, said in *Heckler*, 'however heavy the burden might be when an estoppel is asserted against the Government, the private party surely cannot prevail without *at least* demonstrating that the traditional elements of an estoppel are present' (emphasis added).[105]

Public authorities 'cannot fetter the performance of their duties by contract or estoppel or, without statutory authority, bind themselves to perform them in a particular way'.[106] The Justice—All Souls Report traced this limitation to the decision in *Western Fish*, which it stated 'comes close to excluding for all practical purposes the law of estoppel from the realm of the exercise of statutory powers'.[107] The wording of that conclusion seems to indicate that the Committee thought, as some Australian judges came to do, that the door to equitable relief may still be ajar in the right circumstances. While this has proved to be true only theoretically, and not in any practical sense, in Australia, it has become irrelevant in England as a result of the rise of the doctrine of substantive legitimate expectations.[108] In this respect, the issues mirror those which limit the availability of liability in tort for the otherwise negligent acts of public authorities, although the comparison is not absolute, given the greater remedial flexibility possessed by equity.

The limitations on estoppels being enforced against public authorities are largely policy-based, or as a function of an authority's empowerment by statute, rather than due to the authorities' public *status*. For example, an estoppel cannot be enforced where the enforcement would require the future exercise of a statutory discretion to be fettered, nor may an estoppel be enforced against a public authority where it would have the effect of compelling the authority to act ultra vires.[109] This point is in fact no more than an extension of the principle that an estoppel cannot, as a matter of public policy, compel an unlawful act either by a public authority or a private actor.[110] Therefore, it is uncontroversial that a representation made on behalf of a public authority that it will perform an act that it has neither statutory nor executive power to perform will be substantively unenforceable, just as an estoppel cannot

[104] eg *Commonwealth v Verwayen* (1990) 170 CLR 394.

[105] *Heckler v Community Health Services of Crawford County Inc* 467 US 51 (1984), 60. See also *Re Minister for Immigration, Local Government and Ethnic Affairs v Kurtovic* (1990) 21 FCR 193, 208 (Gummow J).

[106] KR Handley, *Estoppel by Conduct and Election* (London, Sweet and Maxwell, 2006) 22 (citation omitted).

[107] JUSTICE—All Souls, *Administrative Justice* (P Neill (ed), Oxford, Clarendon Press, 1988) 174. See *Western Fish Products Ltd v Penwith District Council* [1981] 2 All ER 204.

[108] See *Reprotech* [2003] 1 WLR 348, 358.

[109] *Southend-on-Sea Corporation v Hodgson (Wickford) Ltd* [1962] 1 QB 416; *Maritime Electric Co Ltd v General Dairies Ltd* [1937] AC 610. See KR Handley, *Estoppel by Conduct and Election* (London, Sweet and Maxwell, 2006) 22–23; P Cane, *Administrative Law*, 5th edn (Oxford, Oxford University Press, 2011) 311–12; *Kurtovic* (1990) 21 FCR 193, 211–16; *Howell v Falmouth Boat Construction Co Ltd* [1951] AC 837, 845 (Lord Simonds); cf *Robertson v Minister for Pensions* [1949] 1 KB 227. These limitations are discussed above in Chapter 7 of this volume.

[110] KR Handley, *Estoppel by Conduct and Election* (London, Sweet and Maxwell, 2006) 296.

give a court or a tribunal jurisdiction that is not permitted by statute.[111] This is particularly evident since an official cannot even have ostensible authority which is inconsistent with his or her statutory limitations.[112]

Where public authorities are subject to estoppel because they are exercising powers held in common with natural persons, refusal to give substantive effect to an estoppel against a public authority is based on the same principle which holds that in Australia soft law cannot be given binding force. This is because decision-makers are given discretion by Parliament which may not be restricted other than by the terms of the statutory grant of power and the procedural requirements of administrative law. Further, this merely procedural effect of soft law can also be avoided with sufficient warning that the decision-maker will disregard it.[113]

Nonetheless, there is need for an equitable remedy where an individual relies, both reasonably and actually, to his or her detriment on a soft law instrument being applied by a public authority. The fact that an estoppel raised in such circumstances cannot be enforced if the public authority would thereby be compelled to act ultra vires does not contradict this argument. The equitable jurisdiction to mould relief leaves open the possibility that justice could frequently be satisfied with a lesser equity, such as equitable compensation.[114]

There is an argument that, given the scope to obtain damages for government misrepresentations in tort, there is no need to stretch equity to provide a monetary remedy, for example because 'common law developments in negligence have substantially replaced the need for a revival of [equitable] compensation'.[115] However, there is a long-established jurisdiction in equity to provide compensation as a remedy for a misrepresentation which causes the breach of an equitable right. Equitable compensation in relation to representations made by public authorities may also be available in circumstances where a duty of care is not owed, although situations in which equity can provide a remedy where none is available at law will be exceptions to the general rule. Soft law representations from which a public authority seeks to depart will frequently see the grounds for a remedy to be made available satisfied both in equity and at law, although equity's remedies will only be applied where those available at law are insufficient.

A renewal of the recognition that equity has the capacity to award compensation for breach of an equitable duty would be a significant improvement to the state of the law. I have responded elsewhere to the possible objections which might be raised to prevent what I consider to be a wholly welcome development.[116]

[111] ibid, 299.

[112] *Attorney-General for Ceylon v AD Silva* [1953] AC 461, 479. See also *Western Fish* [1981] 2 All ER 204; JUSTICE—All Souls, *Administrative Justice* (P Neill (ed), Oxford, Clarendon Press, 1988) 345.

[113] *Lam* (2003) 214 CLR 1, 14 (Gleeson CJ).

[114] *Giumelli v Giumelli* (1999) 196 CLR 101, 114.

[115] IE Davidson, 'The Equitable Remedy of Compensation' (1982) 13 *Melbourne University Law Review* 349, 350.

[116] G Weeks, 'Estoppel and Public Authorities' (2010) 4 *Journal of Equity* 247, 282–86.

9

Private Law Liability: Example 1

Suppose the following factual scenario, which is based upon, but departs from, the facts of *Stuart*:[1]

A. Before dawn, two police officers find a man sitting in his car in a public car-park. The man has taken various steps preparatory to attempting to commit suicide.

B. A police officer has a statutory duty to apprehend a person who is likely to commit suicide. The relevant section of the Mental Health Act reads as follows:

> A member of the police force shall apprehend any person who has recently attempted, or undertaken any act preliminary to attempting, suicide or attempted to cause serious bodily harm to herself or himself or to some other person.

C. The police officers subjectively form the view that the man is likely to attempt suicide.

D. The man tells the police officers that he had considered doing 'something stupid' but has changed his mind and now wants to go home to talk to his wife. The police officers allow the man to drive away.

E. The man returns home and attempts to commit suicide after his wife leaves the house. He is unsuccessful but his attempt leaves him in a permanent vegetative state. Through his wife as his tutor, he now seeks compensation from the police officers for the injuries he sustained.

Let us consider the facts above and address a series of questions based on different permutations of these facts.

I. First, are the police officers liable for breach of a statutory duty or a common law duty of care owed to the plaintiff?

[1] *Stuart v Kirkland-Veenstra* (2009) 237 CLR 215. The allegation that the appellants ought to have adhered to the relevant terms of the Victoria Police Manual was not pressed before the High Court and was therefore not the subject of consideration in any of the judgments in that court.

II. Secondly, suppose that, instead of the text in Fact B, the relevant section of the Mental Health Act states that:[2]

> A police officer may apprehend a person if the police officer has reasonable grounds for believing that the person is likely by act or neglect to attempt suicide or to cause serious bodily harm to herself or himself or to some other person.

Can the existence of such a statutory power to act be converted into a common law duty to act?

III. Thirdly, suppose the following additional facts:

> F. The Police Force issues a copy of the Police Manual, a soft law instrument, to each police officer. It is used to ensure that police procedures are internally consistent. The Police Manual contained the following provision:
>
> > A police officer who encounters any person who has recently attempted suicide, or undertaken any act preliminary to attempting suicide, must contact the nearest Crisis Assessment and Treatment (CAT) service and should, wherever possible, stay with the person until he or she is assessed by that service.
>
> G. The Police Manual is not available to any person other than police officers.

Does the provision in the Police Manual assist the plaintiff in establishing that the officers owed a common law duty of care to him?

IV. Fourthly, suppose that Fact G were instead to read as follows:

> G. The Police Manual is available for inspection at every police station and may also be downloaded from the Police Force's website.

What would be the result, given that the Police Manual was available to the public, if the plaintiff knew of its terms?

V. Fifthly, would the situation in question IV be any different if the plaintiff had *not* been aware of the relevant terms of the Police Manual?

These questions are intended to address the capacity of soft law to create a duty of care. A full consideration of the tort issues involved in this scenario is beyond the scope of this book. In particular, issues of causation and, if the

[2] This is an edited version of Mental Health Act 1986 (Vic) s 10(1). I have omitted the requirement that the person 'appears to be mentally ill'. In *Stuart*, the Court held that the power to apprehend Mr Veenstra under this section was never enlivened because, in essence, he had appeared to the officers to be suicidal but not mentally ill. His right as an apparently sane man to commit suicide trumped the police power to apprehend him.

man's wife were in fact the plaintiff, remoteness would likely be determinative of the case. The following points are concerned only with when and in what circumstances a duty of care may arise on the various sets of facts set out above.

A. WOULD A CLEAR STATUTORY DUTY TO ACT EXPOSE THE OFFICERS TO TORT LIABILITY?

Assuming that the police officers had a statutory duty, rather than a statutory power, to apprehend the plaintiff, a failure to exercise that duty may be remediable in damages under the tort of breach of statutory duty. The first step to making out this tort is to establish that a common law cause of action was intended to be available under the Mental Health Act.[3] To succeed, the plaintiff would then need to establish that:

(i) the duty was imposed on the police officers;[4]
(ii) that the Mental Health Act was enacted to prevent the kind of harm suffered by the plaintiff;[5]
(iii) that the plaintiff was a person for whose benefit the Mental Health Act was passed;[6]
(iv) that the officers did in fact breach the statutory duty; and
(v) that that breach caused the plaintiff's injuries.[7]

Once these elements are established, the tort is usually treated as one of strict liability, although the officers could benefit from a complete defence if they were able to prove that the plaintiff's injuries were caused *solely* by his own conduct, without any independent fault on their part.[8] This would be unlikely where the entire point of the duty was to protect the plaintiff from inflicting harm on himself.

However, the tort of breach of statutory duty is now affected by statutory provisions.[9] These apply the *Wednesbury* standard as a minimum basis for liability on the part of public authorities.[10] Harlow presaged the legislative adoption of the *Wednesbury* standard by two decades, having argued that the courts already 'used this 'public law' test of reasonableness to restrict the growth of liability in negligence'.[11] After the fact, she commented that the Australian experience stood as 'a sharp warning that reforms of public liability are not necessarily beneficent'.[12] This development will probably have the practical effect of placing the final nail in the coffin of the

[3] *O'Connor v SP Bray Ltd* (1937) 56 CLR 464.
[4] *Darling Island Stevedoring and Lighterage Co Ltd v Long* (1957) 97 CLR 36.
[5] *Mummery v Irvings Pty Ltd* (1956) 96 CLR 99.
[6] *Read v Croydon Corporation* [1938] 4 All ER 631.
[7] See generally *X v Bedfordshire County Council* [1995] 2 AC 633.
[8] D Mendelson, *The New Law of Torts*, 2nd edn (Melbourne, Oxford University Press, 2010) 695.
[9] In Victoria, see Wrongs Act 1958 (Vic) s 84(2). In other Australian jurisdictions, see Civil Liability Act 2002 (NSW) s 43(2); Civil Law (Wrongs) Act 2002 (ACT) s 111(2); Civil Liability Act 2003 (Qld) s 36(2); Civil Liability Act 2002 (Tas) s 40(2); cf Civil Liability Act 2002 (WA) s 5Y. There is no equivalent section in Civil Liability Act 1936 (SA).
[10] See E Carroll, '*Wednesbury* as a Limit on Liability' (2007) 15 *Tort Law Review* 77; G Weeks, 'A Marriage of Strangers: the Wednesbury Standard in Tort Law' (2010) 7 *Macquarie Journal of Business Law* 131; M Aronson, 'Government Liability' (2008) 32 *Melbourne University Law Review* 44.
[11] C Harlow, *Compensation and Government Torts* (London, Sweet and Maxwell, 1982) 53.
[12] C Harlow, 'Rationalising Administrative Compensation' [2010] *PL* 321, 323.

action for breach of statutory duty: Aronson contended that it already had 'almost no life in this country beyond its original context of workplace injuries', with the implication that the tort reform legislation had little practical effect in this regard.[13] At any rate, it is safe to say that the tort of breach of statutory duty will never expand to new fields. Indeed, breach of statutory duty does not give rise to a cause of action separate from negligence in either the USA or Canada.[14]

Even if we were to assume that the common law test described above were met and the officers were in breach of their statutory duty to apprehend the plaintiff because he had taken steps towards committing suicide, it is unlikely that their failure to do so would be characterised as so unreasonable that no reasonable police officers in their position would have done the same thing. We can rule out liability for breach of statutory duty.

If the plaintiff sought to establish the officers' liability in negligence, the existence of a common law duty of care would need to be proven separately to showing the existence of a statutory duty, whose breach may be remediable in public law.[15] This will, however, generally be the case absent a clear contrary intention in the terms of the statute.[16] It is unlikely that a duty of care would otherwise be owed by police officers, although this exception applies particularly to circumstances in which the police are investigating criminal activity.[17] Lord Toulson has said that any exception which applies to police investigations in this regard should not be characterised as an 'immunity' which 'is generally understood to be an exemption based on a defendant's status from a liability imposed by the law on others, as in the case of sovereign immunity'.[18]

The reforms by which suicide and attempted suicide were decriminalised by statute in both Australia and England were welcome.[19] They are now decades old.[20] By contrast, if the plaintiff had died and the action were brought by his widow, she would have had a right of action as the deceased's dependent, if he would have been able to sue, but for his death.[21] At common law, no remedy is available where a negligent act leads to the death of the plaintiff; neither the deceased person's estate nor his or her dependents are able to recover damages, by contrast with the position in continental Europe.[22] Remedies where a tortious act results in death have been available under statute since Lord Campbell's Liability Act 1846, which has equivalents in every Australian jurisdiction. I mean to refer here to the capacity of the wife of the deceased man to make out that a duty of care was owed to *her*, consequent to section 16 of the Wrongs Act 1958 (Vic).

[13] M Aronson, 'Government Liability' (2008) 32 *Melbourne University Law Review* 44, 76.

[14] See *Council of the Shire of Sutherland v Heyman* (1985) 157 CLR 424, 459; *The Queen v Saskatchewan Wheat Pool* [1983] 1 SCR 205.

[15] *Crimmins v Stevedoring Industry Finance Committee* (1999) 200 CLR 1, 18.

[16] *Heyman* (1985) 157 CLR 424, 459.

[17] *Brooks v Commissioner of Police of the Metropolis* [2005] 1 WLR 1495, 1509.

[18] *Michael and Others v Chief Constable of South Wales Police and Another* [2015] 2 WLR 343, 355; cf *Hill v Chief Constable of West Yorkshire* [1989] AC 53, 64 (Lord Keith).

[19] cf Lord Denning, 'This Is My Life' (1986) 1 *Denning Law Journal* 17, 21.

[20] See eg Crimes Act 1958 (Vic) s 6A; Suicide Act 1961 (UK) s 1.

[21] eg *Stuart* (2009) 237 CLR 215. See *Crimmins* (1999) 200 CLR 1, 18–19.

[22] D Mendelson, *New Law of Torts*, 2nd edn (Melbourne, Oxford University Press, 2010) 85.

B. IS A MERE STATUTORY POWER TO ACT SUFFICIENT TO IMPOSE A DUTY OF CARE ON THE OFFICERS?

On the assumed facts, the officers did not create the risk and the plaintiff cannot be said to have relied on them exercising their statutory duty to detain him. It remains to ask whether the officers were in a position of such 'control' over the plaintiff that a common law duty to take care of his safety should be imposed on them.

The question of control arose more squarely in *Crimmins* than it had in *Pyrenees Shire Council v Day*, where, as Aronson has noted with some understatement, the Council 'was not in complete control of the situation'.[23] McHugh J stated that he did not regard the result in *Pyrenees* as being dependent on the Council's 'control' of the situation at all.[24] It was in fact the steps taken by the Council in *Pyrenees* which led to a finding that it owed a duty of care, since the questions of whether an authority has 'control', or whether those who rely on it are relevantly and sufficiently 'vulnerable', are only ever relevant to the extent that they establish the existence of a relationship upon which a duty of care can be grounded.[25] This is characterised as the public party's 'entry into the field'.[26] The facts in the hypothetical scenario (and *Stuart* itself) are markedly different from those in *Crimmins*.[27] There was no prior relationship between the plaintiff and the police officers. To whatever extent the plaintiff was vulnerable, this was not a circumstance within the control of the police officers.[28] A duty of care could not be made out using this reasoning.

A duty of care would, however, have been owed by the police officers in any exercise of their statutory duty. The reasons for this are essentially the same as those for which I conclude below that the police officers would have owed a duty of care if they had only a statutory power to apprehend the plaintiff but were required to exercise that power by the terms of a soft law instrument. Ultimately, in either case, it is unlikely that the police officers would be liable in damages. Regardless of whether a duty of care were owed by the police officers, the plaintiff's case would founder at the causation stage, unless he could establish that, had the officers called the CAT service, he would not have succeeded in inflicting harm on himself.

C. CAN A PROVISION IN THE POLICE MANUAL ASSIST THE PLAINTIFF IN ESTABLISHING THAT THE OFFICERS OWED HIM A COMMON LAW DUTY OF CARE?

On the first version of the assumed facts, the plaintiff was unaware of the requirements of the Police Manual and therefore cannot be said to have relied specifically

[23] M Aronson, 'Government Liability' (2008) 32 *Melbourne University Law Review* 44, 71.

[24] *Graham Barclay Oysters* (2002) 211 CLR 540, 581.

[25] *Crimmins* (1999) 200 CLR 1, 22 (Gaudron J); *Stuart* (2009) 237 CLR 215, 254 (Gummow, Hayne & Heydon JJ).

[26] *Pyrenees Shire Council v Day* (1998) 192 CLR 330, 372 (McHugh J). See also ibid, 390 (Gummow J).

[27] *Stuart* (2009) 237 CLR 215, 255.

[28] ibid, 255.

on the officers exercising their statutory power to detain him pursuant to its requirements. He was, however, a member of a class of persons which it is arguable that the police officers should have had in mind in determining whether to exercise their powers.[29] The principle enunciated in *Hill*, as modified in *Brooks* and *Michael*, is that there will generally not be a duty of care owed by police officers to victims and witnesses of crime.[30] The question of whether the officers owed the plaintiff a common law duty of care ought not to be decided simply by applying the principle in *Hill*, which does not extend to circumstances in which such a duty of care is otherwise anticipated.

It may be arguable that, having concluded that the man was suicidal, the officers had 'entered the field' or 'assumed responsibility' over him. In *Brooks*, Lord Steyn noted that 'cases of assumption of responsibility under the extended *Hedley Byrne* doctrine fall outside the principle in [*Hill*]'.[31] This reasoning also applies to circumstances in which an intention that police have certain parties in mind is objectively observable (as to which, see the discussion of *Hedley Byrne* below). The defendant Council was held to have 'entered the field' in *Pyrenees* in a manner with which an analogy may be drawn in these circumstances. However, that aspect of the case was subsequently overturned by statute. In Victoria, the relevant provision states that:[32]

> [i]n a proceeding, the fact that a public authority exercises or decides to exercise a function does not of itself indicate that the authority is under a duty to exercise the function or that the function should be exercised in particular circumstances or in a particular way.

If the officers had entered the field, having done so could give rise to a common law duty of care to take positive action to prevent the man from taking his own life, absent the operation of statute. This reasoning depends on a finding that the officers had commenced exercising their statutory powers.[33] The relevant statutory power in the fact scenario is expressed as follows:

> A police officer *may* apprehend a person if the police officer has reasonable grounds for believing that the person is likely … to attempt suicide (emphasis added).

The best interpretation of this section is that, although the relevant statutory power to apprehend the plaintiff might become available for the police officers to exercise due to their subjective conclusion that he was likely to attempt suicide, they would retain a discretion as to whether they would in fact commence exercising that power. They decided in this case that they would not. This may be because they had concluded, after talking to the plaintiff, that he was no longer likely to attempt suicide in the immediate future. The fact that they were ultimately, tragically incorrect in this assessment does not change the fact that they had decided against exercising

[29] *Chapman v Hearse* (1961) 106 CLR 112.

[30] *Hill v Chief Constable of West Yorkshire* [1989] AC 53, 59 (Lord Keith); *Brooks v Commissioner of Police of the Metropolis* [2005] 1 WLR 1495, 1509 (Lord Steyn); *Michael* [2015] 2 WLR 343, 355 (Lord Toulson).

[31] *Brooks* [2005] 1 WLR 1495, 1509. See *Michael* [2015] 2 WLR 343, 374–75.

[32] Wrongs Act 1958 (Vic) s 85. See also Civil Law (Wrongs) Act 2002 (ACT) s 114; Civil Liability Act 2002 (NSW) s 46; Civil Liability Act 2002 (Tas) s 43; Civil Liability Act 2002 (WA) s 5AA.

[33] *Stuart* (2009) 237 CLR 215, 261 (Crennan & Kiefel JJ).

their power. This discretion was left open to the officers by the terms of the statute. However, the common law has always made an exception to the availability of the defence that the defendant has made no more than a 'pure omission' if s/he has *undertaken* to render assistance. If the Police Force has undertaken to render assistance to persons of a certain class, it follows that the Police Force is liable if certain forms of harm happen to such persons following a denial of the promised assistance.

It remains to be considered whether the soft law requirement that the police officers exercise their discretion in a certain manner has any effect on this situation. Specifically, does the content of the Police Manual form a basis for the existence of a common law duty of care to act, despite the fact that action was not compelled by the terms of the statutory power? Australian law accepts that public authorities *may* sometimes owe a greater duty than would be owed by a private actor due to a superior capacity to prevent harm.[34] By contrast, foreseeability of harm and capacity to prevent it are insufficient bases for finding that a duty of care is owed by a private actor, who would in any case generally have the right to refuse assistance. The question becomes, therefore, whether the proposition 'that a public authority may be subject to a common law duty of care when it exercises a statutory power *or* performs a statutory duty' can be extended to cover soft law obligations in addition to statutory powers and duties (emphasis added).[35] Two issues should be noted in this regard: first, that the plaintiff in *Heyman* was unsuccessful in establishing a common law duty of care on the part of the Council on either basis; and secondly that the existence of a statutory power or duty per se is insufficient to create a common law duty of care.

An orthodox response to this inquiry is that, if the statutory source of the police officers' power to apprehend does not compel them to act, a fortiori a soft law instrument cannot do so. However, the situation should be seen as being more complex than that answer indicates.[36] A finding that the officers owed the plaintiff a common law duty to contact the CAT service might be open to a court, despite the officers' statutory discretion whether to apprehend him. Such a duty would arise subject to a finding that the officers had a moral duty to intervene, as in the hypothetical discussion above based on *East Suffolk v Kent*, because protection of people at risk was a substantial purpose of their jobs. Such a purpose may be revealed in the terms of the Police Manual, which were as follows:

> A police officer who encounters any person who has recently attempted, *or undertaken any act preliminary to attempting*, suicide *must* contact the nearest [CAT] service and should, wherever possible, stay with the person until he or she is assessed by that service (emphasis added).

The Police Manual is a soft law instrument, of which the plaintiff was subjectively unaware, which was designed to guide the discretion granted to the police officers by statute. It is different from a soft law instrument aimed at regulating the behaviour

[34] S Wotherspoon, 'Translating the Public Law "May" into the Common Law "Ought"' (2009) 83 *Australian Law Journal* 331, 334–35.

[35] *Heyman* (1985) 157 CLR 424, 458 (Mason J) (see also 467–68).

[36] See above at Chapter 8.B of this volume.

of a *private* party, which takes its character as 'law' from its regulatory purpose or effect. However, the fact that the police officers possessed powers to protect the plaintiff which are not possessed by private actors is implicit in the terms of the Police Manual. Furthermore, the terms of the instruction to officers contained in the Police Manual are not dependent on them having 'reasonable grounds for believing that the person is likely … to attempt suicide', as the statutory power to apprehend the plaintiff was. Even if they were unable to stay with the plaintiff until the CAT service had assessed him (for example, because the plaintiff declined to remain with the officers and the officers did not exercise any power to apprehend the plaintiff, or because they were required to respond to an emergency situation elsewhere), the Police Manual states that they 'must' still contact the CAT service. There is nothing on the facts to suggest that they could not have done so at the time.

The Police Manual reflects the reality that, in addition to being in a unique position to protect people from committing suicide, police officers are also more likely than most people to encounter persons suffering from mental illness:[37]

> For most community-based Australian police officers, encounters with persons suffering from a mental illness or mental disorder form a regular part of the job. In a society which has largely emptied its asylums for the mentally ill, it remains a sad reality that in the absence of adequate alternative care in the community it is the police who are all too often left with the task of assisting and, where necessary, apprehending those lacking the requisite mental capacity or resources to help themselves. It is a task which they often accept with some reluctance because of the drain it creates on police time and personnel, although most commentators agree that the majority of police perform this sensitive work in a humane and appropriate way.

The reluctance of police officers to undertake this work has not prevented mental health issues from becoming a key element in police training.[38] As I have noted above, it is scarcely accurate to analyse the interaction between police officers and a man preparing to commit suicide in terms of their 'relationship' for the purpose of determining whether the officers owe a duty of care. Rather, the duty of care on the assumed facts arises from the fact that it was a substantial purpose of the officers' jobs to refer people such to the CAT service. This common law duty does not arise *from* the terms of the Police Manual but the terms of the Police Manual indicate the basis for the duty being found to exist independently by a court. Any finding that no such duty was owed, if based on a characterisation of the instruction in the Police Manual as something less than 'law', reflects a gap in negligence doctrine which is both morally and intellectually unsatisfying. This is particularly the case given that an operational duty already exists in practice. It is a very small step in these circumstances to impose a common law duty on the officers.

[37] T Anthony and D Chappell, 'Police Care for the Mentally Ill: the Restricted Vision of the High Court in *Stuart v Kirkland-Veenstra*' (2009) 21 *Current Issues in Criminal Justice* 325, 325 (citations omitted).

[38] ibid, 329.

D. WHAT WOULD BE THE RESULT IF THE POLICE MANUAL WERE AVAILABLE TO THE PUBLIC, AND THE PLAINTIFF WAS AWARE OF ITS TERMS?

The permutation of this scenario above treats the terms of the Police Manual as indicative of a moral, if not a common law, duty on the part of the police officers to take positive action to protect the plaintiff by calling the CAT service. Broadly speaking, I have looked at the first three permutations as examples of negligent omission on the part of the officers. On that analysis, nothing changes by supposing that the Manual were available, whether or not the plaintiff was aware of its terms.

There is another way to approach the soft law Police Manual, however, and that is as a representation. Where the Police Manual was issued only to police officers as a set of operational guidelines and was not available to other persons, there could be no question of it amounting to a representation to the plaintiff. Contrary to the law as regards a duty of care to take positive action, considered above, the relationship between the parties is an essential part of establishing that a representation has been negligently made. In *Hedley Byrne*, the House of Lords referred to the requisite 'special relationship' in general terms.[39] This reasoning has since been criticised as demonstrating a 'fusion fallacy'.[40]

In *MLC v Evatt*, Barwick CJ considered 'the features of the special relationship in which the law will import a duty of care in utterance by way of information or advice' to include several elements.[41] First, the relationship between the parties must have at its heart an 'element of trust' such that the speaker (or a reasonable person in the same position) would realise that s/he:

> is being trusted by the recipient of the information or advice to give information which the recipient believes the speaker to possess or to which the recipient believes the speaker to have access or to give advice, about a matter upon or in respect of which the recipient believes the speaker to possess a capacity or opportunity for judgment, in either case the subject matter of the information or advice being of a serious or business nature.

Secondly, the speaker (or a reasonable person in the same position) must realise that 'the recipient intends to act upon the information or advice in respect of his property or of himself in connexion with some matter of business or serious consequence'. Thirdly, the recipient's reliance on the speaker's utterance must be reasonable in the circumstances. Factors that are relevant to establishing reasonableness might include the 'nature of the subject matter, the occasion of the interchange, and the identity and relative position of the parties as regards knowledge actual or potential and relevant capacity to form or exercise judgment'.

[39] *Hedley Byrne & Co Ltd v Heller & Partners Ltd* [1964] AC 465, 486 (Lord Reid); 502–3 (Lord Morris); 514 (Lord Hodson); 528–29 (Lord Devlin); 539 (Lord Pearce). See *Mutual Life & Citizens' Assurance Co Ltd v Evatt* (1968) 122 CLR 556, 621.

[40] JD Heydon et al, *Meagher, Gummow and Lehane's Equity*, 5th edn (New South Wales, LexisNexis, 2015) 52; cf *Harris v Digital Pulse Pty Ltd* (2003) 56 NSWLR 298, 325–29 (Mason P); 391–92 (Heydon JA).

[41] *MLC v Evatt* (1968) 122 CLR 556, 571.

The decision of the High Court in *MLC v Evatt* was overturned by a bare majority in the Privy Council.[42] This was at a time when dissents in Privy Council advices were both new and rare.[43] The High Court was no longer bound by Privy Council precedent when it heard *Shaddock*, in which Mason J expressly stated that the reasons of Barwick CJ should be preferred to the speech of Lord Diplock for the majority in the Privy Council.[44] Gibbs CJ and Stephen J, by contrast, distinguished the Privy Council's advice but specifically declined to overturn it. Murphy J delivered a brief judgment in which he stated that 'there is no justification for adhering to the error expressed by the Privy Council' but did not specifically approve the approach which had been taken by Barwick CJ in the High Court.[45] The head-note to *Shaddock* in the Commonwealth Law Reports notes only that the Privy Council's advice was 'considered'. However, the decision of Barwick CJ in *MLC v Evatt* was said to have 'regained vitality' by Gleeson CJ, Gummow and Hayne JJ in *Tepko* and now represents the orthodox view.[46]

A majority of the High Court in *San Sebastian* commented that 'there is no convincing reason for confining the liability to instances of negligent misstatement made by way of response to a request by the plaintiff for information or advice'.[47] The plaintiff would need to establish that he had relied on the representation that police officers *must always* contact the CAT service if they encounter persons who have undertaken acts preliminary to a suicide attempt. In these circumstances, his reliance (if established) would likely be viewed as reasonable, provided that the soft law in question could be characterised as an *unqualified* representation made to persons who had read the Police Manual.[48] A disclaimer will usually be effective to eliminate liability for negligent misrepresentations.[49] This conclusion is based, using the test articulated by Barwick CJ in *MLC v Evatt*, on fact that the representation was in the form of an official police document, the seriousness of the subject matter, and the greater position of power held by the police.

However, the plaintiff may not be able to prove that the police 'made the representation with the intention of inducing [people] to act in reliance on the representation'.[50] A planning instrument with statutory force and its various supporting documents were alleged in *San Sebastian* to have induced in the plaintiff an 'expectation of being allowed to develop in accordance with the proposals'.[51] The majority of the High Court held that no representation had been made by making these

[42] *Mutual Life & Citizens' Assurance Co Ltd v Evatt* (1970) 122 CLR 628.

[43] M Gleeson, 'The Privy Council: An Australian Perspective' at The Anglo-Australasian Lawyers Society, The Commercial Bar Association, and The Chancery Bar Association (18 June 2008), available at: www.hcourt.gov.au/assets/publications/speeches/former-justices/gleesoncj/cj_18jun08.pdf.

[44] *L Shaddock & Associates Pty Ltd v Parramatta City Council* (1981) 150 CLR 225, 251 (Aickin J agreeing).

[45] ibid, 256.

[46] *Tepko Pty Ltd v Water Board* (2001) 206 CLR 1, 16; see also 23 (Gaudron J).

[47] *San Sebastian Pty Ltd v Minister Administering Environmental Planning and Assessment Act 1979* (1986) 162 CLR 340, 356 (Gibbs CJ, Mason, Wilson & Dawson JJ).

[48] See eg *Michael* [2015] 2 WLR 343, 375.

[49] *Hedley Byrne* [1964] AC 465.

[50] *San Sebastian* (1986) 162 CLR 340, 358.

[51] ibid, 349.

documents available. Brennan J, by contrast, did not address the issue of whether the alleged representation had in fact been made. Rather, his Honour held that if a representation was made at all, it was merely implied from the fact that the instrument and supporting documents were said to have been 'expertly prepared'. This was too 'limited' a representation to ground a duty of care to the appellants.[52] In *San Sebastian*, the Court did not express this in terms of the policy/operational distinction used in *Anns* and subsequently in *Heyman* because the same work was able be done by the existing concept that a misrepresentation is not actionable in negligence unless the plaintiff's reliance upon it is reasonable.

Similarly to the majority view in *San Sebastian*, in *Unilan Holdings* the plaintiff alleged that it had lost money consequent on relying on a statement by the defendant Minister for Primary Industry and Energy at a conference held in Dubrovnik about the future 'floor price' of Australian wool. Lockhart J noted that:[53]

> Persons in the wool industry who heard statements of the respondent were not entitled, in my opinion, to treat the statement as an absolute and unconditional guarantee and trade on the basis that if they made profits they would belong to them, but if they made losses they would be borne by the respondent or the Australian Government.

This is the reason why statutory prohibitions on misleading or deceptive conduct have always been pleaded so frequently in commercial litigation: in most business contexts, it completely supersedes the effect of *Hedley Byrne*.[54] In short, the case law indicates that not every statement of future intention which does in fact induce another party to act in reliance on the statement's accuracy is sufficient to ground a duty of care. Cases in which reasonable reliance has been established tend to feature a more direct and personal communication of the relevant representation to the reliant party than is the case here.

All in all, treating the terms of the Police Manual as a representation is a less doctrinally satisfactory method of establishing a duty of care. Resort to this approach would likely be necessary only in the event that a court refused to accept that the police officers had a common law duty to act, regardless of whether the plaintiff was aware of the requirements of the Police Manual.

E. WHAT WOULD BE THE RESULT IF THE POLICE MANUAL WERE AVAILABLE TO THE PUBLIC, BUT THE PLAINTIFF HAD NO SUBJECTIVE KNOWLEDGE OF ITS TERMS?

In the event that the plaintiff was unaware of the terms of the Police Manual, the conclusion above is reinforced based on the current state of the law. There are, however, two legal approaches which could get around the requirement of subjective reliance for a duty of care to exist. The first is to breathe new life into the doctrine

52 ibid, 373.

53 *Unilan Holdings Pty Ltd v Kerin* [1993] FCA 19.

54 See eg The Australian Consumer Law § 18 (Schedule 2 to the Competition and Consumer Act 2010 (Cth)); previously Trade Practices Act 1974 (Cth) s 52.

of general reliance. The second is for the courts to develop a stand-alone principle of compensation for administrative misfeasance. The latter option will not be considered here.

The principle of specific reliance in creating a common law duty to act on the part of a public authority has been discussed above. In *Heyman*, Mason J proposed the doctrine of general reliance as an extension of this reasoning:[55]

> [T]here will be cases in which the plaintiff's reasonable reliance will arise out of a general dependence on an authority's performance of its function with due care, without the need for contributing conduct on the part of a defendant or action to his detriment on the part of a plaintiff. Reliance or dependence in this sense is in general the product of the grant (and exercise) of powers designed to prevent or minimise a risk of personal injury or disability, recognised by the legislature as being of such magnitude or complexity that individuals cannot, or may not, take adequate steps for their own protection. This situation generates on one side (the individual) a general expectation that the power will be exercised and on the other side (the authority) a realisation that there is a general reliance or dependence on its exercise of power ... The control of air traffic, the safety inspection of aircraft and the fighting of a fire in a building by a fire authority ... may well be examples of this type of function.

His Honour argued that some duties of public authorities are relied upon by the public at large implicitly and without any (or much) subjective consideration because this is the entire reason why some public authorities exist, for example where public authorities are charged with 'the control of air traffic' or 'the safety inspection of aircraft'. While it offers a somewhat untidy exception to the neatness of a purely rights-based approach, there is no principled reason why a public authority responsible for air-traffic control ought not to be liable to a plaintiff for breach of a common law duty of care where the plaintiff has suffered loss as a result of the authority's less-than-competent performance of its sole purpose. Stevens argued in favour of the general benefits of a rights-based approach to establishing a duty of care, as opposed to a loss-based approach which looks for exceptions to exclude liability in some circumstances, particularly in regard to *X v Bedfordshire CC*.[56] However, the opposing theoretical approaches are relevant only in the case of inaction by, for example, an air traffic control authority: to carelessly direct a collision between aeroplanes would certainly result in liability on either view. The example employed by Mason J is therefore decisive only if the controllers were to abandon their posts during the course of a flight.

Mason J stated in *Heyman* that general reliance will rarely generate a duty of care. Demonstrating specific reliance on a soft law instrument being *positively* applied by government may also be difficult; indeed, it was not established in *Heyman*.[57] General reliance must be reasonable, and the reasonableness of relying on a soft law instrument will naturally be dictated at least in part by the terms of that instrument and

[55] *Heyman* (1985) 157 CLR 424, 464.

[56] *X v Bedfordshire County Council* [1995] 2 AC 633. See R Stevens, *Torts and Rights* (2007) 224–25; cf P Cane, Review of Torts and Rights' (2008) 71 *MLR* 641, 644; JNE Varuhas, 'The Concept of 'Vindication' in the Law of Torts: Rights, Interests and Damages' (2014) 34 *OJLS* 253.

[57] See *Heyman* (1985) 157 CLR 424, 470.

the circumstances in which it has been issued. For example, a soft law instrument may be stated in terms that contain an implicit (or explicit) warning that it should not be relied upon other than at the risk of the reliant party. However, this issue is generally addressed in relation to reliance on a positive, negligently-made statement rather than an omission.

One of the reasons for holding an authority liable in circumstances such as those described above is that individuals will not take any action to protect themselves where it is generally known, or at least assumed, that a public authority has taken charge. More to the point, it will frequently be impossible for individuals to take steps to protect themselves from the relevant form of damage (for example, from unsafely maintained or directed aircraft). This will usually be the very reason why a public authority has been given certain powers in the first place. Even those who reject the concept of a 'general reliance' doctrine accept that a duty of care may arise where the plaintiff is in fact ignorant of the danger against which a public authority owes a duty to protect him or her.[58]

This reasoning underlying the general reliance doctrine is supported by the fact that many of the objections to requiring a defendant to take positive action are inapplicable to public authorities. The refusal to hold the metaphorical Priest and Levite accountable for their failures to act as the Samaritan did in Christ's parable is usually justified on one or more of the following grounds: that it is unfair to require a party who has not caused danger to get his or her 'feet wet' by coming to the rescue; that it offends individual autonomy to require private individuals to solve problems not of their making; and the 'why me?' objection. These objections amount to much the same thing, which is to say that in the absence of an enforceable right against the Priest or the Levite, their freedom to determine how they will and will not act ought not to be interfered with. In respect of individuals, it is difficult to argue against this proposition.[59]

However, as we have seen above, public authorities are not wholly like individuals. They have different capacities and expectations to individuals and this is an important factor in limiting the extent to which they can be treated in 'the same' way as private actors in private law actions. This ought not to be discounted where it serves to remove some of the objections to finding a positive duty to act. Hence, if a public authority is *not* held to owe a positive duty to take action, this cannot be justified on the basis that it infringes on the autonomy of a certain authority or will cause it to get its metaphorical 'feet wet'.[60]

Yet, while these objections are phrased such that they refer only to characteristics of private actors, their inapplicability to some public authorities would not alone be enough to compel a public authority to take positive action. For example, one could not commence proceedings against a highway authority for the negligent failure to inspect premises for risk of fire. It would not infringe upon the authority's autonomy, per se; it just has nothing to do with that particular authority. Modern government is not a monolith. Many public functions are performed by many different

58 *Pyrenees* (1998) 192 CLR 330, 390.
59 cf *Lowns v Woods* [1996] Australian Torts Reports 81-376.
60 M Aronson, 'Government Liability' (2008) 32 *Melbourne University Law Review* 44, 68–69.

authorities. Therefore, the 'why me?' objection is still relevant, unless the public authority's failure to take positive action relates to the very purpose for which it exists. To consider again the hypothetical example based upon *East Suffolk v Kent*, for a failure to repair sea walls with reasonable skill and expedition to indicate to a court that the defendant Board had breached a common law duty to do so, the plaintiff would first need to establish that doing so was a substantial purpose for the existence of the Board.[61]

Unlike the House of Lords, the Australian High Court demonstrated in *Pyrenees* that it is prepared to find that a common law duty of care is owed by public authorities which are able to foresee harm to an individual and also have the capacity to avoid it. By doing so, it has created a legal environment in which public authorities do sometimes owe a greater duty than would be owed by a private actor due to a superior capacity to prevent harm.[62] Foreseeability of harm and capacity to prevent it are insufficient bases for finding that a duty of care is owed by a private actor, who would in any case generally have the right to refuse assistance.

In articulating the general reliance doctrine in *Heyman*, Mason J was at pains to point out that liability for breach of a duty of care where there has been general reliance on a public authority arises in negligence and not as a matter of public law:[63]

> [A]lthough a public authority may be under a public duty, enforceable by mandamus, to give proper consideration to the question whether it should exercise a power, this duty cannot be equated with, or regarded as a foundation for imposing, a duty of care on the public authority in relation to the exercise of the power. Mandamus will compel proper consideration by the authority of its discretion, but that is all.

However, courts and legislators are frequently tempted to carry public law notions across to the law of torts. One example of this would be demonstrated if commission of an ultra vires act were made the threshold for a finding that a public authority owes a common law duty of care. A second would be if public authorities were held to a public law standard in assessing whether they owe a common law duty of care.

Notwithstanding the view expressed by Mason J, other judges have held that, in order to create a common law duty of care, a power to act invested in a public authority must be enforceable by a writ of mandamus. In *Pyrenees*, Brennan CJ built on Lord Hoffmann's speech in *Stovin* to state that:[64]

> [A] duty to exercise a power may arise from particular circumstances, and may be enforceable by a public law remedy. Where a purpose for which a power is conferred is the protection of the person or property of a class of individuals and the circumstances are such that the repository of the power is under a public law duty to exercise the power, the duty is, or in relevant respects is analogous to, a statutory duty imposed for the benefit of a class, breach of which gives rise to an action for damages by a member of the class who suffers

[61] See fn 88 in Chapter 8.C of this volume above.

[62] S Wotherspoon, 'Translating the Public Law "May" into the Common Law "Ought"' (2009) 83 *Australian Law Journal* 331, 334–35.

[63] *Heyman* (1985) 157 CLR 424, 465. See also *Stovin v Wise* [1996] AC 923, 950; cf *Gorringe* [2004] WLR 1057, 337.

[64] *Pyrenees* (1998) 192 CLR 330, 347 (Brennan CJ). See M Aronson, 'Government Liability' (2008) 32 *Melbourne University Law Review* 44, 67–68; *Stovin* [1996] AC 923.

> loss in consequence of a failure to discharge the duty. The general principles of public law establish the existence of the statutory duty to exercise the power and the statute prescribes the class of individuals for whose benefit the power is to be exercised.

Gummow J put the contrary view in the same case that:[65]

> the liability of the Shire in negligence does not turn upon the further (and public law) question whether (as may have been the case) those who later sued in tort would have had standing to seek against the Shire an order in the nature of mandamus. Their actions for damages in negligence are not brought in addition to or in substitution for any public law remedy.

McHugh J also later criticised the importation of public law doctrines into private law in *Crimmins*.[66] In *Pyrenees*, his Honour merely noted that:[67]

> in many cases where the [general reliance] doctrine applies, the public authority will already have a public duty, enforceable by mandamus, to consider whether it should exercise its power or perform its function. In some cases, its knowledge may be such that, though the power or function may be discretionary, it nevertheless has a public duty to act.

Remarking that the doctrine of general reliance frequently has a basis which is more than illusory, as the majority held, because public authorities subject to that doctrine may also be subject to a writ of mandamus is, with respect, a more benign use of public law than using it as the basis for finding a common law duty of care.

Nonetheless, Brennan CJ's use of mandamus to indicate when a statutory power is converted into a common law duty as the result of an implied statutory right of action, while unique in judicial circles, has since provoked a statutory response, albeit 'in mangled form' because the Civil Liability Acts are sets of *restrictions* on the common law rather than *expansions*.[68] The NSW Act imposes a barrier to the recognition of a common law duty to act on the part of a public authority 'if the authority could not have been required to exercise the function in proceedings instituted by the plaintiff'.[69]

General reliance was disapproved by a majority of the High Court in *Pyrenees*.[70] Gummow and Kirby JJ each agreed with the Chief Justice on this issue, but both Toohey and McHugh JJ dissented on the basis that the general reliance doctrine remained a useful concept. Brennan CJ would have preferred to make legislative intent the basis for a finding that a duty of care is owed by a public authority. His Honour cited the dicta of Lord Hoffmann in *Stovin* in which his Lordship seemed to doubt that 'the general expectations of the community', possibly not shared subjectively by the plaintiff, were an appropriate method of establishing whether a duty of care is owed by a public authority.[71]

[65] *Pyrenees* (1998) 192 CLR 330, 390–91 (citations omitted).

[66] *Crimmins* (1999) 200 CLR 1, 35–36.

[67] *Pyrenees* (1998) 192 CLR 330, 371.

[68] M Aronson, 'Government Liability' (2008) 32 *Melbourne University Law Review* 44, 68.

[69] *Civil Liability Act 2002* (NSW) s 44. See M Aronson, 'Government Liability' (2008) 32 *Melbourne University Law Review* 44, 73–76.

[70] *Pyrenees* (1998) 192 CLR 330, 344.

[71] cf *Pyrenees* (1998) 192 CLR 330, 370 (McHugh J); *Crimmins* (1999) 200 CLR 1, 35–36 (Gaudron J).

Indeed, one of the most persuasive objections to the doctrine of general reliance is that to describe the expectations created by the 'situation' in which an individual's interests are within the control of a public authority as 'reliance' is misleading. As Lord Hoffmann commented in *Stovin*:[72]

> the plaintiff does not need to have relied upon the expectation that the power would be used or even know that it existed. It appears rather to refer to general expectations in the community, which the individual plaintiff may or may not have shared. A widespread assumption that a statutory power will be exercised may affect the general pattern of economic and social behaviour.

The doctrine, as proposed by Mason J, requires no subjective reliance on the part of a plaintiff. Lord Hoffmann's starting point was to say that it will be rare indeed for a public authority to owe a common law duty of care where 'Parliament has conferred a discretion [which] must be some indication that the policy of the act conferring the power was not to create a right to compensation'.[73]

The primary objection to the doctrine of general reliance is therefore semantic. It is clear that the doctrine does not describe circumstances in which a plaintiff has 'relied' on the performance of certain acts by a public authority, as that verb is generally understood. Whatever reliance there has been occurs only in the sense that we all rely on government to undertake some tasks that private actors cannot undertake for themselves due to their 'magnitude or complexity'.[74] It should at least be arguable that the plaintiff in the assumed facts 'relied', in this sense, on the police to comply with their soft law obligation to assist persons who had performed acts preliminary to attempting suicide. In fact, the 'reliance' in such a case need be no more than objective, based on 'those in the position of the plaintiff'.[75] His lack of subjective knowledge of the terms of that soft law would not therefore be to the point if he were able to convince a court that people in his position would generally expect the police to protect the suicidal. It is not a task which could effectively be performed by private actors, and is in this way analogous to the examples provided by Mason J.

This is not necessarily to argue that the plaintiff would be able to establish general reliance on the assumed facts. It is strongly arguable that the role of the police was to supplement, rather than supplant, the care that the plaintiff would be expected to take for himself, given that he was not institutionalised and was therefore held broadly to the standards applicable to other members of society.[76] This view, however, fails to take account of the fact that the mentally infirm are now very rarely confined to asylums and that the police are more likely than virtually any other group of people to come into contact with them.[77] French CJ noted that mental health legislation 'does not assume a necessary linkage between mental illness and attempted suicide [which] accords with the long-standing resistance of the common law to the

[72] *Stovin* [1996] AC 923, 954.
[73] ibid, 953.
[74] *Heyman* (1985) 157 CLR 424, 464.
[75] ibid, 463.
[76] ibid, 462. See *Carrier v Bonham* [2002] 1 Qd R 474.
[77] See n 37 above. See also Victoria, Legislative Assembly, *Parliamentary Debates* (Hansard), 30 May 1985, 77; cited in *Stuart* (2009) 237 CLR 215, 232 [34].

proposition that such a connection necessarily exists'; nor does the common law presumptively link mental illness to suicide or attempted suicide.[78] Gummow, Hayne and Heydon JJ further noted in *Stuart* that the Victorian legislation was drafted such that, even if a police officer were to apprehend that:[79]

> a person appears mentally ill and there are reasonable grounds for the officer to believe that the person has recently attempted or is likely to attempt suicide or to cause serious bodily harm to that person or to some other person … there may [nonetheless] very well be circumstances in which a police officer acting reasonably would not exercise the power even if the conditions for its exercise were met.

Although it may be contrary to the current emphasis of the common law on self-reliance, autonomy and personal responsibility, there is much to be said in favour of finding that the police officers owed a common law duty to the plaintiff on the basis of their higher level of contact with the mentally ill, even if it is unlikely in all the circumstances that the police officers breached that duty or that it was causative of the plaintiff's harm.[80] It is unfortunate that the High Court has held that the doctrine of general reliance cannot assist in reaching a conclusion.

[78] *Stuart* (2009) 237 CLR 215, 236–37.

[79] ibid, 247.

[80] See eg *CAL No 14 Pty Ltd v Motor Accidents Insurance Board* (2009) 239 CLR 390; *Roads and Traffic Authority (NSW) v Dederer* (2007) 234 CLR 330.

10

Private Law Liability and Remedies: Example 2

CONSIDER THE FOLLOWING factual scenario, which is based upon the facts of *Waltons v Maher* but supposes that the party in the position of Waltons is a public authority:[1]

A. Emily proposes to build a housing development on the site of property she owns in Mittagong, New South Wales.

B. She contacts the local government authority ('the Council') which has a statutory discretion to approve developments in Mittagong. A Council employee directs her to a document on the Council website entitled 'Mittagong Area Development Approval Guidelines'.

C. Emily reads the Guidelines, which include the following statement:

> The Council will approve any development which complies with all applicable NSW planning statutes and regulations.

D. Emily discusses her proposed development with her lawyer, who advises Emily that her proposed development is legally compliant, but comments that he has heard that changes are about to be made to the relevant State Environmental Planning Policy (SEPP), an instrument made by the Governor of NSW 'for the purpose of environmental planning by the State' and designed to deal with significant matters in environmental planning.[2] Emily's lawyer tells her that her development would not comply with the amended SEPP but that she will have no problem provided that she commences work before the changes take effect, since laws are not generally changed retroactively, whether hard or soft.

E. Emily writes to the Council to ask whether her development has been approved. She receives a written response which states that the Council is not due to meet for three weeks, but directs her to the Guidelines.

F. Relying on the term of the Guidelines set out in Fact C, Emily believes that the Council must approve her development. She commences work

[1] *Waltons Stores (Interstate) Ltd v Maher* (1988) 164 CLR 387.

[2] Environmental Planning and Assessment Act 1979 (NSW) s 37(1).

to ensure that work has commenced on her development before changes to the SEPP, having invested a substantial amount of money and time in obtaining materials and hiring contractors.

G. The first thing that the contractors working for Emily do is to demolish the house that was already on the land. The house had recently been valued at AU$100,000 without taking into account the value of the land.

H. The Council meets and decides not to approve Emily's development. In its written reasons, the Council states that its policy is to disapprove any development which would contravene existing law, or foreshadowed changes to the law. The changes to the SEPP subsequently come into effect.

Can Emily obtain a remedy from the Council? Given that a court cannot require the Council to approve the development, which would now be in breach of the SEPP, is there an appropriate remedy in common law damages or equitable compensation?

A. PRELIMINARY COMMENTS ON PRIVATE LAW LIABILITY FOR RELIANCE-BASED LOSS

There is a large intersection between equitable estoppel (at least as regards promissory estoppel and estoppel by representation) and negligent misstatement. Both doctrines attach liability to a party which has made a representation upon which another has reasonably relied to his or her detriment. In equity, liability accrues as a result of the representor's refusal or inability to adhere to the substance of the representation. In negligence, liability is the consequence of the representor breaching a duty of care not to make a representation if reliance upon it will cause loss to the representee. This doctrine covers both inaccurate statements of current fact and the negligent provision of advice.[3] For example, the reasoning of Lord Haldane in *Nocton v Lord Ashburton* reads as a precursor to cases later in the twentieth century (notably, it was applied by the House of Lords in *Hedley Byrne*) in which the relationship between parties, being neither contractual nor fiduciary, was able to form the basis of either liability in tort (for negligent misrepresentation) or an estoppel.[4] Neither requires any fraud, in the sense of moral obloquy, on the part of the party which has made the representation relied upon.

Frequently, an individual will either rely on a representation of a public authority as the basis for choosing to act or will be directed to a certain course of action by a public authority.[5] Inducing another party to act to his or her detriment may either create a liability in tort for negligent misrepresentation or raise an estoppel remediable

[3] *L Shaddock & Associates Pty Ltd v Parramatta City Council* (1981) 150 CLR 225; *Hedley Byrne & Co Ltd v Heller & Partners Ltd* [1964] AC 465.

[4] *Nocton v Lord Ashburton* [1914] AC 932. See *Hedley Byrne* [1964] AC 465; cf JD Heydon et al, *Meagher, Gummow and Lehane's Equity*, 5th edn (New South Wales, LexisNexis, 2015) 52.

[5] See *Crimmins v Stevedoring Industry Finance Committee* (1999) 200 CLR 1, 30 (McHugh J).

in equity. Deliberate wrongdoing cannot amount to *negligent* misrepresentation.[6] Therefore, to take a well-known example, the plaintiff in *Waltons v Maher* could not have established that Waltons had made a negligent misrepresentation. By contrast, Campbell noted an example of where an action for negligent misrepresentation may have been available although the court would not have enforced an estoppel against the defendant Minister.[7] There is sufficient overlap between the two causes of action that either could apply in many circumstances.

For the stated example, I will assess the likelihood of Emily obtaining a substantive remedy for damage caused by her reliance on the Council's Guidelines both in tort and in equity.

B. TORT LIABILITY

Whether or not an instrument can be characterised as soft law, it may still amount to a negligent misrepresentation. This doctrine has generally become a less important basis of liability since there has been a statutory prohibition of misleading and deceptive conduct.[8] However, the terms of the legislation are limited to conduct 'in trade or commerce' and, with regard to the Commonwealth and Commonwealth public authorities, that they 'carr[y] on a business'.[9] Consequently, negligent misrepresentation is now more prominent as a doctrine which applies to public authorities whose allegedly negligent misrepresentations frequently fall outside the limits of the statutory provision.

A public authority will be held liable in negligence for loss caused by the failure to apply a soft law instrument if the soft law in question includes a misrepresentation that the authority would act in accordance with it and an individual has relied reasonably on that representation to his or her detriment. Traditionally, courts were reluctant to impose a duty of care in regard to negligent statements, as opposed to negligent acts. This reluctance was compounded by the fact that negligent misrepresentations result in purely economic loss.[10] Cane has stated that:[11]

> two principles relevant in many actions against public agencies are, first, that the law of tort in general and the tort of negligence in particular are mainly concerned with personal injury and property damage, and only marginally and exceptionally for economic loss; and secondly that tort law only exceptionally imposes obligations to prevent harm as opposed to an obligation not to cause harm.

[6] *New South Wales v Lepore* (2003) 212 CLR 511, 531 (Gleeson CJ); 603 (Gummow & Hayne JJ). See also *Nationwide News Pty Ltd v Naidu* (2007) 71 NSWLR 471, 485.

[7] E Campbell, 'Estoppel in Pais and Public Authorities' (1998) 5 *Australian Journal of Administrative Law* 157, 164. See *Minister for Immigration and Ethnic Affairs v Petrovski* (1997) 73 FCR 303.

[8] RP Balkin and JLR Davis, *Law of Torts*, 5th edn (New South Wales, LexisNexis, 2013) 432. See Chapter 9, fn 54 of this volume above.

[9] Competition and Consumer Act 2010 (Cth) s 2A.

[10] *San Sebastian Pty Ltd v Minister Administering the Environmental Planning and Assessment Act 1979* (1986) 162 CLR 340, 354.

[11] P Cane, *Administrative Law*, 5th edn (Oxford, Oxford University Press, 2011) 202 (footnote omitted).

The prohibition on recovery for loss caused by negligent misrepresentations has long since been discarded.[12] However, it remains the case that there are more impediments to establishing a duty of care for negligent words than for a negligent act. Importantly, although the High Court has pointed out that whether a duty of care is owed for negligent misrepresentation is decided consistently with the general principles of negligence, the fact that the only loss suffered by a plaintiff is economic has meant that the relevant legal principles have developed 'relatively independently from the case-law which included *Anns*'.[13] They are accordingly much less fraught with debate than, for example, the principles behind liability for nonfeasance by a public authority.

A ready and attentive audience is not limited to those who have requested information, but may include those induced to act.[14] However, inducement is insufficient without more to establish negligence in regard to a representation. In *San Sebastian*, the plurality judgment started by saying that while, unlike in *MLC v Evatt* and *Shaddock*, the information alleged to have been provided by the defendant authorities was not in response to a request from the appellants, 'there is no convincing reason for confining the liability to instances of negligent misstatement made by way of response to a request by the plaintiff for information or advice'.[15] Their Honours noted that an antecedent request 'certainly assists in demonstrating reliance, which is a cornerstone of liability for negligent misstatement', but this is a practical evidentiary issue rather than one of principle.[16] Courts often require something more than reasonable foreseeability of harm before they are prepared to find that the defendant owes a duty of care.[17] In a practical sense, the key to establishing liability for causing another party to rely on a negligently made representation is the reasonableness of that reliance. Reliance is therefore the crux of the action for negligent misrepresentation, since it is the true cause of loss to the plaintiff, rather than the act of the defendant. This is in contrast to negligent acts, which tend to cause damage directly to the plaintiff.[18] However, there is no reason why a representation upon which a plaintiff relies to his or her detriment *must* be preceded by a request for that representation to be made, and the maker of such a representation will be liable if it is incorrect and the plaintiff can demonstrate reasonable reliance.

As in *San Sebastian*, the information provided to Emily in the Guidelines was intended to provoke a response. This will generally be the case where a person relies on a representation which has a regulatory character or can otherwise properly be characterised as soft law. To require Emily to have made an antecedent request in order for her reliance to be classified as reasonable would be to misunderstand the regulatory nature of soft law.

[12] See *Hedley Byrne* [1964] AC 465; *L Shaddock & Associates Pty Ltd v Parramatta City Council* (1981) 150 CLR 225.

[13] M Allars, 'Tort and Equity Claims' in PD Finn (ed), *Essays on Law and Government—Vol 2* (Sydney, LBC Information Services, 1996) vol 2, 49, 69. See *San Sebastian* (1986) 162 CLR 340, 353–54.

[14] *San Sebastian* (1986) 162 CLR 340, 357.

[15] ibid, 356. See *Mutual Life & Citizens' Assurance Co Ltd v Evatt* (1970) 122 CLR 628.

[16] ibid, 356–57.

[17] *Sutherland Shire Council v Heyman* (1985) 157 CLR 424, 466.

[18] *Shaddock* (1981) 150 CLR 225, 231; *San Sebastian* (1986) 162 CLR 340, 353.

The identity of the public entity which makes a representation and the circumstances in which it is made will indicate to some extent which party is expected to bear the risk of that representation ultimately being false. This goes to the reasonableness of the plaintiff's reliance and affects the liability of the defendant. Hence, a representation reasonably relied on will have to be fulfilled or withdrawn with adequate notice. However, it will not be reasonable to rely on a representation which, in effect, contains its own inbuilt warning that it ought not to be relied upon. For example, one case considered the effect of a soft law Code which was subject to a legislative provision which read: 'Nothing in this section or such a code gives rise to, or can be taken into account in, any civil cause of action, but nothing in this section affects rights or liabilities arising apart from this section'. These terms were held to prevent even an inference of fact being drawn from the defendant's failure to adhere to the Code.[19] This construction seems difficult to justify, given that it rendered the existence of the Code otiose.

Some types of communication from public bodies (for example, published rulings by the Australian Taxation Office) are designed to provide the public at large with comfort that they will be treated in a certain way if they act within the terms of the ruling. Encouragement of reliance is the very purpose for which they are issued. Other communications, for example ad hoc approvals of a proposed course of action, necessarily carry the implication that they are given with the proviso that they can be retracted if there is a change in policy. Some types of 'assurance' necessarily come with the unspoken warning that reliance is at the risk of the reliant party.

As Lockhart J pointed out in *Unilan Holdings*, one way to determine reasonable reliance is to ask whether the representation upon which a plaintiff has relied was intended to communicate that the public authority making the representation would bear the risk of that representation being incorrect.[20] Seen through the lens of risk, it is clear that the Minister in *Unilan Holdings* meant to communicate no such message. Rather, the plaintiff should have known that his representation was no more than a statement of policy and was therefore subject to change.

Additionally, there is a significant difference between a statement of policy directed at future conduct—which is naturally always subject to alteration unless its maker is legally bound to it—and a soft law instrument which records an undertaking as to how a public authority will exercise its discretion in current matters. In the assumed facts, the Guidelines represent to Emily that the Council will approve both current and future development applications which are legally compliant. This is not the same as Emily asking, in effect, for the Council to insure her against any loss she may suffer by relying on the Guidelines. Contrary to the facts in *Unilan Holdings*, it was the entire purpose of the Guidelines, and part and parcel of their character as soft law, that people would act in reliance upon them.

The nature of the communication in which a representation is made also has practical importance in ascertaining whether it is reasonable to rely upon it.

[19] *CPT Manager Ltd (acting as trustee of the Broken Hill Trust) v Broken Hill City Council* [2010] NSWLEC 69, [128].

[20] *Unilan Holdings Pty Ltd v Kerin* [1993] FCA 19.

The extent to which the representation, rather than its purpose, is 'public', is therefore a guide to whether a representation can be reasonably relied upon. While a direct and personal *oral* representation by an unknown employee of a public authority will not necessarily be reliable, a direct *written* representation on behalf of that authority is more likely to be so.[21] Reliance on a representation made to and passed on by a third party is less likely to be reasonable than reliance on a direct communication, although communicating a representation indirectly will not necessarily preclude a duty of care from being owed in relation to that representation. In these circumstances, the purpose of the representation is likely to be decisive.[22] On the other hand, a statement of future policy made to the world at large, either by a public authority or a Minister of State will necessarily be less reliable, because, as Brennan J put it in *San Sebastian*, it is generally 'understood that a public authority is free to alter a policy unless the policy is given binding effect by statute or by contract'.[23]

Soft law is of a different order to a mere representation, since it regulates behaviour in a manner that has the practical effect of law but is able to be made without the oversight and inconvenience that are required to pass legislation or even subordinate legislation.[24] Whether an instrument amounts to soft law by having a regulatory purpose or effect, and is therefore more than a mere representation, can be assessed by analogy to the reasoning which courts use to determine whether a decision is 'of an administrative character' for the purposes of the Administrative Decisions (Judicial Review) Act, or 'of a legislative character' for the purposes of the Legislation Act.[25] This is not an exact science: as the Full Federal Court noted in *RG Capital Radio*, 'there is no simple rule for determining whether a decision is of an administrative or a legislative character'.[26] That case listed considerations which had been held in previous cases to shed light on whether a given decision was of an administrative or legislative character, although 'no one decision is decisive of the issue'.[27] Other cases have also attempted to list the considerations which are indicative of the character of a decision or instrument.[28] Aronson and Groves summarised these cases to list 10 factors for determining the character of an instrument.[29] Importantly, none of these factors relies on the reasonableness of the reliance of a person regulated by an instrument, focusing instead on the character of the instrument itself. A mere representation is strictly neither administrative nor legislative in character, although when made by a public authority it is an expression of 'executive' rather than legislative

[21] *Shaddock* (1981) 150 CLR 225.

[22] *Tepko Pty Ltd v Water Board* (2001) 206 CLR 1, 15.

[23] *San Sebastian* (1986) 162 CLR 340, 374. See also ibid, 360.

[24] The issues raised here are discussed in detail in Part I of this volume.

[25] ADJR Act 1977 (Cth) s 3(1); Legislation Act 2003 s 5(1)(a).

[26] *RG Capital Radio Ltd v Australian Broadcasting Authority* (2001) 113 FCR 185, 194 (Wilcox, Branson & Lindgren JJ).

[27] ibid.

[28] See *Roche Products Pty Ltd v National Drugs and Poisons Schedule Committee* (2007) 163 FCR 451; *SAT FM Pty Ltd v Australian Broadcasting Authority* (1997) 75 FCR 604; *Visa International Service Association v Reserve Bank of Australia* (2003) 131 FCR 300.

[29] M Aronson and M Groves, *Judicial Review of Administrative Action*, 5th edn (Sydney, Thompson Reuters, 2013) [2.500].

power, in the sense that it does not rely on power inherent to government.[30] The proper characterisation of the Minister's speech in *Unilan Holdings* is that it was a statement of intention which was not intended to create binding rights or liabilities, enforceable either in tort or as legitimate expectations.[31] The analogy remains useful as a method of discerning whether an instrument has a regulatory purpose, in which case reliance will generally be seen as reasonable.

On the assumed facts, the regulatory purpose of the Guidelines is clear not only from their terms but also from the fact that Emily is twice referred to the Guidelines in response to her inquiries as to how the Council will exercise its statutory discretion to approve property developments. On its face, the relevant term of the Guidelines appears to state a rule of general application and reflects the broad policy consideration that the Council is in favour of all developments and wishes to encourage them, provided that they meet the applicable legal standards. In short, despite the fact that the Guidelines are not legally binding on the Council, they are a clear example of the Council governing through the use of soft law.

In the circumstances, Emily was reasonable to rely on the statement that the Council would approve any legally compliant development proposal. Any contrary conclusion is morally unsatisfying because it does not take account of the way in which soft law differs from other representations. In many ways, it is the same; for example, just as in *Hedley Byrne*, soft law's effect can be 'ring-fenced' by a disclaimer.[32] However, this is an issue which goes to reasonableness of reliance rather than to the public nature of soft law. The key to establishing liability in a public authority which has issued a soft law instrument which it subsequently declines to apply should be simply whether the party which has relied on the soft law has acted as he or she was encouraged to act by the soft law; that is to say, where there has been a negligent inducement. If this question is dealt with as a matter of construction of the soft law, it requires no adaptation of the private law as it stands, save perhaps to establish an agreed upon test for what constitutes soft law.

C. EQUITABLE REMEDIES

Particularly given that negligent misrepresentations by public authorities are not affected by Part 5 of the Civil Liability Act 2002 (NSW), the position in tort will generally be unchanged whether or not the inducing party is a public authority.[33] It is significantly more difficult to obtain a remedy enforcing an estoppel against a public authority. I have noted above that there is no specific doctrine of public law estoppel, although an estoppel may be nonetheless be raised against a public authority. It is

[30] See eg *Unilan Holdings Pty Ltd v Kerin* [1993] FCA 19.

[31] *Patel v General Medical Council* [2013] 1 WLR 2801, 2817–18 (Lloyd-Jones LJ); citing *R (on the application of Bhatt Murphy (a firm)) v Independent Assessor* [2008] EWCA Civ 755, [46]–[47] (Laws LJ).

[32] See eg *CPT Manager Ltd (acting as trustee of the Broken Hill Trust) v Broken Hill City Council* [2010] NSWLEC 69.

[33] See eg *Shaddock* (1981) 150 CLR 225.

frequently generalised that 'common law estoppel operates where [an] assumption is one of existing fact, whereas equitable estoppel operates where the assumption relates to the future conduct of the representor or the legal rights of the representee'.[34] This statement of the law is not universally accepted as being comprehensive. In *Foran v Wight*, Mason CJ said that 'we should now recognise that a common law estoppel as well as an equitable estoppel may arise out of a representation or mistaken assumption as to future conduct'.[35] For current purposes, it is sufficient to acknowledge that a representation as to a future state of affairs creates an equity on which a party relies to its detriment and which speaks to an equitable estoppel, such as promissory estoppel.

Both common law estoppels (such as estoppel by representation and estoppel by conduct) and equitable estoppel are sometimes brought under the heading of estoppel *in pais*.[36] An estoppel at common law is raised by *acts* performed by the party estopped which induce another party to act, whereas an equitable estoppel is raised by a *representation* which induces another party to act. At common law, estoppel by convention requires that parties adopt a mutual assumption as the conventional basis of their relationship.[37] By contrast, in estoppels by representation, 'the relevant detriment is not accepted as the price of … the representor's being willing to be bound to the representation or promise'.[38] An estoppel *in pais* can be raised against a public authority which does not adhere to the terms of a soft law instrument that has caused an individual to rely to his or her detriment on such adherence in the future. The High Court of Australia has pointed out in the context of equitable estoppel that:[39]

> it is the conduct of the representee induced by the representor which is the very foundation for equitable intervention. Reliance is a fact to be found; it is not to be imputed on the basis of evidence which falls short of proof of the fact.

Mason CJ and Deane J each proposed in *Verwayen* a unified 'general doctrine of estoppel by conduct' in Australian law which encompasses both common law and equitable doctrines.[40] However, Dawson and McHugh JJ rejected that proposition, whereas Brennan J stated only that '*equitable* estoppel yields a remedy in order to prevent unconscionable conduct on the part of the party who, having made a

[34] A Robertson, 'Satisfying the Minimum Equity' (1996) 20 *Melbourne University Law Review* 805, 807; cf J Hudson, 'The True Purpose of Estoppel by Representation' (2015) 32 *Journal of Contract Law* 275, 283. See JD Heydon et al, *Meagher, Gummow and Lehane's Equity*, 5th edn (New South Wales, LexisNexis, 2015) 511–19.

[35] *Foran v Wight* (1989) 168 CLR 385, 411.

[36] *Legione v Hateley* (1983) 152 CLR 406, 430. See also E Campbell, 'Estoppel in Pais' (1998) 5 *Australian Journal of Administrative Law* 157, 158; JD Heydon et al, *Meagher, Gummow and Lehane's Equity*, 5th edn (New South Wales, LexisNexis, 2015) 511–12; *Waltons v Maher* (1988) 164 CLR 387, 413.

[37] *Con-Stan Industries of Australia Pty Ltd v Norwich Winterthur Insurance (Australia) Ltd* (1986) 160 CLR 226, 244; JD Heydon et al, *Meagher, Gummow and Lehane's Equity*, 5th edn (New South Wales, LexisNexis, 2015) 512–13.

[38] JD Heydon et al, *Meagher, Gummow and Lehane's Equity*, 5th edn (New South Wales, LexisNexis, 2015) 541.

[39] *Sidhu v Van Dyke* (2014) 251 CLR 505, 522 (French CJ, Kiefel, Bell & Keane JJ).

[40] *Commonwealth v Verwayen* (1990) 170 CLR 394, 431 (Deane J); 410 (Mason CJ).

promise to another who acts on it to his detriment, seeks to resile from the promise' (emphasis added).[41] The proposition has never commanded the support of a High Court majority and the mooted simplification of estoppel has in general been greeted without enthusiasm by prominent equity scholars.[42] The High Court has left the question open since *Verwayen* without showing signs of determining it.[43]

The authors of *Meagher, Gummow & Lehane's Equity: Doctrines and Remedies* (*MGL*) have argued further that the simplification of estoppel proposed by Mason CJ and Deane J was not supported, as they had thought it was, by two 1930s judgments of Dixon J.[44] His Honour's views on estoppel *in pais* applied both to its legal and equitable forms and held that the objects behind each are the same. However, the remedies available in equity are significantly more flexible than at common law, which offers only the 'all or nothing' remedy of holding the party estopped to his or her representation.[45] McHugh J summarised the authorities on this issue by saying:[46]

> What will be required to satisfy the equity which arises against the party estopped depends on the circumstances. Often the only way to prevent the promisee suffering detriment will be to enforce the promise. *But the enforcement of promises is not the object of the doctrine of equitable estoppel.* The enforcement of promises is the province of contract. Equitable estoppel is aimed at preventing unconscionable conduct and seeks to prevent detriment to the promisee (emphasis added).

There is a distinction which must be drawn between the equity which is raised where the conditions giving rise to an equitable estoppel are satisfied and the relief which a court will grant to fulfil the equity thus created. It is my thesis that the mere fact that relief by way of enforcing an estoppel is inapt to be granted against a public authority where to do so would cause the authority to act ultra vires or would require the future exercise of a statutory discretion to be fettered does not prevent a court from fulfilling the equity with an award of monetary compensation.[47]

A public authority being estopped from denying a 'certain state of affairs' at common law is different to holding a public authority to a representation that it will act in future in a certain way if such action would be ultra vires.[48] The capacity of courts with equitable jurisdiction to 'mould' the decree required to do justice between the parties means that courts can provide a remedy, such as equitable compensation, even where it is impossible to hold the relevant public authority to its initial representation.

[41] ibid, 428–29. See E Campbell, 'Estoppel in Pais' (1998) 5 *Australian Journal of Administrative Law* 157, 159 (fn 14).

[42] See JD Heydon et al, *Meagher, Gummow and Lehane's Equity*, 5th edn (New South Wales, Lexis Nexis, 2015) 515–19; J Hudson, 'The True Purpose of Estoppel by Representation' (2015) 32 *Journal of Contract Law* 275, 277.

[43] *Giumelli v Giumelli* (1999) 196 CLR 101, 112–13.

[44] JD Heydon et al, *Meagher, Gummow and Lehane's Equity*, 5th edn (New South Wales, LexisNexis 2015) 516–17.

[45] E Campbell, 'Estoppel in Pais' (1998) 5 *Australian Journal of Administrative Law* 157, 167. See *Waltons v Maher* (1988) 164 CLR 387, 427; *Verwayen* (1990) 170 CLR 394, 454.

[46] *Verwayen* (1990) 170 CLR 394, 501 (citations omitted).

[47] See *Maritime Electric Co Ltd v General Dairies Ltd* [1937] AC 610; *Southend-on-Sea Corporation v Hodgson (Wickford) Ltd* [1962] 1 QB 416.

[48] E Campbell, 'Estoppel in Pais' (1998) 5 *Australian Journal of Administrative Law* 157, 166.

On the assumed facts, an equitable estoppel would be raised against the Council because Emily was induced to act to her detriment (both in her expenditure of money and the demolition of the existing house on her property) by the soft law representation that the Council would approve *all* legally compliant development proposals. To the extent that equitable estoppel is based upon relief against unconscientious conduct rather than enforcing representations, the relevant conduct by the Council was, as in *Waltons*, to remain silent about Emily's erroneous understanding of the Council's policy in the face of the literal interpretation of its Guidelines.[49] Given that an estoppel has been raised against the Council, the next question is with what equity it can be remedied.

The prevalence of soft law emphasises that an equitable remedy is needed where an estoppel is raised against a public authority, even if substantive enforcement of that estoppel is impossible. Frequently, other remedies will suffice. For example, on the assumed facts, Emily would likely establish that she had suffered loss as a result of her reasonable reliance on the Guidelines and her loss would be compensated in tortious damages. This would not be the case, however, if the Council's act had been deliberate rather than negligent.[50] Emily could have argued for a substantive remedy, before the amendments to the SEPP took effect, on the basis that she had suffered prejudice as a result of the fact that she had been unaware of the Council's policy 'to disapprove any development which would contravene … foreshadowed changes to the law', given that that policy had not been published.[51] The requirement to make internal policy documents available would not, however, allow Emily to obtain the substantive remedy of obtaining development approval after the amended SEPP took effect, and is in this sense limited in a similar fashion to equitable remedies.

In the event that the Council were to seek a mandatory injunction to demolish any building work commenced by Emily on the land in respect of which she had not obtained valid development consent, Emily could oppose such an application on the basis that it would cause hardship.[52] A mandatory injunction may be granted at the discretion of the court in appropriate cases to produce a fair result.[53] It will be relevant to the outcome of the application that the Council has acted swiftly to prevent Emily incurring building costs.[54] The issues relevant to whether a mandatory injunction to demolish building work is warranted will also tend to differ where the building has been in breach of a restrictive covenant rather than in breach of a statutory instrument.[55] In *Willoughby City Council*, the third respondent was ordered to demolish and remove partially completed building works which did not comply with statutory requirements, notwithstanding that the local council was aware of

[49] *Waltons v Maher* (1988) 164 CLR 387, 404–5. See *Verwayen* (1990) 170 CLR 394, 501.

[50] *Lepore* (2003) 212 CLR 511.

[51] Government Information (Public Access) Act 2009 (NSW) s 24. At Commonwealth level, the relevant provision would be FOI Act 1982 (Cth) s 10.

[52] *Attorney-General (NSW) (ex rel Wentworth) v Woollahra Municipal Council* (1980) 41 LGRA 376, 394; *Wentworth v Woollahra Municipal Council* (1982) 149 CLR 672, 673.

[53] *Shepherd Homes Ltd v Sandham* [1971] Ch 340, 412.

[54] *Gafford v Graham* (1999) 77 P & CR 73, 79; *Jaggard v Sawyer* [1995] 1 WLR 269, 209.

[55] See eg *Miller v Evans* [2010] WASC 127.

the development and had taken no action to prevent it.[56] Emily is likely to face the same result.

The limitations on the remedies available to Emily do not alter the fact that individuals are apt to act to their own detriment on the faith of soft law issued by a public authority. The fact that a request, demand or instruction comes from an official source will frequently result in compliance from a private actor, regardless of that person's subjective opinion. An instruction from a uniformed police officer to drive the wrong way up a one way street will inevitably be obeyed because we are used to accepting the authority of police officers, particularly in circumstances where there is no practical and immediate means of challenging their authority to give a certain instruction.

There is little difference in effect between this example and soft law issued by many types of public authorities. It is unlikely that the effect of a soft law provision issued by a revenue authority to a small business owner would be challenged, although it would have the potential if incorrect to cause substantial loss.[57] Such soft law may, of course, amount to a negligent misrepresentation compensable in tort; such circumstances have been considered above. The necessity for an equitable remedy is to cover situations where the elements of negligence are not made out.

It is possible that one kind of substantive remedy could be available to Emily, and that is the enforcement of an estoppel raised at common law. Campbell noted that:[58]

> To hold a public body estopped from denying the existence of a certain state of affairs will not always be to sanction *ultra vires* action on the part of that body or breach of its statutory obligations. A body which is empowered to grant pensions to former defence personnel who suffer disabilities attributable to war service cannot really be said to have exceeded its powers if it is estopped, by representation, from denying that X's disability is attributable to such service.

Applied to the assumed facts, this would mean that a court would enforce a common law estoppel raised against the Council by holding that it could not deny that Emily's development was legally compliant. The effect of this is functionally the same as if the court were to apply section 10 of the FOI Act.[59]

This result may in some circumstances be open to doubt. If a statutory power to grant a pension, in the example used by Campbell, is only activated in relation to persons disabled as a result of war service, the power does not accrue to the decision-maker in question *unless* he or she forms the opinion that the recipient of the pension has *in fact* been disabled as a result of war service. To grant a pension on any other basis is to act ultra vires, although it must be remembered that result of a justiciable controversy on these facts would be highly dependent on the statutory definition of the relevant terms. The matter is less relevant in circumstances where

[56] *Willoughby City Council v Minister Administering the National Parks and Wildlife Act* (1992) 78 LGERA 19.

[57] cf *Neil Martin Ltd v Revenue and Customs Commissioners* [2007] EWCA 1041 [67]. This reasoning has been doubted: T Cornford, *Towards a Public Law of Tort* (Aldershot, Ashgate, 2008) 214.

[58] E Campbell, 'Estoppel in Pais' (1998) 5 *Australian Journal of Administrative Law* 157, 166.

[59] FOI Act 1982 (Cth) s 10.

the decision-maker's satisfaction, which grounds his or her jurisdiction, is in relation to a current and changeable state of affairs, rather than an existing fact. A substantive remedy consequent on the Council being estopped from denying the legality of Emily's proposed development would only be possible in the event that the amended SEPP had not yet taken force and, assuming that the SEPP did not have retrospective operation, the approval of the development therefore remained *intra vires* the Council.[60]

The fact that a public authority is unable to have an estoppel raised against it where to do so would require it to fetter the future exercise of a statutory discretion may be seen as a matter of public policy.[61] In public law terms, it is also ultra vires since substantively to enforce an estoppel would effectively prevent the authority from exercising the power granted to it by Parliament at its own discretion.[62] A public authority is capable of being estopped from denying the veracity of its soft law provided that it is not in conflict with the public law doctrines to which a public authority is subject.[63] The result of this is that a private actor mistakenly charged only 10 per cent of the statutorily fixed monthly charge for electricity cannot rely on an estoppel to overcome the price regime set by statute, regardless of his change of position in reliance on the amount charged.[64]

In contrast, a teacher employed by a local government body, who was over-paid due to a mistake and then spent part of the amount overpaid, was able to raise an estoppel by representation to prevent the employer from recovering the overpayment as moneys had and received.[65] Although an estoppel by representation can be raised in such a situation, this might not mean that the entirety of the amount overpaid can be kept.[66] Additionally, it will not prevent a payment from Consolidated Revenue from being ultra vires if made without statutory authority.[67] However, it is notable that mistakes of law are held generally to go to jurisdiction in both England and Australia and payments made consequent on a mistake of law should therefore be considered as being ultra vires and recoverable. Professor Burrows thought that that was the conclusion that should have been reached in *Avon County Council v Howlett*.[68] That is not to say that it would have been the preferable result, since the 'all or nothing' operation of estoppel by representation as a defence has been held to be unsatisfactory. On its facts, *Avon County Council v Howlett* would better have

[60] KR Handley, *Estoppel by Conduct and Election* (London, Sweet and Maxwell, 2006) 296.

[61] ibid, 301.

[62] G Weeks, 'The Public Law of Restitution' (2014) 38 *Melbourne University Law Review* 198, 222–35.

[63] *Minister for Immigration, Local Government and Ethnic Affairs v Kurtovic* (1990) 21 FCR 193, 208–11.

[64] *Maritime Electric* [1937] AC 610; cf *Durban City Council v Glenore Supermarket and Cafe* 1981 (1) SA 470 (D). See KR Handley, *Estoppel by Conduct and Election* (London, Sweet and Maxwell, 2006) 301–2.

[65] *Avon County Council v Howlett* [1983] 1 WLR 605.

[66] ibid, 624. See *Scottish Equitable Plc v Derby* [2001] 3 All ER 818; *National Westminster Bank plc v Somer International (UK) Ltd* [2002] QB 1286; cf J Hudson, 'Estoppel by Representation as a Defence to Unjust Enrichment—The Vine Has Not Withered Yet' (2014) 22 *Restitution Law Review* 19.

[67] *Auckland Harbour* [1924] AC 318.

[68] See A Burrows, *The Law of Restitution*, 3rd edn (Oxford, Oxford University Press, 2011) 519.

been decided by applying the change of position defence against a claim of unjust enrichment, had it been available at the time.[69] Indeed, change of position is generally to be preferred, since it applies *pro tanto*, although it should be remembered that change of position and estoppel by representation are not always simultaneously available.[70] The alternative of allowing estoppel to operate as a *pro tanto* defence has not been accepted in Australia. Hudson has argued that it would be inconsistent with the operation of estoppel by representation as a rule of evidence.[71]

The established reasoning behind the rejection of attempts to extend private law estoppel to the public exercise of statutory powers and discretions is that private actors are capable of being estopped because they are self-regarding, whereas the 'public law ... binds everyone'.[72] With respect, it is difficult to understand why the application of this principle should preclude an estoppel from being raised when, in England, it is not an insuperable barrier to the courts giving substantive effect to a legitimate expectation with a judicial review remedy.

South African courts had also indicated that they were prepared to depart from the traditional position preventing estoppel of public authorities where that would impede the performance of a statutory duty. In *Peter Klein Investments*, Boruchowitz J held that section 39(2) of the South African Constitution required 'that the Court should balance the individual and public interests at stake and decide on that basis whether the operation of estoppel should be allowed in a specific case'.[73] However, this position, which was redolent of the English law relating to the substantive enforcement of legitimate expectations, was subsequently abandoned.[74] The Supreme Court of Appeal returned to the established principle that '[e]stoppel cannot ... be used in such a way as to give effect to what is not permitted or recognised by law. Invalidity must therefore follow uniformly as the consequence. That consequence cannot vary from case to case'.[75]

Regardless, there is no prima facie reason why, where a plaintiff has made out that an estoppel could be raised if the defendant were a private actor, courts should be prevented from providing an alternative remedy in circumstances where it is inappropriate to enforce an estoppel by preventing the defendant public authority from exercising a statutory power or discretion. There are, however, some potential barriers to such a course of action. First, plaintiffs cannot always overcome the essential preliminary requirement.[76] Additionally, there are reasons why public authorities and private actors cannot always be treated in the same way. This, however, has not operated as a blanket rule to prevent individuals from obtaining remedies against public authorities in tort. Fears that estoppel in public law will result

[69] ibid, 554–55.

[70] J Hudson, 'Estoppel by Representation as a Defence to Unjust Enrichment' (2014) 22 *Restitution Law Review* 19, 29–31.

[71] ibid, 34; J Hudson, 'The True Purpose of Estoppel by Representation' (2015) 32 *Journal of Contract Law* 275, 288–89.

[72] *Newbury District Council v Secretary of State for the Environment* [1981] AC 578, 752.

[73] *Eastern Metropolitan Substructure v Peter Klein Investments (Pty) Ltd* 2001 (4) SA 661 (W), [40].

[74] C Hoexter, *Administrative Law in South Africa*, 2nd edn (Claremont, Juta & Co, 2012) 41–42.

[75] *City of Tshwane Metropolitan Municipality v RPM Bricks (Pty) Ltd* 2008 (3) SA 1 (SCA), [23].

[76] See eg *Kurtovic* (1990) 21 FCR 193, 217–18; *Reprotech* [2003] 1 WLR 348, 357.

in courts enforcing the substance of promises made to individuals are overstated, provided always that the scope of public law estoppel is appropriately restricted. A better solution would be for equity, with its characteristic 'remedial flexibility', to exercise its capacity to construct a remedy which is not at odds with the doctrine of ultra vires.[77]

This obstacle could be overcome if the only reason that courts do not currently award compensation in such circumstances were purely for reasons of public policy. After all, strong objections to the extension of equitable estoppel on policy grounds have been overcome. Prior to the decision of the High Court of Australia in *Waltons v Maher*, there were grave concerns that the extension of the doctrine of estoppel to enforce promises as to future conduct outside the realm of contract would have a severely deleterious effect on the contractual doctrine of consideration.[78] More than 20 years after that landmark decision, the law relating to consideration remains recognisable. It has survived the capacity of equity to intervene and enforce a promise upon which another party has relied to his or her detriment (although in *Waltons* itself, damages were ordered in lieu of an order for specific performance).[79]

The Supreme Courts in each Australian jurisdiction have the power, granted by statute in terms derived from Lord Cairns' Act, to award equitable damages where it would otherwise have had power to grant an injunction.[80] The current scope of this statutory power is stated in section 68 of the Supreme Court Act 1970 (NSW):[81]

> Where the Court has power:
>
> (a) to grant an injunction against the breach of any covenant, contract or agreement, or against the commission or continuance of any wrongful act, or
> (b) to order the specific performance of any covenant, contract or agreement,
>
> the Court may award damages to the party injured either in addition to or in substitution for the injunction or specific performance.

The purpose of Lord Cairns' Act, passed in 1858, was stated by Lindley LJ to be 'to enable the Court of Chancery to administer justice between litigants more effectually than it could before the Act'.[82] Additionally, there is an inherent power in the Supreme Courts of each Australian jurisdiction to award equitable compensation, for the breach of a fiduciary duty or other breach of an equitable duty.[83]

[77] *Harris v Digital Pulse Pty Ltd* (2003) 56 NSWLR 298, 304 (Spigelman CJ).

[78] A Mason, 'Estoppel in Public Law' in M Groves (ed), *Law and Government in Australia* (Sydney, Federation Press, 2005) 160, 162.

[79] *Waltons v Maher* (1988) 164 CLR 387, 390.

[80] Chancery Amendment Act (UK) (21 & 22 Vict c 27) s 2. See JD Heydon et al, *Meagher, Gummow and Lehane's Equity*, 5th edn (New South Wales, LexisNexis, 2015) 874–77.

[81] eg Supreme Court Act 1986 (Vic) s 38; Equity Act 1867 (Qld) s 62. See also *Wentworth v Woollahra* (1982) 149 CLR 672, 682 (Gibbs CJ, Mason, Murphy & Brennan JJ); cf PD Finn, 'A Road Not Taken: the Boyce Plaintiff and Lord Cairns' Act (Part I)' (1983) 57 *Australian Law Journal* 493; PD Finn, 'A Road Not Taken: the Boyce Plaintiff and Lord Cairns' Act (Part II)' (1983) 57 *Australian Law Journal* 571.

[82] *Shelfer v City of London Electric Lighting Co* [1895] 1 Ch 287, 316.

[83] L Aitken, 'Developments in Equitable Compensation: Opportunity or Danger?' (1993) 67 *Australian Law Journal* 596, 596 (fn 3); *Bennett v Minister for Community Welfare* (1992) 176 CLR 408, 426–27 (McHugh J). See RI Barrett, 'Equitable compensation' (2000) 74 *Australian Law Journal* 228.

Furthermore, 'literature in the field has differentiated between equitable compensation that is *reparation for loss* and equitable compensation that is in *substitution of performance*'.[84] The principles involved when a court awards compensation for the breach of a fiduciary duty causing loss are well known but will not be addressed here, since they will not generally apply to departures from representations contained in soft law.

The difference in nomenclature between damages and equitable compensation is 'notoriously difficult' but Owen J summarised it as follows:[85]

> Strictly speaking the term 'damages' describes a monetary award for an infringement of a common law or statutory right while 'compensation' denotes a monetary award granted in the inherent jurisdiction of equity as relief for a breach of an equitable obligation.

This distinction has been summarised elsewhere as saying that equitable compensation is to breaches of equitable duty what damages are to breaches of common law duties.[86] The authors of *MGL* have stated that the statutory power to award damages was not intended to empower the courts to award damages 'in addition to or in lieu of injunctions in aid of purely equitable rights'.[87] The statutory reference to a 'wrongful act' is to be read as synonymous with 'tort', a conclusion given force by the fact that the courts had before *Lord Cairns' Act* an inherent power to 'grant damages in addition to, or in lieu of, an injunction in aid of a purely equitable right'.[88]

The function of equitable compensation is compensatory, a point that Mason P characterised as a 'blinding glimpse of the obvious [which] tells you nothing about areas where equity goes further, for example, by granting an injunction, specific performance or account of profits'.[89] Equitable compensation goes beyond the well-understood circumstances where 'property held in a fiduciary capacity is misapplied'.[90] However, 'the limits of the monetary relief capable of being awarded in equity' are not best explored by starting from the compensatory nature of equitable compensation.[91] In his celebrated speech in *Nocton v Lord Ashburton*, Lord Haldane stated that damages are available at common law where loss is consequent on an honest but reckless statement falling short of fraud, in the context of a 'special relationship' which is not of a fiduciary character.[92] His Lordship's statement was

[84] VJ Vann, 'Equity and Proportionate Liability' (2007) 1 *Journal of Equity* 199, 212.

[85] *The Bell Group Ltd (in liq) v Westpac Banking Corporation (No 9)* (2008) 225 FLR 1, 835.

[86] *Coulthard v Disco Mix Club Ltd* [1999] 2 All ER 457, 478.

[87] JD Heydon et al, *Meagher, Gummow and Lehane's Equity*, 5th edn (New South Wales, LexisNexis, 2015) 883; cf *Wentworth v Woollahra* (1982) 149 CLR 672, 676.

[88] ibid.

[89] *Harris v Digital Pulse* (2003) 56 NSWLR 298, 323. See also JD Heydon et al, *Meagher, Gummow and Lehane's Equity*, 5th edn (New South Wales, LexisNexis, 2015) 801.

[90] IE Davidson, 'The Equitable Remedy of Compensation' (1982) 13 *Melbourne University Law Review* 349, 349.

[91] *Harris v Digital Pulse* (2003) 56 NSWLR 298, 324.

[92] *Nocton v Lord Ashburton* [1914] AC 932, 955. See *Derry v Peek* (1889) 14 App Cas 337; F Pollock, 'Nocton v Lord Ashburton' (1915) 31 *LQR* 93.

subsequently used as authority for the recognition of liability for negligent misstatement in *Hedley Byrne*.[93]

In *Nocton v Lord Ashburton* itself, the appellant solicitor was held not to have been liable to his client, the respondent, in the tort of deceit, meaning that damages were not payable at common law. The appellant was, however, liable for breach of a fiduciary duty; this was a matter falling within the exclusive jurisdiction of equity.[94] Mason P concluded that 'Viscount Haldane's speech … exposed the error of thinking that equity lacked power to award compensation for infringement of a right which was recognised exclusively in Chancery in the pre-*Judicature Act* era'.[95] The authors of *MGL* cited the judgment of Dixon AJ in *McKenzie v McDonald* as stating that *Nocton v Lord Ashburton* stood for the proposition that the equitable jurisdiction to remedy breaches of fiduciary duty extended to making an order for compensation in favour of the party whose confidence had been abused.[96] Such an order would also be available in respect of a 'special relationship' which is not fiduciary in nature. Equitable compensation has a broad application.[97]

As I have discussed above, the equity created by an estoppel need not be fulfilled by holding the representor to the substance of his or her representation. The standard view (now seemingly in retreat) had been that a court must award the 'minimum equity' required to do justice in the circumstances, but no more.[98] In *Crabb v Arun District Council*, Scarman LJ stated that courts 'have to determine not only the extent of the equity, but also the conditions necessary to satisfy it'.[99] His Lordship's reasoning was subsequently approved by a majority of the High Court in *Waltons v Maher* but received detailed consideration only from Brennan J, who articulated a reliance-based approach to remedying the breach of a legal obligation owed to the representee in circumstances where the conditions for an equitable estoppel are met. His Honour characterised equitable estoppel as 'the source of a legal obligation arising on an actual state of affairs'.[100]

The decision of the High Court in *Verwayen* is often criticised for its lack of a ratio decidendi beyond what was decided on its facts.[101] Nonetheless, each member of the Court noted the flexibility with which the equity created by an equitable estoppel

[93] See *Hedley Byrne* [1964] AC 465, 484–85 (Lord Reid); 500–502 (Lord Morris); 508–9 (Lord Hodson); 519 (Lord Devlin); 533 (Lord Pearce); cf JD Heydon et al, *Meagher, Gummow and Lehane's Equity*, 5th edn (New South Wales, LexisNexis, 2015) 52.

[94] JD Heydon et al, *Meagher, Gummow and Lehane's Equity*, 5th edn (New South Wales, Lexis Nexis, 2015), 810.

[95] *Harris v Digital Pulse* (2003) 56 NSWLR 298, 323.

[96] *McKenzie v McDonald* [1925] VLR 134, 146. See JD Heydon et al, *Meagher, Gummow and Lehane's Equity*, 5th edn (New South Wales, LexisNexis, 2015) 815.

[97] *Harris v Digital Pulse* (2003) 56 NSWLR 298, 323.

[98] *Verwayen* (1990) 170 CLR 394, 412 (Mason CJ); 454 (Dawson J); cf 443–45 (Deane J); *Giumelli* (1999) 196 CLR 101, 120–21.

[99] *Crabb v Arun District Council* [1976] Ch 179, 199. See *Waltons v Maher* (1988) 164 CLR 387, 404 (Mason CJ & Wilson J); 425 (Brennan J); 460 (Gaudron J). See also A Robertson, 'Satisfying the Minimum Equity' (1996) 20 *Melbourne University Law Review* 805, 820.

[100] *Waltons v Maher* (1988) 164 CLR 387, 416. See A Robertson, 'Satisfying the Minimum Equity' (1996) 20 *Melbourne University Law Review* 805, 821.

[101] cf A Mason, 'The Use and Abuse of Precedent' (1988) 4 *Australian Bar Review* 93, 103–4.

was able to be fulfilled as a result of the wide discretion possessed by courts of equitable jurisdiction as to the grant of remedies.[102] Of the available equitable remedies, Deane J noted specifically that in some circumstances 'the appropriate order may be an order for compensatory damages'.[103] One set of circumstances in which compensation will be an appropriate remedy is where the representor is a public authority and it is inappropriate as a matter of public law to give substantive effect to the representation in question. However, Robertson noted that, in the years immediately following *Verwayen*, courts almost universally satisfied equitable estoppels by granting expectation-based relief.[104] Indeed, the High Court has more recently remarked that, notwithstanding the minimum equity principle, 'where the unconscionable conduct consists of resiling from a promise or assurance which has induced conduct to the other party's detriment, the relief which is necessary in this sense is usually that which reflects the value of the promise'.[105]

The requirement for courts to provide only the minimum equity required to do justice to the plaintiff has therefore become uncertain since Deane J stated in *Verwayen* that:[106]

> Prima facie, the operation of an estoppel by conduct is to preclude departure from the assumed state of affairs. It is only where relief framed on the basis of that assumed state of affairs would be inequitably harsh, that some lesser form of relief should be awarded.

Deane J's doubts about confining relief to the minimum equity in that case were cited with approval by the majority of the High Court in *Giumelli*.[107] Some commentators thereafter concluded that the restriction of relief to the minimum required equity 'has not survived' the Court's acceptance in *Giumelli* of Deane J's dicta in *Verwayen*.[108] By contrast, Handley AJA, acknowledged for his mastery of estoppel, was prepared only to say that the minimum equity principle 'since *Giumelli* is *probably* not the law in this country' (emphasis added).[109] The true position is likely to be that courts must consider whether equitable relief will do disproportionate damage to the defendant by comparison to what the plaintiff has suffered.[110] This is part and parcel of that fact that '[a]ny order made by an equity court is discretionary, in the sense that it is tailored to meet the circumstances of the particular case'.[111]

102 *Verwayen* (1990) 170 CLR 394, 411–12 (Mason CJ); 429–30 (Brennan J); 439, 442 (Deane J); 454 (Dawson J); 475–76 (Toohey J); 487 (Gaudron J); 501 (McHugh J). See A Robertson, 'Satisfying the Minimum Equity' (1996) 20 *Melbourne University Law Review* 805, 807.

103 *Verwayen* (1990) 170 CLR 394, 442.

104 A Robertson, 'Satisfying the Minimum Equity' (1996) 20 *Melbourne University Law Review* 805, 829.

105 *Sidhu v Van Dyke* (2014) 251 CLR 505, 530.

106 *Verwayen* (1990) 170 CLR 394, 443.

107 *Giumelli* (1999) 196 CLR 101, 123 (Gleeson CJ, McHugh, Gummow & Callinan JJ).

108 M Bryan, 'Unifying Estoppel Doctrine: The Argument for Heresy' (2013) 7 *Journal of Equity* 209, 210; cf JC Campbell, '*Waltons v Maher*: History, Unconscientiousness and Remedy—the "Minimum Equity"' (2013) 7 *Journal of Equity* 171, 173.

109 *Delaforce v Simpson-Cook* (2010) 78 NSWLR 483, 493. See L Aitken, 'The Future of the 'Minimum Equity', and the Appropriate 'Fault Line' in Promissory and Proprietary Estoppel' (2010) 33 *Australian Bar Review* 212, 215.

110 JD Heydon et al, *Meagher, Gummow and Lehane's Equity*, 5th edn (New South Wales, Lexis Nexis, 2015) 525–26.

111 JC Campbell, '*Waltons v Maher*' (2013) 7 *Journal of Equity* 171, 208.

Nothing in the debate regarding the role of the minimum equity principle is inconsistent with equitable compensation being available as a remedy to a person who has relied to his or her detriment on a soft law instrument issued by a public authority and amounting to a representation. In such circumstances, the remedy of giving effect to the representation, reliance on which has created an equitable estoppel, will generally be unavailable against the public authority for the reasons surveyed above. It is sufficient to note that what is required to do justice to the reliant individual *need not* be the substantive fulfillment of the representation.[112] Vann summarised the issue (albeit not referring specifically to the situation in which the representor is a public authority) by noting that, in some cases, 'the court has little alternative but to order the payment of a monetary sum, in order to relieve the detriment suffered by the plaintiff' because it is not possible for the promise to be performed.[113]

There is no logical difference between a representation which cannot be fulfilled, for example 'because the subject matter of the promise has disappeared, or because the court has taken into account interests of third parties who might be affected by an order specifically performing the promise', and a soft law instrument whose substance cannot be fulfilled because to do so would require an ultra vires act, or fetter on the future exercise of a discretion, by a public official.[114] The equitable estoppel which has been created by the representation remains. The public identity of the representor does not provide any prima facie basis for denying compensation as the appropriate form of relief. There are other issues in relation to making out that equitable compensation is payable, notably the requirements of establishing causation and remoteness, which will not be addressed in this book.[115]

Emily cannot obtain a substantive remedy against the Council once the new SEPP has come into effect because to approve Emily's development proposal would be ultra vires. An estoppel has nonetheless been raised in favour of Emily by the Council's unconscientious act of inducing her to believe that the terms of the Guidelines would be applied. Furthermore, she has suffered monetary loss as a result of relying on the Guidelines being applied by the Council: she has demolished a house valued at AU$100,000 and incurred liabilities by hiring contractors. If the Council were a private party, a court could enforce the estoppel against it or award a lesser equity, such as equitable compensation. Although the former remedy is unavailable on the facts supposed, a court could nonetheless award equitable compensation in the amount of Emily's loss.

D. CONCLUSION

The possibilities for enforcing the terms of soft law through legal processes in Australia are, at best, few and indirect. The situation is different in England,

[112] cf *Verwayen* (1990) 170 CLR 394, 443.
[113] VJ Vann, 'Equity and Proportionate Liability' (2007) 1 *Journal of Equity* 199, 218.
[114] ibid.
[115] See M O'Meara, 'Causation, Remoteness and Equitable Compensation' (2005) 26 *Australian Bar Review* 51.

although there are still legitimate concerns that the English approach to substantive legitimate expectations is too broad (at least for Australia) and retains in any case a worrisome capacity to be ineffective.[116] While it has seemed clear that legal responses to reliance on soft law are best left in the hands of the judiciary, the ARC concluded that:[117]

> it would [not] necessarily be effective or efficient to seek to extend administrative law review mechanisms to … areas of co- and self-regulation. It would, however, be reasonable to assume that such soft law rules should give rise to an appropriate form of accountability.

Jurisdictions which have come to peace with high levels of judicial autonomy and capacity to intervene in exercises of executive power, like England, are much more likely to be able to deal with the challenges thrown up by soft law than jurisdictions which remain, for a host of reasons, much more conservative. Many changes would need to occur before judicial review could be considered an adequate response to the challenges of soft law in Australia, the foremost of such jurisdictions.

Part II has further demonstrated that, although private law remedies are in some circumstances available for the failure of public authorities to adhere to their own soft law, the examples where this is so are severely limited. On the whole, the existence of such remedies is inadequate protection for individuals who have acted on the faith of soft law. A statutory remedy will likely be required in order to address a problem like reliance on soft law, given that it does not conform to any existing body of legal or equitable doctrine.

[116] See *Davies v HMRC* [2011] 1 WLR 2625.
[117] *Complex Regulation Report* (2008), 15.

Part III

Non-judicial Remedies

INTRODUCTION

It is no great leap, in light of the previous chapters of this book, to conclude that judicial remedies for breach of soft law by public authorities are difficult to obtain, not least in Australia. The reason for this is fundamental: soft law may be 'law' in the sense that it constitutes a norm that is usually followed but it is nonetheless 'soft' and as such is not directly enforceable by courts. The potential judicial remedies described in the chapters above amount to work-arounds rather than affirmative indications that judicial remedies are applicable to breaches of soft law.[1] Significant changes in established Australian legal doctrine will be required to change this state of affairs.

This is not to say that there is nothing that can yet be done to remedy loss caused by a public authority's departure from its own soft law; however, some remedies are granted by consent rather than as of right. I propose to discuss two such remedies in this Part. The first is investigation by the Ombudsman.[2] The second is a substantive remedy in the form of a payment of ex gratia compensation by the government. Indeed, the two will very frequently be linked to one another.

[1] This is in effect a reversal of the circumstances described in M Aronson and M Groves, *Judicial Review of Administrative Action*, 5th edn (Sydney, Thompson Reuters, 2013) [6.730].

[2] This book will adhere to the custom, common to both Australia and England, of using the term 'ombudsman' regardless of the gender of the office-holder and to render the plural of ombudsman as 'ombudsmen'; see A Stuhmcke, 'Ombudsmen and Integrity Review' in L Pearson et al (eds), *Administrative Law in a Changing State* (Oxford, Hart Publishing, 2008) 349, 349 (fn 1); T Buck, R Kirkham and B Thompson, *The Ombudsman Enterprise and Administrative Justice* (Farnham, Ashgate, 2011) 3 (fn 1); P Cane and J Conaghan, (eds) *The New Oxford Companion to Law* (Oxford, Oxford University Press, 2008) 851–52.

11

The Ombudsman

THE OFFICE OF the Commonwealth Ombudsman operates as a mechanism for holding executive decision-makers accountable. It does this under statute through two different but complementary roles: the first for handling complaints and the second for conducting own-motion investigations. There are numerous 'independent oversight agencies' which now operate according to this model.[1] This section will examine how the Ombudsman's accountability role may be of use to a person who has suffered loss due to a public authority's departure from its own soft law.

A. THE DUAL ROLES AND CONSTITUTIONAL LOCATION OF THE OMBUDSMAN

The Commonwealth Ombudsman is one of Australia's 'non-judicial accountability bodies'.[2] It is frequently described as an element of a notional fourth or 'integrity' branch of government.[3] Spigelman CJ first popularised this concept in Australia but it has since been picked up by many others.[4] References to a national integrity branch are in fact inaccurate; it is better to think of the institutions within such a 'branch' as simply sharing a common theme.[5]

The Ombudsman is constitutionally part of the executive branch of government in Australia but it is more or less the standard practice in Australia to note that the office is 'alien' to the established divisions under the separation of powers doctrine and is as a result some sort of 'Constitutional misfit'.[6] In other words, despite the fact

[1] J McMillan, 'Re-thinking the Separation of Powers' (2010) 38 *Federal Law Review* 423, 435.

[2] ibid, 423. See also T Buck et al, *The Ombudsman Enterprise and Administrative Justice* (Farnham, Ashgate, 2011) 3.

[3] JJ Spigelman, 'The Integrity Branch of Government' (2004) 78 *Australian Law Journal* 724, 729; JJ Spigelman, 'The Integrity Branch of Government—The First Lecture in the 2004 National Lecture Series for the Australian Institute of Administrative Law' (Speech delivered at the AIAL National Lecture Series, Sydney, 29 April 2004).

[4] See eg A Stuhmcke, 'Ombudsmen and Integrity Review' in L Pearson et al (eds), *Administrative Law in a Changing State* (Oxford, Hart Publishing, 2008) 349, 349 (fn 4); cf WMC Gummow, 'The 2012 National Lecture on Administrative Law: A Fourth Branch of Government?' (2012) 70 *Australian Institute of Administrative Law Forum* 19.

[5] M Aronson and M Groves, *Judicial Review of Administrative Action*, 5th edn (Sydney, Thompson Reuters, 2013) [1.90].

[6] See A Stuhmcke, 'Changing Relations between Government and Citizen: Administrative Law and the Work of the Australian Commonwealth Ombudsman' (2008) 67 *Australian Journal of Public*

that the executive branch is not conceptually the most appropriate constitutional location for the Ombudsman, it is there of necessity because the Constitution was not drafted to include a fourth branch.[7] The Australian terminology in this regard differs from that used in the USA, where the 'fourth branch' refers to agencies.[8] It follows that, if the USA were to have an ombudsman, that office would be part of a nominal *fifth* branch.

What is meant by the description 'integrity branch' varies. The Swedish origins of the institution are often emphasised.[9] Spigelman CJ noted, however, that, as a genus, guardians of integrity in government have a strong resemblance to what Western scholars generally describe—by inaccurate analogy—as the 'censorial' or 'supervising' branch of the Chinese civil service.[10] Spigelman CJ did not regard the Ombudsman's complaint-handling role as a central feature of the integrity branch:[11]

> Complaint mechanisms are designed to improve the quality of decision-making and are more in the nature of the performance of an executive function, than an integrity function. Nevertheless, many complaint handling bodies, including Ombudsmen, do perform integrity functions, in the course of, or sometimes in addition to, dealing with individual complaints.

His Honour saw the integrity function as being exercised in the main through judicial review (which is to say, through the constitutionally recognised third branch), which has the function of ensuring the legality of the actions of public authorities. Aronson and Groves commented to the contrary that 'fourth branch institutions have a daily impact far beyond that of the courts'.[12] Whether or not the office of the Ombudsman is 'central' to integrity review, it is certainly 'a central component of administrative justice'.[13] I argue below that the Ombudsman is in fact essential to upholding the rule of law.

Administration 321, 322; R Snell, 'Towards an Understanding of a Constitutional Misfit: Four Snapshots of the Ombudsman Enigma' in C Finn (ed), *Sunrise or Sunset? Administrative Law in the New Millennium* (Canberra, AIAL, 2000) 188; D Pearce, 'The Commonwealth Ombudsman: Right Office in the Wrong Place' in R Creyke and J McMillan (eds), *The Kerr Vision of Australian Administrative Law at the Twenty-Five Year Mark* (Canberra, AIAL, 1998) 54, 72; T Buck et al, *Ombudsman Enterprise* (Farnham, Ashgate, 2011) 15.

[7] See R Creyke and J McMillan, *Control of Government Action*, 3rd edn (Sydney, LexisNexis, 2012) 220–23.

[8] SA Shapiro and RE Levy, 'Heightened Scrutiny of the Fourth Branch: Separation of Powers and the Requirement of Adequate Reasons for Agency Decisions' (1987) 36 *Duke Law Journal* 387.

[9] See R Creyke and J McMillan, *Control of Government Action*, 3rd edn (Sydney, LexisNexis, 2012) 202; T Buck et al, *Ombudsman Enterprise* (Farnham, Ashgate, 2011) 3.

[10] JJ Spigelman, 'The Integrity Branch of Government' (2004) 78 *Australian Law Journal* 724, 724; JJ Spigelman, 'Judicial Review and the Integrity Branch of Government' (Speech delivered at the World Jurist Association Congress, Shanghai, 8 September 2005).

[11] JJ Spigelman, 'The Integrity Branch of Government' (2004) 78 *Australian Law Journal* 724, 729; cf A Stuhmcke, 'Ombudsmen and Integrity Review' in L Pearson et al (eds), *Administrative Law in a Changing State* (Oxford, Hart Publishing, 2008) 349, 354.

[12] M Aronson and M Groves, *Judicial Review of Administrative Action*, 5th edn (Sydney, Thompson Reuters, 2013) [1.90].

[13] C Harlow and R Rawlings, *Law and Administration*, 3rd edn (Cambridge, Cambridge University Press, 2009) 480. See AJ Brown, 'Putting Administrative Law Back into Integrity and Putting the Integrity Back into Administrative Law' (2007) 53 *Australian Institute of Administrative Law Forum* 32;

By contrast to Spigelman CJ's views, Stuhmcke argued that integrity review is in practice 'diametrically opposed to the outcomes delivered by an adversarial system of dispute resolution':[14]

> This is because, in the adversarial system, disputes arise precisely because there is a view by the litigant or complainant that the administrative decision was impaired and imperfect. Integrity review requires the opposite—that there is no originating dispute due to imperfection or incorrect administrative decision-makers. Indeed, effective integrity review means that administrative law will operate to ensure that government agency decision-making is perfect from its inception and that this is an ongoing state of government agency administrative decision-making.

Stuhmcke differentiated the reactive complaint-handling role, typical of ombudsmen, from an active 'system-fixing' role.[15] While the first of these roles is the traditional focus of the Ombudsman's office, the latter is assuming an ever greater importance, with ombudsmen making limited funds go further by commencing more investigations on their own motions and attempting to influence systemic change rather than redress individual grievances.[16] The Commonwealth Ombudsman in fact finalised a greater number of complaints in 2011–12 than in the previous year, but additionally released five reports and made a further 13 submissions to Parliamentary Committees or government inquiries.[17] The latter activity is expressly for the purpose of promoting 'good public administration'. The Commonwealth Ombudsman has an unreviewable discretion to refuse to investigate a complaint, a statutory power which enabled the Commonwealth Ombudsman's office to investigate only one in every nine complaints in 2008.[18] However, this active investigative function is the function which conforms more fully to the notion of integrity review.[19]

The Ombudsman's system-fixing role is relevant to an analysis of soft law because soft law remains a legally under-theorised method of regulation. The fact, as I have discussed above, that courts have few current tools for dealing with soft law means that 'integrity branch' authorities like the Ombudsman bear a responsibility for making sure that the steps required 'to ensure that administrative law values are upheld'

D Solomon, 'What is the Integrity Branch?' (2012) 70 *Australian Institute of Administrtative Law Forum* 26; R Creyke, 'An 'Integrity' Branch' (2012) 70 *Australian Institute of Administrative Law Forum* 33; J Wenta, 'The Integrity Branch of Government and the Separation of Judicial Power' (2012) 70 *Australian Institute for Administrative Law Forum* 42; J McMillan, 'Re-thinking the Separation of Powers' (2010) 38 *Federal Law Review* 423.

14 A Stuhmcke, 'Ombudsmen and Integrity Review' in L Pearson et al (eds), *Administrative Law in a Changing State* (Oxford, Hart Publishing, 2008) 349, 353–54.

15 See Ombudsman Act 1976 (Cth) Pt II Div 2.

16 R Creyke and J McMillan, *Control of Government Action*, 3rd edn (Sydney, LexisNexis, 2012) 209. See J McMillan, 'Future Directions 2009—The Ombudsman' (2010) 63 *Australian Institute of Administrative Law Forum* 13, 14–15; A Stuhmcke, 'Ombudsmen and Integrity Review' in L Pearson et al (eds), *Administrative Law in a Changing State* (Oxford, Hart Publishing, 2008) 349, 365.

17 Commonwealth Ombudsman, *Annual Report 2011–12*, (2012) 41; 98–102.

18 J McMillan, 'Future Directions' (2010) 63 *Australian Institute of Administrative Law Forum* 13, 14. See Ombudsman Act 1976 (Cth) s 6.

19 A Stuhmcke, 'Ombudsmen and Integrity Review' in L Pearson et al (eds), *Administrative Law in a Changing State* (Oxford, Hart Publishing, 2008) 349, 355.

are properly understood.[20] In helping to define the norms in accordance with which activity is regulated the Ombudsman fills a protective, rather than a remedial, role.

A significant issue raised by the fact that the Ombudsman is in practice positioned outside the tripartite separation of powers model is that it lacks the determinative power which is possessed by the judicial branch of government. As a result, the Ombudsman's office cannot impose binding declarations of right on the public authorities which it investigates, as the High Court established with regard to the analogous Human Rights and Equal Opportunity Commission (HREOC) in *Brandy*.[21] However, as I will discuss below, ombudsmen are no less effective for their incapacity to exercise determinative powers and, in fact, 'have a potential for *systemic* impact beyond any court's capacity' (emphasis added).[22]

Lawyers, however, tend to examine issues through a formal lens, which does not necessarily reflect their 'special responsibility to be well informed about the assistance which an ombudsman may be able to give to their clients'.[23] When that lens is the Constitution, the consequence is a common perception amongst lawyers that the Ombudsman is a 'toothless tiger'.[24] This allegation 'may illustrate that the culture of the adversary system is not receptive to other forms of dispute resolution'.[25] At the very least, it lacks imagination, since ombudsmen usually find ways to be very effective even without 'teeth' of the sort possessed by courts and tribunals—there is still much that is effective about a tiger before one confronts its teeth. Perhaps the effectiveness of the 'ombudsman model' is precisely *because* of this lack of teeth, and the consequent necessity to find other methods of getting results. A body with the metaphorical teeth of a tiger may become complacent in the efficacy of those teeth; an ombudsman does not have this luxury but finds ways around his or her dental deficiencies such that s/he may in fact possess 'some advantages over courts in securing the rule of law'.[26] Sullivan LJ recognised this point when, in response to the Law Commission's *Administrative Redress* Consultation Paper, he 'agreed with the underlying premise that "a significant proportion of certain types of claim in the Administrative Court would be equally well, if not better, dealt with by ombudsmen"'.[27]

Buck and his co-authors regard as 'uncontentious' the proposition that 'the ombudsman is now an established feature not just of systems of administrative and civil justice, *but also of the constitution*', subject only to the difficulty of 'establishing the full strength of the ombudsman's constitutional worth' (emphasis added).[28] They appear to contend that 'integrity' is simply another way to describe the broad

[20] J McMillan, 'Future Directions' (2010) 63 *Australian Institute of Administrative Law Forum* 13, 18.

[21] *Brandy v Human Rights and Equal Opportunity Commission* (1995) 183 CLR 245.

[22] M Aronson and M Groves, *Judicial Review of Administrative Action*, 5th edn (Sydney, Thompson Reuters, 2013) [1.90].

[23] JUSTICE—All Souls, *Administrative Justice* (P Neill (ed), Oxford, Clarendon Press, 1988) 137.

[24] R Creyke and J McMillan, *Control of Government Action*, 3rd edn (Sydney, LexisNexis, 2012) 217.

[25] M Groves, 'Ombudsmen's Jurisdiction in Prisons' (2002) 28 *Monash University Law Review* 181, 201. See also D Pearce, 'Right Office in the Wrong Place' in R Creyke and J McMillan (eds), *The Kerr Vision of Australian Administrative Law* (Canberra, AIAL, 1998) 54, 65.

[26] J McMillan, 'Re-thinking the Separation of Powers' (2010) 38 *Federal Law Review* 423, 435.

[27] Law Commission, *Administrative Redress* (2010), 55 [5.16].

[28] T Buck et al, *Ombudsman Enterprise* (Farnham, Ashgate, 2011) 4.

rule of law values which underpin the constitution and, on that basis, because the Ombudsman embodies those values, the office is thereby 'constitutional'.[29] In the *Communist Party Case*, Dixon J made the point that the Constitution was framed in accordance with certain explicit and assumed conceptions, the rule of law being an example of the latter.[30] However, his Honour did not propose that assumptions such as the rule of law be given immediate normative operation in the manner of the separation of powers and other traditional conceptions which are given effect by the text of the Constitution and, in the case of the separation of judicial power, are strictly applied.[31] Rather, he appears to have held that assumptions underlying the Constitution, such as the rule of law, have a role limited to informing constitutional interpretation. Nonetheless, Buck and his co-authors argue persuasively (and specifically in regard to jurisdictions without a written constitution) that the Ombudsman's role must be viewed in constitutional terms simply because of the objective importance of its capacity to review proper conduct as a supplement to the more limited supervisory jurisdiction of the courts, which looks generally only at whether conduct is lawful.[32]

The Victorian Ombudsman has constitutional status under the Constitution Act, although the protections that this status provides appear to be minimal, since the Ombudsman's designation as 'an independent officer of the Parliament' and the conferral of 'complete discretion in the performance or exercise of his or her functions or powers' are subject to legislative amendment.[33] Furthermore, to say that a body is 'independent' says little about *from what* it is supposed to be independent, and is not the same as being 'impartial'.[34] To the extent that other ombudsmen can be described as having constitutional status, this is mainly due to acceptance that their functions and role advance the aims of the rule of law rather than because their decisions and recommendations carry immediate legal normative force. Decisions of ombudsmen do, of course, carry *non-legal* normative force and legal enforceability is not, after all, the model for the Ombudsman's office, which tends to achieve much without having determinative powers *because* (rather than in spite) of their absence.

In addition to being unenforceable, however, recommendations made by the ombudsmen are also most unlikely to be the subject of judicial review proceedings in Australia.[35] This is due in part to the nature of the Ombudsman's function but also in part to the limited range of matters over which judicial review's supervisory jurisdiction extends in practice and the limited range of judicial review's remedial options.[36] By contrast, Harlow and Rawlings have noted a 'creeping spread of judicial review' over ombudsmen and like bodies in England, usually on the ground of

[29] ibid, 24.

[30] *Australian Communist Party v The Commonwealth* ('*The Communist Party Case*') (1951) 83 CLR 1, 193.

[31] McMillan, 'Re-thinking the Separation of Powers' (2010) 38 *Federal Law Review* 423, 424–27.

[32] T Buck et al, *Ombudsman Enterprise* (Farnham, Ashgate, 2011) 24–25.

[33] Constitution Act 1975 (Vic) s 94E.

[34] C Harlow and R Rawlings, *Law and Administration*, 3rd edn (Cambridge, Cambridge University Press, 2009) 531.

[35] J McMillan, 'Re-thinking the Separation of Powers' (2010) 38 *Federal Law Review* 423, 427.

[36] ibid, 427–28; 436.

procedural fairness having been denied, and contrary to the common assumption 'that ombudsman systems [are] not amenable to judicial review'.[37] The result of this approach to judicial review of ombudsmen has been that recommendations of the Parliamentary Ombudsman in England have become presumptively binding in a way that those of the Commonwealth Ombudsman in Australia are not. In this respect, they are somewhat analogous to the compensation scheme's non-statutory rule book in *Lain*, in regard to which Aronson and Groves noted that, although 'the rules were not binding ... the government would in fact honour their application by the board'.[38]

The case which 'changed the ballgame' in the evolution of this judicial approach is *Bradley*, in which for the first time the proceedings were not by way of a *challenge* to a discretionary choice made by the Parliamentary Commissioner for Administration (PCA) but 'effectively asking for her findings to be enforced'.[39] The Court of Appeal held that the defendant Secretary of State could not reject the PCA's finding that government maladministration had been the cause of certain pension schemes being underfunded if s/he lacked 'cogent reasons' to do so. This reasoning was based on the close relationship, enshrined in statute, between the PCA and the House of Commons.[40] The reasoning of the trial judge, Bean J, was somewhat different to that of the Court of Appeal in that his Honour would have held that the Work and Pensions Secretary had been *Wednesbury* unreasonable.[41] An Australian court would not have applied the high threshold *Wednesbury* standard as it is understood there. Even after the High Court's revised approach to *Wednesbury* in *Li*—a decision which was based on the inadequacy of a tribunal's reasons—it is unlikely that an Australian court would see as analogous circumstances in which there was at best a convention that the findings of ombudsmen are accepted, despite lacking binding force, and a Minister was therefore under no legal obligation to accept them. Indeed, Bean J slipped easily from a finding that the PCA's findings were 'reasonably open', to the finding that no reasonable Secretary of State could rationally disagree with them.

Harlow and Rawlings pointed out that, even where the convention to accept the findings of ombudsmen fails, 'parliamentary pressure usually prevails'.[42] The result of *Bradley* has augmented this practical position and administrative decision-makers are now open to legal challenge if they reject the findings of ombudsmen unless they are able to justify such a decision 'cogently'. This legal position is not universally popular in England, and has been described as a rare example of a legal development

[37] C Harlow and R Rawlings, *Law and Administration*, 3rd edn (Cambridge, Cambridge University Press, 2009) 482.

[38] M Aronson and M Groves, *Judicial Review of Administrative Action*, 5th edn (Sydney, Thompson Reuters, 2013) [3.250]. See *R v Criminal Injuries Compensation Board, ex parte Lain* [1967] QB 864.

[39] C Harlow and R Rawlings, *Law and Administration*, 3rd edn (Cambridge, Cambridge University Press, 2009) 564. See *R (Bradley) v Secretary of State for Work and Pensions* [2009] 1 QB 114.

[40] See Law Commission, *Administrative Redress* (2010), 65 [5.76]–[5.78].

[41] *R (Bradley) v Secretary of State for Work and Pensions* [2007] EWHC (Admin) 242 [66].

[42] C Harlow and R Rawlings, *Law and Administration*, 3rd edn (Cambridge, Cambridge University Press, 2009) 564.

that nobody wants.[43] For example, in *Bradley*, Wall LJ recorded the unconcealed distress of the PCA that her report had been 'misrepresented'.[44] Some, however, are very pleased with the result in *Bradley*: Buck and his co-authors recorded their view that it is most significant for providing 'further evidence of the enhanced status of the modern ombudsman enterprise within the constitution' and that the 'rebalancing of the constitutional balance of power' is 'entirely appropriate'.[45] This conclusion, of course, has no application in Australia, but even leaving aside Australia's strict approach to the separation of powers, it is a conclusion which is hard to support on a number of bases.

First, far from being a cause for celebration, the conclusion that 'public bodies cannot simply choose to agree to disagree with the ombudsman' begs the question *why* the elected and politically responsible Work and Pensions Secretary ought not to be allowed to say 'I have read the PCA's report; I disagree; and I will proceed as follows …'.[46] Such a course of action would leave the Secretary of State exposed to questions as to why s/he had rejected the PCA's findings but the consequences of such a course of action should be decided in the political realm, rather than in the courts based upon a judicial determination of the cogency of the Secretary of State's reasons. Any contention that this ought not to be the case must be justified.

Secondly, leaving aside the questions of whether ombudsmen can or should be invested with power that they can use to bind elected officials, it is likely that ombudsmen would not readily trade their influence, and the accumulated goodwill upon which it relies, for mere constitutional recognition. Ombudsmen are effective within the current understanding of their powers; the impact of their findings does not need to be strengthened in this way.

Thirdly, giving ombudsmen determinative powers and the attendant constitutional status makes nothing so likely as that they will spend a great deal more of their time and resources defending judicial review actions. This may be where the real battle would be fought, if it came to that, since constitutional recognition of ombudsmen would be entirely counter-productive if it were to lead to increased pressure on their time and budgets.

Buck and his co-authors appear to be well aware of the opposition to *Bradley* and it is fair to say that they occupy a space towards the end of the spectrum of academic responses to the Court of Appeal's decision. I suspect that the concerned statement of Harlow and Rawlings that the courts have been taking an 'activist line' is closer to the middle.[47] It is unlikely that, by employing the term 'activist', Harlow and Rawlings intended to buy into significant and generally 'acrimonious' recent Australian history with accusations of judicial activism.[48] Lee and Campbell would

[43] ibid, 564–65.

[44] *Bradley* [2009] 1 QB 114, 203.

[45] T Buck et al, *Ombudsman Enterprise* (Farnham, Ashgate, 2011) 216.

[46] ibid.

[47] C Harlow and R Rawlings, *Law and Administration*, 3rd edn (Cambridge, Cambridge University Press, 2009) 565.

[48] See eg JD Heydon, 'Judicial Activism' (2003) XLVII *Quadrant* 9; cf M Aronson, 'Process, Quality, and Variable Standards' in D Dyzenhaus et al (eds), *A Simple Common Lawyer* (Oxford, Hart Publishing, 2009) 5, 25–28.

sooner have categorised many of the flashpoint moments as examples of 'judicial adventurism' rather than activism per se.[49] Sackville J thought 'judicial activism' to be no more than a 'slogan', and generally an unhelpful one, usually employed pejoratively and behind the assumptions of which one must look for the true meaning of what is being alleged.[50] It is a term which has now fallen into disuse in Australia among commentators who are not actively looking to provoke a reaction.

This is all to the point that, in both Australia and, at least until the decision in *Bradley*, England, the constitutional status of the Ombudsman has largely been nothing more than a point of academic interest.[51] Predominantly on the basis of the decision in *Bradley*, the Law Commission stated that 'recent constitutional developments mean that the administrative landscape in relation to ombudsmen is currently in a state of flux' and declined to make recommendations about ombudsmen until a further process of review and consultation had been undertaken.[52] Options for holding public bodies accountable which fall outside the traditional scope of judicial review are increasing, rather than falling prey to legislators and members of the executive who would take advantage of their lack of formal constitutional status to abolish them.[53] Harlow and Rawlings have described as 'Ombudsmania' the 'rapid spread of the ombudsman technique' of complaints-handling which has resulted in a variety of ombudsmen created either under statute or in certain industries by analogy to public ombudsmen in both England and Australia.[54] The inescapable conclusion seems to be that the Ombudsman's somewhat unsettled constitutional position neither prevents the office from being effective nor poses any imminent threat to its survival.

B. THE OMBUDSMAN AND THE RULE OF LAW

The question of whether ombudsmen are 'effective' usually carries the unspoken subtext that effectiveness is, in their case, measured against the fact that they lack determinative powers. I have pointed out above that such an approach is driven by the most formal, 'capital-C' variety of constitutionalism. Whether or not ombudsmen are able to be located within such a framework, they are clearly part of the machinery of the rule of law.

Professor McMillan served as Commonwealth Ombudsman between 2003 and 2010, after which he took up the newly created (and subsequently abolished)

[49] HP Lee and E Campbell, *Australian Judiciary*, 2nd edn (Cambridge, Cambridge University Press, 2012) 2.

[50] R Sackville, 'Activism' in T Blackshield, M Coper and G Williams (eds), *The Oxford Companion to the High Court of Australia* (Melbourne, Oxford University Press, 2001) 6.

[51] cf R Snell, 'Towards an Understanding of a Constitutional Misfit' in C Finn (ed), *Sunrise or Sunset?* (Canberra, AIAL, 2000) 188, 189.

[52] Law Commission, *Administrative Redress* (2010), 70 [6.21].

[53] J McMillan, 'Re-thinking the Separation of Powers' (2010) 38 *Federal Law Review* 423, 432–38.

[54] C Harlow and R Rawlings, *Law and Administration*, 3rd edn (Cambridge, Cambridge University Press, 2009) 480. See P Cane and J Conaghan (eds), *The New Oxford Companion to Law* (Oxford, Oxford University Press, 2008) 851; R Creyke and J McMillan, *Control of Government Action*, 3rd edn (Sydney, LexisNexis, 2012) 201, 209.

position of Australian Information Commissioner.[55] He argued over the course of several years, albeit not alone amongst current and former ombudsmen, that the Ombudsman ought not to be forgotten in considerations of how the rule of law is upheld in Australia.[56] There have been numerous suggestions to the effect that upholding the rule of law is a function exclusively exercised by the courts.[57] McMillan opposed the view that these should be held to amount to a serious contention that the rule of law should itself be defined as being the sole domain of the judiciary. His logic is sound: to the extent that the rule of law requires that disagreements between government and those governed 'can be taken to an external forum for an independent ruling or opinion', it is essential that this function be exercised by tribunals and 'independent oversight agencies' like the Ombudsman since '[i]t is not practical to rely on the judiciary for this purpose in all but a minor fraction of the cases that arise'.[58] Tribunals and ombudsmen undeniably advance the aims of the rule of law.

Perceptions that the High Court has suggested that the rule of law is protected *only* by the judicial review provisions in section 75(v) of the Constitution are misconceived. Kirby J remarked that section 75(v) was '*the* means by which the rule of law is upheld throughout the Commonwealth' (emphasis added) but was speaking specifically about the burden of persuasion lying upon applicants for the Constitutional writs.[59] Similarly, Gaudron J's later comment that section 75(v) 'provides *the* mechanism by which the Executive is subjected to the rule of law' (emphasis added) was made specifically by way of contrasting it with section 64 which 'provides the machinery by which a Minister is accountable to Parliament'.[60] The better view of these dicta is that they are simply less precise expressions of Gleeson CJ's statement that section 75(v) 'secures *a* basic element of the rule of law' (emphasis added).[61]

It cannot be denied on any sensible understanding of 'the rule of law' that statutory measures enacted since Federation are capable of upholding it and serve to supplement the role of section 75(v) in this regard. Non-curial accountability mechanisms do not merely mirror judicial review but perform a role that it cannot. It makes no difference to an inquiry whether the rule of law is being upheld that judicial review pursues that end based upon finding *illegality* or *invalidity* in the performance of administrative action, whereas non-judicial mechanisms focus on whether there has been *maladministration*. The point is that the aim of upholding the rule of law can be pursued by the appropriate mechanism, whether in court proceedings or not.[62]

[55] See G Weeks, 'Editorial: The Closure of the Office of the Australian Information Commissioner' (2014) 342 *Australian Administrative Law Bulletin* 5, [8710].

[56] See D Pearce, 'The Ombudsman and the Rule of Law' (1994) 1 *Australian Institute of Administrative Law Forum* 1; J McMillan, 'The Ombudsman and the Rule of Law' (2005) 44 *Australian Institute of Administrative Law Forum* 1; B Barbour, 'The Ombudsman and the Rule of Law' (2005) 44 *Australian Institute of Administrative Law Forum* 17.

[57] See J McMillan, 'Ombudsman and the Rule of Law' (2005) 44 *Australian Institute of Administrative Law Forum* 1, 1.

[58] J McMillan, 'Re-thinking the Separation of Powers' (2010) 38 *Federal Law Review* 423, 433.

[59] *Re Carmody; ex parte Glennan* (2000) 173 ALR 145, 147.

[60] *Re Patterson; ex parte Taylor* (2001) 207 CLR 391, 415.

[61] *Plaintiff S157* (2003) 211 CLR 476, 482.

[62] cf *Fleet Street Casuals Case* [1982] AC 617, 663.

As much is implicit in Callinan J's reference to the protection that we now enjoy from 'measures *both curial and otherwise*, unheard of in earlier times' (emphasis added), which include inter alia

> legislation for freedom of information; the expansion of remedies for the review of administrative action; the greater willingness of the courts to accord status to those who seek the intervention of the court in public affairs; [and] recourse to ombudsmen under ombudsmen legislation throughout the country.[63]

It may be that talk of the Ombudsman's protection of the rule of law is 'invoked for effect as much as for meaning' and that this bears no substantive difference to talking about the Ombudsman's accountability functions.[64] Arguments about the Ombudsman's contribution to upholding the rule of law become otiose at this point, since there can be no doubt that the Ombudsman is effective in holding the government to account, both by responding to complaints and exercising its own investigatory powers. It is perhaps telling that both 'accountability' and the 'rule of law' have been characterised as 'protean concepts'.[65] For reasons which remain unclear, placing the Ombudsman's accountability functions in terms of the rule of law seems to provoke increased responses to the effect that courts are the primary (or sole) upholders of the rule of law. However, if 'accountability' refers to governments being required to account to the public on the basis of the rule of law through an external mechanism, it is hard to deny that the Ombudsman does indeed have much to do with upholding the rule of law. The debate at that point is essentially about no more than labels.

C. THE OMBUDSMAN'S FUNCTIONS AND REMEDIAL CAPABILITIES

I have discussed above the fact that public sector ombudsmen (by contrast to industry ombudsmen, which have determinative powers exercisable as a matter of contract) have no power to *order* remedies because they lack the constitutional capacity to make binding declarations of right.[66] The focus of the Ombudsman is consequently much more practical than that of a court exercising a judicial review function or even that of a merits review tribunal. Within the jurisdictional limits as to subject matter set out in legislation, the Ombudsman has a broad remit to make recommendations which will allow public authorities to 'get it right' as a matter of fact, in the

[63] *Australian Broadcasting Corporation v Lenah Game Meats Pty Limited* (2001) 208 CLR 199, 334 (citations omitted).

[64] J McMillan, 'Ombudsman and the Rule of Law' (2005) 44 *Australian Institute of Administrative Law Forum* 1, 2.

[65] See respectively M Elliott, 'Ombudsmen, Tribunals, Inquiries' in N Bamforth and P Leyland (eds), *Accountability in the Contemporary Constitution* (Oxford, Oxford University Press, 2013), 233; J McMillan, 'Ombudsman and the Rule of Law' (2005) 44 *Australian Institute of Administrative Law Forum* 1, 2.

[66] R Creyke and J McMillan, *Control of Government Action*, 3rd edn (Sydney, LexisNexis, 2012) 217.

sense of delivering fair specific outcomes and better general administration.[67] There are a number of particular issues to note.

(i) Ombudsmen can Recommend Things Courts Cannot Order

The practical limitations upon the scope of the Commonwealth Ombudsman's complaint-handling work are well understood. They should not, however, distract attention from the fact that the office investigates many thousands of complaints every year and, for each of these complainants, the Ombudsman endeavours to obtain a suitable remedy.[68] The Ombudsman Act does not provide much detail about what remedies are within the Ombudsman's purview. Section 8 contains references to the Ombudsman 'consulting', 'informing' or 'bringing information to the attention of' relevant authorities. Section 10(1) contains one of the only hard-edged remedial powers, stating that where the Ombudsman certifies that there has been an 'unreasonable delay' in making a decision or exercising a power, the decision-maker shall be deemed from the date of the certificate to have refused to act or provide the benefit sought, clearing the way for the matter to brought before a tribunal for decision. The references in the Act add up to a picture in which the Ombudsman's capacity to secure beneficial outcomes is predicated on persuasion and recommendation rather than on the capacity to provide 'remedies' as they are usually understood by lawyers.

At least one former Commonwealth Ombudsman did not view the incapacity to provide 'traditional remedies'—defined as court or tribunal orders which quash erroneous decisions, substitute fresh decisions, restrain unlawful conduct, mandate lawful action or declare the law which is to be applied—as a problem. Rather, McMillan regarded them as:[69]

> ill-adapted, for example to assist a person who is caught by an unintended anomaly in a legislative rule, who has fallen through the cracks of a government program, is confused about the advice received from an agency, is disadvantaged by an agency's delay in addressing a complaint, or is disabled by a physical or mental impairment in understanding or accessing his or her legal rights.

Groves, too, doubted that having determinative powers would improve the effectiveness of the Ombudsman and suggested that they would cause the Ombudsman's office to foreshorten its investigative role in many instances.[70] The Ombudsman is currently able to assist in situations like these *because* the role of the office is

[67] See C Harlow and R Rawlings, *Law and Administration*, 3rd edn (Cambridge, Cambridge University Press, 2009) 536–37; T Buck et al, *Ombudsman Enterprise* (Farnham, Ashgate, 2011) ch 5.

[68] J McMillan, 'Future Directions' (2010) 63 *Australian Institute of Administrative Law Forum* 13, 14; Commonwealth Ombudsman, *Annual Report 2011–12* (2012), 40–41.

[69] J McMillan, 'Future Directions' (2010) 63 *Australian Institute of Administrative Law Forum* 13, 17.

[70] M Groves, 'Ombudsmen's Jurisdiction in Prisons' (2002) 28 *Monash University Law Review* 181, 202. See R Creyke and J McMillan, *Control of Government Action*, 3rd edn (Sydney, LexisNexis, 2012) 217–18.

to recommend a course of action to the relevant public authority and is therefore not restricted to statements of legal right. It is this adaptability that makes the Ombudsman of such importance and utility where individuals are adversely affected by applications of, or failures to apply, soft law, which also operate outside the scope of legal rights.

Moreover, just as the Ombudsman cannot *enforce* the usual legal remedies, nor is s/he *confined* to them. The Ombudsman is able to recommend relief that would not be within the power of a court to order or which may only be a possible outcome following litigation. It is axiomatic amongst those who are professionally involved in litigation that there is no such thing as a matter which either party can be guaranteed to win. Litigation is of its very nature an activity filled with doubt, one of the reasons why it is always lengthy and expensive.

Annual Reports of the Commonwealth Ombudsman are replete with examples which illustrate the breadth of the Ombudsman's capacity to recommend the appropriate relief.[71] In one instance, Australia Post compensated a man for the value of a parcel which could only be collected with the signature of the addressee or his agent but which had been released to an unknown third party. In another, Australia Post compensated a man for the value of a diamond ring lost in transit to England, although the man had used an inappropriate postal service and had subsequently made his claim out of time. The intervention of the Ombudsman was vital in both cases, which, in legal proceedings, may have descended into highly technical legal arguments about bailment and fraud, leading in turn to outcomes which would not likely have been satisfactory to either party. This is because litigation of any kind is lengthy and expensive, both financially and emotionally, regardless of whether you 'win'.[72] As it happened, the Ombudsman's investigations revealed that the man in the first matter could not possibly have signed for the parcel, leading to the inevitable conclusion that the post office staff had released it in error, and that the man in the second matter had been actively misled by poor advice from Australia Post employees on at least two occasions, leading directly to the choice he made about posting the ring and the lateness of his claim. In both cases, Australia Post paid compensation, a remedy which is currently beyond the scope of courts hearing judicial review matters.

(ii) Ombudsmen have the Discretion to Decline to Investigate Matters

In Australia, the Commonwealth Ombudsman has a broad discretion to decide not to investigate a complaint, including because s/he forms the opinion that 'an investigation ... of the action is not warranted having regard to all the circumstances'.[73]

[71] See Commonwealth Ombudsman, *Annual Report 2011–12* (2012), ch 5.

[72] M Legg, 'Changes' in M Legg (ed), *The Future of Dispute Resolution* (New South Wales, LexisNexis, 2012) 3, 4; TF Bathurst, 'The Future of Dispute Resolution: Access to Justice, the Role of the Courts and Internationalisation' in ibid,15, 17.

[73] Ombudsman Act 1976 (Cth) s 6(1).

This provision has a broadly similar analogue in every Australian jurisdiction.[74] In practice, this provision provides the Ombudsman with the scope to select which matters s/he will investigate, having regard to the fact that ombudsmen never have a sufficient budget to investigate every complaint that they receive. In general, ombudsmen will refuse to handle an individual complaint until the complainant has examined which other remedial options are reasonably open. In 2011–12, the Commonwealth Ombudsman declined to investigate more than half of the complaints received until the complainant had first taken the matter up with the relevant agency.[75]

A connected issue, addressed above, is that ombudsmen have directed increasingly greater resources to their 'system-fixing role' at the expense of performing their 'complaint-handling role'.[76] This has been explained in a number of ways, although to similar effect. Creyke and McMillan regard the shift as an example of the ombudsmen seeking to make 'more strategic use of investigation resources', which is to say that ombudsmen have concluded that they have a greater influence on a limited budget if they elect to conduct specific investigations on their own motion.[77] Stuhmcke placed a slightly different slant on this issue, arguing that there is an increased emphasis on the integrity functions of ombudsmen, which are performed to better effect through their 'proactive', own motion investigative functions rather than their traditional, responsive complaint-handling functions.[78] Indeed, the capacity to use active means, such as own-motion inquiries, to monitor and prevent maladministration is now seen as essential to an investigative body being accurately described as an 'ombudsman'.[79] Harlow and Rawlings regarded the Parliamentary Ombudsman in England as having both 'an adjudicative and an inspectorial role, in which "firefighting" and "fire-watching" are combined'.[80] Under this analogy, 'firefighting' describes ombudsmen's quasi-judicial activities, filling whatever gaps exist between parliamentary procedures and judicial review, whereas 'fire-watching' describes ombudsmen's 'inspection and audit' capabilities.

The point that emerges on any view (and it is likely that each is accurate to a great extent) is that ombudsmen are spending less time on investigating individual complaints than previously has been the case. In one sense, the complaints-handling function of ombudsmen has always been the point at which that office comes closest to the judicial model, although 'an ombudsman's investigation is very different in its nature from the adversarial processes of a court'.[81] Ombudsmen do not focus on invalidity or illegality alone and do not have the power to make binding

[74] See R Creyke and J McMillan, *Control of Government Action*, 3rd edn (Sydney, LexisNexis, 2012) 206.

[75] Commonwealth Ombudsman, *Annual Report 2011–12* (2012), 42.

[76] See T Buck et al, *Ombudsman Enterprise* (Farnham, Ashgate, 2011). See nn 16–22 above.

[77] R Creyke and J McMillan, *Control of Government Action*, 3rd edn (Sydney, LexisNexis, 2012) 210.

[78] A Stuhmcke, 'Ombudsmen and Integrity Review' in L Pearson et al (eds), *Administrative Law in a Changing State* (Oxford, Hart Publishing, 2008) 349, 354–56.

[79] C Harlow and R Rawlings, *Law and Administration*, 3rd edn (Cambridge, Cambridge University Press, 2009) 529–30.

[80] ibid, 537–42.

[81] Law Commission, *Administrative Redress* (2010), 59 [5.45].

determinations but examine the broad and flexible, but somewhat undefined, scope of maladministration.[82] However, ombudsmen who investigate a specific allegation are engaged in determining a single set of facts and whether a recommendation of compensation should follow. Harlow and Rawlings pointed out that, by comparison to courts and even tribunals, ombudsmen apply a 'bottom-up' complaints-handling approach which is 'truly inquisitorial and investigatory'.[83] By contrast, ombudsmen who are engaged in auditing and reporting on government issues are looking at polycentric issues, which by definition reach beyond the concerns of any individual to the proper governance of the state generally.[84]

(iii) Ombudsmen's Recommendations are Usually Effective

Whatever antipathy (or apathy) may exist in regard to the Ombudsman's office in the legal fraternity, ombudsmen themselves have long claimed that the office is effective precisely because it 'commands a considerable degree of respect and moral authority' with public sector agencies and that this regard only increases the more frequently the Ombudsman's office deals with any given agency.[85] The Commonwealth Ombudsman has reported that agencies adopt 'a majority' of its recommendations and has given examples of 'agency responsiveness to our reports and recommendations'.[86] It has been noted elsewhere that ombudsmen make recommendations for the payment of damages far more often than courts. These can be made in circumstances in which courts could not prescribe a damages remedy, and are usually complied with.[87] Ombudsmen are therefore 'in practice an important source of compensation'.[88]

Indeed, such is the remedial effectiveness of a recommendation from the Ombudsman's office that it has been considered a reason why the coverage of tort law need not be extended. In *Mohammed v Home Office*, Sedley LJ rejected the imposition of a duty of care for maladministration when the claimant could have applied to the Parliamentary Ombudsman to recommend compensation:[89]

> Save in particular circumstances unlike those we are concerned with, the common law has not recognised a concurrent duty of care outside or alongside the statutory framework, even if there is no other means of claiming damages. Nor, adopting the ... test [in *Caparo Industries plc v Dickman* [1990] 2 AC 605], is it fair or just or reasonable to do so when

[82] See T Buck et al, *Ombudsman Enterprise* (Farnham, Ashgate, 2011) 108–12; C Harlow and R Rawlings, *Law and Administration*, 3rd edn (Cambridge, Cambridge University Press, 2009) 534.

[83] C Harlow and R Rawlings, *Law and Administration*, 3rd edn (Cambridge, Cambridge University Press, 2009) 529; cf K Mason, 'Top-Down Legal Reasoning' in N Perram and R Pepper (eds), *Byers Lectures* (Sydney, Federation Press, 2012) 69.

[84] See LL Fuller, 'The Forms and Limits of Adjudication' (1978) 92 *Harvard Law Review* 353, 394–8.

[85] E Biganovsky, 'New Values for Old? Is the Review Genie Trapped Inside the Lamp of Scrutiny?' in S Argument (ed), *Administrative Law & Public Administration: Happily Married Or Living Apart Under the Same Roof?* (Canberra, AIAL, 1993) 285–86.

[86] Commonwealth Ombudsman, *Annual Report 2011–12* (2012), 16–17.

[87] P Cane, 'Damages' (1999) 9 *Otago Law Review* 489, 514.

[88] H Woolf et al, *De Smith's Judicial Review*, 6th edn (London, Sweet and Maxwell, 2007) 910.

[89] *Mohammed v Home Office* [2011] 1 WLR 2862, 2867 [12].

other recourse is in fact available, in the present cases to the Parliamentary Ombudsman, who has power to recommend the payment of compensation.

Sedley LJ appears to have considered the Parliamentary Ombudsman sufficiently effective that the claimant's mere *request* for compensation to be *recommended* amounted to recourse being available in fact rather than only a chance of recourse being available. While I share his Lordship's high regard for the Ombudsman as an institution capable of providing effective remedies, I would hesitate to characterise those remedies as being any more than potentially available. The Ombudsman's greatest tool in seeing recommendations followed is the goodwill built up by the office over the course of years.[90] To the extent that this approach is unsuccessful in any particular situation, ombudsmen are usually restricted to appealing either directly or indirectly to public opinion to persuade the relevant agency to implement a recommendation. This is part and parcel of the fact that ombudsmen are not granted determinative powers.

D. THE OMBUDSMAN'S CAPACITY TO REVIEW MALADMINISTRATION

This chapter has already concluded that the Ombudsman has a central function of protecting the rule of law, regardless of the constitutional status of the office; that s/he lacks determinative powers but is nonetheless extremely effective in providing relief through the mechanism of making recommendations; that the Ombudsman is focused on maladministration generally rather than the specific question of whether certain administrative acts are either legal or valid (indeed, one of the Commonwealth Ombudsman's key performance indicators is the promotion of the principles of 'good administration' in government);[91] and that the Ombudsman has the capacity to recommend relief which lies beyond the competence of the courts. Harlow noted that the[92]

> area where legal liability overlaps with *ex gratia* compensation is a difficult one for the PCA. In the first place, his jurisdiction is in doubt [because] he has no jurisdiction in cases in which the complainant would have a legal remedy but, [under] the Parliamentary Commissioner Act 1967, he may exercise his discretion to investigate if he is satisfied that it is not reasonable to expect the complainant to resort to a court.

The Commonwealth Ombudsman does not appear to have any similar jurisdictional difficulty, given that s/he is empowered to report to the relevant Department, or later to the Prime Minister and Parliament, if inter alia s/he is of the opinion that a certain action 'appears to have been contrary to law' or 'was based either wholly or partly on a mistake of law or of fact'.[93] The conclusion that I draw from these points is that the Ombudsman is uniquely suited to addressing the problem of administrative decision-makers who fail to adhere to their own soft law instruments.

[90] T Buck et al, *Ombudsman Enterprise* (Farnham, Ashgate, 2011) 117.
[91] See Commonwealth Ombudsman, *Annual Report 2011–12* (2012), 9.
[92] C Harlow, *Compensation and Government Torts* (London, Sweet and Maxwell, 1982) 124.
[93] Ombudsman Act 1976 (Cth) s 15(1)(a)(i) and (iv).

The Ombudsman's remit is to investigate 'action that relates to a matter of administration', and maladministration has a broader coverage than legality.[94] These points lead irresistibly to the conclusion that the Ombudsman plays an important role in providing administrative justice. Part II of this book is essentially an account of how judicial procedures are ill-adapted for dealing with the specific problems thrown up by soft law. By contrast, maladministration is sufficiently broad to include, for example, misleading soft law guidance or broken promises. Such complaints are commonly made to ombudsmen precisely because they 'raise problems to which the courts have as yet produced no satisfactory answer', such as 'by reference to principles of estoppel'.[95] To the extent that ombudsmen are able to assist in securing effective remedies for maladministration of this kind, the equally unsatisfactory approaches to the substantive enforcement of legitimate expectations in Australia and England assume a significantly reduced level of importance.

Let us consider again the situation of Ms Tang, which demonstrates that, where soft law is in issue, an equivalently 'soft' and flexible remedial structure is more effective than the usual judicial review remedies.[96] While exercises of power by universities are not inevitably of a public nature, there are solid arguments in favour of that position, including that each jurisdiction's Ombudsman has jurisdiction over university decisions and conduct.[97] In Ms Tang's case, Queensland's Ombudsman Act empowered the Ombudsman to 'investigate administrative actions of agencies'.[98] This included any entity (other than an individual) established either 'for a public purpose' or 'by government for a public purpose' under an Act.[99] Griffith University falls within these statutory criteria, and Ms Tang could therefore have complained to the Ombudsman. This (and like considerations) cannot be conclusive of whether a university's use of public power is otherwise legally significant, since the High Court of Australia has largely been slow to embrace foreign innovations which have extended the coverage of judicial review's remedies beyond public bodies to exercises of public, non-statutory power more generally.[100] However, Ms Tang might have been able to obtain a remedy through the Ombudsman's influence.

What remedy would she have been able to obtain? The Ombudsman lacked the jurisdiction to reverse the University's decision or to impose a decision of its own; indeed, the Ombudsman has no coercive remedial powers at all. However, the Ombudsman's office is, in practice, highly persuasive, due at least in part to the fact that it is not involved in an adversarial process against administrative agencies.[101]

[94] Ombudsman Act 1976 (Cth) s 5(1)(a) and (b).

[95] P Brown, 'Remedies for Misinformation' in G Richardson and H Genn (eds), *Administrative Law and Government Action* (Oxford, Clarendon Press, 1994) 309, 309.

[96] *Tang* (2005) 221 CLR 99.

[97] M Aronson, 'Soft Law in the High Court' (2007) 35 *Federal Law Review* 1, 14–15.

[98] Ombudsman Act 2001 (Qld) s 6(b)(i). 'Agencies' was defined to include public authorities: Ombudsman Act 2001 (Qld) s 8(1)(c).

[99] Ombudsman Act 2001 (Qld) s 9(1)(a).

[100] See *Plaintiff M61/2010E v Commonwealth* ('*Offshore Processing Case*') (2010) 243 CLR 319, 143; J Boughey and G Weeks, '"Officers of the Commonwealth" in the Private Sector' (2013) 36 *University of NSW Law Journal* 316.

[101] M Groves, 'Ombudsmen's Jurisdiction in Prisons' (2002) 28 *Monash Law Review* 181, 202–3.

It uses its stature to obtain remedies, which may include 'an apology, financial compensation, proper explanation, reconsideration of agency action, and expediting agency action'.[102] Clearly, some of these recommendatory remedial options would not work in circumstances where the Ombudsman was empowered only to make determinations.[103] It is also worth noting that not all Commonwealth Ombudsmen have been equally effective, suggesting that a significant element in being a successful Ombudsman may be the personality of the person in that role.

It is worth recalling that Ms Tang's contention was, essentially, that the University had promised her procedural fairness, through its soft law misconduct code, in coming to any decision to cancel her candidacy for a degree and that it had not fulfilled its promise in this regard. The Ombudsman may well have been of much greater assistance to her than the courts could have been, even if they had taken a broad view of their capacity to review the University's decision, because a recommendation from the Ombudsman in a non-adversarial setting that the University abide by its promise may have had no effect on the substantive decision but would have ensured that it was made consistently with the values and principles of administrative law. Ultimately, this would also have avoided lengthy, expensive and (from Ms Tang's perspective, at least) fruitless litigation.

[102] J McMillan, 'Future Directions' (2010) 63 *Australian Institute of Administrative Law Forum* 13, 17. See also T Buck et al, *Ombudsman Enterprise* (Farnham, Ashgate, 2011) 114–17.

[103] R Creyke and J McMillan, *Control of Government Action*, 3rd edn (Sydney, LexisNexis, 2012) 218.

12

Discretionary Payments

AUSTRALIA HAS A set of interlocking and overlapping voluntary compensation schemes which do not rely upon a claimant being able to establish that s/he has had certain legal rights infringed upon by a public authority and which 'can, to some extent, make up for common law's unwillingness to award damages for breaches of public law'.[1] These mechanisms are generally accepted as being appropriate ways of providing relief to those affected by maladministration, without the difficulties inherent in creating an 'overarching' damages remedy at common law or treading into the heavily contested ground of providing substantive relief.[2] This chapter will look at the remedies which are available for maladministration in Australia and their benefits, the legal standing of the various compensation schemes and the possibility of obtaining judicial review of an adverse determination of a request for administrative compensation.

A. PRACTICAL REMEDIES

Chapter eleven pointed out that ombudsmen have been successful in securing redress through the process of making recommendations. However, it does not follow from this that an ombudsman's recommendation that a payment be made to address maladministration is a condition precedent to such a payment being made as an exercise of statutory or executive power.[3] Such forms of compensation are sometimes known generically as 'grace and favour' payments.[4] In regard to these, the Commonwealth Ombudsman has noted that:[5]

> As problems and complaints change, so too must the way that an Ombudsman's office assists people ... It can be pointless or difficult in that setting to focus on whether the complaint is to be resolved in the complainant's or the agency's favour. The more pressing concern is to resolve a person's grievance and to provide a remedy, if appropriate.

[1] P Cane, *Administrative Law*, 5th edn (Oxford, Oxford University Press, 2011) 313. See Administrative Review Council, *Federal Judicial Review in Australia* (2012), [2.53]–[2.57].

[2] Administrative Review Council, *Federal Judicial Review in Australia* (2012), [10.16]–[10.22]; P Brown, 'Remedies for Misinformation' in G Richardson and H Genn (eds), *Administrative Law and Government Action* (Oxford, Clarendon Press, 1994) 309, 313.

[3] cf P Cane, *Administrative Law*, 5th edn (Oxford, Oxford University Press, 2011) 314; but see Law Commission, *Administrative Redress Consultation Paper* (2008), [3.46].

[4] See C Harlow, *Compensation and Government Torts* (London, Sweet and Maxwell, 1982) 119.

[5] Commonwealth Ombudsman, *Annual Report 2006–07* (2007), 122.

However, when the appropriate redress goes beyond, for example, the administrative body providing a clearer explanation of its action, it helps that an ombudsman has something specific to recommend, such as the payment of administrative compensation. The experience of the Commonwealth Ombudsman in this regard does not match the difficulties experienced by the English Parliamentary Commissioner for Administration in the event that there was, for example, both maladministration and the possibility of legal liability.[6] Schemes for administrative compensation must therefore be understood not only in their own right but also as mechanisms for broadening the range of recommendations available to the Commonwealth Ombudsman. Ex gratia compensation schemes, of course, have a history that originates before Australian ombudsmen.[7] Prior to that, they had a somewhat more sinister purpose.[8]

The Ombudsman's office has 'a special interest in the remedies available to members of the public who suffer detriment as a result of poor administration'.[9] In practice, it is also vital to the operation of the Scheme for Compensation for Detriment caused by Defective Administration (the CDDA Scheme) both because a very small proportion of those who deal with government agencies would otherwise know about the scheme and because disappointed claimants under the CDDA Scheme will not generally have any available options for administrative review other than through the Ombudsman.[10] The Ombudsman cannot compel an agency to make a payment under the CDDA Scheme or overturn its decision not to do so.[11] The terms of the scheme formerly recognised that, where the Ombudsman had recommended that a compensation payment be made, that alone was a 'sufficient basis for payment' by the agency.[12] This wording is, however, absent from the 2014 iteration of the CDDA Scheme.

The Ombudsman need not be involved at all in recommending relief under the CDDA Scheme, given that individuals may 'go directly to the relevant department'.[13] If the Ombudsman is involved in a case, s/he can recommend that a public authority provide financial compensation to an individual who has suffered loss as a result of defective administrative action, such as because the authority failed to adhere to the terms of its soft law, in circumstances where the individual has no enforceable legal right to damages for that loss in judicial proceedings. Ombudsmen have often been more inclined to investigate matters where the process of law would be in some way

[6] See C Harlow, *Compensation and Government Torts* (London, Sweet and Maxwell, 1982) 124–29.

[7] eg *R v Criminal Injuries Compensation Board, ex parte Lain* [1967] QB 864.

[8] See nn 32–36 below.

[9] Commonwealth Ombudsman, *Putting Things Right: Compensating for Defective Administration*, Investigation Report No 11/2009, (2009) [1.18].

[10] Commonwealth Department of Finance and Deregulation, '*Resource Management Guide No 409: Scheme for Compensation for Detriment caused by Defective Administration*' (2014) ('CDDA Scheme'). See Commonwealth Ombudsman, *Putting Things Right* (2009) [2.1]–[2.8]; [2.52].

[11] CDDA Scheme, [91].

[12] Commonwealth Department of Finance and Deregulation, '*Finance Circular No 2009/09*' (2009), Attachment A [92]. See also Commonwealth Ombudsman, *Putting Things Right* (2009), [1.17].

[13] M Aronson and M Groves, *Judicial Review of Administrative Action*, 5th edn (Sydney, Thompson Reuters, 2013) [6.730]. See CDDA Scheme, [34].

inadequate.[14] There are legal limitations on the capacity of government to remedy injustice by spending from consolidated revenue.[15]

However, Australia has administrative schemes administered by the Commonwealth Department of Finance and Deregulation which circumvent this problem.[16] These schemes seem in practice often to be considered as being extensively interchangeable, although they do not have a 'linear relationship' and are determined on different bases.[17] It is likely that no consequence will attach to such reasoning, since the CDDA Scheme recognises that government entities 'may receive applications which seek financial assistance under the CDDA Scheme, as well as the act of grace and waiver of debt mechanisms under the [Public Governance, Performance and Accountability Act 2013 (Cth) (PGPA Act)]'.[18] However:[19]

> if a claim is made for an act of grace payment on the basis that an entity's defective administration has caused a loss, the matter should be considered by the relevant entity under the CDDA Scheme in the first instance. Where the Department of Finance receives act of grace claims of this nature directly from a claimant, these will be forwarded to the relevant entity for consideration under the CDDA Scheme.

At Commonwealth level, there are discretionary statutory mechanisms in the PGPA Act for the Finance Minister to authorise waiver or set off of debts or compensatory 'act of grace' payments.[20] Guidance on these mechanisms is provided in the *Discretionary Financial Assistance under the PGPA Act* guidance document issued by the Department of Finance and Deregulation. Act of grace payments are intended as a 'remedy of last resort' and it is expected that potential claimants will have exhausted all other avenues for redress before seeking an act of grace payment.[21] In *Croker*, Rares J heard evidence that:[22]

> the approach of the Department of Finance and Deregulation in cases where a client of Centrelink asserted a legal entitlement to some form of payment, (whether through merits review by the Social Security Appeals Tribunal or the Administrative Appeals Tribunal, or in any legal proceeding in a Court, at the same time as making a request for an act of grace payment) [was to] ... suspend the processing of the act of grace payment request ... [because it] is regarded to be premature and inappropriate. This approach also ensures that

[14] See C Harlow and R Rawlings, *Law and Administration*, 3rd edn (Cambridge, Cambridge University Press, 2009) 539.

[15] *Auckland Harbour Board v The King* [1924] AC 318; and the cases cited at fn 28 in Chapter 1 of this volume above.

[16] CDDA Scheme; Commonwealth Department of Finance and Deregulation, '*Resource Management Guide No 401: Requests for discretionary financial assistance under the Public Governance, Performance and Accountability Act*' (2014) ('*Discretionary Financial Assistance under the PGPA Act*'). These guidance documents replaced '*Finance Circular No 2009/09*' (2009), which had in turn replaced '*Finance Circular No 2006/05*' (2006) and, before that, '*Finance Circular No 2001/01*' (2001). The CDDA Scheme was originally established by '*Estimates Memorandum 1995/4*' (1995).

[17] CDDA Scheme, [24]–[29]; cf *Croker v Department of Families, Housing, Community Services and Indigenous Affairs* [2010] FCA 1136, [25].

[18] CDDA Scheme, [20].

[19] ibid, [26].

[20] PGPA Act ss 63, 64 and 65 respectively.

[21] *Discretionary Financial Assistance under the PGPA Act*, [3]–[4].

[22] *Croker v Department of Families, Housing etc* [2010] FCA 1136, [11].

> there is no risk of a claimant being able to 'double-dip' by having an act of grace payment approved prior to achieving a successful outcome in a legal claim.

Although no court would allow a plaintiff to 'double-dip' in any case, and this practice therefore seems superfluous, it is nonetheless reflected in the departmental guidance.[23] Indeed, sometimes this approach means that the applicant has not 'dipped' at all. The Full Federal Court upheld a decision to refuse an application for an act of grace payment in circumstances where the applicant had been successful in a legal claim against a party which went into liquidation thereafter and was insured by an entity which was neither solvent nor registered in Australia. The Court adhered to the Minister's approach that 'the mere evasion of a regulatory regime does not require the Australian Government to assume responsibility'.[24]

The CDDA Scheme is an additional, non-legislative remedial scheme which relies on the Commonwealth's executive powers under section 61 of the Constitution. Under the CDDA Scheme, a government entity may make a payment to 'a person or organisation [who] has suffered detriment as a result of the entity's defective administration, when there is no legal requirement to make a payment'.[25] By contrast with the discretionary financial assistance which the Finance Minister is able to authorise under the PGPA Act, CDDA Scheme decisions are made by individual portfolio Ministers or their delegates.[26] Each of these legislative and executive schemes is intended to remedy *exceptional* losses, rather than merely as a method of expending money not envisaged by the relevant statute in compensation. The latter approach would run the risk of circumventing the intentions of the Parliament and Government.[27]

A fifth mechanism, known as ex gratia payments and paid as an exercise of executive power, was previously available for giving discretionary compensation payments.[28] Reference to ex gratia payments no longer appears in Finance Department guidance, but an ex gratia payment scheme still exists and is now managed by the Department of Prime Minister and Cabinet.[29] It allows for ad hoc payments to be made on a discretionary basis, in special cases or emergencies, as a last resort (which is to say if no other discretionary payment mechanism is available). A Departmental submission to a Senate review of Government Compensation in 2010 noted that ex gratia payments are 'the most appropriate response for groups of people affected by a common set of circumstances and for unexpected events'.[30] Previously, one

[23] *Discretionary Financial Assistance under the PGPA Act*, [11].

[24] *Quintano v Minister for Finance and Deregulation* [2014] FCAFC 159, [48].

[25] CDDA Scheme, [1].

[26] ibid, [7]; cf PGPA Act ss 63(1), 64(1) and 65(1); *Discretionary Financial Assistance under the PGPA Act*, [1].

[27] See the comments of the Permanent Secretary to the Minister of Transport in the UK Government, quoted by C Harlow, *Compensation and Government Torts* (London, Sweet and Maxwell, 1982) 120.

[28] Commonwealth Department of Finance and Deregulation, '*Finance Circular No 2009/09: Discretionary Compensation and Waiver of Debt Mechanisms*' (2009), Attachment D.

[29] Indeed, this Department handled inquiries about the ex gratia scheme previously; the Finance Department simply dealt with funding issues: see ibid, [19].

[30] Commonwealth Department of Finance and Deregulation, '*Senate Review of Government Compensation: Submission to the Standing Committee on Legal and Constitutional Affairs*' (2010), [2.15].

would expect the emergencies that would be covered by this mechanism to include predominantly natural disasters, but they have been the subject of a specific inquiry and will merit a specific legislative response.[31] What is of particular interest about the way in which ex gratia payments are now managed is that the criteria on which they are made are unpublished. It does not seem unfair to assume that this is a mechanism whose application will respond as much to political necessity on the part of the government as financial necessity on the part of a successful applicant. In any case, the Ombudsman's awareness of the new arrangements will doubtless see him recommend ex gratia payments in the appropriate circumstances.

Methods of extra-judicial redress are not new:[32]

> Prior to [the enactment of the Crown Proceedings Act in] 1947, the efforts of reformers had been directed at Crown immunity as an affront to the rule of law. In practice the effects of immunity were probably limited. Actions in tort lay against local authorities and many other public bodies and where no action lay there were alternative options: public officials remained personally liable (Dicey's celebrated equality principle); the Crown although not vicariously liable in theory, usually stood behind its servants; the courts winked at legal fictions; awards of *ex gratia* compensation were often made.

The inclusion of ex gratia compensation in this catalogue may be initially puzzling, given its overwhelmingly beneficial modern purpose. However, Harlow recorded that, prior to the 1947 reform of proceedings against the Crown:[33]

> the attitude of lawyers to government officials was one of suspicion and hostility. The Crown was called 'a peculiarly relentless litigant' whose legal advisers stood upon unmeritorious, technical defences and used the Crown's legal immunity to drive hard bargains. *Ex gratia* compensation was in principle an evil. It vested in officials an important discretionary power which allowed them to shelter their misdeeds behind the convenient screen of a secret settlement process. Perhaps it was assumed that, the immunity once ended, *ex gratia* payments would dwindle into insignificance.

As it transpired, they did not, although they adopted a significantly different purpose. The 'alternative options' to which Harlow referred in the first quotation above were designed to patch up a manifestly inadequate legal system, in which resort to legal fictions was necessary in order to do justice, even if only for the purpose of obscuring the government's 'misdeeds'. In England, payments of ex gratia compensation are now calculated on a basis the same as that used to calculate damages payable in tort, by placing complainants 'in the position they would have occupied if they had been correctly advised at the outset'.[34] Harlow commented on the unforeseen tendency for ex gratia payment schemes to make inroads into 'areas traditionally earmarked

[31] See the Productivity Commission Public Inquiry into Natural Disaster Funding: www.pc.gov.au/inquiries/completed/disaster-funding#report.

[32] C Harlow, 'Rationalising Administrative Compensation' [2010] *PL* 321, 321 (citations omitted).

[33] C Harlow, *Compensation and Government Torts* (1982) 117; cf Legal Services Directions 2005 (Cth). See Chapter 8 of this volume above.

[34] P Cane, *Administrative Law*, 5th edn (Oxford, Oxford University Press, 2011) 313; P Brown, 'Remedies for Misinformation' in G Richardson and H Genn (eds), *Administrative Law and Government Action* (Oxford, Clarendon Press, 1994) 309, 316.

for the law of torts'.[35] This is likely to be due, at least in part, to the fact that 'maladministration' is a sufficiently broad term to cover mistakes which are not negligent.[36]

The various Australian schemes currently in effect stand in contrast to the English history of discretionary compensation, which even in the 1990s included:[37]

> [a] bewildering number of administrative schemes operating to provide compensation [and in which] the government's guidance to departments and agencies on the granting of redress in cases of maladministration was in fact outdated and directed more to the protection of the public purse than to the rights of the complainant.

The Australian schemes fit beneath a coherent system of merits and judicial review options, serving as 'remedies of last resort' when such options fail. They are a 'safety net', in which sense they play a role amongst remedies analogous to that played by *Wednesbury* unreasonableness amongst grounds of judicial review.[38]

The CDDA Scheme works effectively because it gets around restrictions on expenditure to allow monetary compensation for persons harmed by maladministration.[39] However, it does so through a mechanism which still exerts significant centralised control through the terms of the CDDA Scheme itself.[40] The Commonwealth Ombudsman has pointed out, by contrast, that the bulk of the process of providing compensation has been devolved to individual agencies, which is efficient and promotes responsibility but also carries risks.[41] The CDDA Scheme is itself regularly subject to a range of accountability measures: in the 2009 report following his own motion investigation into the CDDA Scheme, the Commonwealth Ombudsman noted that the scheme had been the subject of three previous investigations since it was established in 1995: by the Ombudsman's office in 1999, by the Australian National Audit Office in 2003–04, and by the Department of Finance in 2004–05.[42]

The CDDA Scheme 'applies across government'.[43] It has been described as 'a vital measure to ensure administrative justice for the public' and 'a valuable and important means of securing administrative justice in a complex system'.[44] Less generously, Dowsett J characterised it as 'designed to avoid public-relations problems involving public bodies and the political consequences of such problems'.[45] On the understanding that there is probably no such thing as a government act which is *purely* altruistic, it is likely that each of these comments contains a strong element of truth.

[35] C Harlow, *Compensation and Government Torts* (London, Sweet and Maxwell, 1982) 117.

[36] See P Brown, 'Remedies for Misinformation' in G Richardson and H Genn (eds), *Administrative Law and Government Action* (Oxford, Clarendon Press, 1994) 309, 332–33.

[37] D Fairgrieve, *State Liability in Tort* (Oxford, Oxford University Press, 2003) 250; citing First Report from the Select Committee on the Parliamentary Commissioner for Administration, *Maladministration and Redress*, Session 1994–95, No HC 112.

[38] See M Aronson and M Groves, *Judicial Review of Administrative Action*, 5th edn (Sydney, Thompson Reuters, 2013) [6.450].

[39] See the text accompanying n 15 above.

[40] cf C Harlow, *Compensation and Government Torts* (London, Sweet and Maxwell, 1982) 119.

[41] Commonwealth Ombudsman, *Putting Things Right* (2009) [2.106]–[2.110].

[42] ibid, [1.20]–[1.23].

[43] ibid, [1.15].

[44] ibid, [1.18]; J McMillan, 'Future Directions' (2010) 63 *Australian Institute of Administrative Law Forum* 13, 17.

[45] *Smith v Oakenfull* (2004) 134 FCR 413, 418. See text accompanying n 33 above.

The CDDA Scheme is particularly apt for situations in which people have relied on soft law but cannot enforce it. It 'will become steadily more important as legislation and government programs grow more complex; government regulation and benefit distribution become more extensive; and people and businesses rely more on government for correct advice, decision-making and regulation'.[46] Agencies are sometimes reluctant to grant compensation under the scheme in circumstances where it would be justified, and sometimes seek to minimise the amount paid. The Ombudsman's office has exercised its 'system-fixing' role by highlighting some of these deficiencies in the *Putting Things Right* report. Of course, the CDDA Scheme is limited to providing financial compensation for *defective* administration, as opposed to mere 'administrative problems'.[47] In circumstances where this is not appropriate (for example, compensation would not have assisted someone in Ms Tang's position very greatly—understanding that it is a federal scheme and therefore was not available at all to Ms Tang herself), the broader remedial focus of the Ombudsman is still able to achieve results: in 2007–08, the Commonwealth Ombudsman recommended a remedy of some sort in 75 per cent of the cases which it investigated.[48] For the purposes of this book, it is important to note that defective administration is expressly defined to include 'giving advice to (or for) an applicant that was, in all the circumstances, incorrect or ambiguous'.[49]

B. LEGAL BASIS OF DISCRETIONARY COMPENSATION SCHEMES

Payments under a scheme such as the CDDA Scheme are to be distinguished from other types of voluntary government payments, such as those made to settle litigation. Take, for example, the case of Shayan Badraie, a boy from Iran who spent time in the Woomera and Villawood immigration detention centres between 2000 and 2002. Litigation was commenced on his behalf in the Supreme Court of New South Wales against the Commonwealth and the operators of the detention centres (Australasian Correctional Services Pty Ltd (ACS) and Australasian Correctional Management Pty Ltd (ACM) respectively).[50] In a hearing before Johnson J, it was claimed that Shayan had suffered severe psychological harm as a result of incidents that he had witnessed while in detention. During the trial, the practices and condition of the detention centre were placed on record in testimony by the former detention camp commander. The Commonwealth elected to offer to settle the claim and Hoeben J made unreported orders which discontinued the hearing.[51]

46 Commonwealth Ombudsman, *Putting Things Right* (2009), [1.18].
47 ibid, [2.43].
48 See Chapter 11 of this volume.
49 CDDA Scheme, [16](c).
50 See *Badraie v Commonwealth of Australia* (2005) 195 FLR 119.
51 It was reported that Hoeben J 'secured the compensation in law during a brief hearing in the NSW Supreme Court': 'Immigration pay boy $400,000', *Sydney Morning Herald*, 3 March 2006. It is likely that what occurred in fact was that the proceedings were discontinued at the application of the plaintiff as part of the settlement agreement; see Uniform Civil Procedure Rules 2005 (NSW) r 12.1.

The Commonwealth ultimately made a payment of AU$400,000 to Shayan.[52] This would have been a 'major claim' under the terms of the Legal Services Directions 2005.[53] The current Finance Department guidance advises that discretionary payments should not be made in relation to: 'claims in which it is reasonable to conclude that the Commonwealth would be found liable, if the matter were litigated. Legal matters should be considered under the Legal Services Directions 2005 on the basis of legal liability'.[54] Such a settlement payment may, however, be recoverable from the Government's insurer (or through government self-insurance arrangements, since governments frequently do not insure), which a CDDA, act of grace payment or a waiver of debt would not.

While the effect may be similar—the government paid a sum as compensation for harm suffered arguably as a result of maladministration, apparently upon realising the strength of the plaintiff's case—the reason for a payment such as the one made to Shayan Badraie is fundamentally different to a payment under the CDDA Scheme.[55] No claim could have been made on Shayan's behalf under the CDDA Scheme because he had *legal* rights, evidently on fairly strong grounds, upon which he could rely and which he could reasonably be expected to pursue.[56] By contrast, the CDDA Scheme allows payments where it is not reasonable to expect the claimant to litigate. The settlement of the matter which Shayan had brought before the Supreme Court is best understood as having a contractual basis: the government's payment was made in consideration for his agreement to cease legal proceedings.

The CDDA Scheme, by contrast, is in place to aid people who have suffered loss as a result of maladministration but have no practical legal means of obtaining redress. Instead of possessing legal rights against the government, there is at best a state of *moral* responsibility on the part of the government to such people.[57] Sometimes, especially in regard to act of grace payments, this is referred to explicitly in a government agency's reasoning.[58] The Commonwealth Ombudsman has noted that, although decisions about whether to deal with claims in accordance with the Legal Service Directions (where the claimant's legal rights have been affected) or under the CDDA Scheme (where the claim is moral in nature) will necessarily be made in light of legal advice, 'a legal frame of reference' becomes inappropriate once it has been ascertained that the claim will be decided under the CDDA Scheme. 'Defective administration' is defined under the CDDA Scheme predominantly in terms of

[52] 'Immigration pay boy $400,000', *Sydney Morning Herald*, 3 March 2006.

[53] Legal Services Directions 2005 (Cth), Appendix C (Handling Monetary Claims) [3]–[4].

[54] CDDA Scheme, [22](b); see also *Discretionary Financial Assistance under the PGPA Act*, [5].

[55] cf P Cane, *Administrative Law*, 5th edn (Oxford, Oxford University Press, 2011) 313. In the English context, Cane elided settling a case out of court and making a payment consequent on a recommendation from the Ombudsman as forms of permissible compensation by government in the absence of legal liability.

[56] See S Major, 'Am I Special Enough? The Payment of *Ex Gratia* Compensation by the Commonwealth' (1995) 6 *Australian Institute of Administrative Law Forum* 14, 16; C Harlow, *Compensation and Government Torts* (London, Sweet and Maxwell, 1982) 121–24.

[57] S Major, 'Am I Special Enough?' (1995) 6 *Australian Institute of Administrative Law Forum* 14, 16.

[58] eg *Croker v Minister for Finance and Deregulation* [2011] FCA 1188 [23]. See Administrative Review Council, *Federal Judicial Review in Australia* (2012), [2.55], [5.32] (submission of the Department of Finance and Deregulation); *Discretionary Financial Assistance under the PGPA Act*, [10]; Commonwealth Ombudsman, *Putting Things Right* (2009), [1.3].

an agency officer's 'unreasonableness' or the 'ambiguity' of an officer's advice.[59] While agency decisions have been found to be 'generally reasonable' in line with the defined standards, the inappropriateness of an unduly legalistic approach is emphasised by the particular scope of soft law and oral advice to become the instruments of maladministration.[60]

The *Putting Things Right* report listed a number of ways in which agencies handle applications under the CDDA Scheme in an inappropriately legalistic way, such as by relying on legal advice as to liability, applying legal principles and concepts (such as those relating to negligence), exclusively using internal or external legal practitioners to handle claims, or relying on agency manuals which go beyond the Finance Department guidance documents and focus inappropriately on legal concepts (such as mitigation).[61] The Ombudsman recommended both that agencies improve their performance in handling CDDA claims, and also 'that Finance review its advice on the nature and effect of *moral obligations* within the circular to guide agencies in the identification and consideration of those obligations' (emphasis added).[62] However, apart from including a process diagram, subsequent guidelines for making a payment under the CDDA Scheme have been no simpler and are just as reliant on legalism as the guidelines to which the *Putting Things Right* report referred. Particular examples include the references to pure economic loss, interest and taxation issues, deeds of release and indemnity, and procedural fairness.[63]

The CDDA Scheme, ex gratia payment mechanism and the schemes under the PGPA Act are each wholly discretionary and there are few review options open to disappointed claimants.[64] The decision by a government agency not to make an ex gratia payment or a payment under the CDDA Scheme cannot be reviewed either in a merits review tribunal or under the Administrative Decisions (Judicial Review) Act (ADJR).[65] The latter form of review is unavailable because such decisions are neither made 'under an enactment' nor made under an instrument made 'under an enactment'.[66] The CDDA Scheme is revocable at will and creates neither legal rights nor obligations, meaning that it is not an 'instrument' for the purposes of the ADJR Act.[67]

Indeed, in *Smith v Oakenfull*, Dowsett J was prepared to treat the relevant attachment to the Finance Circular in which the CDDA Scheme was set out as nothing more than soft law itself.[68] A proposal to the Administrative Review Council (ARC) that the coverage of the ADJR Act be expanded to cover the CDDA Scheme, which caused concern in government agencies and was opposed by the

[59] CDDA Scheme, [16].
[60] Commonwealth Ombudsman, *Putting Things Right* (2009), [2.37]; [2.59]–[2.68].
[61] ibid, [2.74]–[2.90].
[62] ibid, [3.6].
[63] CDDA Scheme, [59], [70](c), [85], [81] and [38].
[64] Commonwealth Ombudsman, *Putting Things Right* (2009), [2.50].
[65] ibid, [1.16]. Regarding the CDDA Scheme, see *Smith v Oakenfull* (2004) 134 FCR 413, 418; *Barron v Commonwealth Department of Health and Ageing* (2003) 176 FLR 192.
[66] ADJR Act 1977 (Cth) s 3(1).
[67] *Smith v Oakenfull* (2004) 134 FCR 413, 418.
[68] ibid. At State level, see *Chubb Electronic Security Australia Pty Ltd v Commissioner of State Taxation* [2012] SASC 164.

Finance Department, was not ultimately endorsed in the ARC's report.[69] The Commonwealth Ombudsman has also stopped short of recommending reforms which would allow for Administrative Appeals Tribunal or ADJR review, stating that the 'CDDA Scheme has worked well' in the absence of these review mechanisms.[70] He did, however, recommend the creation of an inter-agency panel, chaired by a representative of the Finance Department, which would be able to provide a level of independent review of agency CDDA decisions.[71] At the time of writing, there is no indication that this recommendation will be put into effect. There are no known cases in which an applicant has sought judicial review of a decision about whether to make discretionary compensation payment under the CDDA Scheme in the Federal Court's jurisdiction under section 39B of the Judiciary Act.[72] The reviewability of decisions under the PGPA Act is considered below.

There was some concern that, because relief is premised on the assumption that the relevant agency did nothing unlawful or actionable and is therefore not in the 'ordinary and well-recognised' course of government business, following the decision of the High Court in *Williams (No 1)*, the CDDA and ex gratia payment schemes might be vulnerable to constitutional challenge.[73] *Williams (No 1)* required that expenditure of money by government under the authority of section 61 of the Constitution should have a basis in 'the Commonwealth's inherent authority derived from its status as the national government', be connected to a head of power within section 51 (of the Constitution), or otherwise have statutory authority.[74] The CDDA and ex gratia payment schemes arguably possess none of these bases. Aronson and Groves commented that the debates over whether exercises of power are 'more constrained in the hands of government than in a private person's hands' and, if so, whether judicial review would lie for breach of those constraints, 'involve large questions, only one of which was answered' in *Williams (No 1)*.[75]

Following the decision in *Williams (No 1)*, the constitutional validity of over 400 schemes was shored up by special amending legislation, enacted as section 32B of the Financial Management and Accountability Act 1997 (Cth) (FMA Act). These included not only the National School Chaplaincy and Student Welfare Program (NSCP), which had been the subject of *Williams (No 1)*, but also the act of grace and debt waiver schemes in the FMA Act. They did not specifically include the CDDA or ex gratia payment schemes.[76] The programmes covered were catalogued

[69] Administrative Review Council, *Federal Judicial Review in Australia* (2012), [5.32]–[5.34]; [5.42].

[70] Commonwealth Ombudsman, *Putting Things Right* (2009), [2.53].

[71] ibid, [2.55]–[2.58].

[72] Administrative Review Council, *Federal Judicial Review in Australia* (2012), [5.39].

[73] *Williams v Commonwealth* ('*Williams (No 1)*') (2012) 248 CLR 156, 233–34.

[74] S Chordia, A Lynch and G Williams, '*Williams v Commonwealth*: Commonwealth Executive Power and Australian Federalism' (2013) 37 *Melbourne University Law Review* 189. See eg *Ruddock v Vadarlis* ('*The Tampa*') (2001) 110 FCR 491, 542–43 (French J); *Pape v Federal Commissioner of Taxation* (2009) 238 CLR 1, 23–24, 26–27 (French CJ), 88–89 (Gummow, Crennan & Bell JJ); cf 121–23 (Hayne & Kiefel JJ), 193–95 (Heydon J).

[75] M Aronson and M Groves, *Judicial Review of Administrative Action*, 5th edn (Sydney, Thompson Reuters, 2013) [3.60]. See also above at Chapter 5.C.

[76] Financial Framework Legislation Amendment Bill (No 3) 2012 (Cth) Sch 2 [407.059]; cf M Aronson and M Groves, *Judicial Review of Administrative Action*, 5th edn (Sydney, Thompson Reuters, 2013) [6.730] (fn 468).

in Schedule 1AA to the amended Financial Management and Accountability Regulations 1997 (Cth) (FMA Regulations). The validity of this compendium legislation was challenged in the High Court by Mr Williams, the plaintiff in *Williams (No 1)*.

In *Williams (No 2)*, the High Court confirmed certain premises that it had established in *Pape* and reiterated in *Williams (No 1)*:[77]

> They are, first, that the appropriation of moneys in accordance with the requirements of sections 81 and 83 of the Constitution does not itself confer a substantive spending power and, second, that the power to spend appropriated moneys must be found elsewhere in the Constitution or in statutes made under it.

The plaintiff's case was framed specifically, as in *Williams (No 1)*, as a challenge to the validity of a programme under which the Commonwealth paid money to Scripture Union Queensland (SUQ) for SUQ to provide chaplaincy services at State schools, including the one attended by Mr Williams' children, under the NSCP.[78] The Court held that the executive power of the Commonwealth was insufficient to support expenditure under a scheme such as the NSCP, and the government's argument that such expenditure is reasonably incidental to authorised action and expenditure by government departments was unsuccessful. That does not necessarily mean that it would fail in every context.

In *Williams (No 2)*, the High Court again found for Mr Williams on the basis that the challenged amending legislation was not supported by a constitutional head of power. However, the Court had granted standing to Mr Williams sufficient only to determine the matter before it.[79] It was therefore unnecessary for the Court to determine either whether section 32B of the FMA Act was wholly invalid or whether other Commonwealth programmes listed in the FMA Regulations, including those to 'provide access for eligible recipients to discretionary payments in special circumstances or financial relief from amounts owing to the Commonwealth', were valid.[80] The Court's reasoning was restricted to whether the legislative provisions which provided for payments to fund the NSCP were supported by a constitutional head of power. A unanimous Court held that such payments were supported by neither section 51(xxiiiA), which allows the Commonwealth Parliament to make laws with respect to 'benefits to students', nor section 51(xx), which relates to laws regulating or permitting any act by or on behalf of any corporation.

Williams (No 2) explicitly did not address the validity of the legislative attempt to ensure the validity of discretionary compensation schemes following *Williams (No 1)*. The Court did, however, give some indication as to how the validity of such schemes should be addressed when it said that section 32B:[81]

> should be read as providing power to the Commonwealth to make, vary or administer arrangements or grants only where it is within the power of the Parliament to authorise

[77] *Williams v Commonwealth* ('*Williams (No 2)*') (2014) 252 CLR 416, 455.

[78] See text accompanying fns 291–292 in Chapter 5.C of this volume above.

[79] *Williams (No 2)* (2014) 252 CLR 416, 455. See G Williams, S Brennan and A Lynch, *Blackshield and Williams' Australian Constitutional Law and Theory*, 6th edn (Sydney, Federation Press, 2014) [10.117B].

[80] Financial Framework Legislation Amendment Bill (No 3) 2012 (Cth) Sch 2 [407.059].

[81] *Williams (No 2)* (2014) 252 CLR 416, 457.

> the making, variation or administration of those arrangements or grants. To read the provision in that way is to read it within constitutional power. To read it as having a wider operation might take the provision beyond either constitutional power or the meaning and operation which its words can fairly bear, or beyond both constitutional power and the fair reading of its text.

To be valid, the schemes in question must be linked to a head of Commonwealth legislative power. It is part and parcel of the fact that these schemes deal with situations in which the Commonwealth does not have legal liability that there is not obviously a head of constitutional power which supports them. However, there are good reasons to believe that they will not be subject to reversal in the High Court as the NSCP was. First, even the schemes under the PGPA Act should be viewed as exercises of power supported by section 61 of the Constitution and therefore by the express incidental power in section 51 (xxxix).

Secondly, each discretionary compensation mechanism should be understood as using power 'necessary or incidental to the execution and maintenance of a law of the Commonwealth'.[82] In *Williams (No 1)*, French CJ cited authority to support his statement that the executive power referred to in section 61 extends to such powers, although determining what acts are 'necessary or reasonably incidental to the execution and maintenance of a valid law of the Commonwealth' remains a point of practical difficulty. The argument pursued in this chapter leads to the conclusion that, just as it is incidental to the operation of some departments and agencies to cause loss which they did not intend to cause and for which they bear no legal liability, so too is it incidental to their operation to be able expend money to mitigate financially the unintended losses they created. For the discretionary compensation mechanisms to be invalidated would necessitate a court reaching a different conclusion.

Finally, these mechanisms are likely to survive regardless of their constitutionality simply because nobody motivated to challenge them will have the standing to do so. Those who receive compensation through these mechanisms will have the standing to challenge them, but likely will not.[83] Those who have not received compensation will lack the standing to challenge the constitutional status of the mechanisms. This is an issue common to the schemes which now appear in Schedules 1AA and 1AB to the Financial Framework (Supplementary Powers) Regulations 1997 (Cth).[84] It is interesting to ponder the possibility that some schemes which lack constitutional validity will nonetheless remain legal de facto for want of a challenger with standing.

C. CHALLENGING DECISIONS UNDER DISCRETIONARY COMPENSATION SCHEMES

If the discretionary compensation schemes were to prove to be constitutionally invalid, it is unclear whether there would still be a capacity for the government to make

[82] *Williams (No 1)* (2012) 248 CLR 156, 184–85. See *R v Kidman* (1915) 20 CLR 425, 440–41; *Re Residential Tenancies Tribunal (NSW); ex parte Defence Housing Authority* (1997) 190 CLR 410, 464.

[83] cf *Pape* (2009) 238 CLR 1.

[84] See Standing Committee on Regulations and Ordinances, '*Delegated Legislation Monitor*' (2014).

ex gratia payments (in the broad sense of that term). Payments to remedy defective administration in the absence of legal liability used to be authorised 'usually by a Cabinet decision', although that mechanism would not now make up for the lack of an executive or statutory power to expend money.[85] In *Lain*, Diplock LJ reasoned that the Board's decision to authorise a compensation payment was legally significant because it 'makes lawful a payment to an applicant which would otherwise be unlawful'.[86] This dictum has been cited with qualified approval in the High Court of Australia (on the basis that 'no legal rights in any ordinary sense were in question' in *Lain*).[87] The better view is that it is irrelevant for Australia. Whereas the High Court tried to preserve the Senate's powers of review in *Williams (No 1)*, there was no need for the Court of Appeal in *Lain* to consider preserving the House of Lords' right of review because, unlike the Australian Senate, the House of Lords could scarcely have been considered democratic.[88]

Lain has been criticised on the basis that the Crown, like any ordinary person, can spend as it likes. Such a conclusion involves acceptance (unthinkable in a country with both a federal system and a written constitution) of the 'Ram doctrine', which has been interpreted as allowing, subject to statutory limitations, the state and its individual departments to do whatever a natural person can.[89] What is clear is that mechanisms for making discretionary payments are necessary, given the existence of 'grey or black legal holes' over which judicial review has partial or no coverage.[90] It is further clear that their undoubted legal consequences 'warrant judicial supervision'.[91]

Unlike the CDDA and ex gratia payment schemes, which source their power from section 61 of the Constitution, the mechanisms under the PGPA Act are reviewable, both at common law and under the provisions of the ADJR Act.[92] However, judicial supervision of the decision whether or not to make a discretionary compensation payment is generally conducted by Australian courts with a relatively light touch. By contrast, the authors of *De Smith* cited extensive authority to support their contention that, in England, '[d]ecisions as to whether to make payments of statutory or discretionary compensation ... may themselves be susceptible to judicial review'.[93]

[85] S Major, 'Am I Special Enough?' (1995) 6 *Australian Institute of Administrative Law Forum* 14, 14.

[86] *Lain* [1967] QB 864, 888.

[87] *Hot Holdings Pty Ltd v Creasy* (1996) 185 CLR 149, 162; see M Aronson and M Groves, *Judicial Review of Administrative Action*, 5th edn (Sydney, Thompson Reuters, 2013) [3.250].

[88] See *Williams (No 1)* (2012) 248 CLR 156, 205 (French CJ), 235 (Gummow & Bell JJ), 260 (Hayne J), 313, 315–17 (Heydon J), 340, 343 (Crennan J).

[89] See H Woolf et al, *De Smith's Judicial Review*, 6th edn (London, Sweet and Maxwell, 2007) 236; J McLean, *Searching for the State in British Legal Thought* (Cambridge, Cambridge University Press, 2012) 161–62; M Aronson and M Groves, *Judicial Review of Administrative Action*, 5th edn (Sydney, Thompson Reuters, 2013) [3.250] (fn 303).

[90] M Aronson and M Groves, *Judicial Review of Administrative Action*, 5th edn (Sydney, Thompson Reuters, 2013) [3.60].

[91] ibid, [3.250]; Administrative Review Council, *Federal Judicial Review in Australia* (2012), [5.40].

[92] See eg *Toomer v Slipper* [2001] FCA 981.

[93] H Woolf et al, *De Smith's Judicial Review*, 6th edn (London, Sweet and Maxwell, 2007) 910.

In Australia, this reasoning may apply at common law, but executive discretionary compensation schemes are unreviewable under the ADJR Act:[94]

> There are no statutorily prescribed criteria in relation to the assessment of an Act of Grace Payment Claim [then under section 33 of the FMA Act]. In those circumstances, the matters to be taken into account and weight to be given to the evidence as to those matters are generally for the decision-maker, and not the Court, to determine.[95]

In *Toomer v Slipper*, Weinberg J concluded that:[96]

> The legislature has entrusted the power to make act of grace payments to the Minister. Such payments are not based upon any legal entitlement but are *made in response to moral obligations* assumed by the Commonwealth as a result of the actions of its employees or instrumentalities. The power to make such payments is, by its very nature, one which is particularly suited to be exercised by the Minister. The role of the Court is to ensure that the Minister exercises that power lawfully. Provided he does so, his decision cannot be impugned (emphasis added).

These schemes are designed only to fill lacunae where the government assumes a moral duty but has no legal liability, a situation made explicit by statute.[97] Therefore, the courts' reserve is understandable. The same reasoning has, however, previously been used by a Minister on the floor of the House of Commons to justify *refusing* to make an ex gratia payment in a certain case.[98]

There is a role for the courts to play, as illustrated by the lengthy and wholly unfortunate story of litigation commenced by Mr Croker. The Social Security Appeals Tribunal (SSAT) had concluded that Mr Croker was entitled to a small payment (less than AU$2,000) from Centrelink, which he would have received but for the fact that his right to a payment had been incorrectly determined. Centrelink had refused to pay Mr Croker a pensioner education supplement for a disability support pension in April 2008 but the SSAT determined, in June 2009, that he was entitled to that pension.[99] Following the passage of 15 months, Centrelink no longer possessed the power to make the requested payment or an act of grace payment in the same amount, a power which is not delegated by the Minister of Finance to other agencies.[100] Centrelink did, however, provide written support for Mr Croker's application for an act of grace payment. Such payments are able to be authorised in the discretion of the Minister of Finance or his or her delegate in writing.[101] In this case, the Minister's delegate made the decision, subsequently held by Rares J to

[94] *Collins v Department of Finance and Deregulation (No 3)* [2012] FMCA 860 [125]. See *Smith v Oakenfull* (2004) 134 FCR 413.

[95] *Minister for Aboriginal Affairs v Peko-Wallsend Ltd* (1986) 162 CLR 24, 41; *Toomer v Slipper* [2001] FCA 981, [36]–[37].

[96] *Toomer v Slipper* [2001] FCA 981, [47].

[97] *Public Governance, Performance and Accountability Act 2013* (Cth) s 65.

[98] C Harlow, *Compensation and Government Torts* (London, Sweet and Maxwell, 1982) 130–31.

[99] *Croker v Department of Families, Housing etc* [2010] FCA 1136, [2].

[100] *Discretionary Financial Assistance under the PGPA Act*, [2]; see PGPA Act 2013 (Cth) s 65; cf CDDA Scheme, [3].

[101] PGPA Act 2013 (Cth) s 65(1).

be 'inappropriate and unjustifiable on any view', not to exercise his discretion until after the matter had been fully litigated.[102]

His Honour concluded that, to apply a blanket policy as to when act of grace payments would be considered, exposed potential claimants to the stress and inherent risks of litigation. In circumstances where there was already considerable government support for making the payment, in which the absence of legal liability on the part of the government was therefore already privately under consideration and in which Mr Croker's possible liability for costs would far outweigh the benefit he was claiming, there could scarcely be a valid justification for refusing to exercise the statutory discretion.[103]

The benefit of the Court's involvement in these circumstances was not to lay down binding legal principles but to act as a circuit breaker. Rares J compelled the defendant Secretary to file an affidavit sworn personally, thereby ensuring that the matter had been brought to his attention, and included in his reasons (which he directed the Registrar to send to the Minister of Finance) a 'request for the Minister to reconsider the policy' with regard to act of grace payments.[104] It is significant that, when Mr Croker ultimately challenged the refusal of his claim for an act of grace payment by the Minister, Robertson J dismissed his application with a customary unwillingness to interfere in the substance of the Minister's discretionary decision-making.[105]

In later proceedings, Mr Croker claimed to have made an application to the Finance Minister for an act of grace payment, but these proceedings were dismissed by Cowdroy J on the basis that Mr Croker was unable to prove that he had made the application in question.[106] Mr Croker had also requested that the Court compel the Finance Minister to make a payment to him under the CDDA Scheme on the basis that 'the time which has elapsed since he made his claim is excessive'. Cowdroy J dismissed this claim with the comment that 'there could be no suggestion [of] any defective administration by the Minister or her department in the processing of an act of grace payment in the absence of a request'.[107]

D. CONCLUSION

Soft law is highly and increasingly pervasive in Australia, as in other jurisdictions. It is a form of regulation which has become popular for reasons which are readily understandable. It is easily made, and changed, and requires no legislative oversight. It is true that the Legislation Act states that a legislative instrument is 'not enforceable by or against the Commonwealth, or by or against any other person or body, unless

[102] *Croker v Department of Families, Housing etc* [2010] FCA 1136, [22].
[103] Mr Croker's application was ultimately denied: *Croker v Minister for Finance and Deregulation* [2011] FCA 1188.
[104] *Croker v Department of Families, Housing etc* [2010] FCA 1136, [31]–[33].
[105] *Croker v Minister for Finance and Deregulation* [2011] FCA 1188.
[106] *Croker v Minister for Finance and Deregulation* [2013] FCA 429.
[107] ibid, [12].

the instrument is registered' in the Federal Register of Legislative Instruments.[108] However, this may not be a practical issue where a majority of people *think* that an instrument is enforceable. This is why soft law is referred to as 'law'; it has a practical effect which is very much like primary or secondary legislation. The problem is that this effect is not symmetrical. In other words, soft law only has a 'law-like' effect on individuals, but cannot be enforced against public authorities as 'hard law'.

This state of affairs means that the available judicial remedies for breach of soft law by public authorities are fairly unsatisfying. Private law remedies are limited to circumstances in which the soft law instrument can either be understood as a negligent misrepresentation, or as an inducement giving rise to an estoppel which is able to be remedied with an order for equitable compensation. These circumstances are, to say the least, infrequent. Public law is similarly limited, because in Australia its remedies attach only to administrative action which discloses a jurisdictional error. Unlike their English counterparts, Australian courts have refused to provide a substantive judicial review remedy for disappointment of a legitimate expectation, meaning that the most one can say of soft law in Australian judicial review doctrine is that it may in some circumstances constitute a mandatory consideration to be taken into account by a decision-maker. The remedy for breach of this requirement would never be any more than procedural in nature.

It follows that the most effective remedies for breach of soft law by public authorities, considered in this chapter, are also 'soft', in the sense that they are not determinative but are able to be obtained through influence and consent. The role of the Ombudsman in this process is central and serves to emphasise the role that that institution has in ensuring that administrative justice is done in Australia.

[108] Legislation Act 2003 s 31. See also S Argument, 'Delegated Legislation' in M Groves and HP Lee (eds), *Australian Administrative Law* (Melbourne, Cambridge University Press, 2007) 134, 138.

13

Conclusions

A CURSORY EXAMINATION of this book might suggest that it has succeeded only in the modest task of pointing out that an issue exists and the unwelcome task of stating that very little can be done about it. I intend, however, that having reached this point the reader will be left neither so unsatisfied nor so pessimistic. In concluding, therefore, I propose to revisit the major themes of this book and suggest some further developments that require consideration in the future. It is my belief that soft law should not be viewed as something to be feared, but that a legal capacity to hold accountable those who use it in public regulation should exist.

A. THEMES

(i) Soft Law Must Mean Something

More than theory, more than remedies, more than regulation, the theme which unifies this book is that the phenomenon of soft law must itself have meaning. It is soft law's meaning which will ultimately shape the response which the rest of the law makes to it. It is because soft law means something that we care at all whether the law responds to it.

Soft law means something because it is treated by the majority of those faced with it as though it does. We have long moved past the point where lawyers can dismiss as meaningless any form of regulation which does not come from Parliament or is not made under power delegated from Parliament. Megarry was able to say as long ago as 1944 that that 'administrative quasi-legislation' had invaded a legal world previously 'bounded by Acts of Parliament, Statutory Rules and Orders and judicial decisions'.[1] A lawyer could not advise his or her client without understanding this quasi-legislation, because, 'although no Court would enforce [quasi-legislative announcements], no official body would fail to honour them … [The announcements] are intended to apply generally to all who fall within their scope'.[2] Keyes suggested, nearly 70 years later, that courts are now prepared to view soft law as both significant and persuasive, to the extent that it has 'something approaching … binding legal effect'.[3]

[1] RE Megarry, 'Administrative Quasi-Legislation' (1944) 60 *LQR* 125, 125–26.
[2] ibid, 126.
[3] JM Keyes, *Executive Legislation*, 2nd edn (New South Wales, LexisNexis, 2010) 51.

The practical effect of soft law has always been of greater significance than its legal character. If soft law is nothing more than an emperor without clothes, its power stems from the fact that the majority of people simply do not realise. Megarry was prepared to characterise the phenomenon as 'quasi-legislation' because it was legislative in scope and effect.[4] Likewise, when we now use the term 'soft law', the reference to law is made in the same way; it is softer than legislation but, if it is capable of the same effect, it must be considered as a species of 'law'.

Soft law can become 'hardened' as a result of its interaction with other legal processes. In Chapter four, I considered two examples. The first is of tribunals' application of policy, hardening that policy into precedent.[5] The second is less an example of soft law 'hardening' than a recognition that it is already 'legal' in its effect. The FOI Act, like similar legislation elsewhere, requires that agencies publish 'operational information'.[6] This is defined as

> information held by the agency to assist the agency to perform or exercise the agency's functions or powers in making decisions or recommendations affecting members of the public (or any particular person or entity, or class of persons or entities).[7]

The FOI Act provides that failure to publish such information means that a person who acts while unaware of it cannot be prejudiced 'because of the application to that conduct of any rule, guideline or practice in the unpublished information'.[8] Aronson and Groves noted that the existence of this provision 'involves legislative recognition that some statutes implicitly authorise bureaucracies to fetter their discretions'.[9]

The requirement that law must be published is a rule of law principle of long application. English legislation has required for 120 years that every statutory instrument be published and, from 1946, the publication of the 'flood tide of rules and regulations which arrived with the welfare state'.[10] Fuller applied this principle both to hard and soft law, for reasons similar to those expressed by Megarry, namely that 'to predict the outcome of cases it is often essential to know, not only the formal rules governing them, but the internal procedures of deliberation and consultation by which these rules are in fact applied'.[11] The UK Supreme Court has since applied much the same reasoning in invalidating a secret policy upon which the Home Office acted.[12]

4 RE Megarry, 'Administrative Quasi-Legislation' (1944) 60 *LQR* 125, 126.

5 See *Hua-Aus v Federal Commissioner of Taxation* (2009) 75 ATR 886.

6 Freedom of Information Act 1982 (Cth). See M Aronson and M Groves, *Judicial Review of Administrative Action*, 5th edn (Sydney, Thompson Reuters, 2013) [5.250]; JM Keyes, *Executive Legislation*, 2nd edn (New South Wales, LexisNexis, 2010) 55.

7 FOI Act 1982 (Cth) s 8A(1).

8 FOI Act 1982 (Cth) s 10. See R Creyke and J McMillan, *Control of Government Action*, 3rd edn (Sydney, LexisNexis, 2012) 672–73.

9 M Aronson and M Groves, *Judicial Review of Administrative Action*, 5th edn (Sydney, Thompson Reuters, 2013) [5.290].

10 HWR Wade and C Forsyth, *Administrative Law*, 11th edn (Oxford, Oxford University Press, 2014) 752.

11 LL Fuller, *The Morality of Law* (New Haven and London, Yale University Press, 1964) 50.

12 *Lumba v Home Secretary* [2012] 1 AC 245.

Regardless, making soft law is, in a sense, a common law power and it sits alongside the judicially reviewable executive and prerogative powers. The common law will allow the making and application of soft law; sometimes, it may compel it. This will happen on terms set by the common law and these terms should include that exercises of power through soft law are judicially reviewable.

(ii) The Legal Responses are Limited to Inadequate 'Work-arounds'

If soft law can be similar in effect to hard law, it should follow that, when it is, it should also be subject to the same protections and accountability measures as hard law. That is not the case. The difficulty is that legal remedies attach to law's *form* rather than to its effect or substance. An act performed in accordance with soft law cannot be characterised as ultra vires, either on the basis of the act or the instrument being invalid, when (in Wade's phrase) 'it has no *vires* to be *ultra*'.[13] Australia, in particular, has struggled to reconcile the similar but not co-extensive concepts of law and public power. At Commonwealth level, the reason is constitutional.[14] At State level, the ongoing debate about the meaning of *Datafin* has still not been finally resolved, although it has still only been applied once.[15] It is unlikely that it will be applied again.[16] In summary, action under hard law is subject to judicial review, but the exercise of public power through soft law may not be. Furthermore, Australian judicial review is currently limited to providing procedural remedies and has steadfastly refused to follow English precedents which would allow substantive remedies.[17]

Judicial review does in some respects recognise soft law's substance. Soft law may, for example, be a consideration of which a decision-maker is required to take account, or it may create an obligation to provide procedural fairness, or a decision-maker may be found to have acted invalidly by fettering him- or herself to a soft law instrument.[18] The last of these grounds creates difficult issues of its own, because it is in direct conflict with the expectation that decisions in like cases be consistent with each other, an aim facilitated by soft law.[19] However, none of these grounds can lead to anything more than a procedural remedy in Australia and it is most unlikely that that position will change in the short term.

[13] HWR Wade, 'Beyond the Law: A British Innovation in Judicial Review' (1991) 43 *Administrative Law Review* 559, 561.

[14] See J Boughey and G Weeks, '"Officers of the Commonwealth" in the Private Sector: Can the High Court Review Outsourced Exercises of Power?' (2013) 36 *University of NSW Law Journal* 316.

[15] *Masu Financial Management Pty Ltd v Financial Industry Complaints Service Ltd (No 2)* (2004) 50 ACSR 554. See *R v Panel on Take-overs and Mergers, ex parte Datafin plc* [1987] QB 815.

[16] See eg *Chase Oyster Bar Pty Ltd v Hamo Industries Pty Ltd* (2010) 78 NSWLR 393; *Khuu & Lee Pty Ltd v Corporation of the City of Adelaide* (2011) 110 SASR 235. Special leave to appeal the decision in *Khuu & Lee* to the High Court was subsequently refused.

[17] See G Weeks, 'Holding Government to its Word' in M Groves (ed), *Modern Administrative Law in Australia* (Melbourne, Cambridge University Press, 2014) 224.

[18] The classic example is *Green v Daniels* (1977) 13 ALR 1.

[19] See M Aronson and M Groves, *Judicial Review of Administrative Action*, 5th edn (Sydney, Thompson Reuters, 2013) [3.280].

The recent history of tort liability for public authorities is one of traditional principles in retreat. Statutory changes to the law of negligence in Australia have over the course of the decade since the *Ipp Report*[20] meant that, when a public authority is acting in a regulatory capacity, it is now very difficult to prove liability for a negligent act or omission. Even where the UK Supreme Court held that two prisoners had been subject to false imprisonment due to the Home Office applying an ultra vires policy, they received no more than nominal damages.[21] Misfeasance in public office, a tort specifically applicable to public authorities, is so difficult to prove that it has been peripheral to this book.[22]

In Chapter ten, I considered the possibility of equitable compensation being available where an estoppel is raised because a person has relied to his or her detriment on a soft law instrument from which the relevant public authority has since resiled.[23] Given that it is unlikely that a doctrine of public law estoppel will develop in Australia, the concept having been essentially moribund since 1990, this is a possibility worth exploring.[24]

What becomes clear from the assessment of these public and private legal doctrines is that providing a court-based remedy for a public authority's breach of its own soft law would involve developing the law in a way which is essentially inconsistent with centuries of previous developments. The possible remedies amount to nothing more than 'work-arounds', which might produce a remedy here and there, but which effect no lasting or systemic change (and do not aim to so do).[25] Existing legal doctrine is simply insufficiently flexible to accommodate soft law in a systemic way.

(iii) The Most Effective Current Controls on Soft Law are 'Soft'

It is therefore unsurprising that the most effective remedies for maladministration involving soft law are also 'soft', by which, in this context, I mean flexible and discretionary rather than determinative. This is often seen as code for 'ineffectual' but, just as soft law is remarkably effective despite lacking full legal force, so too are ombudsmen more than effective at obtaining remedies where they see them as being necessary. The fact is that public authorities rarely defy the Ombudsman. One soft remedy which the Ombudsman is able to recommend is a discretionary payment by a government agency, for example under the CDDA Scheme. Such payments are made in the government's discretion where, despite having no legal liability, it accepts a moral responsibility for a claimant's loss.

[20] Review of the Law of Negligence (Final Report), September 2002.

[21] *Lumba v Home Secretary* [2012] 1 AC 245.

[22] See M Aronson, 'Misfeasance in Public Office' (2011) 35 *Melbourne University Law Review* 1.

[23] See also G Weeks, 'Estoppel and Public Authorities' (2010) 4 *Journal of Equity* 247.

[24] *Attorney-General (NSW) v Quin* (1990) 170 CLR 1; *Minister for Immigration, Local Government and Ethnic Affairs v Kurtovic* (1990) 21 FCR 193.

[25] M Aronson and M Groves, *Judicial Review of Administrative Action*, 5th edn (Sydney, Thompson Reuters, 2013) [6.730].

These are remedies which are effective and fill the current lacuna in the availability of legal remedies. However, the discretionary payment schemes are not well-known and are limited in their application, both by the fact that payments are made in the unchallengeable discretion of an administrative decision-maker, and by the terms of the soft law instruments which set their terms. It is not acceptable for us to see the soft remedies examined in Part III as being the whole of the response to the issue which is the topic of this book.

B. FUTURE DIRECTIONS

I wish, therefore, to finish by specifying three areas which will repay further consideration, and by making one more general plea.

First, further consideration must be given to a statutory damages remedy in public law—something that has not been done in this book. Not everybody agrees with Lord Bingham's dictum in *X v Bedfordshire CC*:[26]

> It is not suggested that the child could obtain, or ever could have obtained, any redress of any kind against the psychiatrist save by bringing this action. If she can make good her complaints (a vital condition, which I forbear constantly to repeat), it would require very potent considerations of public policy, which do not in my view exist here, to override *the rule of public policy which has first claim on the loyalty of the law: that wrongs should be remedied* (emphasis added).

The 'question-begging' nature of this statement is somewhat beside the point.[27] The real issue is that maladministration can and does result in loss which is not able to be remedied in full by judicial review's suite of procedural remedies, and is not covered by existing private law doctrines. There is a conversation to be had about whether this situation is acceptably met by the existing 'work-arounds', or if the legislature is obliged to find ways in which those wrongs might be remedied.

This shades into the second issue, which is that we need to revise our expectations. The statement that 'wrongs should be remedied' does not equate to a statement that *all* wrongs should be remedied. Harlow and Rawlings' concerns about a 'compensation culture' should not be ignored.[28] As a society, we need to define *which* losses suffered by *which* people should be remedied. This conversation need not, however, be irrevocably tied to existing causes of action.

The third issue for future consideration is restitution, which is an effective remedy where a public authority is unjustly enriched at a claimant's expense and has no applicable defence. The status of the *Woolwich* decision, however, remains uncertain in Australia.[29] In any case, the law of unjust enrichment exists within a rigidly

[26] *X v Bedfordshire County Council* [1995] 2 AC 633, 663.

[27] L Hoffmann, 'Reforming the Law of Public Authority Negligence' (Speech delivered at the Bar Council Law Reform Lecture, London, UK, 17 November 2009) [20].

[28] C Harlow and R Rawlings, *Law and Administration*, 3rd edn (Cambridge, Cambridge University Press, 2009) 791–93. See also fn 59 in Chapter 8.B of this volume above.

[29] *Woolwich Equitable Building Society v Inland Revenue Commissioners* [1993] AC 70. See generally S Degeling, 'Restitution of Overpaid Tax in Australia: The Woolwich Principle' in S Elliott, B Häcker

defined taxonomy and, *Woolwich* notwithstanding, it is hard to imagine enough disputes regarding soft law falling within its boundaries for it to be more than a small part of the response.[30] It is yet to be formally accepted by Australian courts but there does not seem to be a compelling reason why it ought not. Although a person's capacity to obtain restitution where a public authority is unjustly enriched at his or her expense is a limited response to the pervasive effect of soft law, it is not unimportant. It would be nice to see *Woolwich* accepted in Australian courts at the earliest opportunity.

Finally, as desirable as a damages remedy for invalid administrative action may seem, the reasons against adopting it as a common law measure look almost insurmountable.[31] The summary rejection of the Law Commission's work on *Administrative Redress* by the UK Government seems conclusive of the point that, even in a jurisdiction entirely at ease with substantive remedies for legal errors in administrative decision-making, administrative law damages are considered a bridge too far.[32] However, more than the substance of this rejection, there is a very real risk that the vehemence with which the Law Commission's proposals on the issue of *Administrative Redress* were rebuffed will have a negative effect, causing similar bodies to shy away from revisiting these complex and important issues. That must not be allowed to happen. An appropriate agency should be asked to look at the implications of an administrative damages remedy. In Australia, this would once have been the Administrative Review Council but that body was defunded and then abolished by successive governments, a sad result for Australian administrative law's capacity to deal with the kinds of complex issues raised here.[33] In the circumstances, I would suggest that a Law Reform Commissioner be appointed to conduct a comprehensive review. These issues are too important to be left unexplored.

and C Mitchell (eds), *Restitution of Overpaid Tax* (Oxford, Hart Publishing, 2013) 313; G Weeks, 'The Public Law of Restitution' (2014) 38 *Melbourne University Law Review* 198.

[30] See G Weeks, 'The Public Law of Restitution' (2014) 38 *Melbourne University Law Review* 198, 234.

[31] See *New South Wales v Paige* (2002) 60 NSWLR 371 (Spigelman CJ).

[32] The Law Commission, *Administrative Redress*, Report No 322, (2010).

[33] See J Boughey and G Weeks, 'Comment from Australia: Australian Government Scraps Peak Administrative Law Advisory Body' (20 May 2015) *UK Constitutional Law Association Blog*: ukconstitutionallaw.org/2015/05/20/janina-boughey-and-greg-weeks-comment-from-australia-australian-government-scraps-peak-administrative-law-advisory-body/.

Index

www.ingramcontent.com/pod-product-compliance
Ingram Content Group UK Ltd.
Pitfield, Milton Keynes, MK11 3LW, UK
UKHW051240300926
15471UKWH00015B/1110

9 781509 922062